The Critics and Hemingway, 1924–2014

Hemingway burst on the literary scene in the 1920s with spare, penetrating short stories and brilliant novels. Soon he was held as a standard for modern writers. Meanwhile, he used his celebrity to create a persona like the stoic, macho heroes of his fiction. After a decline during the 1930s and 1940s, he came roaring back with *The Old Man and the Sea* in 1952. Two years later he received the Nobel Prize.

While his popularity waxed and waned during his lifetime, Hemingway's reputation among scholars remained strong as long as traditional scholarship dominated. New approaches beginning in the 1960s brought a sea change, however, finding grave fault with his work and making him a figure ripe for vilification. Yet during this time scholarship on him continued to appear. His works still sell well, and several are staples on high-school and college syllabi. A new scholarly edition of his letters is drawing prominent attention, and there is a resurgence in scholarly attention to—and approbation for—his work. Tracing Hemingway's critical fortunes tells us something about what we value in literature and why reputations rise and fall as scholars find new ways to examine and interpret creative work.

*Studies in American Literature and Culture:
Literary Criticism in Perspective*

Brian Yothers, Series Editor
(*El Paso, Texas*)

About *Literary Criticism in Perspective*

Books in the series *Literary Criticism in Perspective* trace literary scholarship and criticism on major and neglected writers alike, or on a single major work, a group of writers, a literary school or movement. In so doing the authors—authorities on the topic in question who are also well-versed in the principles and history of literary criticism—address a readership consisting of scholars, students of literature at the graduate and undergraduate level, and the general reader. One of the primary purposes of the series is to illuminate the nature of literary criticism itself, to gauge the influence of social and historic currents on aesthetic judgments once thought objective and normative.

The Critics and Hemingway, 1924–2014

Shaping an American Literary Icon

Laurence W. Mazzeno

CAMDEN HOUSE
Rochester, New York

Copyright © 2015 Laurence W. Mazzeno

All Rights Reserved. Except as permitted under current legislation, no part of this work may be photocopied, stored in a retrieval system, published, performed in public, adapted, broadcast, transmitted, recorded, or reproduced in any form or by any means, without the prior permission of the copyright owner.

First published 2015 by Camden House
Reprinted in paperback 2020

Camden House is an imprint of Boydell & Brewer Inc.
668 Mt. Hope Avenue, Rochester, NY 14620, USA
www.camden-house.com
and of Boydell & Brewer Limited
PO Box 9, Woodbridge, Suffolk IP12 3DF, UK
www.boydellandbrewer.com

Paperback ISBN-13: 978-1-64014-070-7
Paperback ISBN-10: 1-64014-070-0
Hardcover ISBN-13: 978-1-57113-591-9
Hardcover ISBN-10: 1-57113-591-X

Library of Congress Cataloging-in-Publication Data

Mazzeno, Laurence W.
 The critics and Hemingway, 1924–2014 : shaping an American literary icon / Laurence W. Mazzeno.
  pages cm.—(Studies in American literature and culture: literary criticism in perspective)
 Includes bibliographical references and index.
 ISBN 978-1-57113-591-9 (hardcover : acid-free paper)—
ISBN 1-57113-591-X (hardcover : acid-free paper)
 1. Hemingway, Ernest, 1899–1961—Appreciation. . Hemingway, Ernest, 1899–1961—Influence. 3. Hemingway, Ernest, 1899–1961—Criticism and interpretation. I. Title.

PS3515.E37Z741744 2015
813'.52—dc23

2015020976

Contents

Acknowledgments	vii
Introduction: "The Most Interesting Man in the World"	1
1: Spokesperson for the Lost Generation (1924–1932)	11
2: Writing on His Own Terms (1932–1952)	24
3: The Critics' Darling (1952–1961)	54
4: Posthumous Evaluations (1961–1969)	69
5: Turbulence (1970–1979)	93
6: Calm before the Storm (1980–1985)	116
7: A "Sea Change" in Hemingway Studies (1986–1990)	135
8: "Hemingway": Site for Competing Theories (1991–1999)	157
9: Old Themes, New Discoveries (2000–2010)	185
10: The Undisputed Champ Once More (2011–2014)	215
Conclusion: The Enduring Master	229
Major Works by Ernest Hemingway	231
Works Cited	233
Index	285

Acknowledgments

My first thanks go to Jim Walker and the editorial board at Camden House, who have once again given a vote of confidence to my work. I would like to acknowledge the cheerful support I have received from the staff at Alvernia University's Frank A. Franco Library, especially Roberta Rohrbach, without whose assistance I would still be struggling to locate material important for completing a study of this kind. I also owe a note of thanks to the staff of the Swem Library at the College of William & Mary, where much of this book was written. Though most of them have no idea who I am, I know them well and appreciate their professional competence.

Introduction: "The Most Interesting Man in the World"

> *His charm is so contagious vaccines have been created for it.*
>
> *His beard alone has experienced more than a lesser man's body.*
>
> *People hang on his every word—even the prepositions.*
>
> *He lives vicariously through himself.*
>
> *He is . . . [the] "Most Interesting Man in the World."*

Ron McFarland (2012) cites these epithets (and more) in his essay "The World's Most Interesting Man," an examination of fiction in which Ernest Hemingway appears as a character. Anyone familiar with Hemingway who has seen the Dos Equis beer commercials instantly recognizes in the bearded actor with piercing eyes and chiseled features (actor Jonathan Goldman, as McFarland points out) the larger-than-life writer awarded the Nobel Prize for Literature in 1954.

Hemingway biographer Scott Donaldson (2009) once observed that "Hemingway died the most famous writer of his time, and (we can confidently say now) the most famous writer of the twentieth century" (15). John Raeburn (1974) argues that Hemingway was the first genuine celebrity among American writers, emerging not only as an important author but also as someone in whom the public was interested apart from his writing. Expanding on this idea in *Star Authors: Literary Celebrity in America*, Joe Moran (2000) says Hemingway was the darling of the Luce magazine chain (publishers of *Time* and *Life*), appearing frequently in profiles or news articles. More than fifty years after his death, Hemingway's name remains a kind of shorthand, immediately conjuring up images of the macho, hard-driving, hard-drinking daredevil who lives life to the fullest. Popular books such as Marty Beckerman's (2011) *The Heming Way: How to Unleash the Booze-Inhaling, Animal-Slaughtering, War-Glorifying, Hairy-Chested, Retro-Sexual Legend Within*, Craig Boreth's (2012) *The Hemingway Cookbook*, and Philip Greene's (2012) *To Have and Have Another: A Hemingway Cocktail Companion* rely on the Hemingway image to sell copies even though the content of their books has little to do with Hemingway or his writings. Additionally, new biographies continue to draw attention not only from academics, but from major newspapers and popular periodicals as well. Long reviews in the

New York Times, *Washington Post*, *Atlantic*, and *New Republic*, to name a few, attest to the continuing interest in Hemingway's life and work. Papa, as he liked to call himself in his later years, continues to be appropriated as a fictional character in novels and stories long after his death (McFarland 2014). In marketing-speak, "Hemingway" has become a brand—so much so that he is the only modern literary figure profiled by Robert Cottrell (2010) in *Icons of American Popular Culture*.

The famous "Hemingway style" that influenced more than one generation of writers is often held up as a model for students given to prolixity, careless syntax, and sloppy organization. To "write like Hemingway" has become a kind of gold standard for expository classroom prose (never mind that Hemingway was writing fiction and literary nonfiction). It is no surprise that a twenty-first-century entrepreneur with one eye on Papa's prose and another on his own bottom line has created "The Hemingway Editor," an online editing tool that "makes your writing bold and clear" (www.hemingwayapp.com).

Hemingway still generates sales, too. His books remain in print, and with the blessing (and often through the direct efforts) of his family, his writings are being repackaged along thematic lines in attractive volumes with titles such as *Hemingway on Hunting* (Hemingway 2003a), *Hemingway on Fishing* (Hemingway 2004), and *Hemingway on War* (Hemingway 2003b). The posthumous publication of works Hemingway left in manuscript form at his death has generated significant controversy.

Thanks to the movies and television, many who have never read Hemingway still speak confidently (if not always correctly) about his work. Adaptations of his novels and stories began in 1932 with the production of *A Farewell to Arms*, an early blockbuster featuring established stars Helen Hayes and Gary Cooper. The big screen has provided a way for people to experience the tough-guy Hemingway hero: Cooper again in *For Whom the Bell Tolls* (1943); Humphrey Bogart in *To Have and Have Not* (1944); Burt Lancaster in *The Killers* (1952); Gregory Peck in *The Macomber Affair* (1947) and again in *The Snows of Kilimanjaro* (1952); Tyrone Power and Errol Flynn in *The Sun Also Rises* (1957); Spencer Tracy in *The Old Man and the Sea* (1958); and George C. Scott in *Islands in the Stream* (1977). These male leads played opposite an array of Hollywood's most popular female stars, including Ingrid Bergman, Lauren Bacall, Ava Gardner, Joan Bennett, and Susan Hayward. More recently, a ballet version of *The Sun Also Rises* was performed at Washington, DC's Kennedy Center (Macaulay 2013).

Family and friends have contributed significantly to creating Hemingway's popular image. He was dead less than a year when younger brother Leicester's *My Brother, Ernest Hemingway* and sister Marcelline Hemingway Sanford's *At the Hemingways: A Family Portrait* appeared in 1962. His sister Madeline Hemingway Miller published a more provocative look into her brother's life, *Ernie: Hemingway's Sister 'Sunny' Remembers*, in 1975. Though they waited a decent interval before sharing their secrets with the world, in the late 1970s two of Hemingway's wives finally published their versions of life with Papa. Mary Welsh Hemingway's *How It Was* (1976) offers a portrait that, though colored by her perceptions as a fourth wife, provides useful correctives to some of the stories Carlos Baker got wrong in his 1969 biography. Two years later Martha Gellhorn (1978), Hemingway's third wife, published her account of her years with Hemingway, *Travels with Myself and Another*.[1]

Hemingway's son Gregory's (1976) *Papa: A Personal Memoir* is biased in a way that only sons can be toward their fathers. From a critical perspective, however, its best feature might be Norman Mailer's preface, which offers some insight into the way Hemingway influenced the next generation of American writers. Years later daughter-in-law Valerie Hemingway (2004), Gregory's wife, provided her perceptions of the family in *Running with the Bulls: My Years with the Hemingways*. Grandson John Patrick Hemingway's (2007) *Strange Tribe: A Family Memoir* has the advantage of perspective but still remains close to the family legend.[2]

Friends like longtime associate A. E. Hotchner have also capitalized on their relationship with Hemingway, perpetuating his legend in a series of books with supposedly inside information about him. Jed Kiley (1965), William Seward (1969), Arnold Samuelson (1984), and more recently David Nuffer (2008) have published similar memoirs. Veteran reporter James McLendon's (1972) *Papa: Hemingway in Key West* collects reminiscences by numerous family members, friends, and acquaintances.

It is doubtful, however, whether all this hoopla would have been successful in making Hemingway a literary and cultural icon if his work had been substandard. Hemingway's early novels were well received by American readers and sold well throughout his lifetime. Topping the list was *A Farewell to Arms*, which sold 1.8 million copies in hardback and more than a million paperback—ahead of quite a few notable titles, including all of Faulkner's. *The Sun Also Rises* had sales of 1.17 million copies in hardback, 1.1 million in paperback. Sales of *For Whom the Bell Tolls* totaled 805,400 in hardback; the novel reached number four on the *New York Times* best-seller list for 1940, falling only to number five the following year. Even a work that is today held in low regard, *Across the River and Into the Trees*, was number three on the best-seller list for 1950. Surprisingly, perhaps, *The Old Man and the Sea* was number seven in 1952 despite appearing late in the year and having so many people read it in *Life* magazine, where it was published before being issued as a book. Three years after Hemingway's death, *A Moveable Feast* was number eight on the nonfiction list for 1964 (Hackett 1967). Few who claim to be writers of serious fiction can boast of such sales.

Hemingway's works also achieved a certain level of notoriety early in his career because of actions taken by associations and government agencies who saw his fiction as either unseemly or dangerous. In 1929 several monthly issues of *Scribner's* magazine were kept off store shelves in Boston because they carried chapters of *A Farewell to Arms*. Italy banned the novel "because of the painfully accurate account of the Italian retreat from Caporetto" (Haight 1954, 102). Pressure from the Italian government resulted in private censorship of the screen version as well. A Hemingway story was in a 1932 issue of a Paris quarterly magazine suppressed by customs authorities in Melbourne, Australia (Notice 1932). The Nazis burned his works in 1933 ("Foolish Fuel" 1933, 4). Five years later, officials in Detroit removed *To Have and Have Not* from bookstores and from circulation in public libraries; the book was "preserved" in library collections, however, "among writers of standing" (Haight 1954, 10). In the same year *To Have and Have Not* was banned in Wayne County, Michigan, "on complaint of Catholic organizations"; the ACLU reported that it was the "only book suppressed during the year" (Haight, 103). Coming late to the party, so to speak, the Irish government banned sales and distribution of *A Farewell to Arms* in 1939, and fourteen years later it banned *The Sun Also Rises* and *Across the River and Into the Trees*.

Notoriety and strong sales may be important, but for a writer to remain in the public consciousness, there is no substitute for literary skill. And yet that, too, may not guarantee lasting success. As Robert O. Stephens (1977b) sagely observes, even if one acknowledges "the energy and craftsmanship" of Hemingway's "extraordinary contribution to narrative art in the twentieth century," one must still recognize that his reputation "was also the product of those who read him and told others about him" (ix). The list of contemporaries who reviewed Hemingway's work is formidable: American critics Edmund Wilson, Allen Tate, Dorothy Parker, H. L. Mencken, Granville Hicks, Malcolm Cowley, Louis Kronenberger, Alfred Kazin, Lionel Trilling, Joseph Wood Krutch, Howard Mumford Jones, Mark Schorer, Joseph Warren Beach, Stanley Hyman, and Irving Howe all reviewed his books, as did writers F. Scott Fitzgerald, Sinclair Lewis, Stark Young, Virginia Woolf, William Faulkner, Evelyn Waugh, and John O'Hare. As early as 1937, when Hemingway wrote what many considered his first really bad book, *To Have and Have Not*, reviewer Charles Poore (1937) noted that, conservatively, "twenty times as much is written about Hemingway as by him" and "ten books appear bearing traces of his influence for every one that bears his name" (21). Less than a decade after he published his first book, Hemingway was the subject of an article in an academic journal (Lovett 1932). By contrast, as a search of Jackson Bryer's (1967) *The Critical Reputation of F. Scott Fitzgerald* indicates, while a brief note in a 1932 issue of *Scholastic* provided a biographical sketch, serious academic study of Fitzgerald's fiction was not initiated until 1944, when Leo and Miriam Gurko published "The Essence of F. Scott Fitzgerald" in *College English*. By then, critical articles on Hemingway numbered in the dozens.

Unquestionably, Linda Wagner-Martin (1998) is on target when she notes in *Ernest Hemingway: Seven Decades of Criticism* that "in some academic circles, Hemingway's work lives as much through the secondary criticism devoted to it as through its valid existence as text. The best criticism changes the lenses, and thereby gives readers new ways of reading, seeing, visualizing the art. It is in the interaction between the literature and its criticism that Hemingway's *oeuvre* remains most vital" (10). The trajectory of Hemingway criticism bears out her claim. When Hemingway started writing, critics, especially academic critics, were interested in the aesthetic, moral, and philosophical qualities of a work—elements that ostensibly transcended time, place, and even authorial intention. This rather Arnoldian approach to literary studies gave way in the second half of the century to a variety of critical approaches (structuralism, poststructuralism, feminism, new historicism, narratology—the list could go on), almost all of which viewed a literary work as a social construct, bound by time, place, and in most cases, the dominant ideology of that moment. It is not surprising that attitudes toward Hemingway changed as critics began viewing his work through different critical lenses. As Morris Freedman (2001) notes in his provocatively titled essay "Disparaging Hemingway," the result has not always been positive: "Hemingway has been the target of critical and academic discounting as perhaps no other writer in the English world since Shakespeare while simultaneously becoming a revered icon" (78).

The principal reason for what can only be described as wild swings in Hemingway's reputation lies in his simultaneous claims to literary genius and celebrity status—a combination that does not always bode well for writers who attract the attention of the academic world. An observation made a century after his death by future *Hemingway Review* editor Suzanne del Gizzo (1999) comes very close to defining the problem: "Hemingway is a peculiar literary figure. He is indisputably one of the most popular American writers of the twentieth century, yet there is far from universal consensus, especially within the academic community, regarding his level of skill or status as an artist." While the "dissonance" may be attributable to Hemingway's attempt to "straddle the high/low cultural divide of the twentieth century," del Gizzo finds that Hemingway still "inspires a certain degree of anxiety in the literary establishment." Often, she notes with a wisdom that belies her relatively junior standing in the academic community at the time of her writing, "one's critical opinion of Hemingway is often elided with the degree of one's sympathy for his 'way of life' and/or for Hemingway himself" (35).

It is sometimes hard to know whether a writer's career demands certain critical interpretations or if critical methodologies *au courant* at a given time steer critics to read writers in certain ways. That observation underlies *The Critics and Hemingway: Shaping an American Literary Icon*, in which I examine the way Hemingway and the many reviewers and critics inside and outside academe conspired, and continue to collaborate, in creating and sustaining his reputation as a literary and cultural icon. Its focus is as much on the critics as it is on Hemingway, and provides a critique of their assessments in order to identify the principles, predilections, and biases shaping their judgments.

As the foregoing narrative makes clear, writing about Hemingway's reputation requires one to take a broader view than might be required in studying the work of other authors. Almost from the moment Hemingway published his first collection of stories, he was noticed by both the popular press and the literary establishment. Within a decade he had become a bona fide celebrity, with people paying as much attention to his much-publicized globe-trotting adventures (and his romantic liaisons) as they did to his fiction. His work was the subject of essays in scholarly journals as early as the 1930s, and the stream of academic criticism has not abated. To understand the status of Hemingway's reputation, then, one must look at all these sources, since they tend to feed on each other, constantly revising and reworking critical and popular opinion.

Fortunately, the scholar who chooses to write about Hemingway has several useful guides to previously published work. Foremost among them is Audre Hanneman's (1967) *Ernest Hemingway: A Comprehensive Bibliography* and her (1975) *Supplement*, which are discussed at some length in Chapter 4. Her work was continued in Linda Welshimer Wagner's (1977) *Ernest Hemingway: A Reference Guide* and Kelli Larson's (1990) *Ernest Hemingway: A Reference Guide 1974–1989*. Larson's (1992) "Stepping into the Labyrinth: Fifteen Years of Hemingway Scholarship" provides important commentary on the quality of Hemingway scholarship, which had increased substantially in the previous decade following the establishment of the Hemingway Society and the opening of the Hemingway Collection at the Kennedy Library. Annual bibliographical lists in the *Hemingway Review* and bibliographical essays in *American Literary Scholarship* further extend the important project of cataloging the burgeoning array of criticism devoted to Hemingway and his work.

A number of other bibliographic studies complement these major efforts. In "The Hemingway Industry" William White (1963) highlights some of the books and articles that appeared within two years after Hemingway's death. Philip Young's (1964) annotated summary of criticism published after 1960 is impressively long, and Frederick Hoffman's (1969) bibliographic essay in *Fifteen Modern American*

Authors covers twenty-five pages. Bruce Stark's (1989) lengthy essay on Hemingway in Jackson Bryer's (1989) *Sixteen Modern American Authors* summarizes some of the more influential criticism published between 1972 and 1988.

Hemingway scholars are fortunate to have available a number of reference handbooks that make research easier. Miriam Mandel's (1995) rather formidable *Reading Hemingway: The Facts in the Fictions* is a compendium of information about every person, place, event, or object referred to in the novels and short stories, a handy guide for making sense of the many casual allusions in Hemingway's work and placing the fiction in its historical and cultural context. In *Ernest Hemingway: A Documentary Volume* in the *Dictionary of Literary Biography* series, Robert Trogdon (1999) weaves newspaper accounts, reviews, letters, and snippets from Hemingway's fiction into a factual narrative of his life and accomplishments. Charles Oliver's (2007) *Ernest Hemingway: A Literary Reference to His Life and Work* provides brief sketches of virtually every character Hemingway created, plot summaries of his work, a brief biography, and appendixes providing information on Hemingway's family, a chronology, a list of adaptations, and brief bibliography of the scholarship Oliver considers most helpful.

More directly connected to the present study, Frank Ryan's (1980) *The Initial Critical Reception of Ernest Hemingway* is a useful starting point for investigating ways reviewers responded to Hemingway's works as they were published. Susan Beegel's (1996) exceptionally informative and insightful review of Hemingway's critical reputation in *The Cambridge Companion to Hemingway* is distinguished by her ability to identify, describe, and critique major trends in Hemingway criticism over seven decades. I hope my more extensive analysis will complement and extend her work and be as useful to scholars as hers has been to me. Robert Evans's (2010) survey of Hemingway's reputation in *Ernest Hemingway: Critical Insights* is useful for its judgments about his enduring value but too brief to explain the complexities of the critical debate that has raged at least since the 1930s. In *The Critical Reception of Hemingway's "The Sun Also Rises,"* Peter Hays (2011) does for Hemingway's most widely read novel what I attempt to do on a broader scale: examine what the critical tradition can tell us not only about Hemingway's fiction, but about our presuppositions and expectations as we approach it. One can also get a good sense of critical trends by consulting the four volumes of Henry Claridge's (2012) *Ernest Hemingway*, part of Routledge's Critical Assessments of Major Writers series. More than a hundred essays provide a representative sampling of biographical and historical accounts, reception and reputation studies, commentary on the major novels, and general assessments of Hemingway's achievement.

The Critics and Hemingway explores the dialogue among critics to see how it has shaped subsequent views of Hemingway and the future of "Hemingway studies." While others have reviewed the way Hemingway was treated by reviewers during the years he was alive, I believe it is important to summarize those assessments because they are an important complement to my central interest, the development of Hemingway studies, the academic critique of his work. I have tried to incorporate comments from sources not commonly cited, mostly reviews in newspapers outside New York, Chicago, and Boston. While reviewers publishing in cities like New Orleans or Richmond may not have had the same influence on readership as those writing for the *New York Times* or the *Atlantic Monthly*, their comments certainly played a role in enhancing or deflating Hemingway's reputation among readers of local papers.

Some might object that this approach gives undeserved credence to local reviewers and columnists who may not have undergone rigorous academic training that qualifies one to make informed judgments about literature. I would reply that my focus is on studying Hemingway not simply as a writer but as a cultural phenomenon. The current interest among literary scholars in "cultural studies" suggests to me that a broader look at how Hemingway and his writings have survived for nearly a century will be of interest to scholars and students alike.

Of course, the sheer volume of Hemingway criticism makes it imperative that I be selective in what I cover. Not only does this mean limiting comments on individual books and articles to assessments of how they helped shape Hemingway's reputation; it also means forgoing discussion of the many handbooks and guides available to help students and scholars alike navigate Hemingway's deceptively simple prose. Even though millions of Americans and others around the world have come to know Hemingway from the movies and television shows based on his fiction, I have also chosen not to deal extensively with film adaptations of Hemingway's work. The topic is covered ably in Frank Laurence's (1981) *Hemingway and the Movies*, Charles Oliver's (1989) *A Moving Picture Feast: The Filmgoer's Hemingway*, and Candace Grissom's (2014) *Fitzgerald and Hemingway on Film: A Critical Study of the Adaptations, 1924–2013*.

This book is not intended as an annotated bibliography of Hemingway criticism. Rather, it is an examination of how a reputation was built over a century by a combination of popular and academic commentary. That approach has influenced the methodology used to select and report on the materials I have chosen to highlight. On occasion I devote a page or more to discussing a single work that is seminal or otherwise important in the development of Hemingway studies. My hope is that my brief summaries of selected criticism are representative of what was written at a given time. With rare exception, I have refrained from providing my own analyses of individual commentaries; instead, I try to quote from these so my readers can get a sense of the tone as well as the substance of what was written about Hemingway. Where appropriate, I have offered observations on how critical practice at a given time influenced judgments about his work.

If I seem to have given more weight to negative judgments, I offer as justification only that I find the tribe of Hemingway critics much like Tolstoy's families: the happy ones are all alike, but unhappy critics seem to employ a wide variety of methods to explain what is often a visceral reaction against Hemingway's work. My approach is generally chronological, though at times I have grouped criticism by category (e.g., feminist, new historicist, etc.). One advantage of a chronological review is that it permits one to see how a later critic responds to claims made by an earlier one. Using this approach also helps explain how the reputation of some works shifts over time, rising and falling as new critical methodologies discover the value of a novel or story that might have been hitherto overlooked, or point out faults that earlier critics failed to discern. As a result of my attempt to examine fluctuations in Hemingway's reputation, however, I may be accused of underrepresenting scholarship published in what is certainly the most important single source of Hemingway criticism extant: the *Hemingway Review*. My rationale for what might be perceived as a slight to the community of dedicated Hemingway scholars is that, while work in the *Review* is first-rate, much of it reinforces the high regard for Hemingway held by the impressive line-up of scholars who have chosen to publish in it. Most of them are represented by other works on which I comment at some length.

I am not part of the community of Hemingway scholars that has devoted its professional life to studying and writing about him, though I have on occasion written critiques of individual short stories and novels. I hope that bringing an outsider's perspective to a study of Hemingway's reputation will allow me to record fairly and comment disinterestedly on the sometimes hyperbolic claims for Hemingway's achievements and the equally vitriolic diatribes against him. My hope is that readers of *The Critics and Hemingway* will come away with an understanding of why Hemingway has generated such strong reaction and why, despite serious and often justifiable criticism of his writing, he remains an icon of American literature.

Notes

[1] Hadley Richardson, Hemingway's first wife, wrote no book about their marriage, but did record a series of tapes that were the basis of a book about her, Gioia Diliberto's (1992) *Hadley*. Hemingway's second wife, Pauline Pfeiffer, also wrote

no memoir. However, the story of her relationship with Hemingway is recounted in Ruth A. Hawkins's (2012) *Unbelievable Happiness and Final Sorrow*.

[2] In a harsh review, Philip Young (1966b) called Hotchner's book more fiction than fact. Hotchner fired back at Young in a postscript to the 1983 edition of his book, explaining how Hemingway despised the young academic. For an account of this dispute and a none-too-flattering analysis of Young's work, see Holcombe (1986).

1: Spokesperson for the Lost Generation (1924–1932)

THE STORY OF HEMINGWAY'S STRUGGLES as an aspiring writer in Paris during the early 1920s has been reported in detail by his biographers. Under the tutelage of Gertrude Stein, Ezra Pound, and Ford Madox Ford, he worked at stories and poems, diligently sending them out and collecting rejection slips. Even in these trying times, Hemingway had no interest in being "discovered" by future generations; he wanted to be recognized in his own lifetime, to make money from his fiction, and eventually be acclaimed as one of the great writers of his time. One might not have thought that his first publications—a slim volume of poems and stories followed by a collection of spare tales—would have gained him much attention. Fortunately for Hemingway, however, he had a friend who knew a friend. The novelist F. Scott Fitzgerald, already acknowledged as a writer of some talent, made sure Hemingway's work was noticed by his Princeton acquaintance Edmund Wilson, then establishing a reputation that would one day make him the most respected critic of his day. Without giving too much weight to this connection, it seems sufficient to employ the timeworn cliché, "the rest is history."

Early Reviews

Though two reviews of Hemingway's earliest publications in the first volume of the *transatlantic review* predate Wilson's, his review of *Three Stories and Ten Poems* and *in our time* in the *Dial* (1924) can be considered the first important assessment of Hemingway's ability and an accurate barometer of his potential. Wilson gets right to the point, opening with the observation that "Mr. Hemingway's poems are not particularly important, but his prose is of the first distinction" (340). He writes with a "naiveté of language" that "serves actually to convey profound emotions and complex states of mind." This new style is "a distinctly American development in prose" (341). With this brief notice, Wilson, himself only twenty-eight, anointed the twenty-five-year-old Hemingway the coming man in American fiction.

Wilson's opinion was reinforced by reviews of Hemingway's next publication, the 1925 collection of short stories titled *In Our Time*—the same title as his earlier book, but with conventional title capitalization.

Reviews of *In Our Time* gave wider notice that a distinct new voice had emerged on the American literary scene. Of course, it is hardly surprising that Fitzgerald (1926) would write a glowing review. He had read these stories in manuscript and encouraged Hemingway to send them to his publisher, Charles Scribner's Sons, if Hemingway could get out of his contract with Boni & Liveright. Others less beholden to say good things did so as well. The *New York Evening Post*'s Herschel Brickell (1925) declared that Hemingway "does remarkable things with a mere handful of words" (3). Allen Tate (1926a) celebrated Hemingway's power of observation and spare style, which the *Trenton Sunday Times* reviewer called "as forceful as a pile driver and at the same time exact to a thousandth of an inch" ("Forceful" 5). Gerald Gould (1926) admired Hemingway's technique, which he described as unique, though he found some of the stories "cruel" (8). D. H. Lawrence (1927) said the stories in *In Our Time* were like a "fragmentary novel," with "short, sharp, vivid" sketches; "most of them are excellent" (73).

If there were misgivings, they were of the kind expressed by Margaret Doorly (1926), who observed that "some of us do not care so much for the strong, harsh outline, but like softer effects" and "gentle character delineations." The mere "conviction that characters are plausible and real seems to us not quite sufficient" (6). A majority felt like Louis Kronenberger (1926), who said that, despite echoes of Sherwood Anderson and Gertrude Stein, the Hemingway style "shows no important affinity with any other writer, and it represents the achievement of unique personal experience" (555). Robert Wolf (1926), who saw stronger influence from Anderson and Stein, nevertheless believed Hemingway had "produced in his own right some of the most sensitive and subtle short stories that have come from any young American" (3).

Hemingway's next publication, *The Torrents of Spring*, was a bit of a rush job, written expressly as a parody of Sherwood Anderson in the hope that Boni & Liveright would reject it, thus allowing him to send his work to Scribner. The ploy worked, and Scribner published the brief novel in 1926. Reviews were mixed. Some found it merely a "clever parody" ("An Anderson Parody" 1926, 7F), "high-spirited nonsense" and "delightful entertainment" wholly unexpected from the author of *In Our Time* ("Mr. Hemingway Writes" 1926, 8). Others found the book "tedious" (Latimer 1926, 16). The *New York World*'s Harry Hansen (1926) thought Hemingway should stick to writing short stories. Some found more in the slight volume, however. Ernest Boyd (1926) called it "an elaborate and exceedingly witty parody of the Chicago school of literature" and described Hemingway as "a true humorist and shrewd critic" (694). The *Cleveland Plain Dealer*'s Ted Robinson (1926b) agreed, calling *Torrents* "one of the most successful parodies we have ever read" and noting that behind the "excellent foolery" there is "good and pertinent literary criticism" (3). The reviewer for the *Saturday Review of Literature* described *Torrents* as Hemingway's way of "freeing himself of an influence of which he is obviously conscious" ("New Books" 1926, 12). So did Lawrence Morris (1926a), who called *Torrents* Hemingway's "declaration of independence" (101).

The Sun Also Rises

Hemingway's independence from the tradition of Anderson and earlier writers—and from Victorian mores—was evident in his first real venture into novel-writing, *The Sun Also Rises*. His penetrating assessment of the Lost Generation sent the literary world into a tizzy. The New York papers were almost universal in their praise. Burton Rascoe (1926) said "every sentence" is "fresh and alive" (10). Conrad Aiken (1926) praised Hemingway's dialogue (4). Herbert Gorman (1926) said Hemingway has the "uncanny skill" of making his characters "live with an almost painful reality" (10M). The reviewer for the *New York Times* ("Marital Tragedy" 1926) called the novel "a gripping story, told in a lean, hard athletic narrative prose that puts more literary English to shame." The novel was "unquestionably one of the events of an unusually rich year in literature" (7). Praise came from outside New York as well. "Seldom does one find a piece of fiction with so much hard-edged truth in it," wrote *Cleveland Plain Dealer* reviewer Ted Robinson (1926a); it is "a masterpiece of a new kind of realism" (7). The *Richmond Times-Dispatch*'s Mark Lutz (1926), ecstatic over Hemingway's unsentimental portrait of postwar life and values, believed the novel would "take its place among the more lasting of present-day fiction" (9).

Hemingway received equally high praise from reviews in highbrow journals. Lawrence Morris (1926b) said *The Sun Also Rises* proved Hemingway was capable of developing a theme more completely than he did in his short stories. Bruce Barton (1927) said Hemingway writes "as if he had fashioned the art of writing himself" (12). Cleveland Chase (1926) described Hemingway's prose as "terse, precise and aggressively fresh," his dialogue some of the finest yet written (420). In a somewhat hyperbolic comparison, Chase asserted, "there is a certain Shakespearean absoluteness about his writing" (421).

Not everyone was quite so euphoric. The reviewer for *Time* acknowledged that much was expected of Hemingway in his first novel, but what he produced was disappointing. While the writing is sharp (except for "a few affectations"), his interests "appear to have grown soggy," concentrating on characters that do not deserve such attention ("Sad Young Man" 1926, 48). John McClure (1926), writing in the conservative *New Orleans Times-Picayune,* was pleased that Hemingway has "liberated himself from the artificially literary" and written in "straight prose" that, "not yet perfected into style," remains "full of possibilities." But McClure considered *The Sun Also Rises* "a tour-de-force which proves little," a novel best suited for "open-minded" adults (4). Similarly, the reviewer for the *Chicago Daily Tribune* ("Hemingway Seems" 1926) expressed annoyance that Hemingway's "immense skill" was "hidden under a bushel of sensationalism and triviality" (13). Allen Tate (1926b) had a more nuanced view of the novel, finding it on the whole successful but lacking in sharp characterization. More serious is Tate's charge that in producing "a popular novel"—successful because it is much talked about—Hemingway had done some "violence" to "the integrity achieved in his first book." Perhaps, Tate suggested, it was "the only novel which he could write" (642). The reviewer for the *Dial* ("Briefer Mention" 1927) was less kind, finding that Hemingway created characters "as shallow as the saucers in which they stack their daily emotions" and seemed content to "make a carbon copy of a not particularly significant surface of life in Paris" (73).

British reviewers were more skeptical about the novel's merits than their American counterparts. The reviewer for the *Times Literary Supplement* ("Fiesta" 1927) said *Fiesta* (the title under which the novel was published in Britain) has "moments of illumination" but becomes "tedious after one has read the first hundred pages" (454). Edwin Muir (1927) complained that despite brilliant, natural dialogue and exceptional description, the novel lacked "artistic significance" (452) because the characters simply do not matter to readers. The *Observer's* Gerald Gould (1927) said *Fiesta* "gives us neither people nor atmosphere," and asked rhetorically, "Why does Mr. Hemingway, who *can* draw flesh-and-blood, waste his time on these bibulous shadows?" (8). A curious and clever dissent appeared sometime after the great swell of laudatory criticism. Elizabeth Emmett (1927) never once mentioned the title or the author, instead describing *The Sun Also Rises* as "a bum book about bums, crammed full of conversation" (114). Her review title, "A Reader in Revolt," suggested her real target: the reviewers who overhyped a book she considered not worth the two-dollar selling price.

These few complaints had little effect on the sudden burst of praise for a young writer who went from being unknown in 1923 to the toast of the literary world four years later. Hemingway was described as "our outstanding realist" (Rothman 1928, 338), "the freshest voice since that of Frank Norris and possibly [Ring] Lardner and [Sinclair] Lewis" (Barton 1927, 12). Inevitable comparisons were made (almost always favorably) to Mérimée and Rudyard Kipling by Andre Maurois (1929), to Ring Lardner and even James Joyce by Lawrence Morris (1926b), who proclaimed that "no other American, writing today, can match his dialogue for its apparent naturalness, its intimacy and its concealed power of revealing emotions" (143). The *Bookman's* Charles Ferguson (1927) named Hemingway one of the five rising stars of American fiction, a "new young novelist[ ]" who has "fused new blood into a body of writing which a year ago threatened decadence" (251). English novelist Hugh Walpole (1927) called him "the most interesting figure in American letters in the last ten years" (302). Many agreed with Percy Hutchinson's (1927) assessment that Hemingway's originality, vitality, and dramatic sense combine to predict for him "a career of remarkable brilliancy" (27).

New Stories for a Growing Audience

In 1927 Hemingway followed his remarkably successful novel with a collection of short stories, *Men without Women*, a work that prompted the reviewer for *Time* ("Men without Women" 1927) to declare that "at least one of the Americans who live in Paris can do something more important than sit around in restaurants." Searching for ways to describe these stories, the reviewer called them "clear and crisp and perfectly shaped as icicles, as sharp as splinters of glass" (38). The *New York Times*'s Percy Hutchinson (1927) described Hemingway's art as that of "the reporter carried to the highest degree" (9). N. L. Rothman (1928), writing in the *Dial* (which had panned *The Sun Also Rises*), said the stories convinced him that Hemingway could be a great tragedian. Even Dorothy Parker (1927), not known for heaping praise on aspiring writers, called *Men without Women* "a truly magnificent book" (94). Outside the center of America's literary universe, praise for these stories was equally high. These "stories of supple originality" (Dabney 1927, 3) reveal "a new technique in the writing which for years suffered—one can use no other word—from the much advertised 'mantle of O. Henry'" ("Ernest Hemingway Displays" 1927, F5). By 1927 *Omaha World Herald* critic George Grimes (1927) could observe that "everybody, more or less, is talking about Hemingway now" (6).

H. L. Mencken (1928), who had rejected some of Hemingway's stories submitted to the *American Mercury*, was a bit less enthusiastic. Acknowledging that of late Hemingway and his contemporary, Thornton Wilder, had enjoyed great success—and "a great deal of uncritical homage" for their "technical virtuosity"—he said that they now must engage in some "hard and fundamental thinking" if they wished to make good on their promise (127). Joseph Wood Krutch (1927) also found it hard to reconcile Hemingway's stylistic virtuosity with his pessimistic outlook. Wood considered him the heir to "gaudier sophisticates" like Oscar Wilde and Aldous Huxley, who often seem bored but "never too bored to be voluble." The distinguishing characteristic of his writing is "a weariness too great to be aware of anything but sensations"; in his hands "the subject matter of literature becomes sordid little catastrophes in the lives of very vulgar people." Yet, Krutch admits, he has "an amazing power to make the apparently aimless and incompetent talk of his characters eloquent," and his dialogue is sufficient to make these very short stories "vivid and convincing." Almost begrudgingly Krutch concluded that, "within the limits of what he undertakes in the present volume," Hemingway is "a master" whose stories are "painfully good" (548).

Edmund Wilson (1927) was not surprised by this spate of negative criticism. Within three years Hemingway had already achieved such notoriety that "it has already become fashionable to disparage him" (102). Wilson accused those who did not appreciate Hemingway's hard-nosed view of the world of either misunderstanding him or being unwilling to accept his pessimistic assessment of modern life. Wilson, on the other hand, celebrated Hemingway as an artist of the first rank who uses his "misleadingly simple and matter-of-fact style" to express "subtle and complicated" criticisms of the contemporary world (102). While Wilson had some problems with Hemingway's fixation on cruelty and suffering, he believed readers would find in Hemingway's fiction "the image of the common oppression" that exists "in our time" (103).

With a novel and two substantial story collections before them, by 1927 critics had the opportunity to evaluate Hemingway's skills in both short and long fiction. Several found his strength in the short story, among them the British writer Virginia Woolf (1927). While ostensibly reviewing *Men without Women,* Woolf paid considerable attention to Hemingway's earlier work, particularly *The Sun Also Rises,* which she found overrated. There is nothing really new or "advanced" in it, she suggested. Hemingway's characters are flat—a fault she discovered at times in the short stories as well. He is not "modern" in being able to see his characters' lives from a new angle, though the "candour" with which they are described in this "bare, abrupt, outspoken book" might merit the term. Hemingway is "skilled and conscientious," Woolf admitted, but his people are crude and crudely drawn, fully formed and incapable of growth or change (1). As a novelist, Hemingway simply won't do. In fact, Woolf observed somewhat puckishly and presciently, "After all the high screaming about 'The Sun Also Rises,' I feared for Mr. Hemingway's next book. You know how it is—as soon as they all start acclaiming a writer, that writer is just about to slip downward. The littler critics circle like literary buzzards above only the sick lions" (8). Fortunately, Woolf said, *Men without Women* is actually a fine collection, as was *In Our Time,* though she found Hemingway's ability to create believable characters suspect. While Woolf did not believe (as others did) that Hemingway is "the greatest living novelist," she called him "the greatest living writer of short stories." Of *Men without Women* she concluded, "I do not know where a greater collection of stories can be found" (8).

Woolf's review is often described as unfavorable, although her observations seem more balanced than other critics have suggested. The most controversial of her criticisms, however, was aimed not at the content of

Hemingway's collection but at its title. Bothered by its implications—that women are incapable of facing some of the harsh realities that the men in these stories must confront—Woolf argues that the modern tendency to discriminate among books by assigning some sort of gender preference can be injurious to sales and dangerous in creating a false impression of the writer. By telling a reader that a certain work is "a woman's book" or "a man's," the critic (or publisher, in Hemingway's case) brings "into play sympathies and antipathies which have nothing to do with art." Woolf believed the greatest writers "lay no stress upon sex one way or the other. The critic is not reminded as he reads them that he belongs to the masculine or the feminine gender." Unfortunately, some modern writers (she singled out D. H. Lawrence and James Joyce) "spoil their books for women readers by their display of self-conscious virility"; unfortunately, though to a lesser extent, Hemingway "follows suit" (1). What Woolf found disappointing and disquieting would become an issue that would affect Hemingway's reputation immensely a half century later.

A Farewell to Arms

The period between 1926 and 1929 was one of great personal turmoil for Hemingway—divorce and remarriage, relocations between Europe and the United States—but throughout these years he continued to work diligently at his craft, and in 1929 issued his second major novel, *A Farewell to Arms*. The initial favorable reaction eclipsed that accorded *The Sun Also Rises*. Few critics doubted that this was the big novel Hemingway was expected to write. Most recognized that the war is not Hemingway's real subject, but instead serves as background for his tragic love story. The novel was reviewed favorably across the country, generating praise from papers such as the *Daily Northwestern* in Illinois ("Versatile Hemingway" 1929), the *Dallas Morning News* (Capers 1929), and the *Springfield Union & Republican* ("Poignant Love Story" 1929). William McDermott (1929) said the novel reminded him of a tragedy and suggested that Hemingway should try his hand at writing drama. James Aswell (1929) said reading *A Farewell to Arms* left him "a little breathless, as people often are after a major event in their lives" (25). Ted Robinson (1929) said the book "hit me an emotional wallop such as I have not felt for years" (6). Walter Brooks (1929) believed the novel has "that quality of warmth, of actuality of closeness that only your own personal experiences have for you" (270).

Writing in the *New York Times*, Percy Hutchinson (1929) described *Farewell* as "a moving and beautiful book"; Hemingway imparts "a sort of enamel lustre" to the story, "not precisely iridescence, but a white light rather, that pales and flashes, but never warms" (15). Agnes Smith (1929) said Hemingway writes "with a poetic modern idiom" and creates dialogue of "eloquent simplicity" that makes other writers' dialogue "seem smirking and stilted" (120). The *New Republic*'s T. S. Matthews (1929) called the book Hemingway's "statement of belief" (210) in human nature. He also suggested that this book revealed that Hemingway "is not a realist" (209); instead, *Farewell* possessed a symbolic quality that hints at larger truths beyond the story of Frederic and Catherine.

Many described the novel as an advance over *The Sun Also Rises*. For example, fellow novelist (and sometime friend) John Dos Passos (1929) called it "a first-rate piece of craftsmanship by a man who knows his job" (16). Bernard DeVoto (1929)—never really on the Hemingway bandwagon—believed that, while the former novel lacked passion, in *Farewell* Hemingway "for the first time justifies his despair and gives it the dignity of a tragic emotion" (9). The reviewer for the *Times* ("New Novels" 1929) found it "something entirely original" among war novels (20). Echoing those sentiments, B. E. Todd (1929) observed that "there may be cruder war books, but there are none gloomier than this very great one" which can be used "as antidote to the sickly poison of glory and glamour" (727). The *Times Literary Supplement* reviewer was willing to concede to Hemingway his unrelieved pessimism because it "animates an extremely talented and original artist" ("Some Italian Novels" 1929, 998). Burton Rascoe (1929) described *Farewell* as "a distinguished work of fiction by a writer who is to be counted among the best we have" (124).

English novelist Arnold Bennett (1929) said the novel is "hard, almost metallic, glittering," and "utterly free of sentimentality"; German novelist Thomas Mann (1932), promoting the German translation a few years later, called it "a masterpiece of a new kind." Hugh Walpole (1929) considered it "the finest novel of the year" (747). Clifton Fadiman (1929), an influential critic of the period who had complained about Hemingway's earlier work (Fadiman 1928), was wildly enthusiastic about *A Farewell to Arms*. There was "no reason," he asserted, that the novel "should not secure the Pulitzer Prize" (Fadiman 1929, 498). Unfortunately for Hemingway, Fadiman did not have a vote. The prize went to Oliver La Farge's *Laughing Boy*, a novel about Native Americans.

Balancing these euphoric pronouncements were reviews by a handful of critics still not won over by Hemingway's revolutionary experiments in style or his frank portraits of modern life. H. L. Mencken (1930) acknowledged the superb dialogue but said that "otherwise [Hemingway's] tricks begin to wear thin" (127). Lewis Galantière (1930), too, believed the novel suffered from weak characterization, though he believed the war story "is much more successful," and the book is crafted with great care and superb skill (259). The *Bookman*'s Robert Herrick (1929) found no such redeeming qualities in a novel whose love scenes he described as "hardly more than the copulation of animals," void of any meaning that might redeem them from being "mere dirt" (261). Of course, Herrick admitted that he did not read beyond the episodes set in Milan, so he conceded—sarcastically—he was "not qualified to say whether such a love 'conceived in the muck of war' [a phrase from an early review that praised the novel highly] finally evolved into something which I should call beauty" (261). Though not calling for outright censorship, Herrick declared that "to my way of thinking, no great loss to anybody would result if *A Farewell to Arms* had been suppressed" (262).

That is precisely what happened to *A Farewell to Arms* in Boston, where the Watch and Ward Society, successor to the New England Society for the Suppression of Vice, managed to suppress publication of the July, August, September, and October issues of *Scribner's Magazine* after an installment of the novel appeared in its June issue. Curiously, the society did not raise objections when the book version appeared in October, but that did not stop people from being curious: a "Banned in Boston" label was sure to increase sales in other, less squeamish sections of the country.[1]

Early Assessments of Hemingway's Importance

Even before the publication of *A Farewell to Arms*, but especially after its appearance, Hemingway was treated by the press as a celebrity. Beginning in 1927 his sojournings in America and Europe, divorce from Hadley Richardson, subsequent marriage to Pauline Pfeiffer, and purchase of a home in Key West were reported in papers across the country. A profile in the *Dallas Morning News* in 1927 ran under the title "This Novelist Is a Bull Fighter" ("This Novelist" 1927, 3). Imitations of his style began popping up in periodicals and newspapers (Phillips 1927, 6). Newspapers reported on efforts by American expatriates to identify real-life counterparts to characters in *The Sun Also Rises* ("Stirs Paris" 1927, 9). A syndicated news brief reported that a prominent magazine agreed to pay Hemingway $50,000 annually to write short stories (Kinnaird 1928, 4).

Syndicated columnists abetted the campaign to turn Hemingway into a household name. Burton Rascoe (1927) recounted how Hemingway saved John Dos Passos from being gored at a bullfight and how he beat up writer Charles G. MacArthur in what was supposed to be a gentlemanly boxing match (1927b). In a brief notice O. O. McIntyre (1929), a New York gossip columnist, described Hemingway as a slapdash writer who preferred to spend time fishing and going to bullfights. Several papers carried a notice of Hemingway's being hurt in a car accident in 1930 ("Ernest Hemingway Hurt" 1930, 5).

Hemingway's reputation among readers and reviewers at the end of the 1920s is summed up succinctly in a review of *A Farewell to Arms* that appeared in the *Greensboro Daily Record* ("War Story" 1929). "During the last five years," the reviewer noted, Hemingway "has won an extraordinary place in American letters. He has thousands of adherents among the readers of his own age; there are younger writers of talent who accept his leadership; he is imitated by writers much older than himself—a rare phenomenon—and one finds traces of his influence almost everywhere. His name is generally mentioned with the respect that one accords to a legendary figure" (8). The reasons for this sudden rise to fame are numerous, but the principal one, the reviewer concluded, "lies in his having expressed, better than any other writer, the limited viewpoint of his contemporaries, of the generation which was formed by the war and which is still incompletely demobilized" (8). Probably for all these reasons, Sinclair Lewis, on his way to Stockholm to collect his own Nobel Prize in Literature in 1930, said he was certain Hemingway would be honored by the Nobel committee in ten years ("Sinclair Lewis Says" 1930, 14).

In general, literary assessments added to the notion that Hemingway was the coming man in American letters and the spokesperson for his generation. In the first extended critical assessment of Hemingway, Robert Littell (1927), then an associate editor for the *New Republic*, looked for the qualities that allowed Hemingway to rise rapidly to a position of prominence in American letters. While Littell admitted that Hemingway was limited in his range of interests and sometimes a bit too cynical, his "curious original magic" (303) was endearing to admirers and threatening to a group Littell called "the Virtuous people," who were bothered by Hemingway's success at redefining "the purposes for which Fiction was brought into this beautiful world." Hemingway's combination of sensitivity and objectivity made him something of a "court reporter who doesn't know what is going to happen" but who can "change the present—cutting, polishing, omitting—so that it secretly leads up to and fits in with the future." This combination of "ignorance and art is the chief source of his originality" (304). In contrast to the highbrow who constantly says "more than he knows or feels," Hemingway "derives his strength from being, in this sense, a Lowbrow" who "instinctively mistrusts explicitness, analysis, imputation of motives, investigation of the souls of others, qualifying adjectives and a heart worn on the sleeve" (305). His unique gift lies in "his power to suggest other things while saying, in actual words, almost nothing at all" (305). Calling Hemingway "an architectural far more than a verbal artist,"[2] Littell believed that his strengths more than compensated for his shortcomings, and that those who are urging him to become more optimistic or less hard-boiled were misguided. "If he were more sensitive and amiable and soft," Littell concluded, "he wouldn't be nearly as interesting, so let's let him alone and see what he does next" (306).

Others found similar reasons to praise Hemingway. Walter Lippmann (1929), highly influential in American society in the early decades of the twentieth century as a thinker and social critic, classified Hemingway as one of the novelists "who describes the doings of the more advanced set of those who are experimenting with life," a writer of "tragic farces" that portray a society "in despair" because it has lost its sense of values (283). In *American Literature 1880–1930* A. C. Ward (1932) argued that Hemingway's "significance in contemporary literature" lies in the "part his work is likely to play in helping to set the literary artist free from subjection to irrelevant taboos" (153). In the introduction to the Modern Library edition of *A Farewell to Arms*, Ford Madox Ford described Hemingway as one of "the three impeccable writers of English prose that I have come across in 50 years or so" (quoted in Grimes 1932, 6).

In "The World of Hemingway," another assessment of Hemingway's early achievements, Granville Hicks (1930)—then not yet 30 and Hemingway's junior by two years—made rather sweeping pronouncements on the value of his fiction. Hicks located the key to understanding Hemingway in the character of Nick Adams, with whom, Hicks argued, many of Hemingway's protagonists share personality traits. Hicks said it is possible to discern a "Hemingway hero" (41) and define his characteristics: one who would like to disengage from the world but cannot, who cannot keep himself from thinking and feeling, and who uses a "cultivated reticence" to protect himself from a world out to crush him (41). Hemingway's hero "stands between two worlds," rejecting the qualities commonly associated with civilized society but not yet able to reach "that simple and objective way of thinking, feeling, and acting which is his ideal" (41). Hicks approved of Hemingway's simple style but questioned his decision to limit his focus to the kinds of people that had thus far populated his work. He thought the Hemingway hero was not particularly representative of human nature in general and publicly speculated that Hemingway would grow as an artist only if he moved beyond his present focus.

Robert Morss Lovett (1932) did not share Hicks's reservations. In an academic profile in the *English Journal*, Lovett wrote about the reasons Hemingway seemed to have "so quickly leapt to fame from so slight and casual a spring-board" as the stories of *In Our Time* (609). Lovett explored Hemingway's use of sport and war as subjects and his deceptively simplistic style that appealed to a wide audience of readers. He found literary parallels in the later Elizabethans, Dickens, and nineteenth-century Russian writers. Lovett was certain Hemingway would continue to excel as a writer, using his "critical talent" and "physical vigor" to provide "further food for his robust talent" (617).

Not everyone, however, was ready to accept Hemingway as the leader of a new movement in literature. Among the generation of critics that came to prominence before the First World War, Hemingway's stark style and frank language took some getting used to, and some never reconciled their critical principles with Hemingway's modernist practices. Fred Lewis Pattee (1930) said that attempts by modern writers to throw off older conventions "have gone often to absurd lengths. Realism and literary license have been pressed to extremes by such writers as Ernest Hemingway," whom Pattee accused of "violat[ing] every canon of the old handbooks and even the elementary rules of grammar" (326–27). Hemingway's "extreme realism" has "alienated many readers" (451).

In fact, the first extended study of Hemingway's fiction to appear in a book was hardly flattering. In *The Twentieth-Century Novel* Joseph Warren Beach (1932) titled the chapter in which he discusses Hemingway "The Cult of the Simple," and proceeded to use Hemingway as his prime example of what he believed was a serious degradation in creative prose. In describing the movement toward realist fiction from the more discursive works of the later Victorians, Beach suggested that Hemingway and others like him, "literal and hard-boiled," may have gone too far in reacting against "subjectivism" and the "psychological trend" (531). Hemingway's "notable reluctance to employ abstract nouns and adjectives" and his zeal to "reduce life to its simplest elements" (534) is not a sign of realist writing but "a return to the primitive" (537–38). Noting that Hemingway's people "refuse to be intellectual or esthetic," or even "polite or 'moral'" (537), Beach concluded that the "most correct word to apply" to Hemingway is "uncivilized" (537).

Beach's strictures seemed well founded to critics like Isidor Schneider (1931), who worried that Hemingway was already having a deleterious effect on a generation of writers enamored with his spare style and hard-boiled attitude toward life. Schneider complained about "the fetish of simplicity" that he found among modern authors, who self-consciously cut out "literary effects." This trend, he concluded, was principally the fault of "the writers of the Hemingway school" (184). While Schneider admitted that some fine works had been produced in the style advocated by "the Hemingway school" (a phrase he uses repeatedly), the few great works "are masterpieces for other reasons than their rhetoric" (186). Finding similar fault with contemporary literature, in a lengthy assessment appropriately titled "The Slump in Letters," Harley Gratton (1932)—no fan of current trends in fiction—insisted that if literature was to continue to be relevant, critics and reviewers should stop promoting Hemingway and Faulkner and instead champion John Dos Passos, Edmund Wilson, and Michael Gold.

Finally, in a curious but insightful critique Arthur Dewing (1931) wrote that most people had misunderstood Hemingway's true accomplishments. Dewing appreciated Hemingway's zest for life. Unlike so many of his contemporaries who, enamored with the trend toward interior exploration prompted by developments in psychology, focus on the complexities of characters' minds, Hemingway "finds too much delight in living to be concerned with introspective thought" (366). Stressing "the vitality of physical activity, of sense experience, as opposed to the deadliness and unreality of comparatively isolated processes of thought," Hemingway "has given contemporary fiction a healthy and much needed stimulant" (370). Unfortunately, Dewing continues, most of Hemingway's protagonists seem to be extensions of himself. If he is to develop as an artist, he must "treat life in its broader aspects," and that may mean abandoning the simplistic style and rhythms that have made him successful (371). Whether Hemingway would continue to write the kind of prose that won him international fame (or notoriety) as the spokesperson for the Lost Generation and the harbinger of modernist prose style, or begin, as Arthur Dewing suggested, to "treat life in its broader aspects" in a new style with new rhythms would be answered unequivocally by the publication of Hemingway's next book.

Notes

[1] For a discussion of the activities of the Watch and Ward Society, see Neil Miller (2010), *Banned in Boston*.

[2] The comparison of Hemingway's artistry to architecture is noteworthy, perhaps even prescient, as it suggests the importance of craftsmanship in creating something durable. Andre Maurois (1929) made a similar observation, suggesting that Hemingway's style reminded one of "modern buildings—steel beams and cement" (49). The analogy is most famously made by Hemingway (1932) himself in *Death in the Afternoon*, where he asserts unequivocally that "prose is architecture" (191).

2: Writing on His Own Terms (1932–1952)

To describe Hemingway's next new book after *A Farewell to Arms* as a radical departure may not be strong enough to capture the astonishment many readers felt when *Death in the Afternoon* was published in 1932. It was nonfiction. It showed only occasional flashes of the spare style for which he had become famous. Yet for Hemingway the book was a labor of love, the chance to introduce the wider world to the intricacies of a sport that he considered a metaphor for life itself. *Death in the Afternoon* also allowed Hemingway to claim the mantle of "writer"—a person whose skill with words transcends genres. The mixed reaction to this bravura literary performance shifted the ground among critics, however, and started a downward turn in his reputation.

Death in the Afternoon

To be fair, many reviewers heralded *Death in the Afternoon* as a significant achievement. Ted Robinson (1932) was amazed that Hemingway could make bullfighting interesting to a wide audience. "Hemingway is a real artist," he insisted, someone "who knows what he is doing and where he is going and so is a pleasing contrast to a large number of heavily publicized and aimless moderns" (11). Allen Cleaton (1932) called it "a fascinating volume," written with the "vigorous masculinity, the capacity for seeing things freshly and clearly, the magical quality of communicating sharp emotions, that give Mr. Hemingway his towering position in modern literature" (5). George Grimes (1932) was equally impressed: "who would think," he asked rhetorically, that a book on bullfighting would be "so interesting?" (7). John Adams (1932) believed the book would prove entertaining, and those who were not fond of bullfighting could still enjoy Hemingway's observations on literature.

Big-city reviewers also applauded the novel. Laurence Stallings (1932) described *Death in the Afternoon* as "a superbly colored and capricious essay on human pride" (34). Herschel Brickell (1932) said it "teem[s] with life, vigorous, powerful, moving and consistently entertaining" (12). R. L. Duffus (1932) felt Hemingway had not only explained the nature of bullfighting, but had pictured "the spirit in which it is done and seen" (5), although he was disappointed that the "famous Hemingway style" was not as evident as in his fiction (17). John Clair Minot (1932) observed, however, that while the book was "quite unlike anything that has earlier appeared in English" it was spoiled by "vulgarities, indecencies and obscenities." He said, "Hemingway writes too well to dip down into the gutter that way" (10).

Critics who were or would become influential in literary circles also voiced approval, although several expressed reservations. Malcolm Cowley (1932) wondered why Hemingway was so intent on writing elegiac prose. H. L. Mencken (1932), no fan of Hemingway, called it "an extraordinary piece of fine expository writing"; unfortunately, he said, "it often descends to a growl and irritating cheapness" (506). Mencken believed that if Hemingway would "take out the interludes" *Death in the Afternoon* would be "a really first-rate book" (507). Granville Hicks (1932) argued that the inclusion of philosophy and literary criticism made it fair to ask whether Hemingway "see[s] the world clear and as a whole" (461). Hicks believed he did not, choosing instead to isolate elements of society and focus on them to the detriment of developing a comprehensive worldview.

The reviewer for the *Springfield Sunday Union & Republican* ("Whole Technic" 1932) offered a judgment that many outside the circle of Hemingway aficionados would come to accept over the years: "Unless one is interested in bullfights or in Spain, their natural home, *Death in the Afternoon* is likely to seem excessive in length and in detail" (7E). Though he did not say so directly, *New York Times* reviewer R. L. Duffus (1932) found the book far too technical in its descriptions of bullfighting and too diffuse in introducing philosophy and literary criticism, which only served to dilute the main focus of the narrative. While the book may please "Hemingway addicts," he said, it will probably win few new fans. However, in one of the few early reviews of a Hemingway book published in an academic journal (*Hispania*), C. E. Anibal (1933) considered it unfortunate that critics are unable to "reconcile themselves to so good a novelist" writing in "a frankly expositional mode" (112).

Most reviews of *Death in the Afternoon* are overshadowed by one that has come down in Hemingway lore as one of the harshest attacks launched by a contemporary. Max Eastman, a writer who knew Hemingway, apparently was not impressed with either his personal bravado or his theory of writing. In "Bull in the Afternoon," Eastman (1933) accused Hemingway of violating one of his cardinal rules of writing by not telling the truth. Instead, Eastman said, he romanticizes bullfighting and ignores the brutality of the sport in which the bull has no real chance of survival. "Why then does our iron advocate of straight talk about what things are" (96) go softhearted over bullfighting? Eastman believed Hemingway wrote about bullfighting and other forms of death-sports and war because he had a fetish for killing. This, Eastman suggested, was Hemingway's way of compensating for the insecurity he felt about his manhood. His macho image was a sham.[1]

Early Challenges to Hemingway's Reputation

Sham or not, the image of Hemingway as adventurer permeated popular consciousness. This development was aided by Clifton Fadiman (1933a), an influential critic and early admirer who made the case for Hemingway's significance as a cult figure in an essay published in the *Nation* under the suggestive title "Ernest Hemingway: An American Byron." Fadiman said that, as good as his novels and stories are, "he has triumphed more as hero than as artist." A symbol of his generation, he is "the unhappy warrior that many men would like to be. About him has sprung up a real contemporary hero-myth" (63). The hero of his books is a projection of his own hero-image, a man with no country because all countries have betrayed him by espousing values that the recent war exposed as false and hypocritical. Like Byron, he openly defies conventional morality and values action, passion, and violence over intellectual pursuits.

In the same year, predictions of Hemingway's demise began to appear. Southern historian Lyle Saxon told an audience at a lecture in Baton Rouge that "the work of such men as Ernest Hemingway" and other moderns "is finished. They wrote for a generation that is passing" ("Several Hundred" 1933, 12). Saxon believed that, with the onset of the Depression, America was looking for new writers; perhaps biased by his own roots, he suggested Faulkner might be the coming man. Hemingway's reputation may also have suffered a bit from Gertrude Stein's (1933) somewhat unflattering portrait of him published in the *Atlantic Monthly*. She insisted that what was best about Hemingway was a result of the tutelage he received from her and Sherwood Anderson. Stein's description of him as a sycophantic young writer ingratiating himself with more established authors undercut both the image of the he-man he was creating for himself as a public personality and of the self-made writer whose new style had arisen sui generis.

The publication of a new collection of short stories, *Winner Take Nothing*, gave reviewers another opportunity to ponder if Hemingway had not reached his peak earlier and was now on a downward trajectory. Associated Press reviewer John Selby (1933) said those who consider Hemingway "the white-haired boy of the Franco-American short story" will find these stories great, while "those who don't care for him will have ammunition galore" (6). The reviewer for the *Dallas Morning News* ("Ernest Hemingway's Stories" 1933) agreed, noting that the collection "has the merits and the faults of his earlier books" (4). John Erskine (1933) called the collection "brilliant" but simultaneously "disagreeable," principally because of Hemingway's unrelenting focus on the derelict aspects of life (17). In a review written as a chummy letter to Hemingway, Clifton Fadiman (1933b) suggested that, as good as these stories are, they are "unsatisfactory" (74). Hemingway has developed his ideas about sport and death "to the saturation point" and should move on to new topics (75). William Troy (1933) also believed Hemingway must change his focus and abandon "fiction based on action as catharsis" or readers would abandon him (570).

Reasons for changing critical attitudes are evident in a number of reviews of *Winner Take Nothing*. T. S. Mathews (1933) complained that Hemingway's stories glorified adolescent behavior. John Chamberlain (1933) believed his preoccupation with death was beginning to wear thin; the patterns of his fiction were becoming mannerisms, and the stories in this collection rang hollow. In a long *New York Times* review essay, Louis Kronenberger (1933) made an even stronger case against Hemingway, pointing out that his exceptional skills and insights were being wasted in describing, without commentary, brutal characters from the lowest levels of society. Kronenberger believed his influence had hardly been salutary. "Without Hemingway there could hardly have been, for example, a gangster literature as we know it, or so much melodrama disguised as realism or sentimentality disguised as bravado" (6). While Hemingway had a right to focus on such people from aesthetic or moral grounds, it was wasteful for him to "show[ ] us things without infusing them into a more spacious canvas, without providing them with transcending values" (6). David Garnett (1934), writing in the *New Statesman*, called the collection "disappointing" and compared Hemingway to a Dutch master, adept at describing things he has seen but weak in dramatic effect. Still, he said, each story "has something beautiful in it for which one must be grateful" (192).

Perhaps the most insightful comment—and certainly one that would resonate with future critics—came from Burton Rascoe (1934), whose review appeared in the relatively new men's magazine *Esquire*.[2] While Rascoe applauded Hemingway's "reportorial cleverness," he wished "the war and life had not done so many things to him that he should find it necessary to put his virility so much on parade" (86). Small wonder that, writing after several reviews had appeared, John Adams (1933) was able to observe that "severely critical comments" in early reviews indicate that the "chorus of praise which has greeted Hemingway in the past is being, if not outshouted, at least inharmoniously interrupted by renegades from the faith" (9).

Shouting loudest, perhaps, was Wyndham Lewis (1934), onetime friend of Hemingway and iconoclast par excellence among modernist critics. Lewis's title reveals his intent: "The Dumb Ox: A Study of Ernest Hemingway." The essay condemned Hemingway in several important ways. Describing his work as having the quality of "an animal speaking"

(186), Lewis relegated Hemingway to "the multitudinous ranks of those *to whom things happen*." His much-vaunted stoicism arises from his willingness to accept his place in "the herd" (188). His art is all on the surface, never penetrating the depths of human feeling or intellectual complexity. He is "*the enthusiastic amateur of rude, crude, naked force in men and women*" (190). All of his books contain a figure—often the central character—who is "futile, clown-like, passive, and above all *purposeless*" (190). The Hemingway protagonist (exemplified by the supposedly sensitive Frederic Henry) is characterized by a "really heroic imperviousness to thought" (191).

A second fault, Lewis said, arises from Hemingway's insistence on using first-person narrators. His "first-person-singular" reminds one of a "dull-witted, bovine, monosyllabic simpleton," a "lethargic and stuttering dummy" (196). Both of these shortcomings can be attributed, Lewis said, to Hemingway's poor choice of a mentor, Gertrude Stein, whose work was characterized by "*faux-naif*" prattle (192) poured out in a kind of "infantile, dull-witted dreamy stutter" (195). Lewis believed Hemingway had mimicked Stein to the point that their work was virtually indistinguishable. For Lewis, Stein and Hemingway represented a particular political viewpoint: the "voice of the 'folk,' of the masses," the "cannon-fodder, the cattle outside the slaughter-house, serenely chewing the cud." Can this be art, he asked? Yes, of a certain kind. "The expression of the soul of the dumb ox would have a penetrating beauty of its own, if it were uttered with genius—with bovine genius"—and this is what Hemingway does in his fiction (206). If this was the kind of writing that contemporary civilization admires, Lewis concluded, there seemed little hope for the future.

Lewis's view was not shared by everyone, of course. Allen Tate, an equally astute observer and writer who also knew Hemingway, described him as "one of the most intelligent men I know and one of the best-read" (quoted in Wickes 1969, 169). Yet Lewis's opinion, not Tate's, became the dominant view of Hemingway's intellectual capabilities for at least the next twenty years. Hemingway biographer Jeffrey Meyers (1985) called Lewis's essay "the most damaging attack ever made on Hemingway," and claimed it "influenced all subsequent English criticism on his work" (25–26).[3]

Much criticism of Hemingway written during the 1930s stresses both the stoicism that underlies his approach to the cruel universe he sees around him (Hartwick 1934) and the limited vision he brings to human experience (Jameson 1934). Granville Hicks's (1935a) brief yet insightful assessment in *The Great Tradition: An Interpretation of American Literature since the Civil War* focused on these two attributes. Hicks posited that there are two heroes in Hemingway's fiction: "the autobiographical hero" and "the hero that Hemingway is not but thinks he would like to be" (274). Like Lewis, Hicks saw Hemingway promoting "action for its own sake" as the ultimate antidote for "the disease of his generation" (275). Hemingway did have values, Hicks insisted, but in his fiction he evades rather than examines them. This refusal is a severe limitation on his art.

Green Hills of Africa

The publication of *Green Hills of Africa* in 1935, another nonfiction book featuring a character remarkably like Hemingway, prompted the same kinds of responses that greeted *Death in the Afternoon*. Some reviewers hailed it as fine writing; others thought it a wasted diversion. The dichotomy can be seen in the two reviews in the *New York Times*. John Chamberlain's (1935) sarcastic dismissal plays with Hemingway's juxtaposition of "big game lore" and "salon controversy," noting how "with one hand he tears out the entrails of a gazelle" and with the other "rips the hide from Malcolm Cowley or Waldo Frank." This "overextended book about hunting" contains "some memorable passages," but is "not one of the major Hemingway works." Worse, Hemingway's involvement with "the cult of blind action" and his "animus against 'New York literary men' is keeping him from more important literary efforts." Yet, two days later, *New York Times* reviewer Charles Poore (1935) called *Green Hills* "the best-written story of big-game hunting" he has read, and much more besides. He applauded Hemingway's advance in style from the simple sentences that characterize early works to ones in *Green Hills* that "would make Henry James take a breath."

The book's admirers included Edward Weeks (1935) and Carl Van Doren (1935), who thought *Green Hills* helped dispel the legend of Hemingway as a tough guy. He is actually better, Van Doren insisted, when he lets his sensitivity come through in his writing. His personal exploits are adolescent; Hemingway is "mature only as an artist," able to write prose "that sings like poetry without ever ceasing to be prose, easy, intricate, magical" (3). The *Richmond Times-Dispatch* reviewer ("Hemingway's Fine Book" 1935) called *Green Hills* one of Hemingway's most interesting and revealing books, charming in its "sensuous perception of and delight in the strangeness and the beauty" of Africa (10). David Garnett (1935) complained mildly that he was expecting another nonfiction blockbuster like *Death in the Afternoon* and was disappointed by this book's "limited" subject matter (529).

George Grimes (1935) thought it was "a good deal like a novel," but was actually disguised autobiography—and sure to "repel readers who do not happen to share Mr. Hemingway's absorption with death" (7E). One such reader was the *Greensboro Daily News* reviewer Phillips Russell (1935), who complained about Hemingway's "dragging into the middle of the African scene a quarrel between American writers" who have lived too long in Paris (B5). Another is the *Boston Herald*'s John Clair Minot (1935), who wondered if Hemingway "believes that anything he writes is interesting enough to make it pay," or if he simply does not care what others think. Minot cautioned that he may lose even his devoted readers "if he does not get busy and exercise his undoubted talents on something other than such bloody fol-de-rol as the latest facile effort" (9). T. S. Matthews (1935) said that, while "it used to be exciting" to read a new work by Hemingway, now it is "alarming"; much of what he writes in *Green Hills* seems more appropriate for a letter to a friend (79). While "he thinks he can write about anything," *Green Hills* is not as good as Hemingway believes (80). John Chamberlain (1935) dismissed the book as "all attitude—all Byronic posturing" (19). Bernard DeVoto (1935), who seemed to grow progressively disenchanted with Hemingway over the years, called *Green Hills* "a pretty small book for a big man to write" (5).

Edmund Wilson (1935) expressed in his review what many critics were coming to believe: when Hemingway writes about himself, his prose suffers. Too taken with the legend that has grown up about him, Hemingway has begun to see himself as "Ernest Hemingway, the Old Master of Key West." This pose, Wilson said, makes him look "ridiculous" (135). Yet for all that, Wilson still believed Hemingway must be considered "on the highest plane of imaginative literature" (136). Granville Hicks (1935b) had a remedy for Hemingway's slide into irrelevance: "If he would just let himself look squarely at the contemporary American scene, he would be bound to grow" (23).

That attitude was shared by the Soviet critic Ivan Kashkeen (1935), who, in the same year *Green Hills of Africa* appeared, published one of the most frequently cited foreign assessments of Hemingway. In an argument that presages Philip Young's longer study of the Hemingway hero, Kashkeen developed a portrait of Hemingway and his characters that explains the consistent tragic dimension of Hemingway's fiction. Like a good Soviet critic, Kashkeen made liberal use of Marxist terminology in his critique. His detailed examination had two purposes: to explain Hemingway's vision of life and the techniques he uses to present that vision, and to predict what Hemingway will do next, as he appeared to Kashkeen to have reached a crossroads in his development as an artist. Kashkeen recognized that Hemingway was less interested in psychological development of characters or offering solutions to social problems, but instead evokes in his readers' minds questions about important social issues. Far from being disturbed by Hemingway's loss of popularity in the years following the publication of *A Farewell to Arms*, Kashkeen took pleasure in seeing that the "bourgeois patrons" and "middle-class readers" were losing interest in Hemingway because "his too intent gazing at what is horrible" is more than they can bear (93). Clearly, Kashkeen was hoping Hemingway would drift even further to the left in the future and become another darling of the Marxists.[4]

To Have and Have Not and *The Fifth Column*

No doubt Kashkeen was pleased with Hemingway's next novel, *To Have and Have Not*, published in 1937, which shows the struggles of a working-class protagonist against the forces of capitalism. Academic critics have generally regarded it as one of Hemingway's weakest books. Given its critical history, it may be surprising to see that initial reviews were not as bad as some later critics have suggested. Malcolm Cowley (1937) said the novel "contains some of the best writing" Hemingway had ever done—although he found it "lacks unity and sureness of effect" (306). In a cover story on Hemingway in the October 18 issue of *Time* magazine, Harry Morgan is described as "by far" Hemingway's "most thoroughly consistent, deeply understandable character" ("All Stone's End" 1937, 79). Bruce Catton (1937) believed that beneath this "brutal melodrama" is "a warm and painfully moving picture of a human soul getting backed into a corner by fate" (4). The *Times Literary Supplement* reviewer said that, within the limits Hemingway set for himself, "this is an absorbing and moving book" ("Toughness Is All" 1937, 733). Cyril Connolly (1937), who would later excoriate Hemingway for publishing *Across the River and Into the Trees*, found the book "very excitable and readable," though "not an advance on his other short stories" (606). Though Philip Rahv (1937) believed *To Have and Have Not* was "the least successful of Hemingway's works," he found that in some scenes "the writing is superb" (62).

Others expressed their disappointment more directly. The novel was described as the "bloodiest book to hit the market this year" ("Hemingway's New Novel" 1937, 12E); it revealed "a disappointing lack of development" ("Hemingway's Tale" 1937, 8); it did not suggest that Hemingway was advancing in his craft (Jackson 1937, 8). Associated Press reviewer John Selby (1937) believed there was "some sort of social criticism implicit" in the novel, but "it would be clearer if only, somewhere in this morass, there was a normal human being" (10). Clifton Fadiman (1937) thought "the best stuff should have been planed and chiseled into short stories" (101). Noting that this was "the first full-length book Hemingway had ever written about his own country and his own people," Alfred Kazin (1937) described *To Have and Have Not* as "troubled, sketchy, feverishly brilliant and flat by turns"; Hemingway seemed "less sure of himself than usual" (3). Louis Kronenberger (1937) complained about the novel's structure, as did Sinclair Lewis (1937), who dismissed *To Have and Have Not* as "not a novel at all but a group of thinly connected tales" (34). Perhaps the harshest judgment was that of *New York Times Book Review*'s J. Donald Adams (1937): "Hemingway's record as a creative writer would be stronger if [this novel] had never been published" (2). *New York Times* reviewer Charles Poore (1937) summed up critical reaction succinctly when he observed that the novel "will do more to renew the uproar than to close the case" about Hemingway's achievement as an artist. Of course, some truly devoted Hemingway readers found the negative criticism of *To Have and Have Not* too much to bear. Elliott Paul (1937) unleashed a diatribe against the naysayers in the *Saturday Review*, resorting occasionally to ad hominem attacks and stereotyping to put down those who found the novel wanting.

One reason Hemingway's reputation may have suffered during the 1930s is that larger forces were working against him. In 1936 the president of the American Library Association reported that the American reading public's tastes were changing. The most popular nonfiction works were those dealing with painting and music, and the taste in fiction "has turned away from the realism of Ernest Hemingway and his school to the sheer romanticism of 'Anthony Adverse' and 'Gone With the Wind'" ("Library Expert" 1936, 2).

Prompted by the publication of *To Have and Have Not*, Delmore Schwartz (1938) published a lengthy critique of Hemingway in what was then a relatively new scholarly publication, *The Southern Review*. Although Schwartz dismissed the new novel as "a stupid and foolish book, a disgrace to a good writer, a book which never should have been printed" (123), he made some interesting observations about Hemingway and his protagonists. First, Schwartz insisted, if one is to write "serious criticism of a serious writer," one must "forget about the public figure, the legend, the athlete and sportsman, the American Byron" (114–15). Hemingway's fiction reveals an extraordinary interest in "sensation" and "in conduct and the attitudes toward conduct," almost always studied against "the background of war" (115). In a provocative comparison not often followed up by other critics, Schwartz said that among novelists, Hemingway "most resembles Jane Austen, who was also very much interested in conduct" (117). Perhaps as well as any critic of his day, Schwartz was able to delineate the elements of Hemingway's famous code: "by which characters are judged and by which they judge each other"; "Courage, honesty and skill are important"; and judgments are made in the "historical context" in which a person acts. Schwartz also noted that for a Hemingway character to be admirable "from the standpoint of morality," he—it is almost always a male protagonist who lives by the code—must "admit defeat," be "a good sportsman," "accept pain without an outcry," and "play by the rules of the game" (117).

Reviews of *To Have and Have Not* were still appearing when Hemingway released his next book, *The Fifth Column and the First Forty-nine*

Stories, in 1938. The stories in the volume won almost universal acclaim, confirming most critics' preconceived opinions about Hemingway's mastery of the short story form. Elmer Davis (1938) proclaimed that "nobody else now living could show forty-nine stories that good" (6). Clifton Fadiman (1938) said the volume should convince everyone that "Hemingway is the best short story writer now using English" (95). Edmund Wilson (1938) called the collection "one of the most considerable achievements of American writing of our time" (630). Even the leftist *New Masses* reviewer Edwin Burgum (1938) praised the stories as "the record of the road that Hemingway has traveled through the confusions of modern life to a clearer insight into the relation between democracy and art" (24).

Hemingway's play was not so well received. Several critics had good words for it, among them Alfred Kazin (1938) and Peter Monro Jack (1938). But Malcolm Cowley (1938) believed it would need "a little play-doctoring before production" (367). Cowley proved prescient, as reviews of a 1940 production were hardly stellar. Stark Young (1940) did not think Hemingway's dramatic writing style well suited for the stage. Joseph Wood Krutch (1940), who had earlier proven himself no admirer of Hemingway, pointed out what he perceived as the play's many faults both as drama and as literature. Its protagonist is too much like other Hemingway heroes—grandiose in design but essentially a pedestrian bully. Only its first act shows any inkling of good writing, largely because it is "little marred by that tendency toward exhibitionism which is its author's besetting sin" (371).

Academic Judgments

By the end of the decade Hemingway's work was being discussed in academic institutions, as a notice about an upcoming forum on his work at the University of Iowa's creative writing program indicates ("To Discuss Hemingway" 1939, 17). In a general assessment published in the *English Journal*, J. Donald Adams (1939) balanced praise for Hemingway's abilities with what he described as self-imposed limitations of vision that Adams believed mar his achievement. Hemingway's "attitude toward life" is "basically adolescent" (87), his ostensibly hard-boiled realism a cover for an essentially romantic view of human experience. Some of Adams's phrasing suggests he had read the work of other critics (even if he did not acknowledge them), as when he noted that Harry Morgan was a man "to whom things are done" (88), echoing Wyndham Lewis, or that Hemingway's description of a matador's love of killing in *Death in the Afternoon* was "pure romantic twaddle" (90), as Max Eastman had suggested. Nevertheless, Adams's assessment, published in a journal aimed at college teachers, suggests that the reaction against Hemingway was beginning to take hold inside the academy.

Among academics writing about Hemingway was Columbia University professor Lionel Trilling. Picking up on the distinction Edmund Wilson made between Hemingway the Artist and Hemingway the Man to explain some of Hemingway's difficulties when writing autobiography, Trilling (1939) used his review of *The First Forty-nine* to blast American critics for making unfair and wrong demands of Hemingway. Trilling believed critics were to blame for Hemingway's degradation as an artist, because they had been insisting that his fiction show something other than the unrelieved misery of the human condition. The critics' demand that fiction be a kind of "moral-political lecture" (67) had caused Hemingway to veer away from what he did best—observe and report—to create political statements that rang hollow. Art has no "messianic responsibility" (70), Trilling insisted. The clues to Trilling's approach can be discerned in the phrasing he used (borrowed from Matthew Arnold, the subject of his dissertation): he insists that the "disinterested reader" can see how Hemingway has erred in succumbing to the critics' demands, or that in his best work Hemingway emulates Twain's *Huckleberry Finn*, which is written in "the prose of the free man seeing the world as it really is" (65).

In "Steinbeck, Hemingway, and Faulkner," V. F. Calverton (1939) assessed Hemingway's career in light of other writers who had made a significant impact on American letters in the early twentieth century. While he seems to lament Hemingway's excursion into socialist themes, Calverton described him as a "monadnock shot forth unexpectedly out of the sudden concussions and contortions of a literary earthquake" (37–38). He is sui generis, a perfect illustration of Remy de Gourmont's "declaration that the style and the man are one" (38). Calverton accepted the conventional opinion that Hemingway and his protagonists are men of action, not thought, who love fighting for its own sake, although most of his characters are "largely exteriorized entities" (39). Nevertheless, he is "the most significant writer in the United States today," writing "a stronger, finer, more puissant prose than any writer we have among us" (39).

Perhaps the most influential essay on Hemingway to appear during the 1930s is Edmund Wilson's (1939) "Hemingway: Gauge of Morale," published in the *Atlantic Monthly*. Wilson's aim was to provide an overall assessment of Hemingway's achievement. While not overly laudatory—Wilson seldom offered unqualified praise—his judgment was largely favorable. However, Wilson criticized Hemingway's use of pure autobiography: when he speaks "in the first person in his own character as Hemingway, the results are unexpected and disconcerting" (38). Wilson described the personae in *Death in the Afternoon* and *Green Hills of Africa* as caricatures. Hemingway's unusually clean, precise style is replaced by purple patches and passages that simply go on too long. Wilson believed the same lack of artistic distance marred *To Have and Have Not*, even though the novel dealt with an important contemporary issue: the degradation of social relationships. Nevertheless, Wilson believed it was wrong to accuse Hemingway of "indifference to society." His oeuvre is "a criticism of society" (another Arnoldian judgment). It is easy to misinterpret Hemingway because he emphasizes the physicality of action. But, Wilson pointed out, "ideas, however correct" (46), cannot prevail unless people of courage are willing to act in support of them. Wilson saw Hemingway's protagonists acting out their values in life-and-death situations that call forth qualities of strength and courage. In this respect, Hemingway was a moralist of the first rank.

Wilson also laid out the premises for much future discussion of Hemingway's philosophy and technique. He described what he called "a code" of behavior that exists beneath the surface dissipation and dissolution of Hemingway's characters, who understand and accept a simple principle that guides their behavior in a meaningless and sometimes cruel world: "We suffer and we make suffer, and everybody loses out in the long run; but in the meantime we can lose with honor." This code supplies "a dependable moral backbone" to many of Hemingway's stories and novels (36). The critical framework laid out by Wilson would influence Hemingway criticism for four decades (and perhaps more); more than thirty years later, Jeffrey Meyers (1982) called Wilson's essay "the most important and influential study of Hemingway" (34).

Wilson's positive assessment was challenged by Hugh Allen (1940), whose essay in *Catholic World* reflected that publication's ideological stance. Allen lamented Hemingway's ties to the amoral Gertrude Stein; seeking advice from her was "one of the dumbest things he ever did" (522). In Hemingway's "sub-human world" a kind of "Faustian bargaining" takes place (525), in which physical pleasure is sought at the expense of eternal happiness. Although Allen found some traces of good in Hemingway's most successful stories, he believed too often Hemingway's gifts were wasted on immoral tales. Allen ends by expressing hope that "before Hemingway goes to Judgment" he might "turn his distinguished talent to a theme worthy of his craftsmanship," creating people who "act like intelligent human beings apprised of the freedom of their wills" (528–29).

Hemingway's right to focus on subjects of his own choice was defended in a 1940 article by a newly minted Princeton PhD, Carlos Baker. "The Hard Trade of Mr. Hemingway" surveyed Hemingway's reputation, which Baker noted had already begun to decline. The reason, Baker insisted, was "Hemingway's singleness of artistic purpose and his unrelenting choice of un-genteel subject matter" (10). Baker approved of Hemingway's decision to fight the "quiet conspiracy against the manhood and the personal integrity of every American writer" and his disdain for New York critics (13). In somewhat hyperbolic terms,

Baker described Hemingway's "philosophy of art" as "naturalistic." In his work he "has attempted faithfully and truly to record his observations on the psychology and physiology of men and animals." Hemingway has "concerned himself with the ancient problems which look, but are emphatically not, simple: the loves and hates of men and women; food and drink; sleep and work; war and outdoor sport," and "the great phenomena of birth and death." However, Baker continued, Hemingway's "refusal to theorize about society sets him somewhat apart from most naturalistic writers" (14). While Marxist critics may blame him for "wasting time and talent" (14) writing about African safaris and Spanish bullfights rather than taking up social causes, Baker believed his achievement was "clearly one of the most distinguished in the annals of twentieth-century fiction" (16). That judgment makes it clear why Baker would continue to write about Hemingway throughout what would be a distinguished career of his own at Princeton.

One might dismiss Baker's encomium as the result of youthful infatuation with a power author and his work, were it not that, in the same year, another review of Hemingway's achievements appeared in the *Sewanee Review*, this one by Edgar Johnson (1940). Johnson had been on the faculty at City College in New York for over a decade, and although he was not yet the internationally acclaimed biographer of Dickens and Scott, his work was well respected. Therefore, his "Farewell the Separate Peace" must be considered important in advancing Hemingway's reputation in the academic community. Johnson does not mince words in his assessment. "Few writers reveal a more consistent intellectual development," he asserted. The reason critics inside and outside the academy have been harsh on Hemingway is that they fail to understand him. Far from being a "child of nature," and a "sort of savage endowed with style," he is "an intellectual" who has understood deeply the tenets of modern intellectualism and rejected them consciously (289). His career shows a dialectical movement, first accepting one attitude toward modern life and then rejecting it for something more complex. The simple isolationism expressed in his early works, which culminates in the separate peace Frederic Henry tries to make in *A Farewell to Arms*, is rejected for a more socially engaged response in later works such as *To Have and Have Not*. Even though his heroes—often simple and anti-intellectual men—fail in their efforts to maintain their integrity in the face of modern hypocrisy and comfortable materialism, they are admirable for undertaking the struggle. Johnson argued that, by 1940, Hemingway had rejected the position of "inverted aesthete and intellectual" and the "atomic individualism and irresponsibility foregoing the world" (300). As a result, his new heroes, "the good, the gentle and the brave," may avoid defeat if they do not try to make a separate peace. The implication is that future Hemingway novels are likely to contain protagonists more willing to engage the world rather than run from it. Johnson's predictions would be borne out shortly with the appearance of *For Whom the Bell Tolls*.

For Whom the Bell Tolls

Although not universally praised, *For Whom the Bell Tolls* rehabilitated Hemingway's reputation and in some ways restored him to his position as America's most popular and respected author. The novel was a Book-of-the-Month Club selection, assuring that it would achieve wide readership. Edmund Wilson (1940) expressed a feeling that many shared: "Hemingway the artist is with us again." What is more, he went on, "the book is also a new departure," a full-length novel with complex characters and a strong story (591). The *Nation*'s Margaret Marshall (1940) was similarly impressed, as was Malcolm Cowley (1941), who described the book as "an interesting and very complicated moral document" (89). Robert Sherwood (1940) called *For Whom the Bell Tolls* "a rare and beautiful piece of work" in which Hemingway "has achieved the true union of passion and reason."

New York Times Book Review contributor J. Donald Adams (1940) declared it "the best book Ernest Hemingway has written, the fullest, the deepest, the truest" (1). Longtime Hemingway admirer Dorothy Parker (1940) said "it is a great thing to see a fine writer grow finer before your eyes" (42). Robert Littell (1941) claimed *For Whom the Bell Tolls* was not only Hemingway's best novel, but "one of the best novels" that "any American has written" (vi). Others described the novel as "a tremendous piece of work" (Thompson 1940), "beyond a doubt" Hemingway's "best" ("Hemingway's Best Work" 1940, 4C), "a work of shining literary merit" ("Hemingway's Power" 1940, 8), and "one of the great novels of these times" (Goldstein 1940, 11). The novel transcends time and place, said the *Boston Herald*'s Charles Lee (1940); "in the symbolic sense of the book there are no Spaniards, but only man and woman battling against mechanized doom for their right to live and be human and themselves" (13). Max Miller (1940) said *For Whom the Bell Tolls* should allow Hemingway to "be accepted back into the fold of the literary holy of holies" (7C). Harry Hansen (1940) concurred, observing that it was "Hemingway's turn today to laugh at those who said 'He will never write another great novel'" (6). V. S. Pritchett (1941) praised the dialogue and the political portraits. Desmond Flower (1941) considered it better than *A Farewell to Arms*, and possibly "one of the greatest novels which our troubled age will produce" (4). Graham Greene (1941) called *For Whom the Bell Tolls* an accurate account of what the Spanish Civil War was really like. The distinguished Harvard scholar Howard Mumford Jones (1940) declared that "Hemingway has done for the Spanish Civil War the sort of thing that Tolstoy did for the Napoleonic campaign in *War and Peace*" (19).

There were criticisms, of course. John Squire (1941) expressed mild disappointment that Hemingway seemed once again to be "holding himself in," refusing to become passionate over the horrors of war (420). *Commonweal*'s J. N. Vaughan (1940) felt that most of *For Whom the Bell Tolls* was "infinitely inferior to Hemingway's prior work" (210). Burton Rascoe (1940) called the novel a "melodrama," entertaining but "absurdly pretentious" (493). Leftist critics were even less enamored. *Partisan Review* contributor Dwight Macdonald (1941) believed the novel's treatment of politics was weak—although Lionel Trilling (1941), writing in the same issue, praised the novel for its artistry. *New Masses* reviewer Alvah Bessie (1940) expressed disappointment that Hemingway's only "achievement" in the novel was the perfection of an "extraordinary technical facility"; he felt Hemingway showed no "depth of understanding," no "breadth of conception," and no more than superficial "grappling with the truths of human life" (25). Writing in *Socialist Call*, Sam Romer (1940) noted that readers of his paper, less interested in the novel as literature than in Hemingway's politics, would find that Hemingway failed to pass muster. Though he is hard on the fascists, his portrait of Communists is hardly more admirable. Romer was especially put out by Hemingway's attacks on Communist leaders and disturbed by his characterization of the International Brigade. Additionally, Romer noted, "the Spanish people and the rank-and-file of the International Brigade" fought not only against the Spanish political establishment but also "against the conspiracy of a world capitalism, led by the great 'democracies' of England and America" that chose Hitler over socialist Spain. "Of this," Romer lamented, "Hemingway says not a word" (8). Ironically, the book was on sale at Communist Workers bookshops ("In the Wind" 1940, 634).

The combination of Hemingway's celebrity status and the strong initial reception of *For Whom the Bell Tolls* prompted more than adverse reaction. In the spring of 1941 John Igual de Montijo filed suit against Hemingway and his publisher, accusing Hemingway of pirating the plot of the novel from Montijo's *The Rebel*. Montijo claimed Hemingway heard him read from it at a party in 1934. Hemingway eventually won the suit and was awarded court costs, but Montijo was unable to pay ("Hemingway Novel Brings Big Suit" 1941, 13; Meyers 1985, 339).

Two later reviews are worth singling out for very different reasons. The first, William Lyon Phelps's (1941), appeared in *Esquire*, which had achieved a wide reading audience in its short history in large part because it featured Hemingway's essays, letters, and reports. Phelps complained that other reviewers had praised the novel too highly. Hemingway "is not a great writer," he said, nor is *For Whom the Bell Tolls* "a literary masterpiece" (76). Phelps raises some of the objections that characterized negative criticism of Hemingway for two decades: he is more interested in what humans have in common with animals than what distinguishes them from lower species, the book is too long, the style too staccato and stilted. Phelps believed R. C. Hutchinson's *The Fire and the Wood*, published in the same year, to be a far superior novel.

The second, Mark Schorer's (1941), was published in the relatively new academic journal *The Kenyon Review*. Perhaps to interest his largely academic audience, Schorer focused on the technical qualities of the novel. He claimed it revealed a new style for Hemingway. Missing was the "ascetic suppression of ornament and figure," the "insistence on the objective and the unreflective," the muscular, staccato sentences. Also gone was the glorification of violence for its own sake. In its place a new, more discursive style complemented a new attitude in Hemingway's fiction: "a tremendous sense of man's dignity and worth, an urgent awareness of the necessity of man's freedom, a nearly poetic realization of man's *collective* virtues" (103). Schorer did not think the novel was perfect; its characters had the defects conventional in partisan novels, and Hemingway's signature understatement had been replaced by occasional overstatement. It may be as much a loss as a gain, Schorer suggested, but the new style was necessary and appropriate for Hemingway's new vision of life.

Though most reviewers and readers expected *For Whom the Bell Tolls* to be honored with a Pulitzer Prize, the committee made no award for fiction in 1941. Numerous explanations for the snub were advanced. Some suggested that the Spanish setting may have disqualified Hemingway, since the prize was set up to honor a work about American life. Hemingway biographer Jeffrey Meyers claimed the selection committee unanimously voted to give the prize to Hemingway but their recommendation was vetoed by "the extreme Right-wing president of Columbia University, Nicholas Murray Butler" (Meyers 1985, 339). John Hohenberg, who served for two decades as administrator for the Pulitzer Prizes, recorded a different story. He claimed the press had virtually awarded the Pulitzer to Hemingway but the selection committee passed over *For Whom the Bell Tolls* in favor of two other novels that received equal votes: Conrad Richter's *The Trees* and Walter van Tilburgh Clark's *The Ox-Bow Incident*. Members of the advisory board, which reviewed the recommendation of the selection committee, were outraged and insisted that Hemingway be given the prize. President Butler opted to settle the matter by directing that no prize be awarded (reported in Fischer 2007, 14). However, in what can only be described as a poke in the eye to the Pulitzer establishment, in 1941 the Limited Editions Club awarded its gold medal to Hemingway, citing *For Whom the Bell Tolls* as the book published in the past three years most likely to become a classic (Britton 1941, 4).

While reviewers and critics battled over the value of Hemingway's writing, Hemingway himself got on with the business of writing as the country went to war. One of his first efforts was to contribute the introduction to a collection of stories about armed conflict, *Men at War* (1942). The collection impressed most reviewers, although Hemingway's introduction came in for criticism. Walter Millis (1942) found it the least impressive piece in the book. Herbert Gorman (1942) described it as "interesting" but "badly put together and discursive" (27). Howard Mumford Jones (1942), who had written admiringly of *For Whom the Bell Tolls*, decreed that Hemingway was "too important an artist" to allow himself to be associated with "so shapeless a collection" (11). Unsurprisingly, Carlos Baker (1942) defended Hemingway's role in producing *Men at War*, suggesting the published volume was a compromise between what Hemingway wanted and what his publishers insisted on including. Baker considered the introduction a valuable restatement of Hemingway's standards of fine writing.

Further Academic Assessments

David Daiches's (1941) review of Hemingway's career in the *English Journal* gives evidence of the esteem in which the academic world held Hemingway after the publication of *For Whom the Bell Tolls*. Daiches looked favorably on Hemingway's decision to mine "his own personal tradition" (176) early in his career. He explained away some of the more objectionable aspects of Hemingway's "he-man" philosophy by claiming that it was simply "the most obvious symbol of the kind of intense life for which he was searching" (182). Daiches believed Hemingway's career showed steady development culminating, for the moment at least, with *For Whom the Bell Tolls*; while it may have flaws, the "dialectic" in the novel "is much more complex than in anything that Hemingway had previously written" (185). It is also the first work in which Hemingway shows a willingness to abandon his "personal tradition" in favor of a more mature view of life.

A wider reading audience also received a midcareer assessment of Hemingway from Maxwell Geismar in the *New Republic*. In "No Man Alone Now" Geismar (1941) noted that the early novels and nonfiction feature a "renunciation of social responsibility" and the "acceptance of a profound and complete isolation as the basis for an artist's achievement" (517). Clearly, Geismar was appalled that Hemingway would express such "supreme and final contempt for the common existence of humanity" (518). He posited that root causes for Hemingway's position could be found not in Hemingway's war experiences but in his deep-seated obsession with death and the will to self-destruction. Hence, *Death in the Afternoon* is a central text in the Hemingway canon because it foregrounds his obsessions. Yet, Geismar admitted, Hemingway continually denied these aspects of his artistry and often chose to write around problems that arise from the situations he created. Action almost always substitutes for thought because thinking would require his protagonists (and their creator) to confront their personal demons. As Hemingway's career progressed, however, he became less enamored with themes of isolation and more concerned with social problems. Geismar saw the turning point occurring in *To Have and Have Not* and coming to fruition in *For Whom the Bell Tolls*, where, by returning to "the common fate and common lot," Hemingway is "enriching the potentialities of his work" (533). Geismar hoped Hemingway would find a way to write about ways to live rather than continue to concentrate on ways of dying, because he is a "marvelous teacher"—limited, unfortunately, by "restrictions of temperament and environment which so far define his work" (534).

Most important for the purposes of the present study is Geismar's judgment of Hemingway's stature. "In our literary heritage there are few writers to compare with Hemingway in his intention and achievement," he said. "Of our past, perhaps Hawthorne is closest," and there are affinities with Poe and Melville, while among contemporaries, Geismar cited O'Neill and Faulkner—all writers who, like Hemingway, are "concerned with the depths of man's life" (532). Geismar (1942) expanded this essay into a chapter on Hemingway in *Writers in Crisis*, a lengthy analysis of the changing beliefs of contemporary American writers in what he called "our period of social crisis" (vii).

Alfred Kazin—then a precocious but apparently self-confident critic who felt that at age twenty-seven he was ready to make sweeping judgments on all of American literature—also explored Hemingway's contribution to American letters in his interpretive history of American prose, *On Native Grounds* (Kazin 1942). Noting that "the Hemingway world is in a state of perpetual war" (329), Kazin concentrated on Hemingway's attempt to create a style that would allow him to present the truth about that world as he saw it. Flatly asserting that Hemingway was not a nihilist, Kazin said his great theme is Man attempting to escape from or control the hostile world in which he finds himself. Hemingway had the uncanny and almost unique ability to assimilate information and technique from others and from his own experiences and transform them into art. His distinction lay "in his unceasing quest of a conscious perfection through style" (373). Like Edmund Wilson, however, Kazin thought Hemingway lost his way when he began to treat the legend he had created as "a guide to personal conduct and belief" (335). Reviewing Hemingway's achievement, Kazin described his career as "a half-triumph, because there is no real continuity in him, nothing of the essential greatness of spirit which his own artistic success has always called for" (340). While Kazin's assessment was less positive than the more fulsome accolades used to describe Hemingway earlier in his career, it was endorsed by Cleanth Brooks (1943), then a figure of some renown in academic circles. Though Brooks had reservations about *On Native Grounds*, he made a point to commend Kazin's judgment of Hemingway, which he called "much more knowing than most recent accounts" (52).

While critics like Daiches, Geismar, and Kazin were helping to solidify Hemingway's place as a major voice in American literature, Malcolm Cowley's (1944b) introduction to the Viking Portable Hemingway advanced Hemingway studies by linking him to American literary tradition, particularly Poe, Hawthorne, and Melville, "nocturnal writers, the men who dealt in images that were symbols of an inner world" (40). Cowley suggested that Hemingway's heroes populate enchanted countries, where beneath the surface calm are nightmare scenarios; much of his fiction has "the quality of a waking dream" (42). Anticipating Philip Young's influential assessment of the importance of the wound Hemingway received during the First World War as the central inspiration for his early fiction, Cowley said Hemingway's writing is "an exhausting ceremony of exorcism." The war left him with "painful memories of which he wanted to rid himself by setting them all down" (43). Following a critical practice common for the period, Cowley offered a symbolic reading of Hemingway's fiction. He said Hemingway is an exceptionally good writer of symbolic fiction because, though "his eyes are fixed on the foreground," he "gives us a sense of other shadowy meanings that contribute to the force and complexity of his writing" (46). While other critics had encouraged Hemingway to write more optimistic fiction, Cowley thought that might be a mistake. Hemingway had "earned the right to be taken for what he is, with his great faults and his greater virtues" (51).

Cowley (1944a) also offered a description of the Hemingway hero in a *New Republic* article that outlined the development of a single figure through Hemingway's first four major novels. Cowley argued that the Hemingway hero initially chooses to alienate himself from society where he suffers both physical and psychological wounds. The "real nature" of the wound the Hemingway hero suffers is "moral rather than physical"; he loses "faith in organized society" (758). The extremes to which alienation takes the hero is evident in the death of Harry Morgan, Cowley said, who comes to realize that "complete loneliness is unbearable" (758). Viewed as part of the progression of a single type, Robert Jordan is the first of Hemingway's heroes to be reconciled with society.[5]

Ray West (1944) is another critic who saw Hemingway evolving away from his nihilist philosophy. West made another point worth noting: despite the success of the recently published *For Whom the Bell Tolls*, "there is a reasonable certainty that the final estimate" of Hemingway's achievement "will depend, ultimately, upon his shorter works, for it is in them that emotion is more completely integrated with technique" (573). W. M. Frohock (1947a, 1947b) also believed Hemingway's style was his distinguishing contribution to American literature. Even after two decades, "the familiar contours of the Hemingway style keep turning up in the most unexpected places" (1947a, 89). Yet, Frohock noted, no one had yet captured the discipline Hemingway exhibited. Of course, Frohock did not believe that Hemingway himself had been able to maintain this discipline. He seemed to have lost his way in *For Whom the Bell Tolls*, which "falls short of his best work" (1947b, 189)—in part, Frohock suggested, because he wrote it with one eye on Hollywood and all the money to be made from a movie starring Gary Cooper.

George Snell (1947) was not so cynical. In *Shapers of American Fiction* he argued that Hemingway enjoyed the highest reputation any American writer had ever had. Additionally, beneath the hoopla surrounding his larger-than-life personality lay a serious artist with a sharp temperament that is sensitive to the contemporary world. Hemingway's desire, Snell insisted, "is to inspire a deeper consciousness of reality through an appeal to the nonobjective factors of experience" (161). Although works he produced during the 1930s had not lived up to the high standards of artistic integrity Hemingway set for himself as a young writer, Snell believed he might achieve continued success because he was exceptionally disciplined and "resolutely searches himself for attitudes of integrity" (172).

The 1940s saw the rise of a new critical methodology that would be employed frequently in the next two decades as a tool for assessing Hemingway's work. New Critics sought to expunge from consideration any materials extraneous to the text being examined. What might be considered the high point of New Critical analysis of Hemingway's fiction is the analysis of "The Killers" in Cleanth Brooks and Robert Penn Warren's (1943) *Understanding Fiction*. The detailed, almost line-by-line critique displays the methodology New Critics employed in examining a work of fiction's structure, irony, and symbolism. This approach to Hemingway is explained in detail by Penn Warren (1947) in a long *Kenyon Review* essay that explains what Hemingway had contributed to literature, offers a method for understanding and interpreting his work, and defends him from some of the charges leveled at him by detractors. A chief characteristic of Hemingway's fiction is the focus on a "violent world" in which either "tough men" or "a very young man, or boy" faces defeat and "usually manages to salvage something" (1–2). These characters maintain in defeat "an ideal of themselves," which represents "some notion of a code, some notion of honor, which makes a man a man"; the "discipline of the code" gives the Hemingway hero "a sense of style or good form" (2). For Hemingway, if one can maintain discipline in one's profession, one can "achieve a moral significance" (2).

One of Penn Warren's chief objectives was to undercut the notion that Hemingway is a writer sui generis; hence, much of his essay examined Hemingway's place in the literary tradition. He noted similarities between Hemingway's outlook and that of other writers—Robert Louis

Stevenson, Tennyson, Housman, Hardy, Zola, Dreiser, Conrad, and Faulkner—all of whom confronted, as did Hemingway, "the world with nothing at center" (4). He also provided a long comparison of Hemingway's work with Wordsworth; both, he said, focus on simple characters that stand outside the intellectual tradition. Hemingway's decision to write in a way that had never been tried before was actually part of the "general revolution in style" that was under way at the end of the nineteenth century but that was accelerated by the First World War (14). The famous Hemingway style—with its "short simple rhythms," "succession of coordinate clauses," and "general lack of subordination"—suggests "a dislocated and ununified world" (18) and serves as counterpoint to his heroes' "quest for meaning and certitude in a world which seems to offer nothing of the sort" (18–19).

While Penn Warren felt it was too early to provide "a final evaluation of Hemingway's work" (24), he believed it important to dispel objections that might cause some to reject or avoid him. He countered the charge that Hemingway's fiction was "immoral or dirty" by pointing out that his best work deals seriously with "moral and philosophical" issues (25). To refute the claim that Hemingway's early work has "no social relevance" (26), he asserted that literature need not be overtly didactic; "what good fiction gives us is the stimulation of a powerful image of human nature trying to fulfill itself and not instruction in an abstract sense." That Hemingway's works had sparked widespread interest "is a testimony to their relevance" (27). Penn Warren's strongest defense—and one that explains why Hemingway was appealing to New Critics, who valued lyric intensity over narrative diffusion—is that Hemingway is "essentially a lyric rather than a dramatic writer" whose success depends "upon the intensity with which the personal vision is rendered." While Hemingway may not have documented and diagnosed the Modern age, Penn Warren concluded, "he has given us one of its most compelling symbols" (28). For New Critics, that was often enough.

The novelist Caroline Gordon (1949) was more restrained in her praise. Noting that among popular writers who "as a rule" attain success because "they speak for their age," Hemingway's work had more staying power than many of his contemporaries. He is deeply grounded in his craft, but is somewhat limited by "the temper of his age." A kind of "natural symbolism" operates well in his fiction, but it "refers to a narrow range of experience" and "seems inadequate today" (220). He avoids giving his characters the ability to reflect on the significance of their actions; as such, Gordon concluded in an apt metaphor, he "always hits out from the shoulder, but his reach is not long enough" (225). He suffers by having "limited his field of observation too strictly" (226).

Opposing the growing consensus among critics about Hemingway's success in creating a new and unique hero, Robert Daniel (1947) argued in "Hemingway and His Heroes" that much of the critical commentary is overblown hype. Specifically challenging Brooks and Warren's assessment of Hemingway in *Understanding Fiction*, Daniel argued that the only judgment Hemingway's heroes deliver about their violent world is through their feelings, not through a coherent code of behavior. He believed Edmund Wilson was right to criticize *A Farewell to Arms* for being a poor novel, dismissed the "moral standard" in *To Have and Have Not* as "childish" (483), and said *For Whom the Bell Tolls* suffers from "a radical disharmony between Hemingway's intense imaginative grasp of his material and his ability to evaluate it" (484). Only *The Sun Also Rises*, which he called "the most nearly perfect" (485) of Hemingway's novels, escaped criticism.

Following in some ways the line of reasoning employed by Wyndham Lewis in his famous "Dumb Ox" essay, D. S. Savage (1948) delivered a stinging critique of Hemingway in a *Hudson Review* article. Savage was skeptical of critics like Mark Schorer who gave primacy to technique in judging the value of a work of art, so it should come as no surprise that he seems dismissive of Hemingway's rise to fame as a "stylist" (23). While Hemingway may aspire to be an artist, Savage conceded, he shares many affinities with the writers of pulp fiction that glorify warfare. His typical hero "has no contact with ideas, no visible emotions, no hopes for the future, and no memory. He is, as far as it is possible to be so, a *de-personalized* being" (24), often "drawn from the lowest stratum of human existence, where life is lived as near as possible on an animal, mechanical level" (25). There is no growth in either characters or author; rather, "Hemingway's world is one of mechanical repetition" (28). Characters reflect "profound spiritual inertia," an "inner vacancy and impotence," projecting "a deadening sense of boredom and negation which can only be relieved by violent, though still essentially meaningless, activity" (28). In a sweeping indictment, Savage declared that Hemingway represented "the *proletarianization* of literature: the adaption of the technical artistic conscience to the sub-average human consciousness" (31).

The idea that Hemingway wrote about subhumans because he shared their outlook and intellectual capacity is reinforced in Lillian Ross's (1950) profile of him in the *New Yorker*. Her assessment seemed to take on iconic stature almost as soon as the magazine hit the newsstands. Ross recounted in great detail the time she spent with Hemingway and his wife Mary in New York City, capturing many of Hemingway's thoughts about his writing and reputation: how he managed to cut away from his work all the excess, leaving only the most refined, true accounts of events and people he wished to depict; how, through careful, dedicated practice, he managed to overtop several literary icons (de Maupassant, Turgenev) or rise to the level of some of the greatest (Stendhal). Ross also recorded what seem to be verbatim conversations in which Hemingway spoke a kind of Pidgin English.

Though Ross began her article with the admission that Hemingway "may well be the greatest American novelist and short story writer of our day" (36), many readers thought her portrait depicted him as a boorish, egotistical lout. The backlash was so strong that Ross found it necessary to defend herself a decade later in a preface to *Portrait of Hemingway* (Ross 1961), a reprint of her essay with some explanatory information added. Ross insisted she meant to flatter, not condemn a man who was "generous with his conversation" (12) and extraordinarily accommodating in the two days she spent with him in New York. She says people who thought she was ridiculing Hemingway simply did not like Hemingway—the way he talked, the way he acted, the freedom he enjoyed—all signs, she suggested, of a kind of petty jealousy. Despite such pleadings, however, Ross's portrait entered the Hemingway canon of criticism alongside Max Eastman's 1932 attack and Wyndham Lewis's 1934 lambasting as one of the principal condemnations of the myth of the heroic warrior and sensitive writer who records things the way they were.[6]

In the same year Ross's profile appeared, John McCaffery (1950) published *Ernest Hemingway: The Man and His Work*, the first book of criticism dedicated exclusively to Hemingway. To his credit, McCaffery included some unflattering commentary, but on the whole his collection reflects his belief that "it is impossible for the critic to disregard Hemingway's importance" (10–11). What seems to interest McCaffery personally, however, is the man rather than the work. He seems genuinely proud to have included with an array of academic criticism a trio of personal profiles that present a "picture of Hemingway as a man among men"—something McCaffery found "conspicuously missing in the reports from critics included in this volume" (10). McCaffery's book received several favorable reviews in American newspapers, giving further credence to the notion that any commentary about Hemingway was of interest to the general public. In a *Boston Herald* notice, Arthur Jensen (1950) called *Ernest Hemingway: The Man and His Work* a collection of "brilliant and searching criticism"—though lacking any "really adverse criticism." Jensen was not surprised to see a publication such as McCaffery's, however, since "today [Hemingway] has become more or less an institution" (27). The book was described in the *Trenton Sunday Times* ("Punk and Incense" 1950) as "an important addition to Hemingway literature" (4:10). Scholarly publications also paid heed. *American Literature* carried a note announcing the publication ("Brief Mention" 1951), and Granville Hicks (1951), writing in the *English Journal*, commented on its timeliness. But as Harvard's Harry Levin (1951) observed in a *Kenyon Review* essay on Hemingway, few of the contributors were able to maintain a distinction between Hemingway's works and their author. Instead, quite a few "seem more interested in recapitulating the phases of Hemingway's career, in treating him as the spokesman of his generation, or in coming to grips with a natural phenomenon" (584).

Across the River and Into the Trees

By 1950 any work by Hemingway was sure to be reviewed widely. Such was the case with *Across the River and Into the Trees*. To say it was not well received would be an understatement. Nevertheless, there were several complimentary reviews in important newspapers, including Fanny Butcher's (1950) in the *Chicago Tribune* and Malcolm Cowley's (1950) in the *New York Herald Tribune*. In an early notice, however, Elliott Paul (1950) lamented that this "magnificent" novel was certain to "get the usual disrespectful reception from the boys of English 'A' who have spent their years in New York offices and hate those who have seen or felt other things" (8). For different reasons, Harrison Smith (1950) predicted that "few books this season will be discussed at greater length"—or "more bitterly excoriated"—than this novel, which he found "egocentric and narcissist beyond belief" (7).

Other reviewers were a bit more charitable, like Jack Bilyeu (1950), who described *Across the River and Into the Trees* as one of three disappointing Hemingway works. Robert Ruark (1950), who said he cut his "literary eyeteeth" on Hemingway, found this latest novel evidence that "Papa is getting old" and losing his touch (71). Northrop Frye (1951) believed Hemingway failed to deliver on the potential of his "great theme"—the loneliness of old age—instead creating an "amateurish" work in which "the most articulate character sounds like a mouthpiece for the author" (612). Kate Simon (1950) described it as "a slight, sad book," although "the Hemingway spell still holds" (20–21).

Others dismissed the novel as "disappointing" (Rovere 1950, 104), an "occasion for little but exasperated depression" (Zabel 1950, 230). "The prose is that of Hemingway's most misguided imitators" (Warshow 1950, 884), as much a parody as a genuinely representative Hemingway novel (Jackson 1950). Lewis Gannett (1950) said that "some of the book is Hemingway at his worst, and the whole does not add up to Hemingway at his best" (23). Maxwell Geismar was especially disappointed because he had written a year earlier that "the literary event" of the coming season "should be Ernest Hemingway's new novel" (Geismar 1949, 1). Instead, *Across the River and Into the Trees* was "Hemingway's worst novel," a book "unpleasant to review for anyone who respects Hemingway's talents and achievement" (Geismar 1950, 18). Even Philip Young (1950), then completing what would become the most influential study of Hemingway to appear in the twentieth century, seems forced to admit that "this is a pretty bad book" (55).

These were not the worst judgments. Cyril Connolly (1950), a longtime admirer of Hemingway, dismissed it as "lamentable" (3). Charles Angoff (1950) said it will be almost impossible for the school of realism that Hemingway founded "to outlive the disgrace of *Across the River*" (625). Philip Rahv (1950) believed the novel was "so egregiously bad as to render all comment on it positively embarrassing to anyone who esteems Hemingway as one of the more considerable prose-artists of our time" (400). Victor Haas (1950a) called *Across the River and Into the Trees* "a mass of distasteful piffle" (28C); he disliked the book so much that he wrote a second piece quoting from many of the reviews that panned it (1950b). Lon Tinkle (1950) described it as "arrogant, self-indulgent, trivially bitter and full of irrelevant slaps at things [nearly everything] that Hemingway hates" (3). Alfred Kazin (1950) found the only consolation one could take after reading this novel was that it is not Hemingway's last word.

Despite the general tendency to pan the novel, some fairly prestigious colleagues rose to Hemingway's defense. Evelyn Waugh (1950a, 1950b) observed that it had already become "impossible to approach" the novel "without some prejudice either against the book itself or against its critics" (1950a, 290). Perhaps unconsciously wanting to defend a fellow novelist, Waugh said that even if Hemingway had written "a completely fatuous book, this was not the way to treat it." It may be inferior Hemingway, but it was still "very much better than most of the work to which the same critics give their tepid applause" (1950a, 290). Why, then, do critics all "hate him so?" Waugh thought the problem lay less in what Hemingway had written than in the way he behaved. The critics have "detected in him something they find quite unforgiveable—decent feeling." Hemingway has "an elementary sense of chivalry—respect for women, pity for the weak, love of honour"—that critics, filled with "high, supercilious caddishness," cannot abide (1950a, 292).

The most strident defense came from novelist John O'Hara (1950). Writing in the *New York Times*, O'Hara called Hemingway "the most important author living today, the outstanding author since the death of Shakespeare," the "outstanding author out of the millions of writers who have lived since 1616" (1), unquestionably "a genius" (30). O'Hara's encomium met with howls from critics and readers alike; editorials and letters to the editor filled periodicals and newspapers calling O'Hara misguided—or worse (Maner 1950, A9). Some even suggested that O'Hara's review made the paper only because *Times* Sunday editor Lester Markel was on vacation and not on hand to stop its publication—a claim Markel later denied, though he said he would have questioned O'Hara to make sure he meant what he said (Lyons 1950, 28). William McDermott (1950) said O'Hara's critique was "nonsensical"; he believed no "competent critic" would consider Hemingway equal to Dickens, Thackeray, "or a hundred others who have written since Shakespeare's time." McDermott wondered, "Does anybody think that anything by Hemingway will be read 100 years from now?" (13). While most critics writing during the next decade found little redeeming value in the novel, eight years after it appeared Robert O. Stephens (1958) published a long defense in which he answered some of the charges leveled against it, claiming that the novel is a continuation of Hemingway's exploration of the concept of the hero, a figure "perpetuated in the succession of protagonists culminating in Colonel Richard Cantwell" (92).

Attack and Defense at Midcentury

Fallout from the publication of *Across the River and Into the Trees* continued into 1951. Isaac Rosenfield (1951) used its publication as a springboard for a harsh critique of Hemingway in the *Kenyon Review*. He believed the novel revealed a truth that few critics wished to recognize: "no writer of comparable stature has ever expressed in his work so false an attitude toward life" (147). Hemingway achieved popularity because he presented to the public a view of the Lost Generation that was gladly accepted, and he had been given a pass since then on his false vision of life. Rosenfield claimed Hemingway had created "his own subsection of the Myth of the American Male, supporting everything in this myth which is lifeless, vicious and false—the contempt for women and for every tender feeling, as for something effeminate and corrupt, the apotheosis of the purely forceful, tense and thrusting component of maleness as a phallic bludgeon to beat the female principle into submission" (149). He uses (or abuses) style to "cover[] up" the fact that his characters feel nothing (151). Rosenfield seems to take pleasure in the irony of Hemingway's "fight[ing] off the meanings which his critical audience attributes to him, the very meanings which give one reason to take his work seriously" (152). The spare style and understatement are actually vacuous; "he presents a blank, which his more sophisticated audience returns to him, filled with insight" (153).

On the other hand, Joseph Warren Beach (1951) argued in "How Do You Like It Now, Gentlemen?" that, despite occasional blemishes and mistakes—among which he would put this latest novel—Hemingway was a "scrupulous artist, bent on turning out the best writing he is capable of" (312). Coming only two decades after he had found Hemingway wanting (Beach 1932), Beach's defense shows a turnabout in his opinion. Unfortunately, he said, Hemingway's defenders suffer "under a double handicap" (311) at the moment; the many faults of *Across the River and Into the Trees* compound a growing hostile attitude toward Hemingway's cult of virility. Beach claimed that an unbiased survey of Hemingway's fiction—one that focuses on artistry rather than celebrity—reveals that the focus on competitiveness and virility is "in the main duly subordinated to more important values of living." Hemingway aims consistently at "truth-telling," and his best stories "seem to be devoted mainly to the debunking of sentimental notions" (317). One value Beach found important to Hemingway is love; the best portrayal of it was in *For Whom the Bell Tolls*. Thus, while *The Sun Also Rises* and *A Farewell to Arms* were both strong literary performances, Beach believed that in *For Whom the Bell Tolls*, a novel in which the action is "important enough to bear the weight of the emotion roused, developed in vivid and convincing detail," Hemingway had "done fullest justice to his theme of 'true love,' given it organic relation to the other main concerns of life, and established its place in the scale of human values" (328).

Similarly, Granville Hicks (1951) argued that "the violence of some of the criticisms" of *Across the River and Into the Trees* was "in itself a tribute to Hemingway's eminence." In his retrospective assessment "Our Novelists' Shifting Reputations," Hicks looked at what had happened to the reputations of several novelists whose works were analyzed by Beach in his influential *American Fiction, 1920–1940*. Of those who were "deservedly eminent in 1940" (1), Hicks said only two had risen above the others to a place of prominence in American letters: Faulkner and Hemingway. These two are almost universally considered "the outstanding novelists of the period from 1925 to 1950" (3).

On the other side of the critical ledger, John Aldridge (1951) expressed the view held by a number of his contemporaries who found Hemingway scintillating when they were young but shopworn as they grew older. Many admired him, first as a great writer who captured the *angst* of the Lost Generation and second as a larger-than-life figure whose escapades served as a model of the man of action. But in the 1950s, Aldridge said, "the Hemingway time is dead," as men "stopped reminiscing about the first Great War" to "start thinking about the second Great War," and women stopped trying to emulate Brett Ashley and instead began preparing themselves "for jobs or marriage and motherhood" (25). In Hemingway's fiction, the famous code that gave men a means of staving off the emptiness of a meaningless world devolved into senseless violence. Sadly, Aldridge concluded, "going back over Hemingway's work today is rather like going back to the house where you lived as a child and finding it smaller and somehow less substantial than you always remembered it" (42).

Similarly, in his sweeping study of American fiction during the first half of the century, Frederick Hoffman (1951) found Hemingway's career to have spiraled downward from the promise he showed in the 1920s. That promise was realized in *The Sun Also Rises*, but was inexplicably missing from *A Farewell to Arms*, which is filled with "sentimentality and romantic softness" that are "melodramatically touched by an amateurish philosophy" (98). Hemingway was not a man of ideas, Hoffman asserted. Unfortunately he determined to force himself to write something positive and passably intellectual—a strategy that failed in his next two novels. His only real contribution to literature, Hoffman concluded, was in promoting the "esthetic of simplicity" (102).

Another important essay that used the publication of *Across the River and Into the Trees* to launch a wider discussion of Hemingway's career is Harry Levin's (1951) "Observations on the Style of Ernest Hemingway." In this somewhat discursive piece, Levin, known for his work on the Renaissance, the moderns, and critical theory (as it existed at the time), began with an acknowledgment that *Across the River and into the Trees* is not particularly good, but countered that Hemingway was nevertheless an important figure in contemporary literature. Levin is interested principally in the methods Hemingway employed to achieve success. Chief among them, Levin suggested, was his constant struggle to give his prose a sense of immediacy. Levin devoted paragraphs to careful exegesis of Hemingway's use of grammar, syntax, word choice, metaphor, allusion, paradox, and a variety of other devices available to him to capture the world he experienced.

Levin debunked claims by Hemingway and his devotees that his prose is without precedents—Levin cites several—but, he continued, unlike almost any writer before him, Hemingway fully identified himself with those he wrote about, "allowing them to take possession of him" and "accepting—along with their sensibilities and perceptions—the limitations of their point of view and the limits of their range of expression" (596). This accounted for many of the charges leveled against him that his own vision and range of expression is limited. Even if one granted the limitations of diction, syntax, expression (particularly the avoidance of adjectives and the lack of "energetic" verbs [599]), how did one explain, Levin asked, Hemingway's "indubitable punch, the unexampled dynamics of Hemingway's style?" (600). His particular strength, best revealed in fiction where he employs indirect discourse, lies in his "power to visualize episodes through the eyes of those most directly involved" (604). He may not behave and write like the other moderns; but behind what some have described as an anti-intellectual pose lies the sensitivity of a poet. His power to get readers to experience what he has, has made him a guide for his generation. His style reflects the age in which he writes, an age of fragmented experiences from which one must create meaning. Levin believed that, despite the current movement to devalue Hemingway's work, in time "he will be remembered for a poetic vision which renews our interrupted contact with the timeless elements of man's existence" (609).

Like Levin, E. M. Halliday (1952) was interested in the technical aspects of Hemingway's fiction, particularly the "limitations and privileges" of using first- or third-person narration (202). Halliday found that

Hemingway usually employed both to his advantage. For example, in *The Sun Also Rises*, the "first-person method of narration" is "remarkably effective" in "implement[ing] and reinforc[ing]" the novel's themes of "emotional isolation" and "moral atrophy" (203). The same is generally true in *A Farewell to Arms* but not in *To Have and Have Not*, which Halliday categorized as an "exhibition of technical irresponsibility" (203). In *For Whom the Bell Tolls* Hemingway recovered his technical proficiency, using third-person narration "to express the essential brotherhood of man" (215), though he seemed to wander again in *Across the River and Into the Trees*. The point Halliday makes throughout his analysis is that an important criterion for judging the success or failure of a novel lies as much in the author's handling of point of view as in his selection of subject matter.

Finally, Hemingway's short fiction received special mention in Ray West's (1952) comprehensive descriptive history of the American short story. West linked Hemingway with Faulkner in a chapter subtitled "Two Masters of the Modern Short Story"—the only authors singled out for special treatment. Arguing that "the twentieth century called for" a "re-examination of the moral and aesthetic principles upon which both American life and American art had been established," West dubbed Hemingway and Faulkner as "*avant-garde*" in bringing about that revaluation (106).

Notes

[1] Hemingway's reaction to Eastman's review is well documented. When the two met at the offices of Scribner, Hemingway hit Eastman with a book. Ostensibly, Eastman then pushed Hemingway over a desk. The initial report of the incident in the *New York Times* ("Hemingway Slaps Eastman" 1937) does not corroborate or deny Eastman's claim.

[2] Hemingway's relationship with *Esquire* and the magazine's coverage of him after his death are discussed by John Fenstermaker (2013).

[3] When he first read Lewis's essay, Hemingway reacted by punching a vase at Sylvia Beach's Paris bookstore (Baker 1969c, 259). Later, he repaid Lewis by writing a venal portrait of him in *A Moveable Feast* (Hemingway 1964), describing him as looking like "a frog" with the eyes of "an unsuccessful rapist" (109).

[4] Predictably, Kashkeen's essay was cited with respect (almost reverence) by later Marxist critics of Hemingway. For example, writing twelve years later, Stanley Hyman (1947) called the essay "a remarkable study of Hemingway's work, perhaps the best written to date" (Hyman 1989, 283). However, dozens of critics who have no ideological bias in favor of Marxist readings of literature have also found merit in Kashkeen's study.

[5] The importance of Cowley's assessments of Hemingway should not be underestimated. Granville Hicks (1944), a critic seldom given to praise, called Cowley's

New Republic essay "the best critical discussion of Hemingway I have read" (524). On the other hand, Cowley could be taken in by the man even while admiring the work. In an article for *Life* magazine, "A Portrait of Mr. Papa," written five years later, Cowley (1949) provided a sketch of Hemingway's life filled with tales that had become part of the Hemingway legend.

[6] In a *Paris Review* profile written eight years later, George Plimpton (1958) allowed Hemingway to speak in his own voice—without the grunting, half-formed sentences that pepper Ross's portrait—and presented in somewhat leisurely fashion his ideas about writing. One comes away from reading Plimpton with the sense that Hemingway was a consummate craftsman who never let his status as an international celebrity deter him from his goal to write the best fiction and nonfiction of which he was capable.

3: The Critics' Darling (1952–1961)

NINETEEN FIFTY-TWO proved to be an important year for Hemingway and his critics. Recovering from the debacle of *Across the River and Into the Trees*, Hemingway published a novella that would become his best seller yet and propel him to honors hitherto denied him. His popularity among the general public, hurt somewhat by *Across the River and Into the Trees*, rebounded quickly. Questions by academics about his morality or his limited vision did not seem to bother the thousands who continued to buy his books. The level of his international renown may be measured in some ways by a 1952 poll taken at Oxford University, where Hemingway was the only American among the top ten most-read authors by undergraduates. The year also saw the publication of two books that set the agenda for Hemingway studies for decades—an occurrence that Mark Schorer (1953) described as "remarkable," because, though "written concurrently" by college English teachers, these studies are "so widely different" (514).

The Old Man and the Sea

Unquestionably, 1952 was the Year of the Comeback for Hemingway, at least with the general reading public and reviewers for newspapers and popular periodicals. *The Old Man and the Sea* appeared in the September 1 issue of *Life* magazine and then in book form from Scribner. A number of reviewers saw the work as Hemingway's answer to those who had written him off as finished. The novella was called "an epic" that reminds readers the world is capable of creating heroes (Valentine 1952, 6), a "story of the preservation of human dignity in the face of misfortune" ("Old Values" 1952, 4A). Few seemed more delighted than Ellen Kaupke (1952), who proclaimed that while "many writers outlive themselves," Hemingway "is not one of this breed" (6); when the public derided him after the publication of *Across the River and Into the Trees*, he responded by publishing this wonderful new work. William McDermott (1952) called *Old Man* "a book of power and beauty," and predicted that "this long short story will become a classroom classic" (17). Robert Ruark (1952) said that, having read the book, he was "proud of Papa" for writing this "epic struggle" that ends in disaster but reveals spiritual triumph (4A). The *Trenton Times* reviewer led with the pronouncement that "Hemingway has done it again," and ended by calling the novella "the work of a master" ("A Great New Hemingway" 1952, 10). Though William Maner (1952) believed this brief tale was not a major work in the Hemingway canon, he found it "a rich store of analogy" (8A).

Many reviewers who panned *Across the River and Into the Trees* had nothing but praise for *The Old Man and the Sea*, and over the months acclamations increased. Predictably, Carlos Baker's (1952b) assessment was highly favorable, but so were reviews by Edward Weeks (1952), Harvey Breit (1952), Brendan Gill (1952), and Mark Schorer (1952). The *Chicago Tribune*'s Fanny Butcher (1952), a Hemingway champion since the 1920s, expressed joy at seeing him rebound from his earlier debacle, while Malcolm Cowley (1952) and Robert Gorham Davis (1952) judged the book an advance in Hemingway's concept of heroism. In an appreciative scholarly assessment in the *Kenyon Review*, F. W. Dupee (1953) said the novella affirmed through the image of "the big hunt" the "frontier virtues" and "natural basis of our life" (150).

Most British reviewers were equally impressed. Arthur Calder-Marshall (1952) said Hemingway was "once again 'the champ,'" managing to achieve "the perfection of a lyric poem" (477). Edwin Muir (1952) believed Hemingway "has never displayed" his imaginative powers "more powerfully than in this simple and tragic story" (7). Somerset Maugham considered the book "absolutely first class" (quoted in Clarke 1953, 4A). Even Cyril Connolly (1952) was won over, calling *The Old Man and the Sea* "the best story Hemingway has ever written" (5).

The long list of positive reviews on both sides of the Atlantic should not obscure the fact that not everyone was impressed with the novel. Delmore Schwartz (1952) found the style mannerist. Gilbert Highet (1952) thought the story was derivative. Similarly, Seymour Krim (1952) said *The Old Man and the Sea* simply repeated and embellished Hemingway's best earlier work. While acknowledging that Hemingway had "woven one of his better stories," Harold Gardiner (1952) believed he was guilty of the pathetic fallacy in "the attribution of personality to impersonal objects" (569).

Additionally, the rush to proclaim the novella a symbolic masterpiece was resisted by more than one critic. Henry McLemore (1952), who said he read a hundred reviews of *The Old Man and the Sea* before he wrote his own, expressed disdain for "those who try to read something symbolic into everything written." McLemore insisted "there is no symbolism" in the novella. The marlin is "not good or evil but a big old fish," and Santiago is "just a fisherman with tremendous skill" (6A). Writing less than a year after the novella was published, R. W. B. Lewis (1953) wondered if this "brief parable" could "bear the amount of critical weight already piled on it" (146). Yet Lewis himself resorted to thematic interpretation, calling Hemingway's story an account of his perception of "the stimulating and fatal relation between integrity of character and the churning abundance of experience" (147).

Despite these negative assessments, it would be hard to overstate the universal approbation accorded *The Old Man and the Sea*, including praise from Hemingway's contemporary and chief rival for the title of the century's greatest American novelist. Writing for *Shenandoah*, William Faulkner (1952) speculated that "time may show [*The Old Man and the Sea*] to be the best single piece of any of us" (55). The judges and advisory committee for the Pulitzer also found it exceptional; Hemingway received the 1953 Pulitzer Prize for *The Old Man and the Sea*.

Setting the Critical Standard: Philip Young and Carlos Baker

Unquestionably the most influential book published on Hemingway in the twentieth century is Philip Young's *Ernest Hemingway*, issued by Rinehart and Company in 1952. Young wrote the initial version as his doctoral dissertation at the University of Iowa and corresponded with Hemingway while preparing the manuscript for publication. Hemingway was initially against seeing the work in print (and later complained vehemently that Young misrepresented him). After four years of negotiations, Young received permission to quote from Hemingway's works.[1]

Young justified writing a study of a living writer by asserting that, while some did not admire Hemingway, "it is hard to think of a contemporary American who has had more influence on modern writers." Yet, Young contended, he was "by no means as well understood as he might be" (vii–viii). Like most critics of the period, Young searched for a unifying principle to explain the essence of Hemingway's art, accounting for subject matter, themes, characterization, and technique. He found the key to understanding Hemingway's fiction in his life experience—specifically, the wound he received during the First World War. The physical wound suffered by a number of Hemingway characters is, to Young, a visible manifestation of the wound that every Hemingway hero suffers, "not only physically" but "psychically as well" (12–13). "The Hemingway hero," Young claims, "the big, tough, outdoor man, is also the wounded man" who will "die a thousand times before his death, but from his wounds he will never completely recover" (27). At another point in his study, Young extends the concept of the wound to cover not only individuals but an entire generation—the so-called Lost Generation, which has been psychically wounded and is unable to heal. The antidote to the pain caused by the wound, Young continues, is "the Hemingway 'code'" (28), a pattern of behavior that allows one to face a hostile world and keep functioning. Only a few (often sports figures or tough guys) are able to survive without continuing anguish by following the code, and Young is careful to distinguish between the code hero—often seen as successful—and the Hemingway hero, who struggles valiantly to live by the code but frequently fails and suffers for his failure.

Young's assessment became particularly controversial when he applied the pattern not only to Hemingway's characters but to their creator as well. Writing became "supreme catharsis" for Hemingway, Young asserted; "since 1924" Hemingway had been "writing out the story of one man who is based on himself" (37). Small wonder that Hemingway had serious reservations about Young's book.

Young found in the Hemingway canon numerous examples that demonstrate the accuracy and comprehensiveness of his thesis. But he did more—a fact often unacknowledged by successors enamored with the brilliance of his deductions about characterization. In a chapter on Hemingway's style, Young revealed how earlier writers influenced the creation of the unique form of writing that came to define modern fiction. Also in keeping with critical trends of his time, Young devoted a chapter to exploring "Hemingway's world." He described Hemingway's vision of life as a "world at war" (214), the result of a failure of the American myth of the new man and new possibilities. One might object to Young's special pleading for Hemingway's brutal portrait of America, but it is impossible to deny the influence Young's work had on at least two generations of critics. In retrospect, one can say that, as Hemingway was to succeeding modern writers, Young has been to succeeding Hemingway critics— applaud him or reject him, one cannot simply dismiss him as irrelevant.

Published almost simultaneously with Young's groundbreaking study, Carlos Baker's (1952a) *Hemingway: The Writer as Artist* is both wider in scope and less controversial in its conclusions about the sources of Hemingway's power as a writer. With no disrespect to Young, it is also fair to say that Baker's book displays wider understanding of literary trends and a firmer grasp of contemporary critical methodologies, keeping Baker free from some of the overreach that mars Young's otherwise remarkable tour de force. These differences should not be surprising. When he wrote his book on Hemingway, Baker was already an established scholar who had made his reputation with a highly regarded critical study of Percy Bysshe Shelley. He was already tenured at Princeton, where he would twice chair the English Department and become a leading figure in the study of English and American literature ("Princeton Names" 1952, 4).

Resisting the trend to read all of Hemingway's work autobiographically or concentrate on his celebrity, Baker opted instead to tell "another story of at least equal interest": the "story of what Hemingway has been able to perform" during the three decades between 1920 and 1950 (xiii). The book begins with an examination of Hemingway's apprentice work and ends with a discussion of *Across the River and Into the Trees*.

In subsequent editions (there would be three more—in 1956, 1963, and 1972) Baker would take up *The Old Man and the Sea* and some of Hemingway's posthumous publications. What does not change, however, is his estimate that Hemingway's "virtue as an artist" lies in his "willing assumption of a responsibility to hold the reality of what is knowably real in steady conjunction with the justice of what is esthetically just" (297).

Throughout his critique, Baker focused on tools Hemingway employed to generate the powerful fiction for which he had become famous. He emphasized structure, symbolism, and the "moral and esthetic" qualities that he said allow Hemingway's best work to transcend its historical context (xiv). Baker makes a case that even the lesser work deserves attention, if only to see how Hemingway was continually experimenting with new ways to get at the truths of human existence. However, Baker was willing to admit that some works were not successful: *To Have and Have Not* "shows marked deficiencies as a work of art" (205); *Across the River and Into the Trees* "is not one of Hemingway's major novels" (287). Yet even in these he found something to praise, as Hemingway worked toward larger ends through experiments in form and theme.

At his best, Baker was able to make sense of the two nonfiction works that had been panned by many critics. He said that from *Death in the Afternoon* one can discern Hemingway's idea of the hero and his concept of tragedy. Of even greater significance, *Green Hills of Africa* "undoubtedly established one esthetic principle very firmly in Hemingway's mind. The highest art must take liberties, not with the truth but with the modes by which the truth is projected" (197).

Baker's readings of the works generally considered Hemingway's best confirmed opinions already expressed by many and explain why those conclusions were justified. Only in discussing *For Whom the Bell Tolls* did Baker break out of the armor of disinterestedness in which he attempted to cloak himself and admit that he found this work the crowning achievement of Hemingway's career. Baker compares Robert Jordan favorably with heroes from history and myth, and while he admits that Jordan's problem seems small, Hemingway conceives and projects it in a way that "suggest[s] a struggle of epic dimensions." Baker seems almost euphoric in pronouncing *For Whom the Bell Tolls* a "living example of how, in modern times, the epic quality must probably be projected" (246–47). Unstated but clearly implied is the assumption that Hemingway has risen to a level reached only by the greatest writers of all time: he has produced an epic.

As one might expect, both books were reviewed in *American Literature*, Baker's by Bradford Booth (1953), who found it impressive, Young's by Frederick Hoffman (1954), who predicted it would influence future Hemingway studies. What might be surprising to some, however, is that both books were noticed in newspapers as well. The *New York*

Times, which carried prepublication notices of both titles, also published lengthy reviews by longtime literary critic Charles Poore (1952, 1953). The *Times* also published a review of Baker by Granville Hicks (1952) and one of Young by Delmore Schwartz (1953), who noted that the publication of Young's and Baker's studies gave Hemingway "the kind of attention generally devoted only to dead authors and their masterpieces" (6). *Commonweal* carried reviews of both titles (Quinn 1952; Duggan 1953). Writing about Baker's book in the *Boston Herald* (in late November), John Finch (1952) proclaimed that it was "an occasion for thanksgiving" that "a finely equipped critic has written a full scale study of Ernest Hemingway's work" (18).

Perhaps because he was more widely known, Baker was reviewed in several other publications, including the *New Republic* (Mayberry 1952), the *Saturday Review* (Mizener 1952), and the *Times Literary Supplement* (Connolly 1953). Young received a vote of confidence from Saul Bellow (1953), then coming into his own as a major novelist, who called Young's study "an excellent book" on a difficult topic, a living writer (338). Bellow appreciated Young's psychological analysis, though he believed the attempt to link Hemingway's hero with Twain's Huck Finn was weak. Bellow also used his review to point out why Hemingway had been successful—and why he seemed so self-absorbed as he attempted to "create an image of manhood" and impose it on the American psyche (342).

Other Early Scholarly Books

Often overshadowed by Young's and Baker's studies, the British writer John Atkins's (1952) *The Art of Ernest Hemingway* combined the approaches of the two American critics—although Atkins had seen neither book while he was writing his own rather personal commentary. Atkins's topically organized analysis attempted to explain Hemingway's development over his career from proponent of naturalism to politically engaged writer back to naturalist philosopher. Displaying exceptional familiarity with the history of American, British, and Continental literature, Atkins established Hemingway's place in literary history and assessed his importance not only for his own time but for all times as well. Atkins moves freely among the novels, short stories, and nonfiction to explore Hemingway's handling of issues such as feeling and sensibility, love and sex, women, and politics, explaining how, even though he may write of people who are deluded, Hemingway himself always saw things clearly.

Atkins also provided some noteworthy observations on the state of Hemingway criticism, much of which he found "interesting" (a loaded word to be sure), but which generally gave "the impression, as does most modern American criticism, of having been written by Olympians in bow ties" (252). He excluded Max Eastman and Edmund Wilson from that condemnation, but believed that, on the whole, critics were "annoyed" with Hemingway "for developing so that their carefully stitched essays of a few years ago are now out of date and cannot be reprinted" (252). As cheerfully depressing as all this critical nonsense seemed to him, Atkins concluded with the prescient observation that "the crazy season for Hemingway criticism is yet to come" (xx).

Another critical book on Hemingway published in the early 1950s, Charles Fenton's (1954) *The Apprenticeship of Ernest Hemingway*, is a work of considerable literary and historical scholarship. Fenton's achievement is made even more impressive by the fact that the book was originally his dissertation, written at Yale, where projects about living writers were frowned upon. Additionally, Fenton (like Young) had significant trouble getting Hemingway to agree to let him quote from the stories and novels. Apparently Hemingway was still not keen on having his private life exposed; to put it more kindly, he may have been concerned that the interest in biography (or psychology) would divert readers' focus from his writing.

Operating from the premise that Hemingway's initial writing experiences were as important as his war service in preparing him to emerge in the mid-1920s as a writer of consequence, Fenton analyzed work Hemingway produced in the early years of his career, including his high-school days. Although Fenton waited until midway through his study to explain his rationale definitively, he argued that "Hemingway encountered most of the significant experiences of his personal and professional life before he was twenty-five years old" (224). A major part of Fenton's argument is given over to explaining how Hemingway's early experiences shaped habits and perceptions that would become staples of his career. The key to Hemingway's methodology, Fenton asserted, can be found in the first paragraph of the *Kansas City Star*'s Style Sheet: "Use short sentences. Use short first paragraphs. Use vigorous English. Be positive, not negative" (quoted in Fenton, 30–31). As Fenton demonstrated, "Hemingway's debt to journalism was a large one" (262).

Apparently there was sufficient interest in critical studies of Hemingway to warrant reviews of Fenton's book in widely read publications. John Aldridge's (1954a) assessment appeared in the *New York Times Book Review*. An unsigned review also appeared in the popular periodical *Newsweek* ("Hemingway: The Making of a Master" 1954). The *Springfield Republican* ran a long feature on it, describing it as "an interesting examination of the early influences and writing habits of America's most popular novelist" (McLaughlin 1954, 7C). Writing in *American Literature*, Laurence Holland (1955) called Fenton's a "resourceful," "informative," and "fascinating" study that displayed "an inventive kind of scholarship" that made it useful to those interested in understanding Hemingway's mature fiction (590). Carlos Baker's (1954) critique of Fenton's and Atkinson's books was published in the *Saturday Review*.

Mark Schorer's (1954) review of Fenton's and Atkins's recent publications, which includes brief assessments of Baker's and Young's books, provided a provocative and at times wry commentary on the status of Hemingway scholarship at midcentury. Schorer speculated that Hemingway must be amused—if not infuriated—that he had become the darling of the academic world. While Schorer found Fenton's book of greater value to scholars than Atkins's more discursive study, he concluded that, for all Hemingway's remonstrances, these four books demonstrate that "his famous contempt for critics and for professors of literature is impotent in the grip of their embrace" (51).

How tight that grip could be is on display in the first volume of *Modern Fiction Studies*, a journal inaugurated in 1955 at Purdue University. Hemingway was the first author to be the subject of a special issue. The third issue of the journal contains six articles employing scholarly methodologies popular at the time: two examined recurring images in the fiction and nonfiction, two compared Hemingway's work to other novels and stories, and one argued for a central theme in the Hemingway canon. One that provided a reading of *A Farewell to Arms* proceeds from the premise that "a novel may imply a world order, a scheme of consequential relationships among events which, as we read the novel, seems to be universal and thus enables us to take the novel as a model of human experience" (Russell 1955, 25).

Midcentury Assessments

The status of Hemingway's reputation in the decade preceding his death in 1961 can be discerned from a selection of articles and book chapters that offer assessments placing him among contemporaries or evaluating the quality of his work by standards in vogue at the time. There is a certain touch of irony in the fact that, as accolades poured in and Hemingway was spoken of as having a virtual lock on the Nobel Prize (which he won in 1954), a number of hostile pieces were published. The most scathing appeared in the Marxist journal *Science and Society*. Lois Barnes's (1953) "The Helpless Hero of Ernest Hemingway" attacked Hemingway's fiction for what she described as the oversimplified bathos that characterized the writing and the bourgeois ideology that underlay his characters and themes. The "values and codes that Hemingway teaches" are "very well suited for training the imperial soldier"; he is "a romantic escapist, though he constantly proclaims that he is a simple teller of the truth" (9). In keeping with her ideological perspective, Barnes insisted that "artists have a special function of coaching social classes in the accents and gestures that are appropriate to them in the world-historical drama" (16).

Hemingway's move toward a more responsible social literature during the 1930s had failed, she said, so he returned to the empty pontifications that made his fiction palatable to the masses (including masses of academic critics). His intellectual depth and perceptive vision of modern life were merely inventions of a critical industry that "must invent literature" out of "shop-worn remains" of "sensation," "Nature," and "Mysteries" (23). Barnes believed critical efforts to make him "an epic writer of great scope" (24) were wrongheaded and even unseemly.

Although not as vituperative as Barnes, Van Wyck Brooks (1953) repeatedly cited Hemingway as an example of what was wrong with modern writers: gifted as stylists, perhaps, but afraid to speak candidly and maturely about values. Brooks believed Hemingway was a victim both of the cult of youth, which made writers fearful of growing old, and of the nihilism and anti-Americanism that pervaded intellectual circles in the 1920s and 1930s.

Interjecting himself squarely between Hemingway's defenders and those who wished to topple him from the pedestal on which his supporters had placed him, Ray West (1953) argued in "The Sham Battle over Hemingway" that critics should avoid taking sides and treating their profession as either a game or a battle. There was much to praise in Hemingway, but also much to criticize, and those who could not accept any criticism were doing Hemingway as much harm as those who took great pleasure in pointing out his faults. "Criticism is not a game, nor is it like war," where one is forced to choose sides, West said. Rather it is "an imperfect instrument in the hands of a fallible human being," used to evaluate "an incomplete, but often amazingly successful, human accomplishment" (240). Clearly, West believed his colleagues in the academic world had not recognized their own fallibility or their proper role in evaluating Hemingway's work.

In 1954 Hemingway first became the subject of an article in *PMLA(Publications of the Modern Language Association of America)*, considered by many the premier academic journal for literary criticism. Going beyond typical analyses of metaphor, symbolism, and irony, Frederic Carpenter (1954) attempted to explain what Hemingway meant when he posited in 1935 that it might be possible to achieve a "fifth dimension" in writing. Carpenter interpreted this as the ability to "communicate the immediate experience of 'the perpetual now'" (712) that Hemingway manages in his best fiction, especially *For Whom the Bell Tolls*.

Philip Young's immediate influence is evident in John Aldridge's (1954b) provocative essay "Hemingway: The Etiquette of the Berserk." Acknowledging that Young's recent study paralleled his own, Aldridge laid out a case for understanding the Hemingway code. He rejected arguments like those of Wyndham Lewis that Hemingway's focus on action is a "dumb-ox compromise with the demands of a healthy intellectual and ethical life." Instead, he argued that the code is the "artistic convention or formula" out of which Hemingway's novels "derive their richest and subtlest effects of dramatic irony" (151). Aldridge sees the code operating "as a psychic barricade erected against one of the primary perils of [the hero's] soul—the loss of consciousness leading to a lawless, amok, or berserk condition" (155). Hemingway's best early heroes believe in "love, honor, goodness, truth, gentleness, dignity, and bravery," the "values on which the code is founded" (153), but cannot express these feelings openly in a world that has perverted their meaning. As Hemingway aged, he began to create protagonists who were increasingly less possessed of these intellectual and moral qualities, until, in *The Old Man and the Sea*, the protagonist's struggle becomes only physical, despite the symbolic superstructure. Aldridge's description of the trajectory of Hemingway's career as a writer, supported by his sensitive reading of the fiction, stands in contrast to contemporaries who were arguing that Hemingway had never truly lost his artistic talent or his moral vision.

Moralist critics looked for positive moral lessons in Hemingway's work (with emphasis on the value of the code), but also attempted to relate his views to traditional moral codes. Hyatt Waggoner's (1955) essay in *Christian Scholar* is one such example. Waggoner admitted that, on the surface, Hemingway's work seemed to undercut traditional Christian values. But he believed Hemingway's real target was the illusory and hypocritical Christianity of the Victorians; repeatedly he attacked the comfortable illusions that sustained his forebears but that had been proven untenable in the modern world. Waggoner found that Hemingway's fiction represents "a stage in the twentieth-century rediscovery of Christianity among the educated" (119). That point seems lost on Thomas Moylan (1955), who wrote in *Catholic World* that Hemingway's "message" was that "life is brutal, but men are brave, and can win, even without God" (293)—a position at odds with traditional Christianity.

Noting the importance of Hemingway's outsized personality in shaping readers' opinion of his achievement, Delmore Schwartz (1955) argued that this perception was consciously cultivated by Hemingway through his unique style. Like many before him, Schwartz equated Hemingway's style with "the moral code at the heart of his writing," one that, while neither "primitive" nor "proletarian," is distinctly American and expresses Hemingway's "sense of the quality of modern life" (74). Better than any other writer, Hemingway "has written the most complete moral history of the American Dream in the twentieth century," depicting "the dream, the hope, the anxiety, and the courage" that "began with the discovery of America" (88).

James Colvert (1955) attempted to correct what he described as the dominant critical attitude toward the Hemingway hero, a figure whose "ethical awareness is contained within a moral construct so rigidly definable that its very simplicity is proof of its moral inadequacy" (372). Colvert agreed with Delmore Schwartz (1938), who argued nearly two decades earlier that Hemingway "is concerned above all else with the problem of conduct" (372), but disagreed that Hemingway's code was bound temporally or socially. Instead, he insisted that all of Hemingway's stories "can be read" as a response to the "problem raised by the breakdown of traditional nineteenth-century values." The "ethical attitude" of his heroes is based on both "profound moral skepticism" and a belief in "the efficacy of a strictly empirical approach to value determination" (373). Hence, operating "in a world dangerously uncertain of its morality" and "terrifying in its hostility potential," the Hemingway hero "must test his values" through experience. Colvert said Hemingway deserved credit for his "serious and consistent concern for finding a new morality in action" (385).

In an essay that was initially as part of a lecture series in 1953, Sean O'Faolin (1956) described Hemingway's development of the antihero and his fascination with death. O'Faolin was not taken in by what he called the "mystique of heroism" (131) in Hemingway's fiction, finding Hemingway both inconsistent and shallow in depicting heroism divorced from any value system. It would be possible, O'Faolin argued, to idolize any person who acts bravely, even gangsters or other moral monsters, although in *For Whom the Bell Tolls* Hemingway did present a portrait of heroism that suggests one might be heroic in acting bravely to serve a larger cause. Despite these reservations, O'Faolin concluded that Hemingway was "the only modern writer of real distinction for whom the Hero does in some form still live" (144)—but his fiction suggested that the "only possible hero for our times is the lone wolf" (145).

The essays summarized above share several points in common. One is a fascination with the Hemingway hero and the Hemingway code. Second is a belief in the significance of Hemingway's work—even if, for critics like Barnes, it was overvalued. Another group of critics had a distinctly different impression of Hemingway. Some, like Richard Chase (1957), thought him inconsequential; in his influential study *The American Novel and Its Tradition*, Chase mentioned Hemingway in passing but did not examine a single novel in detail. Others predicted Hemingway's eventual fall from favor, among them Eugene Goodheart (1956), who wrote in "The Legacy of Ernest Hemingway" that at present Hemingway remains in "critical limbo." Goodheart did not believe this was due simply to cultural prejudice. Hemingway had more "serious deficiencies" (212), and once critics fully understood his morality, his "gifts though considerable will not be seen as formidable as they presently appear" (213). Goodheart believed the essence of Hemingway's moral code was little more than "a kind of fluent animal energy" devoid of human intelligence or emotion (213). His withdrawal from the modern world and his primitivism is really "a form of adolescent regression to a more simple state of affairs" (215). While Goodheart thought Robert Penn Warren had adequately identified Hemingway's limited range, he did not go far enough in condemning him for failing to define the humanity in humankind. Goodheart was convinced that "when the image Hemingway has created for himself as a public figure begins to fade from the public imagination—as it most certainly will in time—the extreme limitations of Hemingway's achievement will become more and more apparent" (217).

Goodheart's critique pales beside that of Otto Friedrich (1957). The title of Friedrich's *American Scholar* article "Ernest Hemingway: Joy through Strength" not so subtly links Hemingway with the Nazi regime, whose state-sponsored leisure program designed to boost morale among ordinary Germans was known as "Strength through Joy." He found Hemingway's deepest motivation not in telling the truth but in seeking fame, and suggested his entire career was aimed at making him renowned—often, and especially in his later years, at the expense of his craft. Hemingway was "potentially a great writer" who produced a "half-dozen minor masterpieces" but who "has persistently limited and corrupted himself" (470). Worse, Friedrich continued, "his supposed realism actually consists of describing his romantic concepts as though they were real" (524). His famous "code," which "attempt[s] to maintain some kind of personal standards against a world of brutality and fraud" has "degenerated into a pseudo code that is both brutal and fraudulent." Friedrich admitted that the milieu in which Hemingway lived and worked played a role in creating this fame-seeking opportunist: "The similarities between Hemingway and almost every worst aspect of American culture are so strong that one hesitates to blame everything on this occasionally great writer." Certainly "his influence has been pervasive," but the misuse of his work by lesser writers has "returned to overwhelm him with a false conception of his own nature, his function and his greatness" (530).

Another deflationary critique, Jack Garlington's (1959) "The Intelligence Quotient of Lady Brett Ashley," is worth noting for the tortuous expression of admiration Garlington managed to exhibit in an essay designed to point out significant faults in the Hemingway canon. Garlington said he had discovered, after reviewing a considerable number of novels and stories, that "Hemingway's characters aren't very bright" (24). In Garlington's view, the supposed depth of feeling that cannot be expressed is a cover for general dullness, as Hemingway tries to make much out of little; for example, "one has only to look at bullfighting to realize what a great to-do has been made about nothing." Where Hemingway presents the bullfight as "challeng[ing] something deep and primevally beneficent in man's nature," it is actually "a rather primitive diversion admired chiefly by the more backward nations and the American literati" (27). Garlington insisted (with more than a hint of irony) that "we are devoted to Hemingway" for having "extended the limits of tragedy"—by creating "a place for the dull in world literature" (28).

Responding to such negative assessments, John McCormick (1957) sounded a challenge to critics who dismissed Hemingway as a "gangster of literature, a Neanderthal *Ur-Mensch* of the novel." The "unhealthy and willful confusion between his life and his work" (95) had obscured the value of his writing, much of which dealt sensitively and thoughtfully with great "primitive and basic" themes such as "religion, initiation, war, death, and their attendant ritual." In fact, McCormick argued, as a war novelist Hemingway was almost without equal; "only Malraux and Broch have approximated his achievement, but neither has surpassed him" (213). Likewise, in brief comments in "The Shape of a Career" Granville Hicks (1958) defended Hemingway from charges that his career peaked early and then petered out, largely by faulting critics for having placed too high a demand on writers who produce great works early in their careers and for being too quick to judge every work by the one that immediately preceded it.

By the late 1950s, despite efforts by some critics to deflate Hemingway's reputation, his best work was being acknowledged in academic circles as some of the most important literature not only of its own time but in the American literary tradition. Evidence of this can be found in Charles Shapiro's (1958) collection *Twelve Original Essays on Great American Novels*, a work often cited in critical studies published during the next two decades. While Shapiro's book may not be definitive, it is certainly illustrative of the stature Hemingway had achieved in the academic community, especially for novels like *The Sun Also Rises*, which is discussed at length in *Twelve Original Essays* by Mark Spilka (1958). Judging from the list of titles covered in this volume, Hemingway is in good company: Cooper's *The Deerslayer*, Hawthorne's *The Scarlet Letter*, Melville's *Moby-Dick*, Twain's *Huckleberry Finn*, and James's *The Ambassadors* are among other works discussed. Only two novels by Hemingway's contemporaries are included: Fitzgerald's *The Great Gatsby* and Faulkner's *Light in August*.

In his introduction, Shapiro, reflecting the critical concerns of the day, says these novels were chosen because they reveal something about America and what it means to be American, but also because they help readers "learn about ourselves," and in the case of Hemingway's novel, "about the changing problems of a fast moving society" (viii–ix). Spilka's close reading of *The Sun Also Rises* was shaped by then-conventional attitudes about the nature of Hemingway's fiction. He explored the reaction of character to "the death of love," which he called "one of the most persistent themes of the twenties" (238). He described the novel as "an extensive parable" with protagonists "shaped as allegorical figures" that are given life in "the most concrete style in American fiction" (239).

Spilka concluded that the bullfighter Pedro Romero is "the real hero of the parable, the moral touchstone, the man whose code gives meaning to a world where love and religion are defunct," and where "every man must learn to define his own moral conditions and then live up to them" (256). The critical vocabulary (and gender-biased language) running throughout the essay, as well as Spilka's focus on theme, characterization, and style make this essay representative of the way competent and respected critics were examining Hemingway's fiction during a period when New Humanism still held some sway and New Criticism defined methodology. More than three decades later, Spilka would offer a very different perspective on Hemingway's fiction, particularly his attitude toward gender, in *Hemingway's Quarrel with Androgyny* (1990).

In his brief summary of Hemingway's career in *American Writing in the Twentieth Century*, Willard Thorp (1960) proclaimed that "few important American novelists have had so many detractors," and "few have had so devoted a following, from the readers of *Esquire*"— intended to stand for all of the thoughtless, he-man readers, presumably—to "the eminent critics" (191–92). In "Hemingway: The Critics and the Public Legend," John Jones (1959) attempted to explain why, despite the sometimes offensive public image, a certain group of critics had found Hemingway's work of value. Though critics had always been interested in Hemingway's development as an artist, the "public legend" had always been "lurk[ing] in the shadows," getting in the way of "dispassionate critical interest in Hemingway's fiction" (387). The confusion had affected even the best critical studies, such as those by Lionel Trilling, Edmund Wilson, and Alfred Kazin. Jones highlighted the prevailing attitudes toward critical practice at the time, and discussed briefly how Hemingway was handled by Marxists, psychological critics, sociological critics, and New Critics. Jones's own predilections are apparent in his assessment that criticism must be "dispassionate"—by which he seems to advocate the Arnoldian principle of disinterestedness—and focus on matters of art such as the use of metaphor, irony, and symbolism. Hence, he saw Hemingway's career progressing from the inheritor of a realist/naturalist tradition and the "consummate and mordant realist of the Lost Generation" to "the predominant viewpoint of the middle Fifties when he has come into his own as a naturalist symbolist whose works are rapidly yielding their treasures of myth, symbol, metaphor and ritual to the industrious scholar-critic" (400).

Among those scholar-critics was John Killinger, who in *Hemingway and the Dead Gods* (1960) viewed Hemingway's fiction through the work of existentialist philosophers. Killinger's approach is not surprising, given the heavy interest in existentialism in academic circles in the first half of the century. Hemingway's fiction, filled with hard-bitten heroes struggling to make sense of events in a world without transcendent meaning, provided what Killinger called correspondences to the writings of Nietzsche, Kierkegaard, Heidegger, Camus, and Sartre. Works like Killinger's endowed Hemingway's fiction with a certain gravitas, suggesting that it exposed, rather than explained, a method of living authentically. Hence, reading him could provide not only aesthetic pleasure but guidance for life as well.

As the 1950s passed into the 1960s, many may have wondered what Hemingway would do to top the success of *The Old Man and the Sea*. He had been in the newspapers for escapades that seemed mere shadows of the exploits that brought him great notoriety in the previous two decades, but he had not published a new novel since receiving the Nobel Prize. His work was still attracting significant attention—not all of it positive—when British critic Stewart Sanderson (1961) produced a brief critical study of him in the Evergreen Pilot Books series on writers and critics. Sanderson was a strong defender of Hemingway as a major voice in twentieth-century American literature. Ironically, this book in which he touted Hemingway's staying power appeared just months before Hemingway committed suicide.

Notes

[1] Young provided a detailed account of the sometimes excruciating and often nerve-racking negotiations in a *Kenyon Review* article (Young 1964), which he reprinted in *Ernest Hemingway: A Reconsideration* (1966). He reprised his arguments about the wound theory in a chapter on Hemingway in William Van O'Connor's *Seven Modern American Novelists: An Introduction* (Young 1959a) and in his 1959 pamphlet *Ernest Hemingway* (1959b) in the University of Minnesota Press series on contemporary writers.

4: Posthumous Evaluations (1961–1969)

Hemingway's suicide on July 2, 1961, was front-page news across the country. The *New York Times* accepted Mary Hemingway's explanation that he shot himself accidentally and quoted President John F. Kennedy's statement mourning his loss, in which the president called him "one of the great citizens of the world" ("Hemingway Dead" 1961). On the same day, the *Times* ran a tribute by regular reviewer Charles Poore (1961), who proclaimed that Hemingway "stands now, with William Butler Yeats and James Joyce, as one of the three most influential writers of an era." Poore also observed rather presciently that "a hatful of pedants will find new allegories, new symbols, in Hemingway, year after year after year" (6).

Three days later, the *Times* carried a long article containing tributes from eighteen prominent writers and critics ("Authors and Critics" 1961). Acknowledgments of his status as one of the greatest writers of the century and an influence on prose style around the world came from critics Lionel Trilling, Alfred Kazin, and Van Wyck Brooks and writers John Dos Passos, V. S. Pritchett, C. P. Snow, John O'Hara, William Faulkner, and Robert Frost. Only a few like those of J. B. Priestley and Oliver La Farge contained negative comments. Within months, Mary Hemingway and Charles Scribner announced that Carlos Baker would be writing the authorized biography ("Hemingway's Biographer" 1961, 16). Implicit in the announcement is the notice being given to the world of who would be in charge of keeping alive Hemingway's memory and controlling the manuscripts he left behind.

Although not intended as an obituary tribute, Irving Howe's (1961) "In Search of a Moral Style" paid homage to Hemingway as the "most influential American novelist of our time" (21). Howe explained how the generation of writers after World War I found it impossible to cling to traditional values or develop new ones; destined to "spend their lives in uncertainty," they sought instead to create a "moral style," which is seen in attempts to create rituals and gestures that could substitute for a moral outlook. Learning how to "make do" with grace and courage is "the great problem" (21), and Hemingway's hero is an embodiment of the person who has learned how to solve that problem through his actions, especially in the face of death. Unfortunately, Howe said, Hemingway eventually became too satisfied with his performance and began to imitate himself, causing his writing to become mannerist and "corpulent" (23).

In 1962 the *Mark Twain Journal* published a special issue to pay tribute to Hemingway. A letter from President Kennedy led off the volume, which included praise from more than a dozen scholars and literary luminaries. The editors somewhat ruefully included a smattering of unflattering responses received from some who had been solicited to contribute. Hemingway's 1930 letter to the Mark Twain Society accepting an appointment as an honorary vice president was reprinted on the cover of the special issue.

Initial Assessments

In the year following Hemingway's suicide, Maxwell Geismar (1962) wrote an appraisal with the provocative title "Was 'Papa' a Truly Great Writer?" Geismar's answer is a qualified "yes." Reviewing Hemingway's career, he pointed out how the early work showed great promise, although he found that *The Sun Also Rises* had not shown the staying power of *A Farewell to Arms*. Geismar detected a decline beginning in the 1930s, although he had good words for *Death in the Afternoon*. Where he found greatest merit was in the short stories, which he called "the core of Hemingway's work." Unfortunately, he concluded, "the boundaries of Ernest Hemingway's literary reputation have contracted" over the years: he is "a writer who gets smaller as you grow older." And yet, Geismar insisted, "that perfect cluster of great short stories" are "immune to criticism as they will be impervious to time" (16).

By contrast, Dwight Macdonald's (1962) unflattering portrait in *Against the American Grain* begins with a sketch of Hemingway's life written in parody of the Hemingway style. In more measured prose, Macdonald dismissed the recently advanced idea that Hemingway was a philosophical writer, calling it "a foolish statement even for a professor of literature" (171). He considered Hemingway completely devoid of ideas, valuable only as a stylistic innovator and creator of some admirable short stories. His assessment prompted a strong rebuttal from George Plimpton, which Macdonald graciously included in his book after his own assessment.

Macdonald's criticisms of Hemingway's intellectual prowess were seconded by Canadian critic D. E. S. Maxwell (1963), who argued in *American Fiction: The Intellectual Background* that one might easily be mesmerized by Hemingway's style and taken in by his seemingly attractive heroes. In a sentence that might have made Hemingway cringe, Maxwell insisted, however, that it is important to recognize "how restricted is his canvas, how unrelievedly emotional are his judgments, how far, in seeking, understandably, to avoid uplift, [Hemingway] has strayed into a quite amoral sensualism, sinking, from want of intellectual vigour, into the most insipid romanticism" (269).

But even Leslie Fiedler (1964), who disdained Hemingway's treatment of women and his callous personality, could not escape noting the extent of his influence on popular literature. He introduced his 1964 collection of essays titled *Waiting for the End* with the observation that "it is with a sense of terror that the practicing novelist in the United States confronts his situation today," because Faulkner and Hemingway, who were something akin to "a pair of gods"—"are gone, the two great presences who made possible both homage and blasphemy, both imitation and resistance." But Fiedler could not resist getting in a dig at both, remarking that "the moment of their world fame has not coincided with the period in which they produced their greatest work. In a sense, each received the Nobel Prize posthumously, though both lived long enough to accept it with thanks" (9).

Fiedler also launched one of the earliest salvos in the war against Hemingway for his misogyny. In his famous treatise on American literature, *Love and Death in the American Novel*, Fiedler (1960) excoriated Hemingway for his focus on males to the exclusion of women as thinking subjects. While Hemingway may have reveled in discussing sex, Fiedler said, "there are no *women* in his books" (304). He failed to make his women human; rather, they are all stereotypes, most frequently mothers or bitches. Brett Ashley is the consummate bitch; "no man embraces her without in some sense being castrated" (308). Not even Catherine Barkley escaped Fiedler's withering gaze. Had she lived, Fiedler insisted, "she could only have turned into a bitch; for this is the fate in Hemingway's imagination of all Anglo-Saxon women" (306). Countering such harsh accusations, Alan Holder (1963) defended Hemingway's handling of female characters, citing a number of instances in the short stories where he shows how much he is aware of his characters' insensitivity toward women. Holder pleaded with critics to distinguish between the author and his creations when judging Hemingway's attitudes.

An early 1960s publication significant in Hemingway studies for reasons explained below is Earl Rovit's (1963) *Ernest Hemingway* in the Twayne US Authors series. Begun in 1961, the series presented critical commentary on hundreds of American authors, written with an eye toward students. Rovit provided only a brief summary of Hemingway's early years before launching into topical discussions of themes and techniques. There was, of course, a chapter (almost obligatory by this time) on the Hemingway code. Rovit's lone extended analysis of a novel, a chapter on *The Sun Also Rises*, is a fine example of the kind of criticism being practiced at midcentury. Calling the book "perhaps" Hemingway's "most successful novel," he takes readers through the text to explain how literary technique reveals the principal theme of the tragedy of a generation scarred by the Great War, and how the code operates to save Jake from being morally bankrupt.

Reviews of Rovit's *Ernest Hemingway* were mixed, and E. M. Halliday's (1964) unfavorable assessment in *American Literature* may have turned some scholars away from the study. Nevertheless, the book had great influence on a generation of students attending college during the 1960s through the 1970s (and perhaps beyond). Twayne books were in nearly every college library, and undergraduates assigned a paper on Hemingway would in all likelihood have consulted Rovit's study to learn what they should say to please a teacher. Little wonder that when asked, baby boomers consider *The Sun Also Rises* Hemingway's best novel.

Critical Anthologies

While the obituary tributes and devaluations were making news in literary circles, Carlos Baker was already at work preserving Hemingway's reputation for the scholarly community. At the same time he was compiling materials for his biography of Hemingway, Baker took time to prepare two anthologies of criticism. The first, *Hemingway and His Critics: An International Anthology* (Baker 1961), is an assemblage of nineteen previously published essays that attest to Hemingway's importance as a writer. Perhaps the greatest value of the anthology in advancing Hemingway's reputation was Baker's focus on Hemingway as an artist of international stature. Baker's introduction, "Citizen of the World," makes the point explicitly, and several of the essays focus on Hemingway's stature in Europe and Asia. Baker also tackled head-on the growing number of critics who disparaged Hemingway's talent, defending him against charges of parochialism, anti-intellectualism, and fixation on the vulgar.

Less focused on controversy were the essays in Baker's (1962) *Ernest Hemingway: Critiques of Four Major Novels*, published in Scribner's Research Anthology series. Baker's selection of four to six essays on each of four novels he described as Hemingway's major works (*The Sun Also Rises*, *A Farewell to Arms*, *For Whom the Bell Tolls*, and *The Old Man and the Sea*) was designed to give undergraduate students a sampling of critical commentary and help them develop ideas about these novels in order to write research papers. This eclectic mix of sociological, moral, political, and religious criticism, as well as essays on characterization and technique, represents approaches recognized and practiced by critics during the 1920s through the 1950s. Hence, this volume not only introduced thousands of undergraduates to Hemingway, but also taught them how they should think about his achievements. It should be noted, though, that Baker made a real contribution in this book by including for the first time the alternate ending of *A Farewell to Arms*, providing scholars a chance to compare the published version with Hemingway's discarded conclusion—fodder for anyone interested in publishing history or psychological criticism.

Hemingway and his work were also well represented in collections of previously published essays assembled for Prentice-Hall's two series produced during the 1960s. The Twentieth-Century Views book, edited by Robert Weeks (1962), provided a helpful snapshot of the development of Hemingway's reputation up to the time of his death. Books in the Twentieth-Century Interpretations series were produced for *The Old Man and the Sea*, edited by Katherine Jobes (1968), and *A Farewell to Arms*, edited by Jay Gellens (1970). Gellens's volume is representative of the general organization for these student aids. Gellens's lengthy introduction provided his own interpretation of the work, concentrating on the development of Frederic Henry as a Hemingway hero who follows the code in dealing with the tragedies he faces, first as a soldier and then as a fugitive from the war. Gellens's commentary is followed by a selection of previously published work from critics well known to Hemingway scholars: Philip Young, John Killinger, Earl Rovit, Ray West, Malcolm Cowley, Wyndham Lewis, Frederick Hoffman, and Leslie Fiedler. The Prentice-Hall volumes gave a seal of approval to Hemingway's works as worthy of inclusion in academic curricula. Late in the decade, Scribner capitalized on students' need for solid anthologies by bringing out *Hemingway's African Stories*, in which book excerpts and stories set in Africa were paired with critical commentary by John Howell (1969).

A Moveable Feast

In 1964 the first of several posthumous works were released by the Hemingway family. *A Moveable Feast* is a collection of anecdotes and observations based on Hemingway's time in Paris during the 1920s. While Hemingway once insisted that much of his nonfiction was composed using techniques of fiction because a writer of fiction may tell the truth better than one who tries to stick close to the facts, most readers—and certainly most reviewers—considered *A Moveable Feast* a memoir. The Book-of-the-Month Club made it a featured selection for June, and Clifton Fadiman's (1964) report for the club's membership described it as "an invaluable portrait of the artist as a young man during that most interesting of all periods" (5).

The New York newspapers praised it highly. The *Herald Tribune*'s Alan Pryce-Jones (1964) claimed it was the Hemingway book "we have been waiting for," written in "a bony, unwasteful prose which is a joy to read" (23). The *New York Times*'s Charles Poore (1964) called it "Hemingway at his best," and added that it was "a greater pleasure" to be able to read Hemingway rather than "cope with the folklorists of his mythology" (41). The *Times Book Review*'s Lewis Galantière (1964) described *A Moveable Feast* as "marvelously evocative" (26), although he did question the accuracy of some of Hemingway's portraits and suggested the book be "read as a novel" (26). George Plimpton (1964), writing in the *Herald Tribune Book Week*, believed many of the sketches rivaled Hemingway's best fiction. He praised Hemingway for the accuracy and immediacy of his portraits, which Plimpton said are "observed in tranquility" (1).

Reviews in periodicals were generally positive as well. Jeffrey Hart (1964) claimed it sparked memories of Hemingway's achievement. Robert Fulford (1964) believed it was on par with his early work. Alfred Kazin (1964) praised Hemingway for his ability to turn personal experience into fable charged with energy and meaning. To recognize this quality was important, Kazin said, when approaching Hemingway's memoir, because those who understood Hemingway knew that "autobiography is not the place to look for the 'truth'—not if a talent like Ernest Hemingway's is writing about it." Nelson Algren (1964), a longtime Hemingway admirer, admitted Hemingway could be harsh on his contemporaries and onetime friends, but dismissed all criticism by noting that, unlike others who were merely representing the times in which they wrote, Hemingway "made his time represent him" (560).

However, Frank Kermode (1964) suggested that "there is malice here, recollected in tranquility" (5), although Hemingway wrote with authority and confidence unmatched by any other writer who had attempted to explain the Lost Generation. Tony Tanner (1964) appreciated Hemingway's restraint in keeping the book from being "deliquescent idealization," but found humor used as "a weapon rather than a joy" (72). Cyril Connolly (1964) considered this "one of the best books Hemingway wrote," although it was "about as sentimental as a Mafia-killing" (36). Stanley Kauffmann (1964) called the book "highly affecting and biographically invaluable" but believed it was "an anomalous performance" (17). Morley Callaghan (1964), who knew Hemingway, seemed dismayed by the "frightening sketches of people who at one time knew and liked him!" (696). Maxwell Geismar (1964) admitted it was "always interesting" to read a writer's view of his life, but argued that this book was "sharp, satiric, wholly self-centered," without "compassion" or "understanding" (9). Brooks Atkinson (1964) was more succinct and direct, calling *A Moveable Feast* "extraordinarily mean" (32). The harshest dismissal was Stanley Edgar Hyman's (1964): "It is Hemingway's most insignificant book" (8).

Reviews of *A Moveable Feast* also appeared in academic journals. Although *American Literature* carried only a brief positive note ("Brief Mention" 1964), other publications ran longer commentaries, not all of them positive. Writing for the *Massachusetts Review*, William Van O'Connor (1964) lamented that it was "a sick book" (789) containing many "cruel and embarrassing passages" (790). *North American Review*'s Robert Emmet Long (1964) called Hemingway's attacks on his contemporaries unpleasant, malicious, and in many cases uncalled for. Earl Rovit (1965) began his review in *Books Abroad* by stating flatly that this "first posthumous publication from the estate of Ernest Hemingway forebodes no particular good for whatever yet remains in the unpublished treasure trove of Hemingwayiana" (91).

On the positive side, writing in the *Hudson Review*, Marvin Mudrick (1964) called the book "a beautiful legacy" (572), a "new beginning" (576) in which Hemingway came at his experiences directly. Mudrick defended Hemingway's unflattering portraits of contemporaries (even the one of Fitzgerald) and praised him for writing an "authentic love story" about his relationship with Hadley Richardson. Mudrick was decisive in his final assessment: "This book is not only a new beginning for one of the greatest American writers," he said; it is "his masterpiece" (579). Similarly, in the *Kenyon Review* Philip Young (1964) admitted Hemingway might win few new admirers for his treatment of others, but believed "for the most part the prose glitters, warms, and delights." In recreating his Paris years, "Hemingway is not remembering but re-experiencing; not describing, making" (700). Although some academics may deplore the work, Young said, "the book was not written for specialists," but "for the many who have paid the price of it" (704). Many had tried to capture the spirit of "the great years of Americans in Paris; "the difference is," Young concluded, "that this little collection of anecdotes and reminiscences is a minor work of art" (706).[1]

Critical Books of the 1960s

Despite some negative criticism, interest in Hemingway's work continued to grow in academic circles. Dissertations written in the 1950s were turned into books during the following decade, and a number of scholars already established as authorities on other figures turned their attention to Hemingway. As a result, more than a dozen critical commentaries expanded the academic community's understanding of the subtlety and intellectual power of Hemingway's writings. Almost without exception, these studies reflected academics' interest in psychological, New Critical, formalist, and moralist approaches.

For example, Jungian psychology served as the basis for Joseph DeFalco's (1963) study of Hemingway's short fiction, *The Hero in Hemingway's Short Stories*. Relying heavily on theories of the archetype derived principally from Jung and Joseph Campbell's *The Hero with a Thousand Faces*, and on Baker's and Young's studies, DeFalco examined theme, structure, and symbolism to elucidate Hemingway's aesthetic theory, or as he described it, his Literary Ideal. DeFalco grouped the stories thematically to concentrate on issues such as initiation into adulthood, war, marriage, and heroism. In his assessment of the Hemingway hero,

DeFalco defended Hemingway from charges that his worldview was nihilistic; instead, DeFalco said, true Hemingway heroes accept the fact that death is inevitable, but never give up their ideals. Most of DeFalco's close readings of individual stories support his view that Hemingway was a moralist who wished to share life lessons with readers.

Robert W. Lewis's *Hemingway on Love* (1965) is also typical of Hemingway studies of the 1960s. Filled with references to psychoanalysis, the study traced the growth of Hemingway's "love ethic" (vii) from the early novels through *A Moveable Feast*. Arguing that Hemingway's work was a kind of gestalt in which the whole is greater than the sum of its parts, Lewis made the case for a steady progression of Hemingway's understanding of love, from his early dissolution and rejection of romantic love through his acceptance of the concept of agape. Bound to be controversial if for no other reason than Lewis's privileging later works as more accomplished in dealing with this important subject, *Hemingway on Love* was dismissed by some reviewers as too narrow and filled with the stilted arguments common to dissertations (Halliday 1966; Weeks 1967). But over succeeding decades, the book remained a source of interest to Hemingway scholars. Furthermore, the early reviews did not discourage Lewis, who would go on to become a leading figure in the Hemingway Society and a highly respected Hemingway scholar.

Nelson Algren's (1965) *Notes from a Sea Diary: Hemingway All the Way*, a curious (and critically panned) olio of sea tales, salty humor, and literary criticism, lashed out against critics who had willfully misunderstood Hemingway's work and his importance in the American literary tradition. Too many of the critics—Algren cited Dwight Macdonald and D. S. Savage in particular—were fooled by the image of Hemingway as "the Violent American" to realize what he had accomplished in his fiction. "Only Malcolm Cowley and Maxwell Geismar have perceived that what Hemingway appeared to be"—the celebrator of machismo and bloodlust—"was only the surface of the writer" (168). Beneath that veneer, Algren said, Hemingway carried "within him the whole buried burden of America's guilt, the self-destructiveness of a people who felt their lives were being lived by somebody else" (169). Far from having no memory, as critics charged, he was able to "give new life to John Donne's sermon that no man is an island," and he developed a style that, far from being a "clever trick," filled a vital need for his contemporaries: a need "for light and simplicity" (171). The critics "distrusted his style," his penchant for adventure, his drinking, his lack of politics—and later, his politics. They even came to distrust "his beard" and "his smile" (250). Their distrust, Algren concluded, obscured their envy, because, for all the fame he achieved and money he made, Hemingway was never motivated by anything other than the desire to be the best writer he could be and chronicle his world as accurately as he could. For these reasons, Algren said, that if one could bring back any dead writer, the choice would be easy: "Hemingway *all* the way" (251).

In 1966 Philip Young brought out a new edition of his groundbreaking 1952 study. However, *Ernest Hemingway: A Reconsideration* (Young 1966a) was less a total reconsideration than a reprint of Young's original observations, supplemented by a long foreword about the travails he experienced in getting his original book published and a concluding chapter analyzing *A Moveable Feast*. Both were essentially reprints of essays that Young had published in the *Kenyon Review*.[2] Published in the same year, Constance Cappel Montgomery's (1966) *Hemingway in Michigan* focused on the time he spent in Michigan and his years as a young writer. With care not to overstate her case, Montgomery explained how the environment in which Hemingway spent many of his summers and a crucial period after returning from World War I shaped his early fiction.

Nathan Scott's (1966) *Ernest Hemingway: A Critical Essay*, in publisher William Eerdman's Contemporary Writers in Christian Perspective series, demonstrated that it was possible to see in Hemingway's fiction something other than violence and defeatism. Perhaps because he was looking for evidence of religious themes, Scott discovered that the bulk of Hemingway's work is "powerfully bracing and affirmative" (11); it recalls (for Scott, at least) "a world touched by glory" (19). Beside that glory Hemingway recognizes "the blackness" (29) of modern life, but Scott insisted that critics who focused only on the dark side of Hemingway's fiction often missed the great moral lessons he offered. Scott believed Hemingway's vision of life had had a "gripping effect on the modern imagination" in part because of "its essentially religious seriousness." Hemingway was "a 'spiritual writer'" whose works enacted "just beneath the clenched surfaces of his fiction" the "soul's journey in search of God" (40).

Sheridan Baker's (1967) *Ernest Hemingway: An Introduction and Interpretation*, in Holt, Rinehart and Winston's American Authors and Critics series, is, like many of its predecessors in this critical genre, a brief study that attempted to find a pattern in Hemingway's style, themes, and characterization. Readers—especially ones who subscribed to the belief that Hemingway was the premier writer of his generation—may have been put off by Baker's initial judgment: "Hemingway," he said in his first sentence, "is a limited writer" (1). Baker's readings of individual novels and stories were aimed at explaining his belief that over his career Hemingway moved from what Baker called "the poetry of defeat" to "that of undefeat," although his hero remained "a man alone, against towering circumstance" (134). Within his limited vision, Baker observed, Hemingway had written powerful stories and novels, filled with bitter and often tragic irony that resonated with readers.

For four decades criticism of Hemingway seemed driven by a need to reconcile the writer's life and work, a desire fueled in part by Hemingway himself, who seemed to inject himself in his fiction and nonfiction only to deny that the person he depicted was really himself. The idea of the Hemingway code hero seemed to codify the critical direction of Hemingway studies at least until the late 1970s. Even studies of Hemingway's style looked for autobiographical roots to explain his spare prose. Finding in the man the source of the angst that troubled his protagonists became a dominant mode of critical inquiry.

That approach is evident in Richard Hovey's (1968) *Hemingway: The Inward Terrain*. Written, Hovey said, in answer to the question "What are we to make of Hemingway?" (ix), this psychological reading of the fiction went beyond Young's analysis to impose even more stringent psychological categories upon Hemingway's work. Although Hovey warned against "establishment readings" (xii) because "our authorized version of Hemingway may eventuate in a nearly scandalous misrepresentation" (xiii), his attempt to expose the inner drama playing out in the stories and novels produced a portrait not too dissimilar from Young's. Fixated on Hemingway's "singular and characteristic interweaving of the erotic with pain-wounds-and-death" (5), Hovey exposed a man whose fiction was little more than a displacement of his own Freudian neuroses. Hence, Hovey concluded that the best way to read Hemingway was biographically. "His importance" was "not merely as an exponent of things American nor as the mouthpiece of a certain transient mood or the model for a temporary stance." Instead, he is likely to be read in the future for the "intrinsic value of his writings," for "whatever was both new and true in them" (208). Both an artist and a moralist, Hemingway endures because readers (and critics) admire the way he "sought to win from the death drive itself some affirmation of human dignity" (209). In Hovey's estimation, Hemingway's art was true and morally sound because it came from Hemingway's own experience.

Hovey's book is an example of a thesis-driven approach, examining Hemingway's work within a theoretical framework—in this case, Freudian psychology. Consequently, as Nicholas Joost (1970) noted, the efficacy of Hovey's "moralistic" reading of Hemingway depended on one's willingness to accept the "Freudian doctrine" on which it was based (301). Considered as such, it is not very different from later studies influenced by various theories or approaches that shaped the way critics would read Hemingway's work and come to notably different conclusions about the fiction and its author.

Leo Gurko's (1968) *Ernest Hemingway and the Pursuit of Heroism*, a critical study intended for students, was also thesis driven. Perhaps in an attempt to appeal to his audience (and their teachers), Gurko argued that Hemingway's novels were "not primarily studies of death or simply researches into the lost generation," but that "the central theme in Hemingway's longer work is heroism" (55). His readings of individual novels demonstrate how, instead of providing a "leisurely examination and exposition of character," as one might find in the work of Dickens or George Eliot, Hemingway "evaluated his men and women by their reaction to some deliberately contrived strain." The "main business of his novels" is to show how his protagonists "live with calamity" (228–29). Gurko's readings are characterized by careful exposition in plain language, but his definitive pronouncements about individual works struck the reviewer for *Kirkus* as too facile—and potentially misleading for young people first approaching Hemingway's works from a critical perspective ("*Ernest Hemingway and the Pursuit of Heroism*" 1968). Surprisingly, however, Carlos Baker (1969b) said even the most jaded critic may be "informed and refreshed" by Gurko's study (129)—although Baker devoted almost half his review to pointing out factual errors in Gurko's biographical chapter. Ultimately, Baker judged Gurko's work a "sound introductory study" (130).

Also focusing on the "Hemingway hero," in *Hemingway's Heroes* Delbert Wylder (1969) challenged those who argued that two types of heroes inhabit Hemingway's fiction. Wylder made the case that each hero was somehow unique, or at least sufficiently differentiated from others in the Hemingway canon to dispel notions that Hemingway did not develop his ideas about the effect of suffering on characters. There are two broad types, Wylder argued, the hero and the antihero, but within those categories Hemingway had examined the concept of heroism from different perspectives. Conveniently, for Wylder's purposes, one type predominates in each of the major novels: the sentimental hero in *Torrents of Spring*, the wounded antihero in *The Sun Also Rises*, the guilt-ridden antihero in *A Farewell to Arms*, the self-destructive antihero in *To Have and Have Not*, the mythic hero in *For Whom the Bell Tolls*, the tyrant hero in *Across the River and Into the Trees*, and the hero as saint and sinner in *The Old Man and the Sea*. These fine distinctions made it possible for Wylder to provide close readings that reveal Hemingway's sensitivity toward a major theme, the right way to confront suffering and death. More importantly, *Hemingway's Heroes* provided further demonstration that the characters in Hemingway's fiction were more than mere projections of the author in his work.

In 1968 Robert O. Stephens published the first major study of Hemingway's essays and journalism. Stephens argued in *Hemingway's Nonfiction: The Public Voice* that "Hemingway's work in the essay [a term Stephens uses to describe all of the nonfiction] was an important and parallel form of writing done throughout his career" (ix), and that these journalistic efforts furnished important insights into the fiction. Discussing the major nonfiction (*Death in the Afternoon, Green Hills of Africa, A Moveable Feast*) as well as works like *The Spanish Earth* and Hemingway's introductions, prefaces, and journalism, Stephens found in Hemingway an ambivalence that allowed him to dismiss this kind of writing while still believing that the best journalism had value beyond its immediate publication. One characteristic of these pieces, Stephens said, was that they allowed Hemingway to speak in his own voice rather than mask himself behind one of the characters in his fiction. In the nonfiction Hemingway was always present as "the expert" who has a "right to speak on a topic" derived from "his implied competence and knowledgeability." Hemingway understood that what convinces readers is not "logic or ideology" but rather "the force of personality or character" (45). Stephens identified four ways in which Hemingway presented himself as "expert": as "the model for living one's life"; as the man with "behind-the-scenes information about stories told to the public"; as the master of "how-to" information, a "preceptor" for learning how to do things correctly; and finally as "the giver of expert advice—moral and technical—to those who had to act on knowledge" (46). Stephens provided a lengthy exposé on the way Hemingway transformed nonfiction, especially his journalism, into his fiction. He was sophisticated enough to realize there is no slavish, one-to-one correspondence, but his general argument was that the seeds for much of Hemingway's finest creative writing were planted in the work he did as a journalist and essayist. *Hemingway's Nonfiction* became almost instantly the reference book for anyone interested in exploring the relationship between the two forms of Hemingway's writing.

Among books making a contribution to the history of Hemingway's apprenticeship as a writer, Nicholas Joost's (1968) *Ernest Hemingway and the Little Magazines* is distinguished in two ways. First, Joost used his extensive knowledge of literary history, particularly the history of literary magazines, to explain how Hemingway honed his craft in stories submitted to a handful of these journals between 1921 and 1925. A good bit of Joost's study consists of piecing together information from previously published work, but he also spent considerable time and effort going through files of defunct journals such as the *transatlantic review*, the *Double-Dealer*, and others. Certainly the book was then, and is now, informative for those interested in Hemingway's development as a writer. However, it is distinguished for a second reason. In his review for *American Literature*, Carlos Baker (1969a), the recognized doyen of Hemingway studies, began by praising Joost's sound scholarship before pointing out that, in his view, the most significant piece of new information was contained in a few brief paragraphs in the epilogue and that the book contained at least twelve factual errors. Clearly, during the 1960s anyone brave enough to publish biographical materials on Hemingway ran great risk of running afoul of Hemingway's approved biographer, who seemed to guard his territory fiercely.

Richard Peterson's (1969) *Hemingway: Direct and Oblique* was another extended exploration of the relationship between style and meaning in Hemingway's fiction. Peterson built on work by Young, Baker, and Weeks—taking great pains to explain how his version was more sophisticated than theirs. His nuanced approach allowed him to account for Hemingway's later work as part of his evolution of ideas about human relationships and heroism rather than dismiss them because they were not written in the spare style for which Hemingway had become famous. The early style aptly reflected the "exhaustion of value" that Hemingway wished to portray in his early work (16), but the more complex expression of ideas in later works was also intentional. Peterson was interested primarily in the way Hemingway used "various forms of indirection" along with "overt themes and statements that say the same things directly" (21). He concluded that Hemingway should be considered a romantic writer rather than an existentialist.

Another book that attempted to provide a comprehensive framework for reading Hemingway and appreciating his achievement was Jackson Benson's (1969) *Hemingway: The Writer's Art of Self-Defense*. In what can best be described as an exercise in blended critical analysis, Benson combined insights of psychological criticism and the close reading techniques of New Critics to explain how the power of Hemingway's fiction emerged not from the "sudden, single event of being seriously wounded in war" as Young argued, but rather from "the more gradual accumulated perceptions of the sharp contrasts" between the Victorian world of Oak Park and "a world at war with the individual" (4). Hemingway's fiction was the product of an artist consciously striving to keep powerful emotions in check through the medium of style, structure, irony, and other technical and rhetorical devices. On one level Hemingway's fiction revealed a constant struggle to define masculinity, a concept not modeled in his own home where a domineering mother controlled events. On another level it displayed the unceasing effort of heroic individuals to battle against forces of nature and society that inevitably crushed them. Benson seemed to reject readings that glorify figures such as Jake Barnes and the Lost Generation. At the same time, he cautioned that, while the "Hemingway hero" often found himself "living his life in firm opposition to" the mores of conventional respectability (21), it was unwise to "group together all major and minor characters in Hemingway's work who display courage" or search among all his major figures "in order to codify their conditions or qualities" (149). In essence, Benson rejected the idea that there was a typical Hemingway hero, or code hero. He believed "the most constant demand in all Hemingway's work was the demand for ethical judgment"—a requirement sometimes placed on characters, but always on readers (149).

As important as Benson's arguments about the nature of Hemingway's philosophy are, his observations on critical trends and predictions about future studies were perhaps even more instructive. "Hemingway's work, because of its apparent simplicity, seems destined to attract simplistic labels," he warned (187). The "early failure to perceive him as an intelligent, knowledgeable, and clever craftsman" (188) had obscured his achievement and might continue to influence judgments about his work. What ought to happen, in Benson view, was that Hemingway should be read for what he is: "essentially a philosophical writer who searched for the bedrock of man's experience" and tried to capture it in his fiction. A person of his time, Hemingway "has a valid claim to being one of the authors who has contributed most to identifying and combating the most pressing literary problems of our age": the "bankruptcy of language" and the "superficiality" of much twentieth-century literature," which is "weighed down with romantic historical novels and nostalgic stories of childhood" and "a naturalistic devotion to the 'times'" (189). Benson's Hemingway is the heroic artist—although Benson did not say it, and might object to the comparison—the romantic artist striving to achieve purity of craft and accuracy of vision in a world that little appreciates his efforts.

Audre Hanneman's Bibliography

In 1967 the most important tool for Hemingway scholars to appear before the advent of the Internet was published: Audre Hanneman's *Ernest Hemingway: A Comprehensive Bibliography*. Organized in eight major sections, the book provides detailed information about publications ranging from Hemingway's works (books, stories, writings for newspapers and periodicals, translations of his work, and appearances of individual works in anthologies) to one about him.

While it is now possible to discover reviews or even articles Hanneman missed by doing a variety of online queries, the extent of her diligence in identifying, recording, and summarizing thousands of works from Hemingway's own publications (in several editions), academic scholarship, and references in newspapers and magazines is nothing less than remarkable. In the foreword, Hemingway's publisher Charles Scribner Jr. described Hanneman's work as "a task comparable to one of the fabled labors of Hercules" (vii). Hanneman was notably less effusive, using her preface to outline the work's general organization and thank the dozens of scholars and librarians who helped her compile the information in a book of nearly six hundred pages of relatively small type. A mere eight years later, Hanneman (1975) issued her *Supplement to Ernest Hemingway: A Comprehensive Bibliography*, a work focused almost exclusively on editions and criticism published between 1967 and 1974—and running to nearly four hundred pages.

Over the years, a handful of scholars have taken great joy in pointing out an obscure review or two that Hanneman missed. While such work is important to the community of Hemingway scholars, these ladies and gentlemen bear a remarkable similarity to Gulliver announcing the discovery of minor flaws on those benevolent giants, the Brobdinagians.

Articles and Book Chapters: Dominant Approaches

In addition to the books published on Hemingway, dozens of chapters and articles published during the 1960s provide some idea of the interests that dominated academic study of Hemingway's fiction. A small sample of the hundreds that appeared during the decade offers insight into how New Criticism, myth criticism, and psychological studies continued to influence critics' assessments of Hemingway's achievements.

Among formalist approaches to Hemingway's work, Tony Tanner's (1965) analysis in *The Reign of Wonder* stands out both for its sensitive critique of technique and its ability to place Hemingway's fiction in the larger context of the American literary tradition that traces its roots back to the Transcendentalists. Tanner explained why Hemingway was so focused on describing the sensations of experience, owing to his belief that these were the only reliable ways for capturing reality. His discussion of Hemingway's style removed the stigma that had often been attached to his work as anti-intellectual, suggesting instead that the calculated recitation of selected details creates a more intense experience of the reality Hemingway wished to convey in his fiction.

Concentrating on style, novelist Wright Morris (1963) argued that Hemingway's was unique, distinct, and virtually unchanged during his career. Wright believed Hemingway realized early that the spare style of his earliest stories, characterized by "sublime economy," was, "when dictated by the imagination" (139), the perfect vehicle for conveying his vision of the world. Similarly, Robert Slabey's (1965) "The Structure of *In Our Time*" and Peter Lisca's (1966) "The Structure of Hemingway's *Across the River and Into the Trees*" suggested that every Hemingway work revealed the hand of the artist in crafting his materials. In a lengthy essay on Hemingway's style, Richard Bridgman (1966) claimed Hemingway melded the "two lines" of American literature represented by Henry James and Mark Twain, "shaping the vernacular for general service" (195). Bridgman's technical analysis of Hemingway's use of structural patterns and parts of speech demonstrated how his style evolved as his career progressed. Hemingway's principal contribution to the development of American style was his simplification of expression—a simplification that reached extreme levels in his work.

William Toole's (1967) "Religion, Love and Nature in *A Farewell to Arms*: The Dark Shape of Irony" and Warren Bennett's (1970) "Character, Irony, and Resolution in 'A Clean, Well-Lighted Place'" revealed the influence of New Criticism in the authors' exploration of the text for patterns of irony. Daniel Schneider's (1967) "The Symbolism of *The Sun Also Rises*" demonstrated how one of Hemingway's most respected novels yields to investigations for symbolic patterns, while Rosemary Stephens's (1966) "'In Another Country': *Three* as Symbol" and Malcolm Marsden's (1969) "Hemingway's Symbolic Pattern: The Basis of Tone" made clear the possibility of finding such patterns in less acclaimed novels or in the short stories.

Many scholars continued to be fascinated by the philosophical dimensions of Hemingway's fiction. Witness, for example, how in *The Hidden God*, Cleanth Brooks (1963) found "approximations to Christianity" (18) in a number of Hemingway's novels and stories; however, Brooks did not press the case (as some before and after him would do) that Hemingway is at his core a Christian writer. In his best work, such as *For Whom the Bell Tolls*, "Hemingway gives us real people in their complexity and in their exasperating mixture of good and evil" (19). Similar interest is evident in Barbara LeBost's (1965) "'The Way It Is': Something Else on Hemingway" in the *Journal of Existentialism* and in Bickford Sylvester's (1966) "Hemingway's Extended Vision: *The Old Man and the Sea*" in *PMLA*. David Noble's (1968) discussion of Hemingway in *The Eternal Adam and the New World Garden* found parallels between Hemingway's fiction and Melville's; his heroes, like Melville's Ahab, struggle against death while fully knowing they will lose in the end.

Psychological studies during these years were divided among two camps. Some, like David Gordon's (1966) "The Son and the Father: Patterns of Response to Conflict in Hemingway's Fiction," examined the psychological dimensions of Hemingway's creations. Others, like Stanley Cooperman's (1967) chapter in *World War I and the American Novel*, focused on Hemingway's psychological makeup. Cooperman argued that Hemingway was not really an existential thinker. His excessive focus on ritual "represents a retreat from rather than an acceptance of existential absurdity." His fixation on associating masculinity with action led him to link the passivity of death with the feminine, resulting in his uncomfortable portraits of women.

Hemingway's debt to myth and the epic tradition remained of interest to scholars, as essays by Benjamin Harlow (1966) and Peter Hays (1966) demonstrate. Hemingway's work also prompted a number of readings focused on its religious dimensions. Typical of scholarly explorations that identify characters in Hemingway with Christ was Julian Smith's (1969) "Christ Times Four: Hemingway's Unknown Spanish Civil War Stories." The number of studies comparing Santiago from *The Old Man and the Sea* to Christ runs to at least a dozen. Typical is Edwin Moseley's (1962) "Christ as the Old Champion: Hemingway's *The Old Man and the Sea*"; Moseley argued that Santiago is Hemingway's portrait of the Christian tragic hero, whose "suffering leads to moral victory" (209). Among the more unusual—perhaps provocative—religious readings is William Glasser's (1966) "*A Farewell to Arms*," in which Glasser explores Frederic Henry's growth in achieving a Christian awareness of life.

Robert Holland's (1968) daring argumentative strategy in "Macomber and the Critics" stands out among dozens of articles that attempted to provide definitive interpretations of individual works. Holland began by asserting that Hemingway would have been appalled at the "scholarly ineptitude" and "irresponsible thesis-hunting" of those explaining the ending of "The Short Happy Life of Francis Macomber," certainly "one of the most frequently explicated scenes in all of contemporary literature" (171). After surveying prior interpretations to "illustrate how far astray we may go in our judgments in literature" (171), Holland ended up by deftly syllogizing to reach what in his view was the only possible interpretation: Since Hemingway always wrote clearly, and since the text says Mrs. Macomber shot at the buffalo, then that's what really happened. No further commentary required.

Traditional influence studies appeared on occasion, such as Frederick Benson's (1967) in *Writers in Arms* (1967). Benson discussed Hemingway's involvement in the Spanish Civil War and the impact of his experience on the composition of *For Whom the Bell Tolls*. A similar argument was made by John Muste (1966) in *Say That We Saw Spain Die*, in which Muste cited Hemingway frequently to show how literary artists were impacted by events of war.

Undoubtedly, however, scholars seemed most interested in tracing the development of the Hemingway code in all of Hemingway's fiction. Typical of these is Richard Hovey's (1966) "*The Old Man and the Sea*: A New Hemingway Hero," in which Hovey extended Philip Young's definition of the Hemingway hero to include the fisherman, who in several respects is quite different from characters like Jake Barnes, Frederic Henry, or Robert Jordan. W. M. White's (1969) "The Crane-Hemingway Code: A Revaluation" used techniques of influence study to show how Hemingway borrowed from Crane some elements of the code and transformed them to fit his unique interpretation of human behavior. How far those studies might take one can be seen in Harry Hand's (1966) "Transducers and Hemingway's Heroes," in which Hand argued that Hemingway's heroes behave like "transducers," a term used by scientists to describe devices that transform one form of energy into another.

Finally, the special issue of *Modern Fiction Studies* published in 1968 may serve as a microcosm for identifying dominant critical approaches to Hemingway's writing. Essay titles reveal each critic's approach: Robin Farquhar's "Dramatic Structure in the Novels of Ernest Hemingway" is followed by Daniel Schneider's "Hemingway's *A Farewell to Arms*: The Novel as Pure Poetry." Another examination of structure, Robert

Cochran's "Circularity in *The Sun Also Rises*," precedes one on symbolism, James Green's "Symbolic Sentences in 'Big Two-Hearted River.'" The New Critics' search for unity informs Clinton Burhans's "The Complex Unity of *In Our Time*," while their focus on irony as an important literary device is highlighted in William Ryan's "Uses of Irony in *To Have and Have Not*." Perhaps the most intriguing essay is the first one in the issue, William Gifford's "Hemingway: The Monsters and the Critics." Playing off the title of J. R. R. Tolkien's famous essay on *Beowulf*, Griffin examined Hemingway's development of various stylistic techniques and critiques his worldview. Gifford argued that Hemingway's work has "much in common with that of Old English poetry" (hence the allusion to Tolkien's essay) and that "the elements of his writing" combine to "produce a unified effect of heroic quality" (255). Worth noting as well is Maurice Beebe and John Feaster's "Checklist of Criticism," intended to complement Audre Hanneman's 1967 bibliography; it covers more than thirty pages and is printed in very small typeface.

Publication of Hemingway's Journalism

William White's (1967) edition of Hemingway's journalism, *By-Line: Ernest Hemingway*, was reviewed by a number of well-known critics. Carlos Baker (1967) was quite pleased with the publication. "Rescued from piles of yellowing newsprint and files of superannuated magazines," he said somewhat hyperbolically, "these selections shine like a hoard of gold pieces brought newly to light and still bearing the coin-maker's inimitable imprimatura" (1). Few were as positive as Baker. Like Baker, Granville Hicks (1967) thought the publication of these pieces was likely to enhance Hemingway's reputation. William Kennedy (1967) noted that, while the material in *By-Line* was "not top drawer," it was the raw material from which Hemingway created much of his art (19). The reviewer for *Time* thought the book would be useful principally as "source material for Hemingway biographers and thesis hunters in the Eng. Lit. faculties" ("Hero as Celebrity" 1971, 133). But Philip Young (1967) cautioned readers to recognize these pieces for what they are, "writing that was at first the meal ticket, before long the moonlighting, of a man who had a different job" (6).

British reviewers offered more measured assessments. Malcolm Bradbury (1968) said the book illuminated "the steady search for the right style" and the "paradox" that occurs when Hemingway achieves it: "when Hemingway is his own hero, the work falls off" (386). Maryvonne Butcher (1968) said the best writing occurs early in the book, "cheek by jowl with examples of very amateur reporting," while in pieces written near the end of his career Hemingway "wrote some really terrible passages of near self-parody." These would not be the last words on Hemingway's journalism, but the reviewers seemed to recognize that the best use of this early material was for comparison with the fiction that grew out of these early efforts to explain "the way it was."

Hemingway's Reputation Reconsidered

The ongoing debate over Hemingway's place in American literature continued to interest scholars and the general public during the 1960s. Certainly by the end of the decade, he was, as Robert Weeks (1967) observed wryly, being put to many uses: as "American phenomenon," as "agreeable means to a Ph.D.," as a "giant of American literature," and "as a fruitful subject of psycho-biographical criticism" (265). Two essays provide some insight into the way Hemingway was being evaluated—and say something as well about the status of academic critics' ability to predict the future.

Despite the temporary uptick in critical appreciation shown in some quarters for *A Moveable Feast*, the idea that Hemingway's reputation had actually fallen in recent years is front and center in Malcolm Cowley's (1967) "Papa and the Parricides." Likening Hemingway to a fallen lion surrounded by jackals ready to pounce on a corpse, Cowley noted that each critic who wrote about Hemingway tried to outdo previous commentators by further limiting the works that should be considered worth reading. The general consensus among detractors was that Hemingway's focus on death showed unhealthy morbidity, and his venture into political writing (particularly *For Whom the Bell Tolls*) was a failure. Cowley defended that novel and Hemingway's choice of subjects. In fact, he was particularly impressed with the way the presence of death that hangs over much of Hemingway's work seems to clarify his vision for the "special cleanness and freshness of the physical world" (103). Critics attacking Hemingway's reputation were not showing "more than the customary measure of ingratitude," but Cowley believed the loss would be to American literature, which was "vastly richer now than it was when Hemingway started writing"—yet "not so rich that it can afford to disown and devalue one of its lasting treasures" (162).

In an essay in *American Literature*, Robert Evans (1966) tackled the persistent complaint that Hemingway and his protagonists are anti-intellectual. Evans admitted that, in one sense, the charge that Hemingway was "aesthetically a primitive" (162) was justified. Characters like Nick Adams and Robert Jordan do not like to think—because for Hemingway, to think is to remember, and the pain of remembering is too difficult for men of integrity to bear. As a result, however, Hemingway's characters are diminished. They move in "a bleak and impoverished landscape" (174) and "almost invariably live and act in the specious present" (175). This diminishment ultimately reflects on Hemingway's achievement, Evans argued. Because his heroes exhibit a "fugitive and cloistered virtue that does not seek its adversary but slinks out of the race," for "all its blood and thunder, Hemingway's world is not quite man-sized" (176).

Equally germane to the present study, Evans made several observations about Hemingway's reputation. On the one hand, he described *The Old Man and the Sea* as "overvalued and too heavily symbolic" (168), a judgment with which many subsequent critics would concur. On the other hand, his confident statement that he "doubt[s] strongly whether any posthumously appearing work of Hemingway's will *significantly* alter our present understanding and evaluation of his work" (173) seems hopelessly wrong in light of what has happened in Hemingway studies during the past thirty years. The reasons for Evans's miscalculation are made clear in his own words. "Evaluation of the literary artifact," he asserted with equal certitude, "may proceed under either or both of two modes: aesthetic, or moral and intellectual" (173–74). The strictures of what was then critical best practice limited Evans's ability to conceive that new critical theories would make possible a radical revaluation of Hemingway.

Carlos Baker's Biography

Within months after Hemingway died, his widow selected Carlos Baker to be Hemingway's "official" biographer. The designation is important, because Mary Welsh Hemingway was fiercely protective of her late husband's reputation. As owner of Hemingway's personal papers, Mary Hemingway exercised tight control over access to letters, notes, and other personal documents that are a biographer's best sources. Knowing her husband had found Baker's 1952 critical study the least offensive of the ones produced during his lifetime, Mary allowed Baker the access he needed to write a comprehensive life study of the recently deceased Nobel laureate.[3]

Anticipated for nearly a decade, Carlos Baker's (1969c) *Ernest Hemingway: A Life Story* delivered in providing exceptional details about Hemingway's life. The biography is certainly massive—more than six hundred pages in the first edition—and despite Baker's claims to the contrary, it is not without a thesis. The dominant impression one takes away from *Ernest Hemingway: A Life Story* is that Hemingway was a man's man, a living legend who measured up to all the hype about his larger-than-life personality. Like many biographers, Baker takes exceptional measures to explain how events in Hemingway's life affected his fiction, and while Baker does not strive for literal one-to-one correspondence between life and art, hardly a story or novel escapes his careful gleaning of real-life details that inspired imagined people and events. In the details Baker assembled, one can see how Hemingway worked to craft his art and his legend.

Ernest Hemingway: A Life Story demonstrates fairly clearly that, like the fictional David Copperfield, Hemingway thought of himself as the hero of his own life story and relished the celebrity status he achieved. Hemingway did some truly heroic things in his life, and Baker did not hesitate to celebrate his courage and genuine concern for a number of social causes. At the same time, he is no blind hero-worshipper; on more than one occasion, he presents Hemingway as a self-absorbed prima donna or a bully who loved to humiliate other men and take advantage of women who truly loved or admired him.

The lack of critical commentary is easily explained. As Baker noted in his introduction, he had published a major critical study of Hemingway in 1952 and already updated it twice before releasing the biography. As a collection of biographical details from a wide array of sources (first-person reminiscences, newspaper accounts, published reports, and thousands of letters and personal documents), Baker's biography can hardly be bested. Yet Baker himself observed that his work was not the last word on Hemingway's life. Whether that was merely a disclaimer intended to justify his lack of genuine assessment of Hemingway's character and personality, or an acknowledgment that much about Hemingway's life and work had not yet been made public, it is certainly true that Baker did not possess all the letters, reminiscences, and critical commentary he needed to be definitive.

Despite Baker's disclaimers, many reviewers and academic critics were disappointed in Baker's lack of insight into Hemingway's character and personality. Others were puzzled by Baker's strident attempt to avoid hero-worship, which sometimes caused him to appear almost hostile toward his subject. While *Time* magazine described the book as a "massive and humane critical treatment," a "warts and all" book that made Hemingway more fully human than any previous account ("Ernest Good and Bad" 1969, 102), *New York Times* reviewer Christopher Lehmann-Haupt (1969) said reading Baker's book was "hugely exasperating"; he was particularly frustrated by Baker's unwillingness to "seize the psychological evidence" and tell us something more substantive about Hemingway's personality and how it informed his art (45). Saul Maloff (1969) was almost apologetic, excusing Baker for undertaking such a difficult and thankless task when his earlier work on Hemingway revealed his admiration for a figure whose life provided tabloid fodder. Less kindly, Irving Howe (1969) observed that "for those Americans to whom fishing and hunting are the substance of life, Professor Carlos Baker has written the perfect biography of Ernest Hemingway" (155). Howe was disturbed that Baker focused on external details and failed to get inside Hemingway's mind and explore his imaginative life. Howe insisted that the evidence to do so was at Baker's disposal, but he failed to use it.

Most academics were even less impressed. Harry Moore (1971) found Baker's biography heavy on detail but light on character analysis, although—unlike Lehmann-Haupt—he was grateful Baker did not write "a heavily psychoanalytical biography" (90). A few agreed with A. Robert Lee (1971), who believed Baker presented "a more complex, more various and attractive figure" (223) than the stereotypes of Hemingway created during the past twenty years. Many others, however, were more sympathetic to the position of Charles Thomas Samuels (1969), who described Baker's book as an assemblage of facts with little analysis or insight. Perhaps its best feature, he said, was that it provided the basis for great and useful speculation about Hemingway. George Steiner (1969) called Baker's biography "one of the saddest books I have read in a long time"—sad because it was filled with trivia and interminably long without capturing the essence of Hemingway's achievements as a writer (147).

Nicholas Joost (1970), who was treated rather unkindly by Baker in a review of his book, repaid the favor by noting how much help Baker had in turning *Ernest Hemingway: A Life Story* into a best seller. While some have called Baker's book epic and indispensable, Joost noted (somewhat happily) that others found it "not epic nor indispensable nor essential," but instead "the work of a writer who himself is dull, plodding, and obtuse" (294). Still, Joost admitted that Baker had done a service by assembling so many facts about Hemingway's life—even while displaying "shakiness in dealing with the material of the twenties" (297) and "fail[ing] to destroy the legendary Hemingway" (299). Mark Schorer (1970) described the book as "an extraordinary, an enormous, and finally a frustrating abundance of external fact" (592). Julian Smith (1970) cautioned that Baker was sometimes wrong about facts, and while his "judgments about the stories" tended to be "brief and frequently Olympian" (643), of greater concern was his tendency to read all of them autobiographically, showing a lack of respect for the fiction. Alan Wycherley (1969) simply called it "a very bad book"—and suggested that Baker knew it (15).

Baker did not satisfy everyone in the Hemingway family either. Hemingway's eldest son, John, wrote some years later that while he considered *Ernest Hemingway: A Life Story* "a monument to tireless research and hard work," the book seemed to him to be "about someone I never knew, someone without humor and, in short, someone without life" ("Foreword" in Griffin 1985, v).

Summing Up a Decade of Criticism

The large number of books appearing in 1969 led to the publication of several omnibus reviews that reflect the status of Hemingway criticism at the end of the 1960s. Two reviews may serve as illustrations. Robert Murray Davis (1969) insisted that, now that Hemingway was dead, critics are responsible for "set[ting] the record straight" and determining which works, "independent of the Hemingway legend," are "made to last" (382). Reviewing Baker's biography, Hovey's psychological assessment, Stephens's analysis of the nonfiction, and Joost's study of Hemingway's work for the Paris literary magazines, Davis insisted that none was "anything like definitive" (383). Using the bullfight as his controlling metaphor, he concluded that Hovey's work is a "virtuoso performance" based on "a borrowed method of questionable soundness" (383); Stephens is successful in "overpower[ing] the beast with a solid, wooden, unimaginative but respectable message"; Joost "lacks the equipment necessary for the kill," though he gives a fine performance; and Baker "is for the most part content to let the creature gallop around and around the ring" (383). Davis believed that, with the exception of Baker, these studies would have little impact on the majority of Hemingway's admirers.

William Wasserstrom (1969) also commented on Baker, Hovey, and Stephens, and on Lloyd Arnold's (1968) *High on the Wild with Hemingway*, a memoir by one of Hemingway's hunting companions. Wasserstrom believed each of these writers (and by extension, anyone else writing about Hemingway in the years after his death) had to deal with "the Hemingway problem: how to avoid treating this extraordinary man as just a painful case or merely an inviting target" (532).[4] Arnold's "amalgam of myth and make-believe," he said, did little to address this issue. However, Wasserstrom also had little good to say about Hovey (he "launches himself head-on in attack of the Hemingway problem and ends in a pratfall" [533–34]) or Stephens (another of the many works that "merely simplify or restate classic issues" [535]). Wasserstrom accused Baker of attempting to "circumscribe the problem by treating it as still another datum to be included in his handsome and epic biography" (534). Underlying these criticisms, however, is Wasserstrom's own attitude toward Hemingway, which is hardly adulatory. He insisted there was still unresolved the "question of deciding what remains once the man is stripped bare of his scarcely transformed Oak Park ideas," described, almost gleefully, as "pretty close to those of the *Reader's Digest*" (536).

Given the amount of criticism published during the decade of the 1960s, the results of a survey conducted by Jackson Bryer should surprise no one. To determine which writers should be included in a collection of bibliographical essays, *Fifteen Modern American Authors: A Survey of Research and Criticism* (Bryer 1969), Bryer conducted a poll of scholars. Hemingway got the most votes, beating out William Faulkner 127 to 125 (reported in Hubbell 1972, 282–83).

Notes

[1] The publication of *A Moveable Feast* launched a new round of biographical study, as critics now had access to Hemingway's supposedly nonfiction account of the Paris years to compare to his fictional treatment of Paris in the 1920s. For

an example of this kind of scholarship, see George Wickes's (1969) chapter on Hemingway in *Americans in Paris.*

[2] Although Young eventually moved on to write about other topics, he did not abandon his interest in Hemingway—or perhaps other scholars did not let him get away from pontificating on Hemingway and the critical tradition that continued to grow around his works. Young's essays on Hemingway appeared periodically in journals and collections of new criticism until the 1980s. Several were collected in *American Fiction, American Myth: Essays* (Young 2000), posthumously published by Penn State University Press.

[3] In 1964 Baker wrote a long essay for the *New York Times* detailing the problems a Hemingway biographer would have, noting that "one huge obstacle to seeing him plain is the pile of inexact allegations which bulk on the biographical horizon" (Baker 1964, 4).

[4] Nicholas Joost (1970) defined "the Hemingway Problem" slightly differently, calling it the result of Hemingway's decision "more or less deliberately" to make "his art his life and his life his art" (293–94).

5: Turbulence (1970–1979)

THE 1970s WAS A TURBULENT decade for Hemingway studies. In the academy, a growing number of young Americanists trained in the principles of New Criticism, taught to value literature that dealt with existential issues, and predisposed to admire works where style and substance seemed joined at the hip, gravitated toward Hemingway's work as fertile ground for serious scholarship. His mistakes from the 1930s and 1940s and the "disastrous" *Across the River and Into the Trees* were acknowledged but often ignored in favor of extended analysis of the stories and novels that had made him the darling of the moderns. At the same time, the emergence on campus of "new critical theory," as the collection of theoretical (and political) approaches to literary study came to be called, led to a backlash against Hemingway's work and the philosophy underlying it.

Islands in the Stream

The same kind of controversy that erupted at the publication of *A Moveable Feast* greeted the publication of *Islands in the Stream* in 1970. The book was reviewed in dozens of newspapers, periodicals, and academic journals and was a Book-of-the-Month Club special selection. In reporting to club subscribers, Clifton Fadiman (1970) gushed that reading *Islands in the Stream* "is a moving experience." Its finest episodes "are at least as good as any comparable ones to be found in [Hemingway's] entire body of work" (2). Robie Macauley (1970), whose laudatory assessment appeared in the *New York Times*, believed the novel was "a contender with [Hemingway's] very best" (51). The United Press International review that was published in newspapers across the country called the novel "very, very good" ("Last by Hemingway" 1970, E8). Outdoorsman and writer Archie Satterfield (1970) made even larger claims, insisting that this was the "big book" Hemingway had promised. Satterfield thought Scribner and Mary Hemingway were wise to issue the three stories that make up *Islands in the Stream* in a single volume so "the reader can feel the full impact of Hemingway's genius as a storyteller"—a talent that extended to his ability to write love scenes, which "no one" can do "more convincingly" (H4). Satterfield ranked *Islands in the Stream* as one of Hemingway's three greatest novels.

Malcolm Cowley (1970), who had read the original manuscript, was delighted with the published version, which he considered more unified and certainly reflective of Hemingway himself, the "great man in public" who spent so much time "standing alone at his work table," trying to "summon back his early powers" (108). Roderick Nordell (1970) was less effusive but still positive, asserting that "after all the caveats have been entered, *Islands in the Stream* remains as likable and heartbreaking a book as Ernest Hemingway ever wrote" (13). Robert Emmet Long (1970) thought the novel accurately reflected "the grand Hemingway manner—the sharp, chiseled style that has been one of the most admired and imitated in the world" (99); unfortunately, he said, the subject was not worthy of Hemingway's talent. Edmund Fuller (1970) said *Islands* contained "scenes and passages as good as anything" Hemingway had written; and even at points where Hemingway was bad, "it is the idiosyncratic badness of a great writer which is quite another thing than the badness of mediocrity" (10).

Less enthusiastic reviewers described *Islands* as "mawkish, sentimental and tasteless" (Oldsey 1970, 376), "mediocre work" (Rubin 1970, E1), filled with slack writing, only occasionally rescued by "charming passages" (Howe 1970, 125). John Aldridge (1970) was only slightly less harsh, describing the novel as "neither very good nor very bad"; in some places it is "downright wonderful, in others as sad and embarrassingly self-indulgent as the work of any sophomore" (23). The reviewer for the *Times Literary Supplement* ("Hemingway's Unstill Waters" 1970) thought the section titled "Cuba" the "very worst piece of writing we have seen by Hemingway so far" (1193), but still judged the novel the "most interesting" Hemingway work since *For Whom the Bell Tolls* (1194). However, Maxwell Geismar (1970) said the publication of this novel "may be hailed as the literary sensation of the fall season," but that it "is not major fiction. It is not even good" (1).

Christopher Lehmann-Haupt (1970) noted that Hemingway did not think it ready for publication, and he could see why: it was at best a "first or second draft" in which Hemingway had not yet found "any universal meaning in the still-private experiences it records" (41). *Richmond Times-Dispatch* book editor Maurice Duke (1970) believed that the publication of *Islands in the Stream* would cause Hemingway's already damaged reputation "to suffer even further" (F5). However, Duke said, the fault was not Hemingway's; he did not publish this book. Jonathan Yardley (1970) believed the Hemingway family and Scribner were "motivated by an urge to shore up, magnify and embroider" the legend that had grown up around Hemingway himself (25). Guy Davenport (1970) thought while *Islands* may remind readers of the old Hemingway, it fell flat—perhaps *because* it was too much of the old in a time when something new was demanded of writers: "It is not Hemingway, but the world that has changed" (1215). Echoing those sentiments, the writer John Updike (1970) lamented that, after reading *Islands*, "few readers younger than myself could believe, from this sad broken testament, how we *did* love Hemingway and, after pity feels merely impudent, love him still" (489).

Columnist Smiley Anders (1970) of the Baton Rouge *Daily Advocate* believed the root of the controversy over this novel lay outside the book itself. Since Hemingway's suicide, Anders noted, "there has been a considerable debunking" of his reputation, with critics seeming to take great pleasure in finding him a "weakling" beset with "psychological problems," his preoccupation with death "a sign of madness" (2F). Anders believed readers not affected by the mania to cut down Hemingway's image would find the stories in *Islands* "will do nothing to harm the Hemingway reputation" and might "even add to it." They would certainly "make you realize, in case you've forgotten, just how gifted a writer Hemingway was" (2F).

As for its place in the Hemingway canon, reviewers could not agree. Addressing the wisdom of posthumous publication, Malcolm Bradbury (1970) contended it was "a major addition to the Hemingway canon," yet it was "worse than the best, better than the worst" (18). Edward Corbett (1970) was not so generous, finding it "painful to admit that this novel will do little to enhance Hemingway's reputation but may do a great deal to diminish it" (382). John Wain (1970) concluded "there is nothing new in it—nothing that a seasoned reader of Hemingway has not met before" (33). Joseph Epstein (1970) believed, however, that the novel would prove "salutary" for Hemingway's reputation (1). Anatole Broyard (1970) seems to have been accurate in his prediction that *Islands*, "less disciplined than *The Old Man and the Sea*, less disastrous than *Across the River and Into the Trees*" was "unlikely to affect Hemingway's standing" (10).

Despite the mixed reception of *Islands in the Stream*, a consensus about Hemingway's staying power was growing among some—but definitely not all—critics and fellow novelists. In a long essay following the publication of *Islands*, Reynolds Price (1972), who admitted to having not always been enthralled by Hemingway, concluded that Hemingway produced "a body of fourteen volumes which, in my guess, will winnow to eight and then stand as an achievement so far unexcelled in American letters, certainly by no one in his own century" (66).

Advances in Hemingway Scholarship

In 1970 the editors of *Rendezvous*, a journal published in Idaho, brought out a special issue dedicated to Hemingway. This olio of scholarly essays by Philip Young, Delbert Wylder, Robert W. Lewis, and Jackson Benson, accompanied by poems and artwork, was intended as much as a tribute to Hemingway nearly a decade after his death as an attempt to advance scholarship. More significant to Hemingway studies, a year later Taylor Alderman of Youngstown State University and Kenneth Rosen of Dickinson College launched *Hemingway notes*, a twice-yearly publication that was part journal, part newsletter, devoted to further study of Hemingway and his works. From its inception *Hemingway notes* was eclectic in approach, although the earliest issues tend to reflect the strong bias for traditional literary study, including a fair number of close readings and biographically based essays. The journal also served as a source for bibliographical information, as each issue carried lists of recent publications and a generous sampling of reviews.

Hemingway notes lasted for ten years. Eventually Alderman and Rosen gave up the editorship to Charles Oliver, under whom the publication was transformed into the *Hemingway Review*, which has become one of the finest scholarly publications devoted to a single author. Oliver continued the editorial policy of accepting submissions that represented an array of critical approaches, and as new critical theories emerged during the 1970s and 1980s the *Hemingway Review* became a forum for debating Hemingway's achievements. Unlike some other publications that focus on one figure, it attracted first-rate work by established and emerging scholars. For thirty-plus years the *Hemingway Review* has remained the best source for scholars wishing to keep abreast of the latest developments in Hemingway scholarship.[1]

In 1970 Matthew Bruccoli, known throughout academe for his bibliographical work on American writers (most notably F. Scott Fitzgerald) and his editorship of several literary dictionaries, and his publishing partner C. E. Frazer Clark Jr. brought out the first issue of the *Fitzgerald/Hemingway Annual*. This intriguing scholarly miscellany appeared regularly until 1979. Following Bruccoli's editorial policy—"save everything"—the *Annual* printed critical commentary, scholarly notes, some seemingly offhanded observations, and other materials that helped round out the portrait of Hemingway's life and writings before the opening of the Hemingway Papers at the Kennedy Library.

Over four decades, Bruccoli made significant contributions to Hemingway scholarship by collecting fugitive pieces by and about him. Bruccoli made no apologies for publishing even the most obscure or ephemeral work. "Everything Ernest Hemingway wrote is important because he wrote it," Bruccoli (1971) said in his introduction to *Ernest Hemingway's Apprenticeship: Oak Park 1916–1917*, a collection of Hemingway's high-school writing. A year earlier Bruccoli (1970) collected some of Hemingway's early journalism under the title *Ernest Hemingway, Cub Reporter*, valuable for anyone interested in seeing how Hemingway's work as a journalist prepared him to write the fiction on which his fame rests.

Collectors were no doubt grateful for Bruccoli's (1973) *Hemingway at Auction, 1930–1973*. Similarly, literary historians and Hemingway scholars benefited from his collections of conversations with Hemingway (Bruccoli 1986a) and letters between Maxwell Perkins and Hemingway (Bruccoli 1996; Bruccoli 2004). In *Hemingway and the Mechanism of Fame*, a collaboration with Judith Baughman, Bruccoli (2006) published statements, public letters, introductions, forewords, prefaces, reviews, endorsements, and miscellaneous blurbs written by Hemingway between 1922 and 1961. Making no claim for their enduring literary merit, Bruccoli and Baughman defend their decision to publish these pieces by describing them as the work Hemingway did between his major undertakings.

Traditional Criticism of the Early 1970s

Two books published in 1971 employed the mainstream approach to Hemingway that dominated critical circles in the previous two decades. In *The Flesh and the Word: Eliot, Hemingway, Faulkner*, Floyd Watkins (1971) provided a sensitive analysis of Hemingway's use of language, explaining how, as his career progressed, Hemingway moved toward a more abstract language in which "details and good sensuous images" become more scarce and ideology more prominent (162). Watkins described the pattern of Hemingway's career as a steady movement away from the successful early novels that rely on description and spare language to carry meaning. The "late career," he argued, "is a decline and fall and a rise again in *The Old Man and the Sea* if that book is the last fiction he wrote" (165). Of course it was not, although one has to wonder what the posthumously published works would have been like had Hemingway lived to see them through the press. As they stand, however, *Islands in the Stream* and *The Garden of Eden* lend credence to Watkins's judgment that, as he aged, Hemingway moved further away from the style that characterized the earlier work. In *Ernest Hemingway and the Arts*, Emily Watts (1971) employed ideas of philosophers Étienne Gilson and Jacques Maritain to create a taxonomy of Hemingway's theory of art, which she said is based on the close relationship of modernist painting and techniques of style that create emotion and sensation.

Also focused on a topic of traditional interest, in *Hemingway's Spanish Tragedy* Lawrence Broer (1973) explored the influence of Spain on Hemingway's work. Working from the assumption that much of Hemingway's fiction was autobiographically based, Broer demonstrated how early Hemingway heroes suffer from the kind of trauma described by Philip Young, but later ones seem to possess a resilience and stoicism that allow them to act in the face of horror and death. The change occurred, Broer argued, as Hemingway became familiar with the Spanish character and psyche, represented most fully in the figure of the matador, who projects a sense of dignity even in the face of death. Broer cautioned, however, that Hemingway did not subscribe wholly to the idea that death was acceptable—especially when the hero is forced to inflict death, whether on animals or other humans. In later works, Hemingway's commitment to "the primitive and militant outlook of the matador" began to clash with a recognition that living out this "reckless and rebellious lifestyle" (111) has negative consequences. Sadly, Broer concluded, Hemingway himself felt this conflict more acutely as he grew older; it affected his ability to write, and eventually led to his suicide.

The dominant critical methodologies of midcentury are reflected in other works published in the early 1970s as well. Morse Peckham (1971) examined Hemingway's depiction of sexual behavior, carefully distinguishing between love, eroticism, and sexual experience to demonstrate that Hemingway used sexual experience as a means of addressing the problems of human identity and the ability of one individual to relate fully with another. Writing about Hemingway in *The Middle Distance*, a book in a multivolume series of American literary history, John McCormick (1971) asserted that "with the exception of T. S. Eliot and William Faulkner, no recent American writer's place in literary history is more secure than Ernest Hemingway's." Regardless of the controversy surrounding Hemingway generated by his larger-than-life personality, he was "foremost and finally a deeply serious writer" (43). The determining factor in his success and enduring importance lay in "his ability to project through style the illusion that complex matters of conscience and conduct can be reduced to their elements, ordered, and dominated" (49). McCormick said Hemingway was essentially a religious writer: "his heavily disguised dialectic is spiritual rather than logical, specifically Christian but not theological" (52). Four years later, in *Fiction as Knowledge*, McCormick (1975) repeated his claim that Hemingway was essentially an ahistorical novelist.

Commentary on Hemingway figured prominently in the 1971 Stratford-Upon-Avon Studies volume *The American Novel and the Nineteen Twenties*, but not always in a positive way. In this collection of essays focusing on the social and aesthetic aspects of postwar fiction, editor Malcolm Bradbury (1971) linked Hemingway with Fitzgerald as spokespersons for the postwar generation and noted the importance of his developing a new style to express the values of his age. However, Brom Weber (1971) believed Hemingway's books "no long seem to penetrate too deeply and steadily below the surface of existence," and wondered if "they ever did so significantly in the nineteen twenties." The fault was Hemingway's, Weber asserted; he "became a dupe of his culture rather than its moral-aesthetic conscience," and as a result "the import of his work had diminished" (151). Fraser Sutherland (1972) made a similar claim, stating as if it were an accepted fact that "by 1929 Hemingway had produced his greatest work" (5); nothing he wrote afterward measured up to those early accomplishments.

Malcolm Cowley (1973) countered these assessments in *A Second Flowering: Works and Days of the Lost Generation*, a retrospective on the 1920s. Cowley reprised many of the favorable comments he had made about Hemingway in a series of reviews and essays over the preceding forty years. Noting that some critics had shied away from dealing with Hemingway's public image, Cowley asked rhetorically: "Why shouldn't it be studied?—considering that the image has played an important part in fifty years of cultural history" (225). For Cowley, whose criticism was always more broadly focused than that of most academics at the time, the public image is "an essential part of the truth about Hemingway" (227). Hugh Kenner's (1975) assessment of Hemingway in *A Homemade World* echoed Cowley's sentiments. Studying Hemingway as one of the modernists who reshaped literature at the beginning of the twentieth century, Kenner said Hemingway's greatest achievement "consisted in setting down, so sparely that we can see past them, the words for the action that concealed the real action" (156). Kenner believed Hemingway, more than any other writer, was responsible for turning the modern short story form into a work of art.

By the early 1970s books like Young's and Baker's stood atop a growing pile of specialized analyses of the Hemingway hero, the Hemingway code, the Hemingway style, and the Hemingway personality type. Occasionally an alternative reading would be offered, such as Jan Bakker's (1972) *Ernest Hemingway: The Artist as Man of Action*. In taking on Young and Rovit, Bakker's study found neither Young's description of the Hemingway hero nor Rovit's analysis of contrasting tutor and tyro protagonists "completely satisfactory" (6). Instead, Bakker constructed a reading of Hemingway's fiction that stressed the developmental nature of Hemingway's concept of the hero. Like Young, Bakker believed Hemingway had a fixation with suffering and death, but his examination placed more stress on *Death in the Afternoon* as the pivotal work in the Hemingway canon.

A half dozen other books published on Hemingway in 1972 and 1973 offer more conventional judgments of his work. The tradition of examining technique and concentrating on artistry was continued by Sheldon Grebstein (1973) in *Hemingway's Craft*, one of many books on twentieth-century literature published by Southern Illinois University Press during the 1960s and 1970s. Chapter titles reveal Grebstein's methodology: "Structure of the Short Stories," "Structure of the Novels," "Narrative Perspectives and Narrators' Voices," "Dialogue," "Other Observations on Style and Method." Grebstein's close readings of individual texts highlighted ways Hemingway used the tools available to shape readers' experience. In the preface, Harry T. Moore, editor for SIU Press's series on "Modern Critiques," celebrated this book as a long-needed study "devoted principally to Hemingway's art as such—his techniques as well as his ideas"—because too many critics had given "scant attention" to the "organic artistic elements of Hemingway's fiction" (Grebstein 1973, ix–x).

Samuel Shaw's (1972) *Ernest Hemingway*, in publisher Frederick Ungar's Modern Literature Monographs series, a competitor to the more popular Twayne series, can serve as a good example of what undergraduates were being taught about Hemingway in the early 1970s. Shaw summarized accepted critical opinion about the Hemingway style, Hemingway hero, Hemingway code, and the role personal experience played in shaping Hemingway's fiction. Shaw was quick to point out that Hemingway's nihilism was balanced by his "compassion and romanticism" (8), a will to believe that humankind could be better than the twentieth century had shown us to be. Students who went to Shaw for an explanation of the essential Hemingway came away with a sense that the tough-guy image was a pose to help a sensitive writer deal with a world that had lost its way.

While not necessarily intended as such, the culmination of traditional critiques of Hemingway's fiction can be found in Arthur Waldhorn's (1972) somewhat misnamed *A Reader's Guide to Ernest Hemingway*. Unlike most guidebooks, Waldhorn's is a sophisticated, detailed, analytic assessment of Hemingway's fiction through the publication of *Islands in the Stream*. Intended for general readers as well as other scholars, the book offers a chronological survey of Hemingway's career, pointing out (but not overstressing) the influence of Hemingway's life on his writing. Like most critics of this period, Waldhorn was concerned with the timeless aspects of the fiction; hence, he relied heavily on the idea of the hero's quest and the hero's code as underlying principles for explaining the meaning of individual stories and novels. Waldhorn's (1973) *Ernest Hemingway: A Collection of Criticism* brought together under a single cover eight previously published essays or book chapters by scholars recognizable to their contemporaries for their work on Hemingway or American literature. Although Waldhorn said the intent of the collection was to provide "thoughtful and divergently oriented analyses" of Hemingway's work (viii), the relative homogeneity of these essays gives further testimony to the hegemony of traditional critical approaches to Hemingway prevalent during the middle decades of the century.

Focus on the Short Fiction

The appearance of *The Nick Adams Stories* was the culmination of a project conceived by Philip Young nearly a quarter century earlier but only brought to fruition when he finally received permission from

Hemingway's publisher and widow to collect both published and unpublished stories in a single volume (see Young 1972b). Reaction among critics was mixed, although the volume generally received less negative criticism than *Islands in the Stream*. William Nolan (1972), writing in the Writers Guild of America publication, said all writers "owe a solid debt of gratitude" to Young for "pushing his idea through to completion," because in this volume the young Hemingway shines through his fiction. Jeffrey Hart (1972) described the fragment "The Last Good Country" as a "tremendous narrative" that exhibits Hemingway's ability to "suggest the deeper emotions and meanings beneath the simplest statements" (801). Louis Rubin (1972) called the collection "fascinating" and suggested the "fragmentary nature of the new pieces does not really interfere seriously with one's enjoyment" (C6). Digby Diehl (1972) said that this volume, like others containing previously unpublished materials, continues to "dazzle" readers with Hemingway's "scope and literary brilliance"—though he admitted that some of the new materials would do little to advance Hemingway's reputation (45).

Others had greater reservations. Harry T. Moore (1972) was happy to see the volume in print, though it is clear he preferred the published works to those Hemingway chose not to publish in his lifetime. William Abrahams (1972) called the new material "recognizably lesser or apprentice work" (98). G. E. Murray (1972) dismissed the previously unpublished stories as "second-rate," but admitted "even the worst of Hemingway deserves attention, and some interesting biographical notes can be garnered from this collection" (18). Margaret Manning (1972) said the unpublished materials were "really unfinished," although they demonstrated Hemingway's ability to write gorgeously about nature (23).

Other critics thought Young's project misguided. Jonathan Loesberg (1972) objected to publishing fragments, noting that only one new story was actually finished but not published; he was particularly exercised about "On Writing," which he called "an almost intolerably boring fulmination" on Hemingway's ideas about his art (H21). Some later critics would complain about Young's alteration of the name "Hadley" in the manuscript to "Helen," a change Bernard Oldsey [1979] believed justified because in his opinion it was simply a mistake on Hemingway's part. Edmund Fuller (1972) agreed, calling "On Writing" "just awful—the worst unconscious self-parody" (10). George Higgins (1972) complained that the decision to override Hemingway's judgment was unseemly. Quentin Anderson (1972) blasted the project as "a case of insatiability pushed to the limit of indiscriminate greed: not simply commercial greed, but a desire to make Hemingway just the kind of imaginative commodity he is not" (13). Anderson was particularly bothered by Young's decision to include materials that Hemingway cut from published stories, since Hemingway obviously thought those passages not worthy of publication.

The first important collection of essays on Hemingway's short fiction, Jackson Benson's *The Short Stories of Ernest Hemingway: Critical Essays*, appeared in 1975. Concerned that much of that which had been written was "too general, too trivial, or too heavily focused on a few of the most popular stories to be of much value to the serious student of the stories as a whole" (xiv), Benson saw himself exercising a kind of Arnoldian discrimination, intended to put in one volume the best that had been thought and said to date on the short fiction. Reaching back to materials published in the past thirty years, Benson brought together commentary from books by Carlos Baker, Philip Young, Charles Fenton, Norman Grebstein, Richard Hovey, Earl Rovit, and Ray West and previously published essays by nearly two dozen scholars, including Clinton Burhans, Robert W. Lewis, and Warren Bennett. He also reprinted Cleanth Brooks and Robert Penn Warren's highly influential explication of "The Killers." Benson's own essay, composed for this volume, provided a sensitive, informed analysis of Hemingway's achievement in the genre.

The Feminist Assault

The radical revaluation of Hemingway beginning to take shape in 1970 was all but lost in the frenzy of commentary that surrounded the publication of *Islands in the Stream*. The reassessment began, as it did with so many male authors, with the rise of feminist scholarship, which proposed other ways of reading authors and works that had been accepted almost without question into the canon of British and American literature. Looking at ways women had been portrayed in literature in the past, and insisting that women's writing be given the same serious consideration that men's had enjoyed for centuries, feminist literary critics had a profound impact on Hemingway's reputation—though hardly a positive one.

The generation of feminists that emerged in the 1960s and 1970s seemed to take special delight in taking shots at Hemingway. An allusion in Kate Millett's (1970) *Sexual Politics* signals the way Hemingway had become the personification of the macho image of primitive men partaking in male-only bonding rituals. Millett noted that when a character in Norman Mailer's *Why Are We in Vietnam?* experiences the blood-ritual of a hunt in the forest, he "join[s] the ranks of the Hemingway cult" (321). Obviously Millett assumed her readers would know exactly what she meant by the reference. Cynthia Ozick (1969) used Hemingway as her example to illustrate how women, even in university settings, were circumscribed by gender in expressing opinions. "If I said I didn't like Hemingway, I could have no *critical* justification, no *literary* reason; it was only because, being a woman, I obviously could not be sympathetic toward Hemingway's 'masculine' subject matter" (309).

In *The Female Eunuch* Germaine Greer (1970) dismissed Hemingway—and D. H. Lawrence—as mere romantics incapable of explaining the realities of sexual relations. They simply possessed a larger vocabulary than pulp novelists like Barbara Cartland (182). In her Marxist argument for sexual revolution, *The Dialectic of Sex*, Shulamith Firestone (1970) made similar disparaging comments, calling Hemingway one of the "paper tigers" who "consciously present a 'male' reality" as a "backlash" to the "growing threat to male supremacy—Virility, Inc., a bunch of culturally deprived 'tough guys,' punching to save their manhood." Firestone condemned Hemingway and others like Norman Mailer, Joseph Heller, and Henry Miller for attempting to mystify their experience, which in her opinion "makes their writing phony" (182).

In cataloging examples of the bitch in literature, Elizabeth Janeway (1971) cited Hemingway's "The Short Happy Life of Francis Macomber" as a classic text (199). Similarly, Dolores Barracano Schmidt (1971), in a widely cited article titled "The Great American Bitch," used Hemingway's Margot Macomber as her first example of the archetype of the "man-eater" (900) in classic American literature. Schmidt argued that in all of Hemingway's fiction, no man's relationship with "an emancipated American woman is ever satisfying" to either partner (903). Male writers like Hemingway see this type of woman as the cause of "marital unhappiness, infidelity, divorce, alienation"; she is a "fabrication used to maintain the *status quo*" (904). She claimed she did not mean to "denigrate the literary accomplishments" of writers like Hemingway. Instead, she simply wanted to point out that they do not represent universal views, only "a specifically *male* view"—and certainly in Hemingway's case, "a threatened male view of their times" (904–5). Joanna Russ (1972) dismissed Hemingway with the acerbic assessment that "Hemingway, whom we call a realist, spent his whole working life capitalizing on the dramatic lucidity possible to an artist who works with developed myths"—such as the stereotype of the "Bitch Goddess" (11) who preys on the "Failed Man" (12) in "The Short Happy Life of Francis Macomber." That story is reprinted in Mary Anne Ferguson's 1973 anthology, *Images of Women in Literature*, as an example of fiction featuring the dominating wife, or the "bitch," which Ferguson defined in her introduction as a beautiful woman who "uses her 'weapons' of tongue and sex to diminish a man's sense of worth" (2).

Feminist jabs at Hemingway continued throughout the decade. Wendy Martin (1972) argued that *A Farewell to Arms* "reveal[s] that the stigma of original sin still taints American heroines." Catherine Barkley's agony and death in the labor room scene, which "depict[s] the consequences of God's wrath on adulteresses, could be right out of a Puritan sermon" (269). Norma Willson (1974) included in her "Majority Report: A Liberated Glossary: Guide to Feminist Writings" a definition of "Maria": "The 'ideal' woman described in *For Whom the Bell Tolls* by

Ernest Hemingway, a twentieth century writer of fantasy whose men were virile and strong and whose women were either despised mothers or Maria's who say, 'I will do anything for thee that thou wish. . . . But thou must tell me for I have great ignorance'" (14).

Cheri Register (1975) sketched obliquely the rationale for a feminist revaluation of Hemingway's fiction. She noted that some midcentury feminists (Millett among them) found it possible to admire writers like Hemingway and Lawrence even if they did not subscribe to their presentation of women. Register cited Ann Pratt as a critic who believes one should not "withdraw her attention from a work which is resonant and craftsmanlike even if it is chauvinistic" (quoted in Register, 7). A dissenting view was expressed forcefully by Lillian Robinson, still three years away from publishing her influential feminist Marxist critique *Sex, Class and Culture*: "I do not believe we have hitherto had objective standards by which to judge literary art, and the application of a feminist perspective will not mean adding ideology to a value-free discipline" (quoted in Register, 7). Register wrote that the debate over whether "literary competence is a redeeming virtue" (7) for misogynistic writers was not settled.

The most frequently cited feminist critique of Hemingway is Judith Fetterley's (1977) essay on *A Farewell to Arms*, published originally in Arlyn Diamond and Lee Edwards's *The Authority of Experience* and the following year in Fetterley's widely read and influential feminist manifesto *The Resisting Reader*. Fetterley asserted that the novel reveals what feminists have known for some time: that "idealization is a basic strategy for disguising and marketing hatred," and that behind "the novel's surface investment in idealization" of Catherine Barkley lay "an immense hostility whose full measure can be taken from the fact that Catherine dies, and dies because she is a woman" (258). Fetterley's careful if at times tendentious reading reveals how Hemingway subtly jostles readers into a position to identify with Frederic Henry, whose egocentrism and passivity Fetterley documents extensively (and somewhat vituperatively). In this "anti-romantic" (259) novel, women are either villains or inconsequential characters holding men back from realizing the glories designed for their gender alone. Hence, she points out, where men who die in battle are eulogized, the death of Catherine is tragic only because it leaves Frederic unfulfilled and alone. "If we weep at the end of the book," Fetterley asserts, "it is not for Catherine but for Frederic Henry abandoned in a cold, wet, hostile world. All our tears are ultimately for men because in the world of *A Farewell to Arms* male life is what counts" (262). There is hardly a kind word for Hemingway in Fetterley's resistant reading.[2]

Critical Anthologies and Other Studies

Criticism published during the mid-1970s reveals the growing split over the value of Hemingway's fiction and the burgeoning influence of critical approaches outside what was then the mainstream. As noted above, a number of feminists insisted on revising what they considered ill-conceived judgments about Hemingway's merits. Marxist critic Fredric Jameson (1971) claimed that both detractors and supporters of Hemingway miss the essential truth about his writing. "It is a mistake to think," Jameson said, "that the books of Hemingway deal essentially with such things as courage, love, and death; in reality, their deepest subject is simply the writing of a certain type of sentence, the practice of a determinate style." Hemingway's primary interest is in *"literary* production" (409). Content is simply a means of reaching that end. By implication, Jameson suggested that Hemingway was not really interested in the subjects he chose to write about, but only in the way he could use those subjects as a means of perfecting his style—and selling books. Jameson believed Hemingway thought of writing as a skill to be mastered like boxing or bullfighting. Furthermore, his "ideology of technique clearly reflects the more general American work situation," in which "the American male is conveniently evaluated according to the number of different jobs he has had, and skills he possesses" (412).

Despite the growing importance of new theoretical approaches, one could still find essays like Harold McCarthy's (1974), which argued that Hemingway's fiction showed a gradual movement from "alienated critic" to "a man who is at the same time creator and actor in the drama of his social being" (136). Seeing himself "engaged actively in resolving the basic existentialist problem of alienation," Hemingway repeatedly wrote metaphorically about the "game of life," using the rules of play and sport as a means of demonstrating how one might control and provide meaning for one's existence (137). McCarthy argued that Hemingway found American culture excessively serious and sought to counter that tendency by stressing "life as play" (150). As a second example, Sarah Unfried (1976) argued in *Man's Place in the Natural Order: A Study of Hemingway's Works* that Hemingway developed a consistent philosophy of life through the early works that culminated in *For Whom the Bell Tolls*. Hemingway saw individuals as parts of something much larger, a universe that humans can only know partially. Unfried's Hemingway is a writer committed to describing the human condition realistically yet optimistically.

Even those practicing traditional criticism found it necessary to recognize that the low-hanging fruit had been picked, so to speak, by earlier scholars studying theme and technique. Richard Astro and Jackson Benson (1974) attempted to refocus Hemingway studies in *Hemingway in Our Time*, a collection of essays originally presented as papers at a 1973 conference. Admitting that the proliferation of criticism had resulted in "little of Hemingway's iceberg remain[ing] intact" (v), the editors hoped these essays could help shift focus from the much-studied early novels and stories to the later fiction and some work hitherto considered unpopular. However, while their subject matter is in many cases different from that typical of Hemingway criticism from the previous two decades, the contributors employed decidedly traditional approaches to Hemingway's work: biographical essays, examinations of philosophy and theme, and comparative studies. Some offered new pairings, such as Faith Norris, who examined parallels between *A Moveable Feast* and Proust's *Remembrance of Things Past*. The essays that frame the collection—Benson's introduction and Richard Lehan's examination of Hemingway's reputation among his contemporaries—are of special value to anyone interested in the reasons for Hemingway's continuing appeal.

Benson's assessment not only expressed a majority opinion among Hemingway scholars but also revealed the basis for their belief: "Hemingway will continue to be read," he predicted, because "his position is in a closer alignment with our felt positions than that of any other modern writer." His "style, imagery, descriptive patterning, and narrative strategy all relate directly to the task of carving out a defensible position from which the forces of chaos can be excluded and within which the power of justice and virtue can be established and sustained" (9). In essence, those who examine Hemingway's technical methods can appreciate the universal appeal of his existential position in the modern world. Those kinds of examinations describe the essays on the short stories in editor Bates Hoffer's (1976) collection *Hemingway's Experiments in Structure and Style*. Hoffer said in his introduction that the volume was intended to help students gain greater appreciation for the stories by showing them that "Hemingway packed even more into his stories than you had seen before."

The appearance in 1974 of *Ernest Hemingway: Five Decades of Criticism*, edited by Linda Welshimer Wagner (Linda Wagner-Martin), is noteworthy for several reasons. First, it launched a series that continued through three more volumes, providing decennial snapshots of Hemingway criticism as it has evolved over time. In its own right, *Five Decades* collects some of the better critical commentary published over the half century since the appearance of Hemingway's first volume of stories and poems. Naturally Wagner is highly selective, choosing fewer than thirty essays to represent the history of Hemingway criticism. A more appropriate title, though, might have been "The View of Hemingway by Critics Writing after 1950," since all but one of the essays were published after that date.

This observation may seem caviling, however, when one realizes that, inside the covers of one book, it is possible to see the mainstream of Hemingway criticism during the middle decades of the century. The collection is divided into three sections. In the first, dealing with Hemingway's development as a writer, Wagner included an essay on Pound's influence, one on Hemingway's debt to literature, and a third on the influence of Spain. In a second section focusing on studies of his work as a whole, Robert Penn Warren's (1947) assessment is one of five that look at overarching concerns in his writing. A third section examining method and language contains a chapter from Richard Bridgman's (1966) *The Colloquial Style in America*, two essays from the *Journal of Modern Literature* (including Wagner's assessment of Hemingway's revisions of *For Whom the Bell Tolls*), and an essay from the *New York Review of Books*. The final section features eight selections that focus on individual works, including all of the novels and the short story collection *In Our Time*. Wagner also reprinted the first important critique of Hemingway's work, Edmund Wilson's 1924 review "Mr. Hemingway's Dry-Points," a work that was otherwise difficult for scholars to locate.

Wagner made two telling observations that offer another insight into the status of Hemingway's reputation and the impact of critics in shaping it. First, although posthumous works had appeared and been reviewed, "Hemingway criticism pays slight attention to them, seeming to feel that any work not finished by Hemingway the craftsman is truly not finished, and therefore not worthy of being judged beside the acknowledged masterpieces." Wagner said this attitude emphasizes critics' current predilection for "judging Hemingway as skilled craftsman" (5). The second key point Wagner made is also reflective of the time at which *Five Decades* was published: "[Hemingway's] writing has not gone through the slack periods, the fall from critical favor, of the work of Fitzgerald, Faulkner, Dreiser, and countless others" (3). Again one might argue that there were periods during Hemingway's lifetime that reviewers (and the public) wondered if he had lost his touch, but Wagner's focus here is (rightly) on criticism, by which she means the enterprise of evaluating a writer's merits regardless of current popularity.

A sampling of reviews of Wagner's critical anthology is also enlightening for what they expose about critics' attitudes toward Hemingway at this time. For example, Bernard Oldsey (1974) calls *Five Decades* a mixed bag but credited Wagner with preserving some otherwise fugitive pieces and making them more accessible. James Tinsley (1975) complained about the lack of a bibliography and the absence of more extensive information about contributors. He also wondered why Wagner included so many essays that seem openly hostile toward Hemingway—a fact he attributes to "either literary insensibility" or "essential hostility to the principles of Hemingway's art" (117). Tinsley made allowances for the inclusion of negative criticism by noting that, since the collection is designed for students and for professors with limited access to major libraries: "After all, someone must be wrong, and students must be allowed to discover error" (117). More appreciative of Hemingway and Wagner—but more cynical in his reading of Hemingway's contributions to literature—Alan

Wycherley (1976) observed that, judging from the "torrent of Hemingway criticism" of the last decades, one might conclude that his reputation "is far from being a settled matter" (78). Wycherley believed Hemingway would continue to be read and taught because he is "interesting," "teachable," and "has something to say to us whose destiny is to live and die in this most regrettable of centuries" (78–79).

Wagner's 1975 collection, *Hemingway and Faulkner: Inventors/Masters*, explains how each author exhibits the qualities Ezra Pound identified as distinguishing two types of artists. Wagner was concerned throughout with the way each "learned and followed his craft, the experiments they made in various genre and techniques, and the eventual writing which resulted" (xiii). Some observations in her preface, however, suggest the problems many critics outside the circle of devoted readers had with Hemingway's fiction. While both Faulkner and Hemingway "began their writing careers in search of innovation" (vii), the "contrast between the lives of these men" (viii) had made it hard to consider them as equally committed to art. Wagner said it is "easier to see the artist in the withdrawn and relatively quiet existence of Faulkner" (viii). That statement exposes contemporary critical prejudices regarding what an artist should be, and it reveals much about why Hemingway had difficulty being accepted by a wider academic establishment more attuned to the notion of the artist as a lonely struggler rather than a garrulous celebrity.

Important New Voices in Hemingway Scholarship

Two studies that appeared within a year of each other became instrumental in reshaping Hemingway scholarship in the coming decades, and the authors emerged as major new authorities on the Hemingway canon. The first appeared in 1976, Michael Reynolds's *Hemingway's First War: The Making of "A Farewell to Arms"*. Part scholarly investigation, part textual examination, and part literary criticism, the book was the first of more than a dozen published by Reynolds over the next twenty-five years. He began with a thesis that, while not unique, was still uncommon among Hemingway critics: he insisted that to read *A Farewell to Arms* as autobiography "is to misread the book" (16). "*A Farewell to Arms* is, in part, a researched novel," Reynolds declared, "and eventually one must ask what sources Hemingway used to write of places he had not seen and battles he had not fought" (136).

Reynolds cataloged an impressive list of sources that provided Hemingway the information he needed about wartime actions he did not witness personally. Reynolds did not claim to be the first to point out the works that inspired Hemingway; that was done, he said, by Hemingway himself, "but no one paid attention": Stephen Crane's *The Red Badge of Courage* and Stendhal's *The Charterhouse of Parma* (134).

However, Reynolds was certainly the first to document the novelist's extensive reading in historical accounts and newspapers that produced a novel that has the ring of authenticity. He included a long discussion of Hemingway's relationship with Agnes von Kurowsky, explaining how Hemingway transformed his real-life experiences into fiction so that there is no point-by-point correspondence between Agnes and Catherine Barkley. A section on technique explains how careful use of foreshadowing, echo scenes, and role reversals among characters allows Hemingway to construct a tightly woven tale in which every detail seems to work in support of plot and theme.

Reynolds's contemporaries recognized the importance of his work. Writing in *American Literature*, Richard Lehan (1977) suggested that Reynolds's book "may very well lead to a new way of reading Hemingway's novels" (471). Robert O. Stephens (1977a) called it "the harbinger of a new generation of Hemingway criticism" (280). Jeffrey Meyers (1977) said it was "an original and valuable book," especially since "virtually all the significant works of the modern period have been thoroughly analyzed and interpretive literary criticism has almost come to a dead end" (269). Because Reynolds employed different methodologies—textual study, historical and biographical research, and an interdisciplinary approach to his subject—his work was among those that, in Meyers's view, now provided "the most useful and innovative ways to discuss modern literature" (269). Walter Sullivan (1977), however, offered a contrarian view, praising Reynolds for his diligent work but asserting that he "repeats himself, elaborates the obvious, and overstates his case" (677).

These Hemingway experts were only partially right. Reynolds's techniques would certainly be used by others to provide new ways of understanding individual Hemingway novels and stories, but his interdisciplinary approach grounded in traditional methodologies would be challenged by a generation of critics that believed that what one brought to the critical enterprise—in terms of (often unconscious) political or gender bias—could very well predetermine the outcome of one's assessment. The kind of "interpretive literary criticism" Meyers refers to might have been "at a dead end," but other methodologies were already being employed to turn traditionalist readings on their heads and create new ways to view the established canon, Hemingway's works included.

A year later, scholars who grumbled about the inadequacies of Carlos Baker's biography of Hemingway were placated somewhat by the publication of Scott Donaldson's (1977) *By Force of Will: The Life and Art of Ernest Hemingway*. Rather than challenge Baker's extensive assembly of facts about Hemingway's life, Donaldson instead presented a complementary portrait that treats Hemingway not as a larger-than-life action figure but as a thoughtful writer interested in the problems of living in the modern world. Donaldson believed Hemingway's celebrity status worked against acceptance of his work as serious fiction. In some ways *By Force of Will* is an intellectual biography, and its serious treatment of Hemingway's ideas is a useful corrective to the emphasis on action over thought prevalent in most accounts of his life and work. Donaldson organized his book topically in order to "discover and record" what Hemingway thought about love, war, politics, money, and other matters. His methodology was traditional in that he looked to Hemingway's writings to identify the author's views on these issues. While he insisted that the stories and novels are not strictly autobiographical, they have "autobiographical relevance" (191). With exceptional skill and a sound familiarity with the Hemingway canon, Donaldson created a portrait of Hemingway as someone who thought widely and at times deeply about modern life. While it may be true, as Townsend Ludington (1977) remarked in reviewing *By Force of Will*, that "the end result of the book is to weld the image of Hemingway more firmly than ever to his fiction" (36), Donaldson's Hemingway is far more complex—and perhaps more likable as well—than the self-aggrandizing bully so frequently described in other accounts.

Walter Sullivan (1977) made the bold claim that Donaldson's book "comes as close as any is ever likely to come to a final answer concerning the connection between Hemingway's complex personality and the characters and actions of his novels." He believed there is "no way to overpraise this excellent book" (679), which provided "the most vivid and complete picture of Hemingway that has yet been drawn" (680). George Monteiro (1978) called *By Force of Will* "the very best book to put into any beginner's hands after he has experienced the magic of Hemingway's finest work as well as the peculiar fascination of his literary failures" (288). Robert Fleming (1978) was also enthusiastic about Donaldson's book, although not quite so effusive as Sullivan. He believed Donaldson had "found a fresh approach" and offered truly "new readings for some of Hemingway's most thoroughly discussed works" (603). Yet he believed his topical approach was "not without its pitfalls" (604) and cautioned against placing too much stock in biographical readings of Hemingway's fiction. The importance of the book for scholars is best summed up by Richard Hovey (1978) in *American Literature*: this may not be "*the* biography" of Hemingway, but until that is written, Donaldson's study "will do very nicely indeed!" It is, Hovey asserted, "the best general introduction to the writing and the man who did it" (667).

Shifting Critical Perspectives

By the end of the 1970s, conventional approaches to interpreting Hemingway's fiction were competing for space in academic publications with ones employing new critical methodologies. Older forms dominated, however, as a survey of publications during the final years of the decade indicates. For example, Hemingway's psychological makeup continued to attract attention long after his death, and it was probably inevitable that a study by trained psychologists would one day appear. Richard Hardy and John Cull's (1977) *Hemingway: A Psychological Study* is a "personality portrait" (5) by two professional psychologists. Their evaluation used multiple techniques of analysis to conclude that Hemingway was complex and prone to depression. What is missing from their commentary—for good or for ill, depending on how one views studies that relate literature to life—is any significant mention of the fiction other than to point out that it was Hemingway's means of achieving fame and exploring life's possibilities.

In *Gide and Hemingway: Rebels against God* (1978) Ben Stoltzfus argued that the two writers are alike in sharing a "faith in man and what he can accomplish, an inordinate pride in the will to be human," and a desire to "fulfill specifically human potentialities" (4). Stoltzfus's highly symbolic reading of *The Old Man and the Sea* critiqued Hemingway's attempt to determine how faith (or the lack of it) influences people in the modern world. In a chapter on Hemingway in *The Writer as Social Seer*, Robert Wilson (1979) described him as the writer most in touch with his age. He categorized Hemingway as an existentialist writer concerned about establishing meaning in a meaningless world and defining what it means to be human. Wilson was careful to point out, however, that while Hemingway was "firmly bonded to the first half of this century" and "many of his assumptions are now unfashionable" (especially those about women), the "universal qualities of his themes and perceptions outweigh the time bound." Wilson is certain that "the best part of Hemingway" will "live on in the clear language, if not forever, at least for a very long time" (55).

Another view of Hemingway's professional career is provided by Scott Berg (1978) in *Maxwell Perkins: Editor of Genius*. The details of Hemingway's life follow closely the narrative in Carlos Baker's book—not surprisingly, since Berg was Baker's student at Princeton. In Berg's book, however, Hemingway is seen as one of many writers competing for attention and advice from an editor who had a knack for picking not only authors of intellectual and creative merit, but in many cases ones able to generate good sales. Hemingway appears a bit petty in this narrative, especially as his reputation (and the myths about his hypermasculinity) grew. Perkins comes off as genuinely concerned about all his writers—but especially Fitzgerald and Wolfe. Only occasionally is Berg direct in assessing Hemingway, and his comments are hardly flattering. Writing about *Death in the Afternoon*, Berg said Perkins never suggested any deletions to the manuscript; "if he had, he might have improved the book further by reducing Hemingway's literary pretentiousness." In Berg's view, the book showed clearly that Hemingway "had become self-obsessed, and the writing lacked its former control" (195). Even more than in Baker's biography, Hemingway comes off as petulant, vain, and in need of constant coddling by a self-effacing editor whose heroic efforts blunted the criticism that could make Hemingway so incensed.

The fiftieth anniversary of the publication of *A Farewell to Arms* in 1979 brought forth a number of tributes, reappraisals, and fresh assessments ranging from traditional appreciation studies and close technical analyses to more daring theory-based critiques. Once again entire books were devoted to discussion of a single Hemingway novel. Bernard Oldsey's (1979) *Hemingway's Hidden Craft* is certainly traditional (some might say old-fashioned) in its approach, operating from the premise that "close examination of the writing of one truly worthwhile novel can reveal something about the nature of all worthwhile novels." Oldsey explored the sources that inspired Hemingway, his methods of composition, and "the structure into which [the novel] was composed" (ix). Echoes of Martin Heidegger's existentialist philosophy resonate through Oldsey's reading of a novel that in his view deals with "the metaphysical question of all times" (88)—the question of creation. Such a weighty reading runs counter to the notion of Hemingway as either dumb ox or misguided misogynist.

Totalizing critiques—those that employ a single interpretive strategy to read an author's entire oeuvre—were still being published, as Raymond Nelson's (1979) brief *Hemingway: Expressionist Artist* attests. Nelson challenged the notion that Hemingway was a realist, claiming instead that his "primary concern was to communicate emotion, not rational themes which might require objectivity and disinterestedness" (ix–x). Nelson looked at techniques Hemingway employed that link him with Expressionists like Cézanne to create fiction that "leads the reader through a vicarious experience, recreating for him what the writer had originally felt" (11). Nelson exposed the Expressionist themes and images running through the Hemingway canon, noting how these inextricably link him to that tradition, allowing him to conclude that "Hemingway was doing in words what his friends were doing in paint" (74).

As one might expect, the constant criticism of Hemingway by feminists was sure to rankle those who admired him for the virtues traditionally associated with his life and writing, and occasional rebuttals appeared in books and journals. Among them was James Tuttleton's (1977) brief assessment of Hemingway's treatment of women, in which he suggested that for Hemingway male-female relationships were essential but dangerous—for men. Hemingway feared "the emasculating power" of women (283), yet at the same time was "the tender poet of heterosexual love" in novels like *A Farewell to Arms* and *For Whom the Bell Tolls*, "celebrat[ing] that love tragically, poignantly, and perhaps even sentimentally" (284). Hemingway's enemy was "the New Woman" because she challenged "masculine independence," which Hemingway valued highly (285). In a riposte to the relentless attack by feminists on patriarchal notions of the value of fiction and their insistence on creating standards for a feminine mode of writing, Peter Schwenger (1979) used Hemingway to illustrate how one might create a masculine mode that would also have value. If the "maleness of experience" means "the infusion of a particular sense of the body into the attitudes and encounters of life" (623), Hemingway's work can serve admirably as an example of the male mode, where minimalist style reflects something about the expectations associated with maleness. Unlike Tuttleton's commentary, Schwenger's is moving toward the methodology later employed by practitioners of men's studies.

The Marxist view of Hemingway at this time is summarized succinctly in Brent Harold's (1980) "The Marxist Survey of American Fiction," a brief guide for creating radical revisions of the standard canon of American literature. Harold insisted "the only way to fight the hegemonic critical version of the classics [including Hemingway's fiction] is to teach them from an alternative—a Marxist—perspective" (44). Critiquing Hemingway's fiction, Harold claimed he "seems to have no memory of identification with America as a progressive society" and often is "not interested" in the "sociological perspective" of his characters. Unfortunately, his "political novel," *For Whom the Bell Tolls*, which purported to have "one of his alienated men" act as "a politically motivated being," missed the mark. Harold believed Hemingway may have meant well, but "the novel fails either to help us understand political action or to inspire us to become politically engaged ourselves" (49). It may best be read, Harold admitted sadly, as just another "existential drama" with "political struggle as its backdrop" (49).

Creeping in among the traditionalist pigeons were a few stray cats like Eric Rabkin (1977), whose examination of narrative techniques presaged later, more extensive narratological studies of Hemingway's fiction. Rabkin wrote appreciatively of Hemingway's use of a technical device new in twentieth-century literature, the introduction of a narrator with pronouns and antecedents for which the reader has no immediate reference. Referring specifically to the opening of *A Farewell to Arms*, Rabkin explained how Hemingway used the device to foreshadow the personal aspects of his story and force the reader to adopt, if only momentarily, the narrator's view of events, creating sympathy for his protagonist.

A Call for New Approaches

As the decade came to a close, Michael Reynolds (1980) provided scholars what he considered a road map for future Hemingway studies. In "Unexplored Territory: The Next Ten Years of Hemingway Studies," adapted from his book *Hemingway's Reading* and published in *College Literature*,

Reynolds offered strong direction for ways scholars should and should not proceed in the coming decade. He began by asserting that the kind of scholarship that characterized Hemingway studies through the 1960s and into the 1970s had been "at least temporarily exhausted" (189). He urged scholars to turn to new pursuits that could truly illuminate Hemingway's life and provide new ways to read his work. His belief was that the best use of time would be to develop good texts and create computer databases of Hemingway's work and criticism, giving future scholars a more objective basis from which to devise more sophisticated analyses. With a nod toward—and apology to—Carlos Baker, he also encouraged further study in "literary history and literary biography" (192) to create "the literary biography of Ernest Hemingway" (193). He advocated studies of the "various fictions" (195) of the 1930s, a neglected decade, and examinations of Hemingway's relationship with European and world writers, particularly Joyce, Pound, Stein, Dos Passos, MacLeish, Fitzgerald, and Eliot. He did not think Hemingway's relationship with Spain or Africa had been fully explored. He called for a thorough examination of Hemingway's relationship with Scribner's (a suggestion taken up by Robert Trogdon in *The Lousy Racket* [2007]).

Reynolds was even willing to see more work on "that illusive topic," the "Code"—so long as it did not simply revisit what had been written. He called for analyses of Hemingway's "economic relationship with Scribner's" (200) and studies of the way his reading (which Reynolds notes was voluminous) influenced his imaginative work. What he proposed, he acknowledges, would be much harder to do than the work already done. But he insisted "the gold rush" was over, and "nothing is left on the surface for the picking" (191). Perhaps his most serious challenge, however, was for those trained in literary studies to stick to their profession. "We are not psychoanalysts, nor are we society columnists," he said. Exploring the psychoses of Hemingway or his characters and focusing on "nostalgia" by revisiting the haunts that Hemingway made famous were, in his view, counterproductive. Critics and scholars should explore what is now available—"manuscripts, letters, reading lists, biography, and texts"—to produce scholarship that truly makes a contribution to understanding Hemingway and his art.

Certainly Reynolds was aware of a new way of reading emerging at the time he wrote his prescription for future Hemingway studies, but he was silent about a movement that would change once again the perception of Hemingway and his writing. That revolution began quietly, with an article nestled in the pages of a 1970 issue of *Arizona Quarterly*. In "Hemingway's 'The Sea Change': A Sympathetic View of Homosexuality," J. F. Kobler (1970) explored what he called an "interesting but generally overlooked" (318) phenomenon: Hemingway's objective presentation of homosexuality and his reluctance to pass harsh judgment on a homosexual character. Kobler said evidence in this story revealed that Hemingway had "a much deeper understanding of the nature of homosexuality than his public reputation as a fist-in-the-face hater of it seems to indicate" (318). Kobler was careful not to claim that Hemingway approved of homosexuality, but he believed this story revealed "a much greater forbearance" than had been discovered in most of his work (324).

Seven years later the subject was in front of a much wider reading public. Often cited as the groundbreaking study of Hemingway's fascination with androgyny, Aaron Latham's (1977) *New York Times Magazine* essay, appropriately titled "A Farewell to Machismo," provided hints of what was soon to come in revolutionizing the study of Hemingway's fiction. Latham was granted limited access to the manuscript of *The Garden of Eden*, and from his perusal and some clever sleuthing through published materials he came to the conclusion that beneath the he-man image Hemingway projected lay a complex, even tormented figure who worked all his life to understand gender issues. As Latham acknowledged, timing had much to do with the impact of his study. While Hemingway "haunts our culture the way our own fathers haunt our individual lives," his reputation had been "sagging," in part because some critics had begun to question whether his supermasculine pose hid a deep secret: "Was Hemingway overcompensating for some sexual ambiguity?" (54).

Knowing that the opening of Hemingway's papers at the Kennedy Library would result in a flood of new criticism, Latham wondered if the unpublished *Garden of Eden* "might not change the way we look at him" (54). Latham discerned from what he had seen and read that Hemingway had a lifelong fascination with androgyny, as the unpublished novel made clear. Furthermore, his works revealed a continuing interest in homosexuality as well. As a result, Latham believed "there is yet another Hemingway which yet another generation will have to come to terms with" (99).

Notes

[1] A brief account of the founding and activities of the Hemingway Society and the Hemingway Foundation is available in Charles M. Oliver, "*The Hemingway Review* and The Ernest Hemingway Foundation and Society" (in Moddelmog and del Gizzo, 2013).

[2] In *Gaps in Nature: Literary Interpretation and the Modular Mind*, Ellen Spolsky (1993) provided an extended analysis of Fetterley's argument and described her impact on feminist interpretation of the Hemingway canon.

6: Calm before the Storm (1980–1985)

THE PROBLEM HEMINGWAY'S critics faced in the early 1980s was summed up succinctly by James Cox (1984) in a review of several of the titles discussed below: scholars are "now, or should be, at the point of comprehending Hemingway" (486), he said. Unfortunately, surveying recent criticism leads one to conclude that "Hemingway was better understood at the outset" than he has been in recent years, "because good early reviewers were actively engaged in the business of making value rather than being burdened by it" (488). Whether Cox is correct may be open to question. However, a review of the literature of the five-year period before the publication of *The Garden of Eden* reveals that many critics were covering the same ground already well plowed during the previous fifteen years, offering nuanced readings but doing little to change perceptions among either Hemingway's admirers or those who had written him off as outdated and irrelevant.

There were exceptions, of course. David Lodge's (1980) exhaustive examination of "Cat in the Rain" in "Analysis and Interpretation of the Realist Text" applied what he described as "the whole battery of modern formalism and structuralism to bear upon a single text" (6). There were also advances in textual study. The opening of Hemingway's manuscripts to scholars in 1976 ushered in a new round of criticism that allowed academics and others to address age-old questions such as: Which of the writer's texts is the 'authorized' one, the one he most wanted to leave as his testament? How did the published text evolve from draft to printed work? Why did some works remain unpublished—and should they stay, or have stayed, that way?

Scholarly and Critical Books

The first responses to some of these questions were provided at a 1980 symposium held under the auspices of the Kennedy Library in Boston. The gathering included an imposing array of scholars. Presentations from that conference, assembled by Bernard Oldsey and published as *Hemingway: The Papers of a Writer* (Oldsey 1981), included George Plimpton's essay on Hemingway and President Kennedy, observations on Hemingway's relationship with Ezra Pound and on his work for the *Toronto Star*, comments on his library, historical studies of Hemingway in Europe during the 1920s, an intriguing and definitely not feminist study of Hemingway's women (by Linda Wagner), and some reminiscences by Philip Young. In "Unexplored Territory: The Next Ten Years of Hemingway Studies," Michael Reynolds repeated the call he made a year earlier for scholars to focus on unexplored areas of Hemingway scholarship rather than rehash topics that he believed had been done to death. One of his exhortations was that someone undertake "the literary biography of Ernest Hemingway" (15)—a project he was already working on when he made these observations. He admitted as much in noting that he hoped to publish "Hemingway's literary biography between 1910–1929" within three years (15).

In 1981 James Brasch and Joseph Sigman published another resource for Hemingway scholars that ranks beside Hanneman's annotated bibliographies as a principal source for research on the literary sources of Hemingway's art: *Hemingway's Library: A Composite Record*. In addition to cataloging the nearly 7,400 items in the library left at Finca Vigia in Cuba when Hemingway died, Brasch and Sigman provided important information on Hemingway's reading habits and documented previous scholarship aimed at linking his fiction with its sources. They also described Hemingway's efforts to assemble his collection and described briefly other locations where Hemingway primary and secondary source materials may be found. The matter-of-fact descriptions Brasch and Sigman provided belie the extraordinary scholarship that went into producing this important documentary sourcebook.

In the same year, Reynolds (1981) published what might be viewed as a preparatory study for his biographical work: *Hemingway's Reading, 1910–1940*. The book was intended as a road map for scholars who want to trace the influence of Hemingway's reading on his work. Reynolds does not make that trek himself, although he speculated in his introduction about ways Hemingway may have used some of the thousands of books he read, particularly the ones he owned. The bulk of *Hemingway's Reading* is a list of more than 2,300 books Hemingway is known to have handled at some time in his life. Reynolds said he undertook the project as a prelude to writing a biography of Hemingway—his first volume was still five years away—but also as an attempt to reduce what he called "the production of absurd source studies" (vii) that seemed (to him at least) to have proliferated in the past thirty years.

Although Reynolds is whimsically self-deprecating—"*Hemingway's Reading* will not stun you with its brilliance," he says in the preface (vii)—his introductory essay displayed once again his deep understanding of Hemingway as an artist familiar with literary tradition and the background in history, biography, travel, and culture that form the basis for fiction. The overarching premise for Reynolds's work was simple—yet bold, especially in the face of four decades of criticism that celebrated Hemingway as a master of fiction while often ignoring or belittling his knowledge of people and books. Where Reynolds argued in *Hemingway's First War* that Hemingway's reading was as important to his art "as Coleridge's was to his" (quoted in *Hemingway's Reading*, 3), he now claimed Hemingway's reading "was more important to his art and to his life than Coleridge's was to his" (3). The comparison was not arbitrary. The influence of Coleridge's reading on his art was the subject of one of the great scholarly studies of the early twentieth century, John Livingston Lowe's (1927) *The Road to Xanadu*, in which Lowe identified virtually everything Coleridge read and explained how it influenced his most important poetry. However, Reynolds did not follow slavishly in Lowe's footsteps. Instead, armed with these reading lists, Reynolds set out to write a biography of Hemingway that would get beneath the surface chaff of Hemingway's extraordinary and well-documented public escapades to identify and understand the artist who said once that he would rather read than do anything else but write.

Although not likely to have been influenced by Reynolds's latest book, Wirt Williams's (1981) *The Tragic Art of Ernest Hemingway* was based on the premise that Hemingway was quite familiar with literary tradition. Williams argued that the most satisfying way to understand Hemingway was to see him as a writer of tragedies (in the traditional sense of the word). He believed that for Hemingway, "life is tragedy, in the face of which men must measure and define themselves" (28). Williams read all of Hemingway's works as either full-blown tragedies or what he called subtragedies—works that contain some but not all elements of tragedy. Typical of his handling of individual novels is his assessment of *The Old Man and the Sea*, where he sees tragic form allowing for the exposition of multiple themes played out on several levels simultaneously; the novel is at once a critique of humankind's existential situation, a study of the fate of the artist who has created a masterpiece, and a Christian parable about the need for endurance and faith.

A traditional focus on characterization and theme informed Joseph Flora's (1982) *Hemingway's Nick Adams*. Accepting that these stories are in some ways autobiographical, Flora explained how Hemingway's deep understanding of the terrain Nick traverses (both in Michigan and, though only alluded to, overseas during the war) allowed him to create a fictional biography of a man whose childhood, adolescence, and early adult years bear striking psychological similarities to his creator. Nick Adams is both the inheritor of an American tradition (suggested by his name, which he shares with one of the country's most famous families) and "*Adam*, the primal man" (20). Organizing his study according to the chronology of the stories created by Philip Young in *Nick Adams Stories* (1972), Flora explored Nick's (and Hemingway's) growth in understanding his psychological traumas and his situation as a modern man, the product of a tradition from which Nick seems hopelessly detached.

In 1983 Jan Bakker published *Fiction as Survival Strategy: A Comparative Study of the Major Works of Ernest Hemingway and Saul Bellow*, in which he used the fiction of these two apparently dissimilar authors to examine how protagonists in their novels sought to establish and define identity in a world that no longer provided "ready-made answers" (1). Bakker explained how in some ways the Hemingway hero, popular until the end of the Second World War, became supplanted by the Bellow hero, opposite in temperament but equally concerned with fundamental questions about developing a sense of self. Bakker's conclusion is worth restating, since it helps place Hemingway squarely within the mainstream of American literature and the American psyche: Despite their differences, Bakker said, both Hemingway and Bellow "write within that particular tradition of American literature designated as the frontier experience" that deals with the "establishment of the American identity" within the territory not still savage but not yet civilized (209). Whether one reads this literally or metaphorically, Bakker corroborated Hovey's thesis in *Hemingway: The Inward Terrain* that the struggle to nail down a healthy identity was at the heart of Hemingway's best work.

Gerry Brenner's (1983) *Concealments in Hemingway's Works* was principally concerned with exposing several issues that Brenner said Hemingway worked hard to conceal: his constant experimentation with various art forms, his zeal to disguise the artistry with which he constructed his writings, and his lifelong oedipal struggle. In the first two thirds of his study, Brenner emphasized structure, technique, and theme. In the final part of *Concealments*, however, he shifted radically, using techniques of psychological criticism to explain how Hemingway's "lifelong ambition to prove himself superior to his father" (19) was "the inspiriting and tormenting genius behind his art" (223). Brenner even hinted that Hemingway's penchant for self-revelation, a practice he seems to have controlled carefully to promote his image as a man's man, might be concealing the fact that he was "latently homoerotic" (19). Whether one agrees with Brenner's zeal to pin Hemingway's successes and failures on a single fixation, it is certainly true that his conclusion about Hemingway's sexual tendencies would move to center stage in Hemingway criticism just a few years after *Concealments* was published.

One of the earliest studies based on the manuscripts at the Kennedy Library is Frederic Svoboda's (1983) *Hemingway and "The Sun Also Rises": The Crafting of a Style*. Carefully examining the various iterations of the novel, Svoboda explained how Hemingway developed not only a "new style and technique" that would reshape the American literary landscape, but also "followed and shaped a new set of principles that he was to follow and elucidate for the rest of his life" (4). Whether Svoboda's claim can be substantiated after the release of *The Garden of Eden* may be open to question (and Svoboda admitted in a later work [del Gizzo and

Svoboda 2013] that estimates of Hemingway had been altered radically by this novel's publication), the fact remains that his study, like Michael Reynolds's 1976 critique of *A Farewell to Arms*, reflected the possibilities that careful manuscript analysis and scholarly investigation could have on literary interpretation.

In 1984 Robert Gajdusek published *Hemingway and Joyce: A Study in Debt and Payment*. Gajdusek was already a familiar name to Hemingway scholars, having published articles in the *Hemingway Review* and elsewhere, as well as a photo essay on Hemingway's Paris years (Gajdusek 1978). A student of Carlos Baker, Gajdusek was little impressed with recent developments that in his view moved the focus off Hemingway's writing as a form of art. In his essay on Joyce's influence, Gajdusek demonstrated not only an appreciation for Hemingway but a deep understanding of the milieu in which he lived and worked during his formative years in Paris. Of interest to those following the development of Hemingway's reputation, Gajdusek mentioned in his epilogue that the Hemingway Society offered to publish his work in the *Hemingway Review*, but he opted for private publication, "the better to reach the specific audience I wish to address" (52). There is a touch of irony in this. If Gajdusek thought a separately bound booklet would have more staying power, he may have miscalculated; his pamphlet is hard to locate in libraries, while the *Hemingway Review* is widely available. Nearly twenty years later, in his collection *Hemingway in His Own Country*, Gajdusek (2002) reprinted the essay on Hemingway and Joyce as chapter 1. No doubt its placement in that volume gave it the potential for wide readership that Gajdusek originally sought in the separate publication.

Despite efforts by some scholars like Gajdusek to get critics and readers to focus on Hemingway's writings, it remained impossible for many to read Hemingway's works without thinking of the man who wrote them. John Raeburn (1984) dealt directly with this phenomenon in *Fame Became of Him*, a systematic examination of the public image Hemingway cultivated during his lifetime. In the 1930s, works like *Death in the Afternoon*, the *Esquire* articles published between 1933 and 1936, and *Green Hills of Africa* were written with an eye toward establishing that public image. Over the course of his career, Hemingway appeared to the public successively as a "dedicated young writer" in the 1920s, "sportsman and *bon vivant*" in the 1930s, social activist and "combat-wise veteran" in the late 1930s and 1940s, and finally, after the publication of *The Old Man and the Sea*, "a sage who seemed to speak with the authority of all the ages" (143).

Raeburn seems less concerned with the unconscious motives that may have driven Hemingway to seek out attention from the public than with his conscious attempts to make himself a celebrity. He attributed Hemingway's actions to his competitive spirit, which drove him to set himself apart from other writers and from the stereotype of the modern writer who was often seen as aloof from life. In dealing with the publication of Hemingway's major works, Raeburn's methodology was to set the reaction of literary critics against that of the general public. The great value of this approach is that it allowed Raeburn to collect materials from popular magazines such as *Time*, *Life*, and *Look*. These widely read publications made Hemingway one of the most recognizable figures in America. His exploits in Africa and Spain and on the battlefield during the Second World War, his divorce from Pauline Pfeiffer and marriage to Martha Gellhorn, and later his divorce from Gellhorn and marriage to Mary Welsh received the same coverage as Hollywood stars might have. For newspapers and magazines, Hemingway made "good copy" (28). Unfortunately, Raeburn said, the "patronage" of the mass media turned Hemingway into a "caricature of himself" (108), and that image had a deleterious effect on his critical reputation.

The UMI Research Press Series

In 1985 UMI Research Press began publishing critical assessments of Hemingway in its Studies in Modern Literature series. Originally written as PhD dissertations, the ten books on Hemingway issued by the press added to the growing body of criticism. Some, like Larry Grimes's (1985) *The Religious Design of Hemingway's Early Fiction*, J. F. Kobler's (1985) *Ernest Hemingway: Journalist and Artist*, and Stephen Cooper's (1987) *The Politics of Ernest Hemingway*, expanded on topics covered by other critics. Others filled in what had hitherto been lacunae in Hemingway criticism. For example, John Gaggin's (1988) *Hemingway and Nineteenth-Century Aestheticism* explored Hemingway's fascination with the concept of aestheticism and his unacknowledged debt to the late-nineteenth-century movement that celebrated "art for art's sake." In *Hemingway and Turgenev: The Nature of Literary Influence*, Myler Wilkinson (1986) applied Harold Bloom's theory of influence to explain the ways Turgenev, a writer Hemingway openly admired, served as a model for Hemingway. Harriet Fellner's (1986) *Hemingway as Playwright* extended critical commentary on Hemingway's work as a playwright. Although the topic has been covered by others, Fellner's work makes available in a single volume information about the publication, production, and critical reception of Hemingway's single venture into dramatic literature.

Chapters and Essays on Hemingway's Work

Reading many of the essays and book chapters published on Hemingway in the first half of the 1980s may create a sense of déjà vu. Topics and approaches seem remarkably similar to what one might have found in journals and books ten, twenty, or even thirty years earlier. For example, in an intertextual study, William Stafford (1981) compared Hemingway's narrator in *The Sun Also Rises* with ones from novels by Faulkner and Fitzgerald, explaining how each represents innocence in some form. Stafford went out of his way to celebrate Hemingway as the "dedicated artist," "true and pure" in his quest to render his material "honestly as he sees it" (42), elevating what some might find distasteful subject matter into refined art. In *Pathways to Suicide*, psychiatrist Ronald Maris (1981) provided a brief clinical description of the causes for Hemingway's suicide, using his case to illustrate "the role of work problems in self-destruction among males" (165). Christian Messenger's (1981) *Sport and the Spirit of Play in American Fiction* celebrated him as an important figure in demonstrating how sport is integral to the homegrown culture of the modern United States.

Bridging the gap between older historicist analysis and the new approach taken by practitioners of cultural studies, Paul Marx (1980) offered an explanation for Hemingway's apparent bigotry in his treatment of American minorities and people of other nations. Marx pointed out that, with the exception of *The Sun Also Rises*, extreme intolerance is shown largely in the short stories. While he did not excuse Hemingway for his racism or anti-Semitism, Marx argued that the use of bigoted language arose from ideology that dominated the age in which Hemingway wrote, and that the stories show a more nuanced attitude and often an appreciation for people of other races and nationalities than the language itself might at first suggest.

In his book on the modern American novel, Malcolm Bradbury (1983) stressed the importance of Hemingway's new, economic style as a reflection of the age that sought authenticity as an antidote to the hypocrisy of a previous generation and a means of achieving some certainty in an uncertain age. In a chapter on Hemingway in *From Fact to Fiction*, Shelley Fishkin (1985) identified those stylistic qualities and attitudes toward writing that Hemingway learned as a journalist and transferred to his fiction. The implication in her analysis was that journalism served as a means of keeping Hemingway grounded for his more important and lasting work. In his essay on the American short story in the 1920s, Thomas Gullason (1984) suggested that Hemingway's contributions to the genre in one area had been overlooked: in creating stories where a single effect dominates.

A handful of general assessments offered some refinement to the portrait of Hemingway that had become established by this time. Daniel Weiss's (1985) "Ernest Hemingway: The Stylist of Stoicism," originally delivered as a lecture in 1962, provided an overview informed by Freudian insights into his life and fiction. Weiss argued that the psychological approach to Hemingway was justified by Hemingway's fascination with violence and death. In *An American Procession*, Alfred Kazin (1984) seemingly overcame the problems he had with Hemingway's work forty years earlier in *On Native Grounds*. Kazin said Hemingway's "greatest gift, the foundation of all his marvelous pictorial efforts, was his sense of some enduring injustice, of some fundamental wrongness at the heart of things" (362). Kazin offered a sympathetic assessment of Hemingway's insistent need to confront violence, arguing that his approach to life and art were essentially identical: "Mastery lay in the moment's triumph over danger; in life as in art, Hemingway needed one deliberate trial of himself after another" (359).

Among the dozens of tried-and-true (or same-and-lame) commentaries, one might occasionally stumble upon an assessment that views Hemingway's work through a new critical lens. In *The Narrative Act*, a highly regarded study of the role point of view plays in the construction and effect of fiction, Susan Sniader Lanser (1981) included an extended discussion of "The Killers" as well as shorter comments on other Hemingway works, demonstrating the unstated but nevertheless important relationship between ideology and technique in a Hemingway story. Hemingway's works are cited throughout F. K. Stanzel's (1984) *Theory of Narrative*, an extensive analysis of the way narratives are constructed and how they influence readers. Robert Scholes (1982) used Hemingway's "A Very Short Story" to illustrate how approaching a literary text from the angle of semiotic criticism opens up the work to interpretations closed off by the rigorous demands of New Criticism or hermeneutic criticism, each of which seeks to define the text's meanings in different but equally limiting ways.

In *Animals in American Literature*, an early foray into what would emerge as a new branch of critical inquiry, environmentalist criticism and animal studies, Mary Allen (1983) explained one of the great paradoxes of Hemingway's life and one of the more troubling aspects of his fiction: the constant focus on suffering and death inflicted on animals. Hemingway repeatedly made clear his admiration for the great animals whose lives are sacrificed in the bullring or on safari. Allen believed Hemingway could admire animals being killed because he subscribed to an ideal that no longer holds force with most people, "The heroic idea that once made it an honor to meet death boldly" (193)—ritual death dignifying what otherwise would be mere brutality.

Essay Collections

Jeffrey Meyers's (1982) introduction to *Hemingway: The Critical Heritage*, which is really a brief monograph on the history of Hemingway criticism up to 1980, offers important insights into the reasons why many find Hemingway immensely appealing but others consider him infuriatingly bad. The 122 reviews and essays that he reprinted or excerpted attest to the immediate and enduring interest in Hemingway's work. Meyers demonstrated his own familiarity with the tradition in his introductory remarks, extending beyond the material he collected to offer a balanced portrait of critical responses. And yet his judgments about the value of published critical commentary and predictions about the future of Hemingway studies seem curiously out of step with his ability to appreciate the nuances of Hemingway's fiction. Acknowledging that Hemingway had been "exhaustively anatomized in the vast number of books that have appeared since 1952," Meyers asserted that the "pioneering critical studies" by Carlos Baker and Philip Young remain "the best books" on Hemingway—though he admitted that Michael Reynolds's *Hemingway's First War* was "original and valuable." Most others were simply noted without comment or lumped into the category of "specialized studies"; a few general overviews he dismissed as "bland" (57). Meyers concluded that unless the unpublished materials contain some undiscovered gems, "the essential work on Hemingway has already been done" (58).

The intent of the essayists in Robert Lee's (1983) *Ernest Hemingway: New Critical Essays* (1983) was to provide an assessment of Hemingway's achievements (and acknowledgment of his shortcomings) two decades after his death. Lee noted in his introduction that the furor surrounding Hemingway, often caused by his behavior rather than his fiction, seemed to have died down, though he admitted that recent feminist studies had returned him "to that fray" (9). The ten contributors provided some sense of what is good in Hemingway's major fiction and what defines his place in American letters. The most controversial of the essays, Faith Pullin's, ascribed Hemingway's failure to deal honestly and compassionately with women to his limited vision: "His work reveals a progressive repudiation of people in general and of women in particular"; it is the vision of the "loner fighting against a hostile world and an indifferent nature" (192). The last word on Hemingway in this volume, however, was reserved for Frank McConnell, who concluded that Hemingway ultimately became more than an influence on American literature. He was "a paradigm" for "the most serious American writers of the post-War years," largely because, "more than any American novelist of the age," he "represented and lived the vocation of art as *risk*, as a deliberate gamble with one's chance for sanity in a mad world" (211).

Continuing the practice of collecting important (or simply unusual) essays about Hemingway's fiction, in 1983 Michael Reynolds edited a collection of criticism on *In Our Time*. Published as part of publisher G. K. Hall's Critical Essays on American Literature series, the surprisingly hefty volume contains more than three dozen selections, from initial reviews of the various versions of Hemingway's first short story collection to essays on the book's structure and themes. Nearly two dozen entries explicate individual stories. While most contributors focused on traditional issues such as structure, characterization, and theme, a modest number employed tools of psychological criticism, giving *Critical Essays on Hemingway's "In Our Time"* some semblance of diversity in critical approach.

The opening of the Hemingway collection at the Kennedy Library seems to have provided the impetus for several other conferences at which a general revaluation of Hemingway's work was undertaken. The results of one held in Alabama in 1980 are collected in Donald Noble's (1983) *Hemingway: A Revaluation*. Supplementing ten papers from the conference with three previously published articles, Noble's collection helped fill in gaps that had existed despite the "flood of Hemingway criticism which has swept over us all in the last few years" (1). Jackson Benson's essay, subtitled "Getting at the Hard Questions," took issue with a number of earlier critics. Not all were misguided, he noted, but many were incomplete. The major problem Benson found is that Hemingway criticism was becoming extremely repetitive—and consequently, irrelevant. Other contributors attempted some reassessment of early works and offered readings of later ones. Philip Young's "Hemingway: The Writer in Decline" is notable for expressing Young's belief that Hemingway lost his creative powers in the last decade of his life—a notion soon to be challenged by critics writing about *The Garden of Eden*, which at this time was three years away from publication. What is perhaps most striking about Noble's collection, however, is the absence of critical commentary informed by what was at the time "new" critical theory, particularly feminist perspectives. The call to revisit Hemingway's relation to the arts and to existentialism may have been justified, but efforts in that direction would become a minor rivulet in the wide river of critical commentary that would dominate Hemingway studies in the next thirty years.

Just as the 1980 Hemingway Society Conference in Boston prompted publication of Bernard Oldsey's *Ernest Hemingway: The Papers of a Writer*, the 1982 conference at Northeastern University in Boston provided the substance for another collection, *Ernest Hemingway: The Writer in Context*. Edited by James Nagel (1984), the volume included essays by Charles Scribner Jr. and Patrick Hemingway, and one by playwright Tom Stoppard. The scholarly papers, once again heavily indebted to manuscript sources, offered observations on Hemingway's composition process and new interpretations of his life and work. Several explored Hemingway's relationship with other writers. Taken as a whole, the contributions seem to confirm Michael Reynolds's prediction from the first conference that the most fruitful line of inquiry for those interested in Hemingway was to come from a careful examination of manuscript sources. Max Westbrook's essay in defense of Grace Hemingway's behavior in the summer of 1920, when she ostensibly banished her son from the family, demonstrated how such study could explode myths and provide a more balanced view of Hemingway's character. Carol Smith's "Women and the Loss of Eden in Hemingway's Mythology" and Millicent Bell's "*A Farewell to Arms*: Pseudoautobiography and Personal Metaphor" dealt with his views on gender. The impact of this groundbreaking collection was not lost on future Hemingway scholars. Writing nearly a decade later, Rose Marie Burwell called Bell's critique "a brilliant study" (Burwell 1992), while in *Hemingway's Quarrel with Androgyny* Mark Spilka (1990) called Westbrook's account "the *locus classicus* of scholarly adjudication" and the "point of departure for all future discussion of this apparently crystallizing episode in a great writer's youth" (171).

In 1985 Harold Bloom, the distinguished critic turned prolific editor, brought out the first of more than a half dozen collections of essays on Hemingway's fiction. The initial volume, simply titled *Ernest Hemingway*, contained an eclectic group of previously published essays and Bloom's brief but provocative introduction. Over the next twenty years, Bloom's Chelsea House publishing company issued four updated versions of *Ernest Hemingway* (Bloom 1999a, 2003a, 2005, 2011a), separate collections of essays on Brett Ashley (Bloom 1991) and Nick Adams (Bloom 2004), and volumes on *The Sun Also Rises* (Bloom 1987b, 1996c, 2007, 2011b), *A Farewell to Arms* (Bloom 1987a, 1996a, 2009, 2010), and *The Old Man and the Sea* (Bloom 1996b, 1999b, 2008). There is a certain irony, however, in Bloom's decades-long project to capitalize on Hemingway's continuing popularity. In his 2003 book *Genius*, a collection of brief vignettes about a hundred creative men and women, Bloom (2003b) praised Hemingway as a writer of short stories but criticized his "highly deliberate mythmaking" and lamented the fact that most American writers after him "have been contaminated" by him (570). One writer Bloom might have had in mind was Norman Mailer. In the same year Bloom's *Genius* was published, Mailer (2003) wrote that "Hemingway's style affected a whole generations of us. . . . His style had the ability to hit young writers in the gut, and they weren't the same after that" (261).

Lingering Controversy over "The Wound"

In 1981 Carlos Baker published *Ernest Hemingway: Selected Letters 1917–1961*, providing perhaps a glimpse behind the mask of Hemingway as macho American adventurer. Using the letters as evidence, Kenneth Lynn (1981) excoriated Malcolm Cowley as the leader of a group of critics (including Philip Young) that had perpetuated a wrongheaded interpretation of Hemingway's fiction by stressing its dark side and attributing the source of Hemingway's angst to the wound he received in 1918. The letters tell a different story, Lynn insisted, one showing that Hemingway's real battle was waged against his domineering mother. Six years later Lynn would flesh out the arguments he outlined in this essay into one of the most widely acclaimed—and controversial—biographies of Hemingway to be published in the twentieth century.

Cowley (1984) felt compelled to defend himself against Lynn and other "critical revisionists," whom he described as "a contentious sect" (223). He acknowledged that the idea that Hemingway's wound was the clue to understanding his fiction, which he said originated with him, was bound to generate strong reactions. He objected to Lynn's revisionist reading, however, because it tended to ignore literary imagination in favor of psychotrauma. Where Cowley said he was attempting to "suggest an underlying quality that helped to give [Hemingway's fiction] literary stature," Lynn "almost never discusses literature in its own terms." Instead, he looked for "psycho-political motives to excoriate" (226). But Cowley's ace-in-the-hole was the existence of letters between himself and Hemingway in which Hemingway acknowledged (at least partially) the validity of Cowley's interpretation. With a certain degree of glee, Cowley said Lynn's "accusation" was "obstinately ill-informed" (231).

Hemingway's Women: Continuing Critical Debate

If one were to read Jeffrey Walsh's (1982) analysis of three Hemingway novels in *American War Literature: 1914 to Vietnam* without any critical context, one might not be aware that any controversy existed over Hemingway's treatment of women. Walsh examined the narrative methods Hemingway employed in *A Farewell to Arms, For Whom the Bell Tolls,* and *Across the River and Into the Trees* to illustrate ways war serves as a catalyst for exploring important themes and illustrating human characteristics that transcend the battlefield. No mention is made, however, about the way women are depicted in these works, suggesting that the ordeals that Hemingway's male protagonists undergo can stand for universal human experience.

By contrast, Joyce Wexler (1981) confronted the problem of Hemingway's treatment of women head-on, challenging feminists who she said were substituting "female chauvinism for the male variety" (111). Specifically refuting Judith Fetterley's reading of *A Farewell to Arms,* Wexler demonstrated how Catherine Barkley could be seen as a fully developed character who "becomes Frederic's model of courage" (116). Wexler pointed an accusatory finger at fellow feminists (and other critics as well, to be fair), claiming that the tendency to see men and women as opposites blinds many to accepting Catherine for what she is. A truly feminist reading, Wexler suggested, would highlight her strengths and "rescue[] her from the stereotyped role of the hero's mistress" (122). A similar line of argument runs through Charles Nolan's (1984) "Hemingway's Women's

Movement," a brief article offering an alternative reading of Hemingway's early fiction that stresses his sympathetic treatment of women. While acknowledging Hemingway's many misogynist traits, Nolan insisted that throughout his work up to the late 1930s "there runs a strong sympathy for the plight of women, a sympathy that at one point, in fact, is expressed in feminist rhetoric and rage" (14). Nolan's catalog of previously published scholarship in support of his point is a useful reminder that feminists were not the first critics to consider the role of women in Hemingway's fiction. While it might be true, Nolan admitted, that "the legendary Hemingway is anti-woman," evidence from the fiction revealed that "Hemingway the writer is much more sympathetic to women and their plight than readers have generally recognized" (22).

Published in the midst of the feminist reaction against Hemingway, Bernice Kert's (1983) *The Hemingway Women* filled in details about Hemingway's relationships with the important women in his life. Relying not only on documents recently made available at the Kennedy Library but also on interviews with numerous women who knew Hemingway, Kert stitched together profiles of these remarkable figures whose influence on Hemingway, she said, had not yet been adequately documented. Although her narrative closely followed Hemingway's life, Kert's well-researched and sensitive portrait of his four wives, his mother, and several other women with whom he was linked (often romantically) explained how Hemingway relied on these women for material comfort and inspiration. Kert found two important common traits among these women: "relinquishment" and "resilience." All of them—including Hemingway's mother, she insisted—gave up something of themselves to serve him, and all were able to bounce back from the sometimes shameful treatment they endured at his hands.

Kert's portraits of these women may be favorable, but they hardly rank as feminist revisionism. Kert was not an academic, although she studied English at the University of Michigan and published fiction before she married in the 1940s. Like many women of her day, however, she gave up her career to support her husband, returning to her first love only after her children were grown (Nelson 2005). Perhaps that is why she could be sympathetic toward the women in Hemingway's life without condemning Hemingway for his abominable behavior toward them. She did not see any of them as victims. Still, there is a certain irony about Kert's book suggested by its title. While the women she described may be strong, creative, and likable, all deserving of admiration in their own right, they are remembered principally because of their relationship with Hemingway. As Christopher Lehmann-Haupt (1983) of the *New York Times* observed, regardless of how successful Kert had been in making these women come alive, the fact remained that Hemingway "continues to bestride their world like a colossus."

The responses to Kert's book are worth noting; in fact, Lehmann-Haupt shrewdly suggested, *The Hemingway Women* "functions fascinatingly as a kind of Rorschach test of the reader's attitude toward Hemingway." Longtime *Oregonian* book review editor Paul Pintarich (1983) was happy to see these women "receive long-deserved attention" in this "excellent collection of profiles" (16). The *Chicago Tribune*'s Clarence Petersen (1986) said Kert "has made an enduring contribution to the Hemingway legend in a book that moves with the swiftness of a well-told tale and is surprisingly fair to Hemingway." James Frakes (1983), an academic who reviewed the book for the *Cleveland Plain Dealer*, dismissed it as a poor attempt at pop psychology and gossip, in the vein of Dr. Joyce Brothers and Louella Parsons. He found the book tiresome, and concluded somewhat snidely that he wished "Hemingway had lived all of his life alone on the top of Mt. Kilimanjaro so that we could read his prose clean and not the gossip he engendered" (B17).

Other academics were more cautious or simply less receptive to Kert's brand of biography. Linda Wagner's (1985) appreciative assessment in the *Hemingway Review* celebrated *Hemingway's Women* as not only the definitive biography of the women in Hemingway's life, but perhaps the definitive biography of Hemingway as well. Wagner seemed happy to report that Kert's Hemingway is a "spoiled, egocentric male, so insecure as to need proof of his worth from a wide gallery of constantly changing admirers" (56). The only "flaw" she pointed out is "Kert's tendency to forgive Hemingway" (56) and assert that each of his wives was better off for having been married to him—a judgment she found Pollyannaish. Jeffrey Meyers (1983) seemed to be metaphorically patting Kert on the head for a nice try in getting her arms around such a meaty and controversial subject. Her book was "original and useful," but she failed to "extract the maximum meaning" from all the new materials available to her. Instead, Meyers said, she adopted the "conventional view of Hemingway given in Baker's biography" and had "a very limited understanding of Hemingway's work" (1027). Apparently Meyers was of the opinion that the scholarly world would have to wait a couple of years to get the definitive biography of Hemingway—his own, of course.

The year after Kert's book appeared, Roger Whitlow (1984) published a modest study that portended to offer a via media between the simplistic (and often dismissive) assessments of Hemingway's female characters by pre-1970s critics and the vitriol of feminists who seemed bent on knocking him off his perch as representative Modern American writer. *Cassandra's Daughters* "explore[d] what [Hemingway's] language actually says about his female characters and the way they deal with the circumstances of their lives" (15). Using the accepted classifications of passive helpmate or unadulterated bitch employed by both traditionalists and feminists, Whitlow offered brief sketches of more than a dozen women in Hemingway's fiction, concentrating on the way they are actually portrayed. He argued that women like Catherine Barkley often have a more accurate and mature outlook than the men with whom they associate, and that some of the "so-called bitches" (including Margot Macomber) "are considerably more complicated than the label implies" and in some cases "are actually morally superior to the male characters with whom they are associated and by whom, in large part, they are judged" (49). The conclusion to be drawn from this assessment, of course, was that Hemingway was not the chauvinist that radical feminists made him out to be, nor the simplistic he-man earlier critics described in their assessments. Arguing for moderation in an age given to radicalism and controversy, however, did not bode well for Whitlow's study, which is cited much less frequently than others that deal with gender issues in Hemingway's life and fiction.

Wilma Garcia (1984) also defended Hemingway in *Mothers and Others: Myths of the Female in the Works of Melville, Twain, and Hemingway*. Employing the tools of myth criticism, Garcia found parallels between Hemingway's work and both classical and Christian mythic tales. Her emphasis was on the importance of the hero and the hero's quest. In this light she saw female characters as "an important part of the hero's efforts to complete his quest" (151). Despite her generally positive assessment of Hemingway's treatment of women, Garcia seemed almost sad to conclude that while Hemingway may have been aware that "women may have ways of being that differ from men's—no small awareness for any man," he "seldom questioned traditional assumptions about women" (173). However, Garcia placed the ultimate blame for this myopia (or willful blindness) outside Hemingway, finding him one of many who are victims of "mythologies" that "furnish us" with so few accurate "perceptions of the female" (173).

Though published in the UMI Research Press series, Mimi Gladstein's (1986) assessment of Hemingway's treatment of women was not simply the reprint of her dissertation but a revision completed thirteen years after Gladstein earned her doctorate. While she wrote the initial version in 1973, when the feminist backlash against Hemingway was rising, her delay in publication allowed Gladstein to provide some perspective on the significance (and appropriateness) of some of the most strident criticisms of Hemingway's portrayal of female characters. *The Indestructible Woman in Faulkner, Hemingway, and Steinbeck* was not a feminist attack, but neither was it an attempt to claim that Hemingway and his contemporaries were "nascent feminists"; rather, Gladstein argued, the "indestructible woman" in Hemingway's work is a "projection" of his sexist attitudes toward women (xi). This figure is conceived as "the other," part of the natural, primitive world that man must conquer (7). All of Hemingway's work, Gladstein argued, is concerned with the quest of the hero, a search for meaning. In most of his fiction, the woman either "knowingly" or "unknowingly" serves as a destructive force, "distract[ing] or otherwise keep[ing] the hero from his goal" (50). Following the line of argument that can be traced back through Elizabeth Janeway (1971) and Dolores Barracano Schmidt (1971) to Leslie Fiedler (1960), Gladstein found two types of indestructible women in Hemingway: the "bitch mother" and the "nurse mother" (65), both of whom were more symbolic, aligned with "the earth and its animal creatures" (73) than individualized characters.

The Dangerous Summer

In 1985 Scribner issued another "new" Hemingway book, *The Dangerous Summer*, a nonfictional account of bullfighters Luis Miguel Dominguín and Antonio Ordóñez. Edited from manuscripts written in 1959 and 1960 while Hemingway was on assignment for *Life* magazine, which published a series of articles that Hemingway extracted from the manuscripts in 1960, the book received the usual prepublication fanfare and was reviewed widely—though not always appreciatively. Novelist William Kennedy (1985) had kind words for *The Dangerous Summer*, praising Michael Pietsch's editing job and calling it "one of the best sports books I have ever read" (35). Ronald Curran (1985), however, dismissed this edited version of *The Dangerous Summer* as "estate-bottled Hemingway" (115).

A more detailed and thoughtful analysis of the book is offered by Edward Said (1985), best known for his groundbreaking analysis of Western imperialism, *Orientalism* (Said 1978). Noting Americans' obsession with learning how things operate, Said commented on both *The Dangerous Summer* and its predecessor, *Death in the Afternoon*, as books in which Hemingway explained the intricacies of bullfighting for those unfamiliar with the sport, adding that "the massive edifice of *Death in the Afternoon* stands, like a tower on a rock, on top of Hemingway's obsession with death" (233). In Said's view, *The Dangerous Summer* did not quite measure up to the earlier book in the intensity of the experience it conveyed, but in it Said detected beneath the retrospective's description of the rivalry between the two bullfighters a "deeper contest": one between the earlier Hemingway, "a man obsessed with the *corrida* as tragedy," and the later Hemingway, "a world-famous writer more celebrated than his material, tired, yet courageously risking self-repetition and self-parody as he seeks to resurrect dead impulses, forgotten gestures, true qualities buried beneath commercialism" (234). Said seemed saddened by the attempt, which he believed did not succeed as well as Hemingway may have hoped. He was much more annoyed, however, that Hemingway's heirs chose to publish the manuscript. He said the original power of *Death in the Afternoon*, where "the shock of recognition derived from knowledge and converted into how-to-ism" is quite effective, had simply been reduced to a "product" for the marketplace (238).

A Bevy of Biographies

It is certainly not a surprise to Hemingway scholars that by the mid-1980s biographical studies of Hemingway began appearing with great frequency. The opening of the Hemingway Papers gave many scholars an opportunity to examine documents that formerly had been seen only by a privileged few. Between 1980 and 1992, more than a dozen biographies were published. Peter Griffin's (1985) *Along with Youth: Hemingway, the Early Years* and Jeffrey Meyers's (1985) *Ernest Hemingway* appeared almost simultaneously. One important difference between them was certainly the authors' résumés. Griffin was a newly minted PhD whose 1979 dissertation served as the basis for the ambitious project he mapped out: a multivolume biography that would bring Hemingway to life in a way Baker had failed to do. Meyers was already a seasoned biographer who had already published more than a dozen books, including *Hemingway: The Critical Heritage* (1982).

True to his plan, Griffin wrote Hemingway's story as if he were crafting a novel, using various techniques of reportage to give some zest to the narrative. Concentrating on the formative years of Hemingway's career, Griffin combined historical research with literary critique to give readers a sense of how Hemingway achieved the insight and discipline that made him the most formidable American writer of his generation. If there was anything unique about *Along with Youth*, however, it was the inclusion of five previously unpublished Hemingway stories, all written during the 1920s. Griffin also reproduced numerous letters to and from Hemingway and lengthy copies of drafts that Hemingway corrected. What emerged is a portrait of a young writer honing his craft and making the most of his personal experiences.

Virtually every reviewer pointed out Griffin's most important contributions, his inclusion of five unpublished Hemingway stories and his inclusion of what Robert W. Lewis (1987) called "unique interviews and letters" (47). That coup resulted from Griffin's ability to win over Mary Hemingway, who gave him access to personal papers and the five stories, and John Hemingway, who not only wrote a flattering preface to *Along with Youth* but also gave Griffin access to letters exchanged between Hemingway and Hadley Richardson, John's mother. Nevertheless, Lewis thought Griffin was sometimes given to hyperbole and was at times too dependent on Hemingway's fiction to interpret his life. Given a chance to review Griffin's book, Meyers (1986a) was less than charitable, calling both "the method and the accuracy" of *Along with Youth* "radically flawed" (60). That might have been expected, of course, when Meyers read the publisher's claim that Griffin's would become the definitive biography.

Although Meyers never said so in his biography, his *Ernest Hemingway* was clearly intended to supersede Carlos Baker's 1969 *Ernest Hemingway:*

A Life Story as the primary interpretive study of Hemingway's life. Meyers began without preface or introduction, launching immediately into his narrative with a brief description of Hemingway's grandparents. His account, like Baker's, was heavy on details about Hemingway's life and light on literary criticism, although he did on occasion offer interpretations of individual works. His main interest in Hemingway's fiction, however, was in explaining how Hemingway's life served as a source of inspiration for his writing.

One reviewer described Meyers's biography as an attempt at "out-psychoanalyzing Philip Young and the many Hemingway scholars who have speculated on the psychological development of such a literary and charismatic phenomenon" (Butts 1986, 334). Meyers insisted on reading the fiction as Hemingway's means of coping with the traumatic experiences of his wartime service. Meyers was also particularly insistent on portraying Hemingway at his worst during the final decades of his life. Nevertheless, Meyers won over *New York Times* reviewer Christopher Lehmann-Haupt (1985), who called his biography "an absorbing tragic portrait" and "a relief" after Baker's "shapeless gathering of a million facts." Lehmann-Haupt was concerned, though, that Meyers dismissed out of hand the possibility that Hemingway's extreme masculinity might have been a cover for homosexual tendencies, because it tended to vitiate his "otherwise impressive treatment" of his subject. Robert W. Lewis (1987) described Meyers's account as useful, but provided a catalog of faults, mostly errors that Lewis believed could have been avoided by careful fact-checking. Also, Lewis continued, Meyers had the annoying habit of "mak[ing] assumptions or generalizations and then determinedly find[ing] evidence or mak[ing] assertions to demonstrate (if not prove) his points" (57).

Contrasts between these two biographies were highlighted in a number of combined reviews. Matthew Bruccoli (1986b) admired both books, although he faulted the authors for following Young in ascribing the source of Hemingway's inspiration for writing to his war experience—a myth, Bruccoli says, already dispelled. R. W. B. Lewis (1985) was not fully supportive of either book. He appreciated Griffin's lively writing style but found his book disorganized. Lewis found Meyers better able at assembling his data and organizing his account, but believed his book would not supplant Baker's. Writing in the *New York Times*, Raymond Carver (1985) called Griffin's book "wonderful and intimate," a study that "brings to life the young Hemingway with all his charm, vitality, good looks, passionate dedication to writing, like nothing else I've ever read about the man." By contrast, Carver complained that Meyers's "strictly Freudian" approach and his sometimes plodding account of Hemingway's many faults and transgressions made for depressing reading. The book "fairly bristles with disapproval of its subject," Carver said.

The only antidote he could recommend was for readers to go straight back to Hemingway's fiction. The best work—"clean serene and solid"—will remind readers why Hemingway "will last," and why biographers like Meyers "might just as well write the biography of an anonymous grocer or a woolly mammoth."

7: A "Sea Change" in Hemingway Studies (1986–1990)

ON SOME FRONTS, 1986 seemed to be another quiet year for Hemingway scholarship. The January 1986 issue of the *Wilson Quarterly* carried an article by Frank McConnell (1986) with the intriguing title "Hemingway: Stalking Papa's Ghost." McConnell traced Hemingway's influence over two generations of American writers, finding the ghost of Papa lurking in the background of figures as diverse as Saul Bellow, Norman Mailer, Kurt Vonnegut, and Thomas Pynchon. Additionally, he continued, "Both Hemingway and the Hemingway style have exercised a strong, probably determinative, effect on the whole course of the American detective story" (165). Unfortunately, while Hemingway himself was able to control through irony the tendencies toward cruelty and irresponsibility that characterized his vision, others had not always been so successful; witness, McConnell noted, the inane immorality of the work of Mickey Spillane. What had made Hemingway so memorable as both a person and a writer was his willingness to "live[ ] the vocation of art as *risk*, as a deliberate gamble with one's chances for sanity in a mad world" (172).

Another work appearing that year, Earl Rovit's (1986) second edition of *Ernest Hemingway* in the Twayne US Authors series, on which Gerry Brenner collaborated, did little to challenge traditional readings or advance critical understanding of Hemingway's work. Most of the text was repeated verbatim from the first edition, although notes were expanded and the bibliography updated to include recent commentaries. The one new chapter, on the posthumous work, gave Rovit a chance to explain how his "tutor and tyro" theory of the Hemingway hero extended to the later fiction, in this case *Islands in the Stream*. The Hemingway community may have been disappointed, though, to discover no serious acknowledgment of the changes in Hemingway criticism brought about by feminists and others who had for more than a decade engaged in a campaign to despoil Hemingway's reputation and legacy.

The tide changed radically in May 1986 when Scribner issued a previously unpublished Hemingway novel: *The Garden of Eden*. Edited by Tom Jenks, who had been hired by Scribner as part of its move to increase sales, the novel would generate radically new readings of Hemingway's fiction—and revaluations of his life.

The Garden of Eden

As they did with the publication of *Islands in the Stream*, Hemingway's family and publisher created a media buildup to the release of *The Garden of Eden*. An advance notice sent out by the *New York Times* trumpeted the fact that "the novel's bisexual theme is a stark departure from the masculine themes popularly associated with Hemingway" (McDowell 1985). Publisher Charles Scribner Jr. noted in the release that the theme was "not as strange today as it was 25 years ago" (D15)—perhaps to explain why Hemingway's heirs and his publisher waited so long to bring out this work. In retrospect, the decision showed remarkable foresight and good business savvy. While a number of newspaper reviewers were disquieted by the new book, the academic community in the 1980s—a far different group than those who wrote admiringly about the Hemingway code during the 1940s through the 1960s—could not have been more delighted.

Reviews were mixed. The appearance of this new Hemingway novel is "one of the major literary events of 1986," announced *Parade* magazine (Kupferberg 1986, 15). One reviewer observed that *The Garden of Eden* read like Hemingway but is "definitely different stuff" (Pettit 1986, E5); another thought the book "a very fine novel"—although "not a lost masterpiece" (Ryan 1986, 12P). In his *Time* magazine review, Lance Morrow (1986) described the novel as "an odd, interesting ingredient in the Hemingway psychomyth" and confessed that "Hemingway's books are easier to know and love than his life." That this complicated man would venture to write about androgyny is one more piece of evidence showing how difficult it was to truly understand him. Morrow pleaded that Hemingway "be spared further Freudian autopsy" and that his works be appreciated for what they are: some of America's finest literature (70).

Some reviewers questioned the editorial job done by Jenks. Robert Merritt (1986) believed the book would have "a certain scholarly appeal and should, if anything, add to" Hemingway's "mystical image"; but it "can't be called a Hemingway novel," because Jenks has essentially eviscerated a manuscript that Hemingway thought not worthy of publication (F5). Novelist Barbara Solomon (1986), who read the manuscript at the Kennedy Library after the novel was published, was more blunt: the publisher "has committed a literary crime" (31); the book is "a travesty" (34).[1] Even those who did not find Jenks's editorial decision making suspect still thought the novel weak. Joe Wheelan (1986), writing for the Associated Press, said the principal lesson one could learn from the publication of *The Garden of Eden* was that "the lode of unpublished Hemingway works is about played out." Whelan believed the problem lay in Hemingway's decision to abandon his "dependable themes" to experiment with the "tricky subject of sexual ambiguity." He would have been better off continuing to focus on the "strong, masculine characters and values" that characterized his best work (DD2). The *New York Times*'s Michiko Kakutani (1986) was less bothered by the change in theme than by the weak story line and flaccid writing. The new novel seemed to her a parody of Hemingway; furthermore, she argued, readers would have a hard time caring about the "careless narcissists" who populate the book (E8).

The reaction of the academic community, however, was decidedly more positive. Almost coincident with the novel's publication, the *Boston Review* published Hemingway scholar Allen Josephs's highly appreciative review, and the *Hemingway Review* reprinted it almost immediately (Josephs 1986). The following year the journal published Tom Jenks's (1987) defense of his editorial job, a lengthy explication of the novel by Frank Scafella (1987), and critiques by Robert Gajdusek (1987) and Robert Jones (1987). In his review for the *New York Times*, the writer E. L. Doctorow (1986), who held positions at a number of distinguished American universities, devoted considerable space to reviewing (with a certain degree of admiration) Hemingway's career before launching into a critique of Jenks's editing job, largely, it seems, to exonerate Hemingway from the book's many faults. Doctorow found it remarkable that Hemingway, "the great outdoor athlete of American literature," could create a female character like Catherine Bourne, which suggested to him that Hemingway possessed "the rudiments of a feminist perspective" (45). While there was evidence that Hemingway had not completed this work, Doctorow was heartened by signs he detected of Hemingway's conscious decision to strike out for new territory as a writer. Jeffrey Meyers (1986b) was one of the few academics who found the novel weak, more interesting for what it revealed about Hemingway's life than for its literary merits.

Major New Biographies

If there is one thing Hemingway's biographers agreed on, it was the elusiveness of their subject. Hemingway was a complex man who frequently drew on personal experience in his work. Anyone wishing to know the man behind the fiction faced a daunting task, and no one seemed to have gotten everything right in biographies published in the 1960s through the 1980s. Hardly any scholar thought Carlos Baker's "official" biography the last word on Hemingway, even though most admitted it contained a slew of facts on which a better biographical study might one day draw. Some new biographies were better than others—Scott Donaldson's work brought high if qualified praise from academic circles, while A. E. Hotchner's (1966) was almost universally dismissed as fanciful and too prone to hero worship. Jeffrey Meyers's book was also well received, but many thought the essential Hemingway had not yet been discovered.

Some opinions were changed by the work of Michael Reynolds and Kenneth Lynn. In 1986 Reynolds published the first installment of his five-volume biography of Hemingway. Carlos Baker's detailed study pales in comparison to Reynolds's meticulous assessment that runs more than 1,700 pages with minimal repetition between volumes. The Hemingway that emerges from Reynolds's work is a mixture of Horatio Alger and Sir Lancelot, a self-made celebrity and accomplished writer who is at the same time a valiant champion of right always looking for new worlds to conquer and new foes to vanquish. In addition to its length, what sets Reynolds's work apart from other biographies (except, perhaps, Griffin's, whom he never mentions or cites) is his approach to writing about his subject. There is a sense of immediacy about his portrait, designed to let readers share the suspense and uncertainty that Hemingway himself felt as he moved forward in his personal and professional life.

In the first volume, *The Young Hemingway* (Reynolds 1986), much is made of family relationships. Reynolds notes that Hemingway never wrote about the nineteenth-century atmosphere of the sheltered Chicago suburb where he was raised. Nevertheless, his fiction about youth was grounded in the ideals he learned growing up. Reynolds portrays Grace Hemingway sympathetically, noting that she extolled virtues that Hemingway gave to many of his characters. Grace was no angel, however, and Reynolds details the tension between mother and son that led Hemingway to describe her later in life as evil. What stands out, however, is Hemingway's determination to "create[ ] himself anew, arranging and modifying his life to become the person he saw in his private mirror" (111). Considerably less attention is paid to Hemingway's war experiences except as they left him feeling like an outsider upon his return to Oak Park. In discussing Hemingway's development from juvenile to professional writer, Reynolds takes care to explain how early models were replaced by new ones, nudging Hemingway to embrace Modernism and its spare techniques of presentation. Urged to write about what he knew, Hemingway drew upon his experiences for his fiction—but the finished products, Reynolds insists, are not purely autobiographical.

Reynolds (1989) makes that point again in his second volume, *Hemingway: The Paris Years*, which covers what he calls the years of Hemingway's apprenticeship. Following Hemingway through the cafés of Paris, the cities and countryside of Spain, the slopes of the Alps, on trips to Russia and the Middle East as a reporter for the *Toronto Star*, Reynolds writes of how Hemingway learned from his mentors and developed his craft. Throughout his narrative Reynolds intersperses interpretations of Hemingway's fiction; however, he avoids equating Hemingway's life with his art, always looking for evidence outside the fiction to corroborate what might seem like autobiographical detail. Reynolds also notes how, when it suited his purpose, Hemingway developed his own version of events to explain his successes and failures. "Early in his career," Reynolds observes, "Hemingway began revising and editing what would become his longest and most well-known work: the legend of his own life, where there was never a clear line between fiction and reality" (272).

Reynolds's (1992) third volume, *Hemingway: The American Homecoming*, deals with only four years—1926 to 1929—but these are formative in Hemingway's development as an artist and crucial in his personal life. During this period he divorced Hadley Richardson and married Pauline Pfeiffer, whose uncle Gus Pfeiffer provided support until Hemingway became financially independent. This volume takes the Hemingway story from the publication of *The Sun Also Rises* to the final drafts of *A Farewell to Arms*, and Reynolds pays special attention to the links between the author's life and the emotional states of his characters. For those interested more in the literature than the life, Reynolds traces the changes in the Hemingway hero, who moves from vulnerable, wounded warrior to a tougher, more active participant in his world.

The fourth volume, *Hemingway: The 1930s* (Reynolds 1997), covers the decade when Hemingway moved from "literary cult figure" to "American icon," and explores what Reynolds calls the "dark side" of Hemingway's American dream (xx). During the 1930s Hemingway lived life largely while trying to expand his literary repertoire, intentionally aiming, Reynolds says, to become known as a man of letters. Reynolds goes out of his way to emphasize Hemingway's literary acumen and his passion for learning everything he could about a subject. "When Hemingway's interest focused on new material or a new genre," Reynolds asserts, "he first read broadly and deep to find what not to write" (169). This is the portrait of a writer sincerely committed to his craft. At the same time, his immense popularity made him a target for everyone with an idea about what he ought to be doing. Reynolds makes a special effort to place events in Hemingway's life against the larger canvas of national and international affairs as the world stumbled through the Great Depression and toward a second worldwide conflict. The story of Hemingway's sudden fascination with journalist Martha Gellhorn is paired with his growing interest in the Spanish Civil War, which provided him materials for *For Whom the Bell Tolls*.

The final volume, *Hemingway: The Final Years* (Reynolds 1999), focuses on the last twenty years of Hemingway's life when growing international adulation, crowned by the award of the Nobel Prize in 1954, was balanced against the deep depression that beset Hemingway, caused by a growing fear that his talent was spent. One might accuse Reynolds of rushing to complete the work without exhausting the patience of reviewers who had complained that earlier volumes covered so few years. However, when examined from the perspective of Reynolds's principal interest, the compression of these years makes sense. Hemingway the writer was fully formed by 1940. Instead, Reynolds offers some intriguing insights into Hemingway's dealings with the group of scholars (Baker, Fenton, and Young) who were making him the subject of their academic study.

By the time one reaches the end of Reynolds's biography, one might begin to think of Hemingway as a protagonist in a Greek tragedy, gifted and highly capable but possessed of one fatal flaw that inevitably led to his downfall. That Reynolds thinks so as well is made clear in his coda, where he describes Hemingway as "the embodiment of America's promise" who realizes his dream of becoming "the best writer of his time." Sadly, the imagination that allowed him to "remodel[ ] the American short story, change[ ] the way characters speak," and confront "the moral strictures confining the writer" also "created his paranoia." Reynolds concludes that Hemingway's immense success led inevitably to his demise when he could not meet the demands his fame brought. His is not a unique story, however, Reynolds insists. "It is an old story, older than written words, a story the ancient Greeks would have recognized" (360).

This nearly poetic conclusion offers some clue as to why Reynolds's study has struck a positive chord with so many scholars. His portrait of Hemingway is not only well researched but also sympathetic—and safe. Reynolds is not taken in by Hemingway's machismo and makes no excuses for his boorish behavior. He does not look for a grand design to explain Hemingway's fiction. Rather, he keeps his focus on his primary goal: to discover and present the writer and thinker inside the man of action and explain the motives for Hemingway's becoming a writer, choosing his subjects, and developing his unique style.

The year after Reynolds published his first volume, Kenneth Lynn (1987) issued what became the most controversial of the Hemingway biographies of the twentieth century. Unlike Jeffrey Meyers, Lynn wrote about Hemingway with admiration and at times even affection. He also seemed to have greater appreciation for Hemingway's complex personality. Lynn's explanation of that complexity is made easier by timing; his biography appeared a year after publication of *The Garden of Eden*, in which Hemingway dealt openly with matters of gender. A revaluation of Hemingway's life based on an appreciation of his complex feelings about gender made Lynn's study both valuable and contentious. Lynn added fuel to the fires of controversy by chastising other biographers for perpetuating myths about Hemingway—particularly about some of the exploits on which his "man's man" image had been created. Like Young, Lynn found in trauma an overarching theme for explaining Hemingway's life and writing. But the "wound" Lynn focused on was not the one Hemingway received on the battlefield but one he experienced as a child raised by a mother whose treatment made him doubt his gender, causing him great anxiety that he never really outgrew.

Lynn did not subscribe to the notion that the fiction is simply disguised autobiography, although he admitted that some of Hemingway's writings come close to being little more than reworkings of events from his life. At the same time, he recognized a subtlety in Hemingway's fiction not often noted by many critics who focus on the Hemingway code. For example, Lynn detected an undercurrent of irony in the title of Hemingway's second major short story collection, *Men without Women*. While it highlighted his focus on "the self-sufficiently masculine worlds of crime, boxing and bullfighting," it also suggested the "alienation from women" that troubled Hemingway so much (365). At the same time, Lynn considered Hemingway's legacy beyond dispute: "Through the enormous curiosity and gusto with which he pursued new adventures and the valorous dedication he brought to his art," he said, Hemingway "affirmed the possibilities of life in this tough world" (593).

Many in the scholarly community applauded Lynn's accomplishment. Writing in the *Hudson Review*, William Pritchard (1988) called Lynn's biography the best book on Hemingway's life to date, finding that his focus on Hemingway's permanent wounding by his mother did not preclude Lynn from offering sensitive readings of individual novels and stories. Among Lynn's foremost champions, Frederick Crews (1987) declared that because of Lynn's biography, "nothing will be the same in any branch of Hemingway studies" (30). Lynn's warts-and-all portrait not only debunked myths but exposed new truths that made Hemingway understandable if not likable, and offered sensible revaluations of some of the fiction. Even more noteworthy, Crews concluded, Lynn had "provided a model of the way biographically informed criticism can catch the pulse of works about which everything appeared to have been said" (37).

Crews's review prompted immediate and hostile response from two well-known Hemingway scholars. In "Pressure under Grace: An Exchange" (1987) Peter Griffin, whose work Crews called superficial, claimed he provided valuable help to Lynn and had actually been responsible for first revealing facts about Hemingway's relationship with his mother. Philip Young railed against Crews for giving Cowley credit for first suggesting that Hemingway's fiction drew its power from the psychological trauma he suffered as a result of his wounding. Given a chance to respond, Crews chided Griffin for being so sensitive and accused Young of coming close to "naïve hero worship." No doubt this kind of exchange could have gone on for quite some time if editors at the *New York Review of Books* had provided these three squabblers sufficient space to continue their argument.

Other Biographies

In 1988 Denis Brian published a biography designed, he said, to elucidate Hemingway's character. *True Gen: An Intimate Portrait of Ernest Hemingway by Those Who Knew Him* (published in England as *The Faces of Hemingway*) is not a traditional narrative of his life, but a compilation of interviews by people who knew Hemingway or who had written extensively about him. The participants are certainly an impressive group: three of Hemingway's wives, members of his family, his sons, high-school classmates, individuals who knew him in the United States and overseas, fellow journalists and novelists, and a handful of academics who had spent the better part of their careers studying his work. Any person's account of events is liable to be biased, but Brian attempted to overcome that problem by seeking multiple sources for each topic he covered. The method did not impress scholars, however; it is hard to find a positive review of Brian's book in any academic journal.

Additional source material of a particularly intriguing period in Hemingway's life was made available to scholars in 1989 with the publication of *Hemingway in Love and War: The Lost Diary of Agnes von Kurowsky, Her Letters, and Correspondence of Ernest Hemingway*. Edited by James Nagel and Henry Serrano Villard (1989), the book documented Hemingway's relationship with the nurse who cared for him in the Italian hospital where he was brought after being gravely wounded in 1918. Villard, a fellow patient at the hospital, provided background on conditions at the institution where Hemingway convalesced, but the materials in the diary and correspondence do not confirm speculation (much of it fueled by Hemingway) that his affair with von Kurowsky was consummated or that she reciprocated his youthful advances. At the same time, for scholars wishing to speculate from available evidence, the material helps explain some of Hemingway's feelings about war and love, both important influences on his early work.

Though not intended as biography, Edward Stanton's (1989) *Hemingway and Spain: A Pursuit* blended scholarly writing and personal essay to explain the importance of Spain as a formative inspiration for much of Hemingway's work. Although sometimes reductive in making simplistic correspondences between Hemingway's personal experiences in Spain and the fiction modeled on them, Stanton nevertheless demonstrated once again that it is impossible to fully appreciate Hemingway's work without understanding the culture that fascinated him so much.

Peter Hays's (1990) *Ernest Hemingway* in Continuum's Literature and Life series redacted earlier biographies in an abbreviated sketch of Hemingway's career and relied on previously published scholarship for many of the critical interpretations. In this introduction to Hemingway's life and work, Hays argued that Hemingway's principal contribution to American literature was not any individual novel or story, but in developing a new style that affected not only professionals but everyone learning how to write. "The sentence structure taught in schools now, without elaborate modification, without carefully balanced clauses, but with an emphasis on clarity, concision, and illustrative detail," Hays said, is modeled on Hemingway's prose. "Hemingway changed the way writers of English in the twentieth century used the language" (137).

The plaudits that accompanied the publication of Peter Griffin's first volume in his planned multivolume biography of Hemingway were notably absent when the second installment, *Less Than a Treason*, appeared in 1990. Griffin (1990) covered a scant seven years, from the time Hemingway took his first wife, Hadley, to Paris in 1921 until the breakup of their marriage six years later. Some scholars thought Griffin should have waited until he had completed his research on a larger segment of Hemingway's life, but many were vocal in their distaste for his presentation style, which tends to mimic Hemingway's in *Green Hills of Africa*: nonfiction presented through the techniques of fiction. Griffin admitted in his preface that he did not "analyze" Hemingway's "well-examined life"; "I try instead," he said, "to recreate it." The tell-tale disclaimer follows almost immediately: "In this book I have told *a story of* Ernest's Paris years" (viii, my emphasis).

In the midst of the flurry of new biographies, Jackson Benson (1989) offered a cautionary note to scholars about literary interpretation. Recognizing that "never in recent times has a life had so much influence on our perception and evaluation of the work" (345), he observed somewhat disappointedly that "some of our most sophisticated critics" have viewed Hemingway's heroes as "essentially 'disguised' personal histories"—a mistake that has resulted "not only in flawed criticism" but also "weak interpretation" (346). Rather than trying to find correspondences between the life and the art, Benson said, "we need to concentrate for a change on the authorial mechanisms by which biographical matter is transformed into art" (347). Sadly, he noted, even Young's influential and often insightful study had been "inadvertently misleading" (350), encouraging critics to read the literature as an extension of Hemingway's psyche. Benson said Hemingway "writes out of his life, not about his life" (350). Additionally, Hemingway suffered through more than one traumatic experience as a young man, and it is possible that his best work—that of the 1920s—was an attempt to establish his own self-worth. Unfortunately, Benson said, when Hemingway started to confuse his fiction with his life, his writing began to suffer, because he failed to maintain sufficient distance from his own work to create art.

Critical Books

Four of Hemingway's novels were subjects of separate volumes in the Twayne Masterwork Studies series, which was designed to provide extended critical commentaries on important works: Michael Reynolds's (1988) *"The Sun Also Rises": A Novel of the Twenties*, Gerry Brenner's (1991) *"The Old Man and the Sea": Story of a Common Man*, Robert W.

Lewis's (1992) *"A Farewell to Arms": The War of the Words*, and Allen Josephs's (1994) *"For Whom the Bell Tolls": Ernest Hemingway's Undiscovered Country*. Although the organization of these volumes is formulaic (a section on "Literary and Historical Context" followed by one titled "A Reading"), scholars selected to write them were given considerable leeway in choosing a critical perspective. That freedom resulted in four distinctly different approaches. As a group, however, these volumes attest to the continuing belief that these novels represent the best of Hemingway's long fiction and reinforce the idea that they remained important in the curriculum of high-school and college classes.

Published as part of UMI Research Press's initiative to bring dissertations into print, Susan Beegel's (1988) *Hemingway's Craft of Omission* is a careful study, made possible by the recent opening of the Hemingway manuscripts to scholars, of the transformation of four stories between initial draft and publication.[2] Arguing that the goal of any manuscript study is "to reconstruct an author's process of composition" (9), Beegel looked at four short pieces not often examined by Hemingway scholars. She claimed that almost everything Hemingway wrote started out as something he experienced directly or learned of from a friend or associate. Following a practice he learned from Gertrude Stein, he often wrote automatically without initial concern for the final shape of the tale. Comparing his drafts to the finished stories, Beegel said, demonstrates that "revision for Hemingway" was "principally a business of omission, of discovering the story in the stream of consciousness, and eliminating the personal material leading to and sometimes from it" (11).

In an intriguing comparative study, *Tales Plainly Told: The Eyewitness Narratives of Hemingway and Homer*, classics scholar Kathleen Morgan (1990) identified correspondences between the two writers. Morgan located an important similarity in the shared practice of what she describes as the "eyewitness style" (5), which she said is characterized by two elements for which Hemingway is well known: the insistence that writers succeed when they write about what they know and when they practice "judicious selectivity" (6). Morgan provided evidence of Hemingway's knowledge of Homer's work, demonstrating that the connection between them is more than merely casual allusion on Hemingway's part. A careful reading of Hemingway's fiction, she said, reveals "an appreciation of Homeric style and technique acknowledged by Hemingway himself" (80).

In what can only be described as a contrarian polemic, Carl Bredahl and Susan Drake (1990) argued in *Hemingway's "Green Hills of Africa" as Evolutionary Narrative* that, far from being one of Hemingway's minor works, this book is "the central piece of the larger Hemingway story, the piece upon which all the others turn" (viii). It is an "evolutionary" narrative, revealing Hemingway's "commitment to change and growth"—a commitment that links him with Einstein and Heisenberg (7). Bredahl and Drake insisted that "*Green Hills of Africa* does not discuss or define the new; it does the new," forcing readers to abandon previous notions about the book's merits and seeing its true value "in itself, within Hemingway's own work, and within the ongoing enterprise of American narration" (118). The potential for lasting impact of this revaluation of *Green Hills* was not lost on longtime Hemingway scholar Charles Oliver (1990), who commented somewhat enigmatically in his review of this "fascinating and too short work of criticism" that, since "so little depth has been achieved in previous interpretations" of the book, Bredahl and Drake's critique "comes as a shock to the system, one difficult to react to on a first reading" (73). One might read that judgment as an endorsement or a polite dismissal.

Less argumentative than Bredahl and Drake's study, Ronald Weber's (1990) *Hemingway's Art of Nonfiction* revisited *Green Hills* and other nonfiction works that had for decades caused consternation for many Hemingway scholars and no small number of devoted readers. Acknowledging the fine work of his predecessor Robert O. Stephens in treating Hemingway's nonfiction at length and with great seriousness, Weber argued that the nonfiction books were not merely "curious diversions or unfortunate lapses from the main business" of Hemingway's career, but were intended by Hemingway to be, like his long fiction, "works of lasting value" (2). Where Stephens found the chief importance of the nonfiction works in the insight they provided into Hemingway's fiction, Weber insisted that they should be read for their own merits. Furthermore, he believed Hemingway wrote them as part of a larger plan to show that, like other American men of letters, he was capable of producing first-rate works in multiple genres.

The extent to which Hemingway's fiction was subjected to careful scrutiny by postmodern critics is evident in Wolfgang Rudat's study of *The Sun Also Rises*. Rudat's close reading of this single text takes up two volumes: *A Rotten Way to Be Wounded: The Tragicomedy of "The Sun Also Rises"* (Rudat 1990) and *Hemingway's Alchemy: Gold in "The Sun Also Rises"* (Rudat 1992). In these critiques Rudat, a European-trained scholar who specialized in identifying and interpreting allusions in literary works, took readers on a guided tour of the novel, commenting on individual passages (and even individual words) to construct a comprehensive reading that incorporates many earlier interpretations and accounts for not only Hemingway's serious criticism of postwar life but also the considerable amount of humor in the novel.

Essays, Chapters, and Collections

One of the strongest endorsements of Hemingway's status not only as a writer but also as a cultural icon appeared in historian Paul Johnson's

(1988) *Intellectuals*, a study of "the moral and judgmental credentials of certain leading intellectuals to give advice to humanity on how to conduct its affairs" (ix). Although Johnson drew most of his details about Hemingway's life and writing from biographers Baker, Meyers, and Lynn, and memoirists who knew Hemingway, his observations and insights are original—and thought-provoking. While at first glance it may be hard to see Hemingway as an intellectual, Johnson said, "on close inspection, he is not only seen to exhibit all the chief characteristics of the intellectual but to possess them to an unusual degree, and in a specifically American combination." Hemingway is "a writer of profound originality" who "transformed the way in which his fellow Americans, and people throughout the English-speaking world, expressed themselves," largely through his "new personal, secular and highly contemporary ethical style" (143). Hemingway believed he had "inherited a false world" embodied in his parents' religious beliefs and lifestyle; his mission as an artist was to replace this false "moral culture" with "a true one" (146). In his early years, Hemingway created both his unique style and his ethic, which placed high demands on anyone who attempted to live by the code he created. Unfortunately, Johnson said, Hemingway became "the victim, the prisoner, the slave of his own imagination, forced to enact it in real life" (152); he ended up "a man killed by his art" (172). Nevertheless, his success in creating "a new way of writing English, and fiction" was "one of the salient events in the history of our language and is now an inescapable part of it" (171). Johnson asserted that Hemingway "came to embody America at a certain epoch rather as Voltaire embodied France in the 1750s or Byron in the 1820s" (143).

One novel receiving significant critical attention at this time was *The Sun Also Rises*. In *Fiction and Historical Consciousness*, Emily Budick (1989) described it as Hemingway's attempt to rewrite *The Great Gatsby*. She placed the novel in the tradition of American romance, calling it a statement of a new American covenant that established the nation's relationship with prior generations of Americans and with history. David Lynn (1989) included a chapter on the novel in *The Hero's Tale: Narrators in the Early Modern Novel*, claiming Hemingway's Jake Barnes was part of a tradition beginning with Conrad that moved the concept of heroism into the twentieth century, when dealing with dissolution and meaninglessness became the modern quest. In *Dying Gods in the Twentieth Century*, a work of myth criticism, K. J. Phillips (1990) read *The Sun Also Rises* as a modern-day reinterpretation of what he called "the tradition of a dying god in bull form" (65), claiming that Hemingway used "the myth of Cybele and Attis" (65) as a unifying device in the novel. With a bit of critical dexterity, Phillips assigned classical roles to Hemingway's major characters.

The availability of Hemingway's manuscripts allowed for new readings based on careful comparisons of the finished novel or story with earlier drafts. One such was William Balassi's (1990) "Hemingway's Greatest Iceberg: The Composition of *The Sun Also Rises*," in which he explained how the composition of the novel exhibits Hemingway's famous iceberg principle. Through a series of writing and revision, Hemingway was able to create a tragedy that is often misread but always challenging to readers intent on understanding its understated or unstated meanings.

On occasion Hemingway's fiction was used to illustrate larger theoretical principles about literature. For example, the ideology of the Nick Adams stories is the subject of Catherine Zuckert's (1990) chapter on Hemingway in *Natural Right and the American Imagination*, a philosophical inquiry into questions surrounding the validity of the concept of the social contract. Zuckert believed Hemingway found the idea of the social contract inherently false, because ultimately each human being is alone and alienated from others and incapable of making meaningful, lasting bonds required by a communitarian philosophy. Similarly, *The Sun Also Rises* served as an exemplary text for narratologist Peter Messent (1990) to point out the complexities of characterization. Relying principally on the work of Jewish literary theorist Schlomith Rimmon-Kenan, Messent exposed weaknesses in structuralist and formalist theories of characterization by citing the many (and sometimes conflicting) ways in which Hemingway described, either directly or in most cases indirectly, the characters in the novel. Louis Renza (1988) applied new theories about the writing process to develop fresh interpretations of *In Our Time* and *A Moveable Feast*, suggesting that they were linked by the shared interest Hemingway had in creating a new form of writing in the earlier work and reliving that experience in his late-in-life memoir.

Although attempts to explore (or discover) religious elements in Hemingway's fiction died down after the 1960s, Henry Idema's (1990) chapter on Hemingway in *Freud, Religion, and the Roaring Twenties* used his work to argue that the "spiritual debacle" that occurred after the First World War "had a strong connection to the breakdown of communities, especially religious communities" (136). As Hemingway's fiction demonstrated, his generation sought secular rituals to replace religious ones that had lost meaning for them. Glen Love's (1987, 1990) studies of Hemingway's use of Native American traditions demonstrated Hemingway's conscious effort to use style as a way of ordering reality and subtly promoting the values he espoused.

In *Fictions of Capital*, a Marxist reading of modern American literature, Richard Godden (1990) presented Hemingway as a principal example of a writer caught in the web of American capitalism. Hemingway's paltry attempts to critique moneyed society are negated by the many examples from his writing that show the overpowering influence of the economic values on which his fiction is based. Godden's rereading of the Hemingway canon locates Hemingway's "central preoccupation with perception and the perceived object" in the "context of consumption" (45). Interested in exposing "the hegemony of price in Hemingway's fiction" (45), Godden recast the Hemingway hero as a good consumer who acts "without much thought" because "to think too much might be to waken numerous anxieties" (46). Whatever one thinks of Godden's approach (which at times requires some stretching to find appropriate examples to support his Marxist interpretation), his identification of the many references to money and exchange in Hemingway's fiction exposed how grounded Hemingway and his characters are in a world dominated by the cash nexus.[3]

Linda Wagner's (1987) second decennial collection, *Ernest Hemingway: Six Decades of Criticism*, is longer than its predecessor and covers more ground. Perhaps making up for a lacuna in the first volume, Wagner included essays from the 1920s and 1930s, and a handful from the 1950s as well, alongside an eclectic mix of more recent work. While still focusing on craftsmanship, this collection, unlike *Five Decades*, emphasized what Wagner called the "newest directions in Hemingway criticism, those in gender-based approaches and those in manuscript study" (6). There was also an attempt to take into account advances in theory. Curiously, though, the focus on women's issues was represented by well-argued and thoughtful essays that defended Hemingway's portraits of women— Charles Nolan's (1984) "Hemingway's Women's Movement" and Robert Crozier's (1984) "The Mask of Death, the Face of Life: Hemingway's Feminique"—but none that represented directly the kind of attack launched against Hemingway by Judith Fetterley and other feminists.

In the same year Wagner, now Linda Wagner-Martin (1987), published *New Essays on "The Sun Also Rises"*. Among its more notable contributions, Wagner-Martin's introduction offered a reading of the novel, while Scott Donaldson's and John Aldridge's contributions sketched out the historical background. Wendy Martin's essay explained the importance of gender relations. In 1990 Scott Donaldson published a similar collection, *New Essays on "A Farewell to Arms"*. The four essays paired traditional critical studies by Paul Smith and Sandra Spanier with new theoretical approaches to Hemingway's fiction: James Phelan's analysis of narratology and Ben Stoltzfus's examination of the novel's language.

Editor Robert W. Lewis's (1990) *Hemingway in Italy and Other Essays* can serve as a touchstone for exploring scholars' interest in Hemingway as the last decade of the twentieth century opened—or, more precisely, of those scholars who seem to have admired Hemingway. Drawn from presentations at the Second International Conference of the Hemingway Society held in Ligano, Italy, in 1986, the seventeen essays are organized into four broad sections. The four essays collected under the rubric

"Hemingway's Women" illustrate the influence of the feminist revolution, although most argue against extremist notions that Hemingway was little more than a chauvinist. Essays in the section on Hemingway's relationship with other writers reveal the critical establishment's continuing interest in issues of influence, although Eugene Kanjo's contribution is really a deconstructionist analysis of *The Sun Also Rises*. Predictably, the volume includes a section on "Hemingway's Texts" in which scholars continue to demonstrate how careful analysis of materials at the Kennedy Library can shed new light on the Hemingway canon. In the final section, "Hemingway in Italy," five scholars explore the importance of place in shaping character, action, and theme in some of Hemingway's novels and stories.

New Collections on the Short Fiction

Four new essay collections focusing on Hemingway's short stories appeared in the closing years of the 1980s. The first, Kenneth Johnston's (1987) *The Tip of the Iceberg: Hemingway and the Short Story*, provided close readings of individual stories and traced Hemingway's development as a writer of short fiction. Collecting essays he had published in journals over the previous fifteen years, Johnston made strong claims that Hemingway is a master—perhaps *the* master among American writers—of this genre. Joseph Flora's (1989) *Ernest Hemingway: A Study of the Short Fiction*, part of a new series sponsored by Twayne to complement their US Authors and English Authors series, extended the work he began in his 1982 study of Hemingway's Nick Adams stories. Working chronologically, Flora explained how, over the course of his career, Hemingway honed his craft both technically and thematically in a genre particularly suited to his spare style and unstated subtext. Flora's volume made available to students a convenient source of criticism—his own, plus excerpts from a half dozen other critics—as well as Hemingway's own comments from his introduction to *The First Forty-nine* and a previously unpublished manuscript on his concept of the short story.

Paul Smith's (1989) *A Reader's Guide to the Short Stories of Ernest Hemingway* appeared two years later. Displaying exceptional familiarity with the Hemingway short story canon (published and unpublished in his lifetime), Smith selected for inclusion in his *Guide* fifty-five stories written between 1921 and 1957. For each of the stories, Smith provided information on composition, publication history, sources and influences, and critical studies. The last section offered summaries of what Smith believed are the most important analyses of each story. This discussion was followed by a list of commentaries, some running for two or more pages of small type. Smith cautioned his readers, however, that some of these are "redundant" (xi). Beyond the scholarly acumen Smith displayed in dealing with individual stories, he was also shrewd and perhaps provocative in challenging the community of Hemingway scholars on the question of the canon for Hemingway's short fiction. His identification of fifty-five stories worthy of discussion is slightly half of the 109 pieces of published and unpublished materials Jackson Benson mentioned in his 1975 essay collection on the short stories. Smith rejected the sketches from *in our time* in his *Guide*, as well as a handful of other works that he believed were either too slight or too diffuse to warrant study. More notable was his rejection of some of the stories Philip Young included in *The Nick Adams Stories* and his relegation of stories published in Peter Griffin's *Along with Youth* to a brief discussion in his introduction.

Published in the same year, Susan Beegel's (1989) *Hemingway's Neglected Short Fiction* brought together twenty-five essays on stories that—relatively speaking—had not received as much critical attention as "The Snows of Kilimanjaro," "The Short Happy Life of Francis Macomber," or "A Clean, Well-Lighted Place." One might quibble about the accuracy of the title, since the volume includes an essay on *The Torrents of Spring* (short in comparison to Hemingway's longer novels, but approaching the length of *The Old Man and the* Sea) and two on "Out of Season," which had been the subject of several earlier critiques. These bring fresh perspectives, and highlight one of the strengths of *Hemingway's Neglected Short Fiction*: the use of new critical theory to illuminate stories that might otherwise have fallen into academic oblivion. Notable among these theory-based essays is Bruce Henricksen's "The Bullfight Story and Critical Theory," a Bakhtinian analysis of the six interchapters in *In Our Time*. Also of significance is Lawrence Broer's "On Writing: A Portrait of the Artist as Nick Adams," which argues that "On Writing" should be considered an independent story (not simply a discarded fragment from "Big Two-Hearted River") in which Hemingway "illuminate[s] the formative process of the generic artist while using art to exorcise personal demons and to reshape a world of failed traditional values" (134). Other contributions, many of the same high caliber as these selections, make Beegel's collection valuable for its insights into aspects of Hemingway's fiction not always discussed by critics focused on so-called major works.

The final important collection of essays devoted to Hemingway's short fiction appeared in 1990. In *New Critical Approaches to the Short Fiction of Ernest Hemingway*, Jackson Benson (1990) compiled a representative sampling of the best critical commentary on the short stories published since he issued *The Short Stories of Ernest Hemingway: Critical Essays* in 1975. In the new volume, Benson gave primacy of place in the new collection to Hemingway's own assessment of short fiction, "The Art of the Short Story," written originally as a preface to a collection of his stories (never published) and printed for the first time in the *Paris Review* in 1981. Benson followed with more than two dozen previously published essays and five written expressly for this volume. Nineteen essays focus on individual stories; six focus on technique. What is truly new about Benson's new volume is the inclusion of eight essays that highlight various critical approaches that had come to prominence in academic circles during the previous two decades with what Benson calls the rise of theory: Debra Moddelmog's on narrative voice in *In Our Time*, Robert Schole's semiotic analysis of "A Very Short Story," Ben Stoltzfus's Lacanian reading of "After the Storm," Oddvar Holmesland's structuralist interpretation of "Cat in the Rain," Susan Beegel's textual analysis of "A Natural History of the Dead," Hubert Zapf's theoretical assessment of the reception of Hemingway's fiction, Nina Baym's feminist critique of "The Short Happy Life of Francis Macomber," and William Braasch Watson's historical-biographical analysis (a term created by Benson) of "Old Man at the Bridge." Like Benson's 1975 volume, *New Critical Approaches* also contains an overview essay; authored by Paul Smith, it provides an informed assessment of the burgeoning criticism in books, chapters, and scholarly journals—although, as Benson observed in 1975, many are repetitive because "so many critics have written while largely unaware of what has already been said" (xvi).

In addition to assembling what some consider an indispensable collection of secondary work on Hemingway's short fiction, which Benson called his "greatest contribution to our literature" (xiv), Benson offered some observations in his introduction that shed light on the status of Hemingway studies in 1990. Speculating on the growth of Hemingway criticism, he suggested that it reflects a rehabilitation of Hemingway's reputation in academic circles. "Antagonism inspired by the Hemingway public persona" had "turned many academics and critics against his work." The animosity had "gradually, nearly three decades after his death in 1961, dissipated," however, and "it is no longer an embarrassment in intellectual circles to be identified as someone who has written about Hemingway, and suddenly those who write about him no longer feel the need to be as defensive of their subject as they once were" (xiv).

Backlash against Feminist Readings

While feminist approaches to literary study became more sophisticated and nuanced between 1970 and the 1990s, Hemingway's attitude toward and treatment of women in his life and his fiction remained controversial and affected study of his work. Commenting on feminist efforts to revise or open up the canon of American literature, Lawrence Buell (1987) suggested that one of the salutary effects of feminist studies may be "to foment reorderings in the prefeminist canon (the demotion of Hemingway, for instance)" (114). In what might be seen as an indirect retort to Buell's dismissal of Hemingway, in "Demoting Hemingway: Feminist

Criticism and the Canon" Robert Merrill (1988) provided a polemical critique of the feminists' attacks on him. Merrill claimed the consistent efforts by feminists to "demote Hemingway" (255), and even have him eliminated from reading lists in American literary studies, were based on willful efforts "to 'see' what is not there" in his work (261). While Merrill claimed to sympathize with the feminists' attempt to revise a traditional, male-oriented reading of a canon made up largely of writing by men, he hoped it was not to be achieved "by misreading as well as demoting writers such as Hemingway" (262). He found a more balanced approach in the work of Annette Kolodny, who did not insist that all the "old masters" be tossed out or that "we should abandon aesthetic questions altogether" (263). Merrill, an old-school formalist and moralist, was unwilling to accept the idea that a work should be judged only as a cultural object, worthy of attention only insofar as it furthers a particular cultural or political agenda.

Similarly, in "Emasculating Papa: Hemingway at Bay" James Tuttleton (1988) excoriated the entire wave of new theorists who would replace the traditional image of Hemingway with a more politically correct version. Tuttleton seemed openly angry with those who dismissed Hemingway's traditionally feminine heroines (Catherine Barkley, Maria) but venerated Brett Ashley for "tak[ing] her pleasure wherever she finds it." Tuttleton attributed such perverted readings of Hemingway to larger forces within the academy; Brett's apparent bisexuality "has been officially endorsed by the Modern Language Association, which has embraced sexual deviancy with all the fervor of a new religion" (141). Tuttleton claimed he was happy to see a renewed focus on gender issues in Hemingway's work because the move highlighted the complexity of Hemingway's character and artistry. He insisted, however, that—despite what Kenneth Lynn and other academics had said—"Hemingway's predilection for masculine activities does not add up to the perversion his detractors have insinuated" (257). To support his argument, he noted that Jeffrey Meyers found no evidence that Hemingway had any "covert homosexual drives or overt homosexual relations" (257). Tuttleton urged those who wanted a more accurate picture of Hemingway to read the biographies written by women who knew him; these were much more even-handed about and appreciative of his masculinity "than one might have gathered from reading the academic lit.-crit" (254). Tuttleton (1992) was equally harsh on feminists in a *New Criterion* essay, claiming "the radical-feminist call for the ejection of Ernest Hemingway from the canon of classic American writers does not seem to have had an effect on American book publishing" (23). Noting that more than twenty critical books on Hemingway and several biographies appeared during the previous decade, he reported—almost gleefully—that "if we turn away from outraged literary criticism by women to biographies of Hemingway (or of his wives) *by* women, we note a curious fact: there is more sympathy for the writer than one might have supposed" (25). Despite efforts by "lesbian ideologists in the academy" to straitjacket Hemingway as "a macho fake and a sexist pig," new facts about his life and work reveal "a complex, deeper and more difficult writer" (23).

While a significant number of scholars in departments of literature, cultural studies, and women's studies tended either to applaud the new, more sensitive and androgynous Hemingway represented in *The Garden of Eden*, those engaged in the new field of men's studies found value in Hemingway's portrayal of the masculine. For example, James Riemer (1987) argued that, if one viewed literary works as "social documents reflecting our society's ideals of masculinity," Hemingway's *The Sun Also Rises* provides a mirror into the changing ideas about masculinity that arose after the First World War (290). Reading the novel as a sociological document also allowed revisionist readings of similar novels that challenge the universalist (and perhaps wrongheaded) notions about manliness that existed until later decades of the century. Of course, as with any critical approach, the renewed focus on the importance of masculinity must be viewed with a degree of skepticism, as some proponents of men's studies seem to go to extreme lengths to glorify Hemingway's portrait of manliness. Witness, for example, the use Harvey Mansfield (2006) makes of *The Old Man and the Sea* in his book *Manliness*, published nearly two decades after Reimer's study. Mansfield claimed that most readers find Santiago's courage in the face of defeat quite admirable, even inspirational. In him, Mansfield said, "we see the definition of man summed up" in this Christlike figure, "the best one of us" (54).

Toward a New Future for Hemingway Studies

If Kenneth Lynn set Hemingway studies askew with his revelations about Hemingway's androgynous tendencies, Mark Spilka (1990) completed the shift in focus, setting a new direction for critical inquiry into Hemingway's work with the publication of *Hemingway's Quarrel with Androgyny*. The product of ten years' research, Spilka's book included previously published work that telegraphed the course he was charting, so the revelations he made did not come as a surprise to Hemingway scholars.[4] In *Hemingway's Quarrel with Androgyny* Spilka created a comprehensive theory to explain why Hemingway lived and wrote as he did. Spilka's psychobiography made use of the work of Baker, Griffin, Meyers, and especially Lynn to document the facts of Hemingway's life and explore his complex personality. Accepting the accuracy of Lynn's assessment regarding the influence Hemingway's immediate family had in promoting notions of androgyny, Spilka explained how Hemingway's early reading combined with the culture of his parents and their community to shape his ideas of heroism—a notion more akin to the muscular Christianity promoted by the Victorians rather than the rough-and-tumble, exclusively male culture of the frontier, which also attracted him. In separate chapters, Spilka explained how six authors influenced Hemingway's ideas about heroism and romance and fostered his interest in androgyny: Frederick Marryat, Rudyard Kipling, John Masefield, Emily Brontë (*Wuthering Heights*), Dinah Mulock Craik (*John Halifax, Gentleman*), and Frances Hodgson Burnett (*Little Lord Fauntleroy*).

Spilka's interpretations of Hemingway's major fiction reinforce his thesis. Androgynous characters take center stage in *The Sun Also Rises* and *A Farewell to Arms*, but fade away in later work as Hemingway elevates masculine ideals at the expense of the feminine. The most important works that provide insight into his continuing fascination—and struggle—with feelings of androgyny, however, are two not published during Hemingway's lifetime: "The Last Good Country" and *The Garden of Eden*. In his long chapter on that novel, Spilka went to great lengths to explain differences between the long manuscript Hemingway left unfinished when he died and the heavily edited text published in 1986. The real keys to understanding Hemingway lay in that manuscript, Spilka insisted, and once one reads it one realizes that, as James Mellow suggested in a 1988 essay, "critics have been reading Hemingway with one eye closed for years." His "peculiar world of men without women was in fact founded on relations with women that we are just now beginning to understand," just as critics are only beginning to understand Hemingway's "sense of himself in relation to women" (quoted in Spilka 1990, 328). This new realization is comforting to some, Spilka noted, but at the same time creates "a kind of growing anxiety" that those who admire Hemingway the man's man "are about to lose him" (327).

From the standpoint of the history of Hemingway criticism, the radical nature of Spilka's assessment is best seen in his comments on Hemingway's "wound." In writing about *A Farewell to Arms*, a novel in which he found numerous examples of androgynous behavior in the protagonists, he asserted that Catherine's death is necessary so that "Frederic/Ernest may regain his maleness." He follows with an important rhetorical question: "What, then, does it mean, at this point, if the 'wound' is androgyny and not, as Philip Young so early established, the actual physical wounds that Hemingway himself sustained at Fossalta?" (219). If Spilka is right, then forty years of Hemingway scholarship becomes immediately questionable—if not incorrect, at least only tangentially accurate. Yet Spilka, who at one point called himself a "neofeminist" (171), did not wish to be seen as too extreme a revisionist, occasionally going to great lengths to challenge some of the more radical feminist readings of Hemingway's fiction.

The community of Hemingway scholars welcomed *Hemingway's Quarrel with Androgyny* with praise not seen in scholarly journals since the publication of Young's 1952 study. *American Literature* reviewer James McKelley (1992) said this "elegant investigation" (177) was "crucial to an even-handed apprehension, and an even-handed appreciation, of its elusive subject" (178). In a long review in *Studies in the Novel*, Leonard Butts (1991) praised Spilka for having "no preconceived psychoanalytical thesis" and avoiding "inherent flaws of contemporary biography and criticism" (509) that assign negative connotations to terms such as lesbianism and homosexuality. Butts found Spilka's reconstruction of Hemingway's childhood "remarkable" (510) and his lengthy argument demonstrating how Hemingway continued to experiment in his fiction throughout his career both convincing and much needed. "This book," Butts concluded, "will undoubtedly open additional avenues of exploration for scholars who are interested in *why* Hemingway wrote what he did" (512). Albert DeFazio (1991), writing in the *Hemingway Review*, called Spilka's case for androgyny as the impetus for Hemingway's vision "compelling" (78). Linda Wagner-Martin (1991) offered an unqualified endorsement of Spilka's book: this "unique study" of Hemingway and his fiction, she said, "considerably enriches the world of Hemingway criticism" (323). Rose Marie Burwell (1992) concurred, trumpeting Spilka's book as "a study that will change our understanding of [Hemingway's] fiction," signaling "the beginning of the end for the kind of obtusely resistant masculine appropriations of Hemingway" and opening "a new era in Hemingway scholarship" (259).

The resistance to the line of studies being pursued by Spilka and others—and especially to the conclusions they were reaching—can be seen in the review of *Hemingway's Quarrel with Androgyny* that appeared in *Studies in Short Fiction*. Gerald Locklin and Charles Stetler (1992) called the book "valuable yet infuriating"—valuable for its "thorough analysis of the significance of certain key works in imprinting on Hemingway the feminine definition of the heroic male, the 'muscular Christian,'" but infuriating because "Spilka's feminism is so doctrinaire" as to make him "incapable of sympathy for traditional male values." Locklin and Stetler believed Spilka should have revealed his biases more clearly to readers. They lamented, too, the possibility that, given the current state of Hemingway studies, *The Garden of Eden* "could, in our age of political correctness, become his most popular work" (138).

Notes

[1] The manuscript runs to 1,500 pages and contains what Rose Marie Burwell (1996) described as a mirror plot, cut from the published version, in which another artist and his female companion serve as counterpoint and reinforcement to the David Bourne–Catherine plot. Jenks's edited version is only 247 pages.

² Certainly Beegel is not the first to show interest in the composition process, but before 1987 Mary Hemingway almost invariably denied permission to quote from Hemingway's manuscripts. As Beegel suggested in her introduction, that prohibition may have been encouraged by Scribner, which saw potential profit in releasing unpublished works. That practice has proven lucrative for the press and Hemingway's heirs. Nonetheless, even before Beegel's study appeared, the Hemingway community was able to get a good sense of what might be learned by careful comparison of manuscripts to finished products from Baker and some of his successor biographers. The best systematic study along these lines that appeared while restrictions were still in place is probably Gerry Brenner's (1982) "Are We Going to Hemingway's Feast?" Brenner outlined the many changes in the published version of *A Moveable Feast* from the manuscript on deposit at the Kennedy Library.

³ Godden is not the first to discuss the importance of money in Hemingway's work. The topic was treated extensively by Claire Sprague (1969), Scott Donaldson (1971), and Richard Sugg (1972). In "The Economics of Survival" Nancy Comley (1979) claimed Hemingway transformed his "personal concern with money into the structure of his fiction," where it manifested itself in "an economic structure of exchange values" (244). Dominant in the early fiction, this theory of "exchange values" that Hemingway used to describe male-female relationships was finally replaced in his later unpublished work by a simpler "exchange system": androgyny (253).

⁴ See, for example, Spilka's 1982 article, "Hemingway and Fauntleroy: An Androgynous Pursuit." At that time, however, unable to work directly with the manuscript of *The Garden of Eden*, Spilka said he doubted if the unpublished novel "represents an advance in Hemingway's grasp and penetration of issues raised in the earlier fiction" (342).

8: "Hemingway": Site for Competing Theories (1991–1999)

WRITING IN 1992, PETER MESSENT (1992b) said that one positive aspect of recent Hemingway criticism was that it had begun the process of replacing the image of him as the poster boy for the all-American male with a more nuanced view of his life and work. No longer was there universal agreement that Hemingway's work presented a monolithic picture of "an existentialist figure" confronting "an indifferent world" in a stoic fashion (270). Messent cited the contributions of feminist criticism, the new psychoanalytic approaches of Kenneth Lynn and Ben Stoltzfus, Spilka's analysis of the influence of androgyny, the efforts of critics (like Messent himself) to rehistoricize him, and the work of structuralists to provide sophisticated analyses of the fiction. A new portrait of Hemingway was emerging, he said, "that of a self-reflexive but also a self-divided writer, deeply concerned with the subject of modernity and its meaning, writing fictions which obsessively explore issues concerning the instability of gender roles, which deny epistemological coherence, and where repetition and renewal exist in dense and unresolvable relations to one another" (275).

An excellent snapshot of the status of Hemingway studies can be seen in editor Frank Scafella's (1991) *Hemingway: Essays of Reassessment*. Although not comprehensive, the volume provides insight into the broad lines of inquiry being pursued after the opening of the Hemingway Papers at the Kennedy Library and the publication of *The Garden of Eden*. Scafella pointed out the importance of these events, noting that Hemingway's unpublished writings present a writer radically different from the one known by his own contemporaries and the scholarly world for nearly six decades. Established and emerging Hemingway scholars, including Scott Donaldson and Michael Reynolds, explain how, even with the new evidence, writing Hemingway's life story remains a complicated task. A group of essays loosely focused around the topic of "psychology" examine Hemingway's life and fiction from various theoretical viewpoints. James Phelan's narratological examination of *A Farewell to Arms* and Ben Stoltzfus's Lacanian reading of *The Old Man and the Sea* illustrate how new approaches to literary study could be used to expose hitherto undiscovered dimensions of Hemingway's oeuvre.

At the same time, while academics found more nuanced ways to interpret Hemingway's achievements, many outside the academy continued to offer almost unqualified praise. For example, in a long *New York Times* article, Frederick Busch (1992) acknowledged that Hemingway was bigoted, chauvinist, reckless, violent, and ungrateful. Nevertheless, "he gave the century a way of making literary art that dealt with the remarkable violence of our time. He listened and watched and invented the language" that allowed modern Americans to "name ourselves." He was "a writer who made the ethos of his fictive world a matter of living or dying." He wrote "because it meant his life to him"—and when he could not write, Busch said with a note of sadness, he took his life because it no longer had meaning.

The books and essays cited above offer a snapshot of the growing divergence of opinion on the "best" way to read Hemingway. This chapter records some of the disparate ways Hemingway has served as a site of critical controversy among scholars working to establish the value of his writing for succeeding generations.

New Biographies

James Mellow's (1992) *Ernest Hemingway: A Life without Consequences* had the advantages and disadvantages of being produced by someone outside the academic community. Mellow spent his career as a reviewer and biographer, producing an award-winning life of Nathaniel Hawthorne and two volumes of a trilogy on the Lost Generation; his biography of Hemingway was meant to conclude this endeavor. Mellow believed Hemingway was one of the greatest writers of what he called America's greatest artistic generation. Despite the curious title, Mellow actually found Hemingway admirable in many ways, particularly in his dedication to his craft. Studiously avoiding direct reliance on the techniques of other biographers, Mellow placed the young Hemingway among the circle of creative people who transformed the arts and created the idea of the Modern. The price Mellow paid for doing so, however, is the creation of a biography heavily weighted toward the years when Hemingway lived and worked in Paris.

Mellow received almost universal praise from newspaper and magazine reviewers. In the *New York Times Book Review* Christopher Lehmann-Haupt (1992) described the book as "fresh and powerfully coherent"; it "stands with the best work done on the writer to date." Gannett News Service reviewer Doris Batliner (1993) and the *Hartford Courant*'s Jocelyn McClurg (1992) gave Mellow's book high marks, as did the *New Leader*'s Brian Morton (1992), who called it "intelligent, engaging, respectful yet not uncritical" (23). *American Spectator* reviewer Donald Lyons (1994) said Mellow's book proved that "intelligent biographies, books that know what art is and what life is, are possible" (73).

Academics were divided in their judgments, however. Among those who admired Mellow's work, Benjamin Anastas (1993) said his "understanding of Hemingway's life and work is singular in its scope and execution" (170). Despite minor reservations, Paul Smith (1993), writing in the *Hemingway Review*, called the book "one of the very best" accounts of Hemingway's early career (83). James Tuttleton (1992) found that, though Mellow's biography reflected current interest in matters of gender, it was nonetheless rich in insight and exceptionally well researched and well written. On the other hand, Edward Galligan (1993) called Mellow a writer "woefully deficient in imagination" (283) who at times "thinks of himself as superior to Hemingway" (284). Robert Murray Davis (1993) dismissed Mellow's book as reductive and devoid of any real new insights, successful only in a financial sense—for Mellow—since "commercial publishers will give big advances for superfluous biographies" (615).

In 1994 Matthew Bruccoli jumped on the biography bandwagon again, enlarging and reissuing a study of the Hemingway-Fitzgerald friendship. Unlike his 1978 *Scott and Ernest: The Authority of Failure and the Authority of Success*, which Bruccoli said was hindered by his inability to quote from Hemingway's letters and his unfortunate decision to forgo footnotes, *Fitzgerald and Hemingway: A Dangerous Friendship* (Bruccoli 1994) offered a detailed, candid examination of a friendship important to both writers even if they were not always willing to admit it. In the 1994 study Bruccoli quoted copiously from letters and other documents to provide firsthand exposure of Hemingway's and Fitzgerald's attitudes toward each other. In some ways Bruccoli used this volume to defend Fitzgerald from charges leveled at him by Hemingway in *A Moveable Feast*, and so did not always paint Hemingway in the best light. Nevertheless, for Hemingway scholars the volume provided another way to appreciate his accomplishments by comparing and contrasting him with the writer who had become for academics his rival for the title of chief architect of the modern American novel.[1]

Like Kenneth Lynn's biography and Mark Spilka's study of Hemingway's fascination with androgyny, Rose Marie Burwell's (1996a) *Hemingway: The Postwar Years and the Posthumous Novels* created significant notice among Hemingway scholars. This "critical biography of Ernest Hemingway's postwar years" (xi) focused on the unpublished work that occupied most of his time and creative energy during the last fifteen years of his life. Burwell argued that the four manuscripts Hemingway left at his death are actually connected and, when read in the order in which he worked on them, provide a kind of metatext of his struggle to come to some understanding of why his creative powers had failed him. Constructed from careful and exhaustive archival research, Burwell's book documented Hemingway's growing realization that the source of his failures lay not in others (not even the women whom he always thought were destructive to creativity) but in himself. Burwell contended that Hemingway suffered from a "double bind of dependency and distrust" (30): he could not live without the company of others (especially women) but was unable to live comfortably with anyone as an equal partner. Much of the angst he suffered was reflected in the unpublished fiction, which Burwell said was in part—but only in part—autobiographical.

Burwell's contributions to Hemingway scholarship are manifold. First, she uncovered new clues to understanding Hemingway's composition process during his later years. Additionally, she offered cogent analysis of the unpublished manuscripts that revealed the extent to which published versions of *Islands in the Stream* and especially *The Garden of Eden* differ from materials in the archives—so much so that, in her view, Hemingway's intent was seriously distorted. She was particularly critical of the editorial process that led to publication of a version of *The Garden of Eden* that overplays Hemingway's exploration of androgyny at the expense of a more basic theme, the process of artistic creation. "Unfortunately," she lamented, editor Tom Jenks excised what Burwell called a "mirroring plot." She believed "the androgynous sexual activities of the three characters that remained in the novel" shifted attention "away from the metafictional nature of the work. The androgyny, presented without adequate context in the published work, became a magnet" and led to numerous misconceived readings (99). Burwell's own interpretation stressed the importance of David Bourne's coming to understand the nature of the creative process and the pitfalls that lie in wait for any serious artist trying to pursue a profession that demands every ounce of talent and focus one can muster.

Burwell wrote approvingly of "the unpublished African book" (129), which she described as another attempt—this time using comic irony—at evaluating the creative process. In this manuscript Hemingway recognized "the heavy and destabilizing burden" that his readers had created for him; his fame, long sought after, was also his curse. Facing that burden became too much for Hemingway to bear, and he found "a temporary reprieve" (148) by turning back to his early years, producing the vignettes that became *A Moveable Feast*. That work, too, caused problems, Burwell said; as he wrote about his experiences in Paris, he came to experience "remorse for what he had done to others" (184). This realization, coupled with problems exacerbated by treatment at the Mayo Clinic, led him to take his own life.

Despite the controversial claims Burwell made throughout her book, the response from the Hemingway community was almost universally positive. Admittedly, Thomas Meier (1997), writing in *American Literature*, believed many would take issue with her "psychological and compositional theories," especially her reading of the four manuscripts as an unfinished tetralogy. On the other hand, in the *Hemingway Review* Carl

Eby (1996) pronounced Burwell's book "required reading for anyone interested in Hemingway's postwar career" (108). Nancy Comley (1998) was pleased that Burwell's exposition of differences between manuscripts and printed versions of posthumous works had allowed scholars to realize "how much they have been cut or manipulated in ways which Hemingway is unlikely to have approved" (454). Jamie Barlowe (1996) believed Burwell had done critics and Hemingway's fan club alike a great service in exposing "Hemingway's self-excuses" (140) so that a proper revaluation of his work could be undertaken. Perhaps the most fulsome tribute was Earl Rovit's (1997); he called Burwell's study "a superb work of scholarship, a sensitive and enlightening piece of criticism" that "jarringly alters the accepted clichés of Hemingway studies" (432).

Critical Books

When in 1980 Michael Reynolds urged scholars to forgo the kind of critical inquiries of Hemingway prevalent in the previous two decades in favor of work based on newly available manuscripts, he might have been imagining a study such as Jacqueline Tavernier-Courbin's (1991) *Ernest Hemingway's "A Moveable Feast": The Making of a Myth*.[2] Tavernier-Courbin's aim was to explain how the book "came into being, trace its conceptualization and the myth surrounding it," "examine the periods of time Hemingway actually devoted to it," and scrutinize "the many posthumous alterations made by his editors and by Mary Hemingway" (x). The larger questions she attempted to answer were ones that have fascinated (or plagued) scholars since this memoir was published: Is it truly autobiographical? How much is fiction?

Combining the talents of the historian and literary scholar, Tavernier-Courbin re-created Paris of the 1920s from sources outside Hemingway's work as well as from *A Moveable Feast*, sorted fact from fiction, and explored the creation of the manuscript that Hemingway left at his death. While casual readers may have little interest in this kind of exhaustive inquiry, Tavernier-Courbin insisted, "for anyone interested in the man behind the book it is important to know what happened to the facts, to the man, and to his text after his death" (110). Possibly the most important conclusion she reached (perhaps not new with her, but in her case well documented) was that "*A Moveable Feast* is not entirely Hemingway's" (182). Mary's heavy hand in reshaping the manuscript ("perhaps misguided rather than ill-intentioned" [182]) changes the impression one gets of several key figures, including Hemingway himself. In Tavernier-Courbin's judgment, "rather than building up Hemingway's positive qualities," the published memoir "diminishes him as a human being" (183).

Peter Messent's (1992a) brief study *Ernest Hemingway* in St. Martin's Press's Modern Novelists series approached him topically and thematically rather than chronologically. Messent examined Hemingway's naturalist style, using as his template the theoretical work of Georg Lukács to produce a view of Hemingway's characters quite different from conventional arguments. Messent argued, "the more his characters try to escape from history into a pure reliance on immediate reaction and direct sensation, the more they have to accept its conditioning presence" (43). Following the lead of contemporary theorists, Messent devotes chapters to examining identity and gender in the fiction, and concludes with one focused on Hemingway's use of place or setting. In his coda on *A Moveable Feast*, he examines Hemingway's aims and achievements as a writer, which he considers substantial.

Wendolyn Tetlow's (1992) *Hemingway's "In Our Time": Lyrical Dimensions* is an extended argument for the organic unity of the story collection. Applying formalist theories of poetic unity developed decades earlier—appropriate, Tetlow asserts, because Hemingway himself described the work as poetry disguised as prose—Tetlow makes the case that, considered as a whole, the completed sequence "presents a precisely patterned succession of emotionally charged units that echo, readjust, and modulate one another, all the while moving toward an organic balance" (98).

Robert Fleming's (1994) *The Face in the Mirror: Hemingway's Writers* tackles an issue that often divided critics of Hemingway: his attitude toward his craft. For those who believe writers should be outside the mainstream critiquing society rather than existing at the center of events, Hemingway was always the "Peck's Bad Boy" of the twentieth century, making himself the most important character he created. Hemingway's more ardent admirers could always counter by pointing to the nonfiction for Hemingway's clear statements on the importance of craftsmanship and the need to present the world one encounters clearly and without prevarication. Fleming acknowledged that the nonfiction provided evidence of Hemingway's commitment to writing, but argued that a better source for understanding Hemingway's continual struggle with his vocation could be found in the fiction. Taking his examples from some of the more widely admired texts (*The Sun Also Rises*; "The Snows of Kilimanjaro") and others less highly thought of (*To Have and Have Not*, for example), Fleming explained how Hemingway's portraits of writers revealed his lifelong struggle to reconcile that role with others that one chooses to play, or is forced to play, in life (father, husband, son, friend). His assessment confirmed what Hemingway's supporters had long believed: that Hemingway fully recognized the toll that writing took on one dedicated to the profession.

Fleming's book also provided an opportunity to see how a book that in succeeding years came to be quoted often by other scholars was received initially by some leading lights in Hemingway studies. Writing in *American Literature*, Allen Josephs (1995) acknowledged the difficulty of the task Fleming set for himself, but asserted that Fleming "fudges on his own system" and "wants it both ways" by discussing *A Moveable Feast* while ignoring earlier nonfiction (160). That criticism pales beside that of Robert Gajdusek (1994), whose longer assessment in the *Hemingway Review* acknowledged the legitimacy of the problem Fleming examined but ran quickly from high praise—"it is always a joy to herald a new critical work that accurately addresses the man and his world" (101)—to sharp critique. Gajdusek accused Fleming of misreading *A Moveable Feast* and holding Hemingway to an impossibly high standard—as evidenced by his criticism of that book "on moral grounds" (106). It is certainly possible that Gajdusek's judgment is accurate, but it is hardly disinterested; one need only read the introduction to his *Hemingway's Paris* (1978) to see how enamored Gajdusek was with the experience Hemingway described in his memoir. Small wonder he was not pleased with Fleming's rather arch critique of that book.

Among works attempting to appropriate Hemingway for extraliterary purposes, none was more determined or provocative than Frank Kyle's (1995) *Hemingway and the Post-Narrative Condition: An Unauthorized Commentary on "The Sun Also Rises"*. Kyle argued that Hemingway's novel was perhaps the first postnarrative work of fiction—narrative in this case referring to the Grand Narratives that have traditionally been the foundation for explaining the meaning of life in Western societies. Asserting that the First World War effectively erased the efficacy of Grand Narratives often expressed in myth, religion, and literature, Kyle argued that in *The Sun Also Rises* Hemingway explored the "philosophical and psychological implications" of the loss of narrative as a controlling ideology for existence. Kyle's book is steeped in philosophical commentary on the ultimate meaning of the experiences undergone by Hemingway's characters. In Kyle's estimation, Hemingway was not simply a great modern; he was the first postmodern American novelist as well.

In another appropriation of sorts, *Reading "The Sun Also Rises": Hemingway's Political Unconscious*, Marc Baldwin (1997) offered an extended Marxist reading of Hemingway's first major novel. Arguing that Hemingway was political without ever acknowledging it, Baldwin demonstrated how the writing style and approach Hemingway took toward his subject linked this novel to the Marxist tradition of total societal critique. The novel celebrates honest work, he insisted, while excoriating capitalism and classism. Published in the same year, Leonard Leff's (1997) *Hemingway and His Conspirators* offered a more commercial view of him. Leff focused on the activities of Scribner, the Hollywood movie industry, and Hemingway himself to transform the virtually unknown writer from Oak Park into an international celebrity. Noting how changes in the publishing industry and the rise of the movies as a principal source of mass entertainment changed both the production and marketing of fiction in America, Leff explained how a network of publishers, reprint houses, photographers, and movie companies catapulted Hemingway into the international spotlight.

Collections of Criticism

In nearly every year during the 1990s a new collection of critical essays on Hemingway and his writing became available to scholars and students, providing easy access to critical commentary. Typical of these is Kenneth Rosen's (1994) *Hemingway Repossessed*, which is held together thematically by what editor Rosen described in the preface as the freedom given to each contributor to demonstrate what Hemingway means for them. As a result, numerous critical methodologies are employed in the sixteen essays, but all approach Hemingway as a major writer who, even in minor work, has touched readers with his insight, command of language, and wide-ranging knowledge of the arts, philosophy, and humor.

Several collections were assembled from papers given at scholarly conferences, such as Rena Sanderson's (1992) *Blowing the Bridge: Essays on Hemingway and "For Whom the Bell Tolls"*. Contributors explore Hemingway's involvement with and use of the Spanish Civil War as the source of his novel, his attitude toward women, and his commitment to his vocation as a writer. The novel is the subject of essays employing deconstructive analysis and psychoanalytic criticism, as well as ones exploring the importance of the Myth of the Frontier in Hemingway's life and writing. The introductory essay by Kurt Vonnegut provides insight into ways Hemingway influenced succeeding generations.

Editor George Monteiro's (1994) volume of previously published essays on *A Farewell to Arms* collects reviews that appeared shortly after the novel was published and ten studies published between 1951 and 1994. James Nagel's (1995) *Critical Essays on Ernest Hemingway's "The Sun Also Rises"* includes several initial reviews of the novel, nine previously published essays, and three commissioned for this collection. Curiously, though these essays were written over a span of sixty years, the approaches taken by contributors do not vary widely, except for recognition of the influence of feminism during the previous two decades on readings of Hemingway's fiction. A year later, in *Ernest Hemingway: The Oak Park Legacy*, Nagel (1996) collected eleven essays from scholars who participated in a 1993 conference held in Hemingway's birthplace. Focusing on the importance of Oak Park as a laboratory for developing Hemingway's values and influencing his style and subject matter, contributors offered new interpretations of a number of Hemingway's most popular works as well as some unpublished ones.

The title of Frederic Svoboda and Joseph Waldmeir's (1995) *Hemingway: Up in Michigan Perspectives* is slightly misleading, because only nine of the twenty-four essays deal with Hemingway's life in Michigan or the stories he set there. Svoboda and Waldmeir's book gathered material from a Who's Who of Hemingway scholars attending a 1991 conference; their observations on Hemingway's accomplishments and failures provide an accurate, insightful snapshot of Hemingway's reputation at the time. Of special note, however, is Mark Spilka's withering riposte directed at feminist critiques of Hemingway.[3] Spilka's argument was based on his belief that the best way to understand Hemingway's fiction is to understand the man who wrote it—a position shared by many Hemingway critics long after biographical and psychological criticism had given way to more fashionable approaches to literature.

Among collections devoted to the study of Hemingway's fiction, Scott Donaldson's (1996) *The Cambridge Companion to Ernest Hemingway* is distinguished for the breadth of coverage and insights of contributors, almost all of whom are authors of well-received books on Hemingway. Donaldson's introductory essay, "Hemingway and Fame," offers an excellent synopsis of how Hemingway's pursuit of notoriety both enhanced and cheapened his status as a writer. Donaldson believed Hemingway's stories and novels had "managed to outlive the burden of celebrity" (477) and were likely to remain a part of the American literary canon for some time to come. Other contributors provided literary analysis of individual works, reviewed important events in Hemingway's writing life, and consider him in light of new critical interest in matters of gender and politics. Particularly noteworthy was Kenneth Kinnamon's assessment of Hemingway's politics, a subject little discussed except by Marxists. Susan Beegel's excellent assessment of his critical reputation, cited in the introduction to the present study, rounded out a volume that, at the time of its publication, succeeded as well as any collection can in explaining its subject to the academic community.

Linda Wagner-Martin's (1998) third decennial collection, *Ernest Hemingway: Seven Decades of Criticism*, offered an excellent snapshot of the expanded interests of critics at century's end. No longer confined to matters of theme and technique, many examined Hemingway's work from broad cultural perspectives and offered new ways of reading the fiction. As she had done in previous volumes, Wagner-Martin included a sampling of work from earlier decades, such as Gertrude Stein's 1923 review of *Three Stories and Ten Poems* and D. H. Lawrence's 1927 review of *In Our Time*. The majority of the selections are essays and chapters published during the 1980s and 1990s. Broad category groupings recall those of earlier collections, but individual essays have a decidedly contemporary focus: gender issues dominate, while ethical criticism and matters of race are represented: Amy Lovell Strong's "Screaming through Silence: The Violence of Race in 'Indian Camp' and 'The Doctor and the Doctor's Wife,'" Thomas Strychacz's "Dramatization of Manhood in

Hemingway's *In Our Time*," and Debra Moddelmog's "Reconstructing Hemingway's Identity: Sexual Politics, the Author, and the Multicultural Classroom" are a sampling of the new emphasis. An entire section was devoted to essays on the posthumously published *The Garden of Eden*. Six essays on the novel, including Kathy Willingham's "Hemingway's *The Garden of* Eden: Writing with the Body," Carl Eby's "'Come Back to the Beach Ag'in, David Honey!': Hemingway's Fetishization of Race in *The Garden of Eden* Manuscripts," and Mark Spilka's "Hemingway's Barbershop Quintet: *The Garden of Eden* Manuscript" suggested that the stricture placed by earlier critics on writing about works not finished by the author during his lifetime (a practice noted by Wagner-Martin in *Five Decades*) had been happily abandoned.

A sense of humor (or resignation?) shows in Wagner-Martin's titles for sections of her book: one is "The Inevitable Consideration of Hemingway's Style," in which Wagner-Martin reached back into the 1970s to choose two of the four selections. A second, "The Inevitable Consideration of Hemingway's Biography," includes an excerpt from a standard biographical study, Michael Reynolds's *Hemingway: The 1930s*, but also reprints essays by Susan Beegel on the effect that undiagnosed hemochromatosis, a disease that if undetected can cause serious depression, may have had on Hemingway's life, and Wagner-Martin's assessment of Hemingway's relationship with Gertrude Stein from her book on Stein. Another important observation by Wagner-Martin reflected the changing nature of Hemingway scholarship: with few exceptions, the criticism in earlier volumes was composed by men, whereas in *Ernest Hemingway: Seven Decades of Criticism*, 40 percent of the essays are by women. Apparently after a dip in popularity with the opposite sex, Hemingway was once again drawing interest from women.

New work filled two volumes published in 1998. Editor Paul Smith's (1998) *New Essays on Hemingway's Short Fiction* is informed by study of the manuscripts available in the Kennedy Library. In fact, Smith justified the publication of his volume by noting that when Hemingway's manuscripts and unpublished letters were opened to scholars, "a cottage industry was born": new, revisionist readings that pointed out flaws in published versions of Hemingway's work, but more importantly, flaws in our understanding of Hemingway, who was "more literate and complex than we suspected" (1). *French Connections: Hemingway and Fitzgerald Abroad*, edited by veteran scholars J. Gerald Kennedy and Jackson Bryer (1998), contains seventeen essays on American modernism's two greatest writers. Focusing on works by Hemingway and Fitzgerald from the 1920s to the 1940s, contributors examined the lasting effects these writers had on each other as a result of their years spent in Paris, and the influence Paris had on each of them. As George Wickes said in the collection's first essay, Paris was "the right place at the right time" (12) for both.

Robert Fleming's (1999) work in selecting and editing papers from the 1996 International Hemingway Conference resulted in the publication of a provocative collection of ecocritical commentary, *Hemingway and the Natural World*, a volume that established incontrovertibly the importance of place and environment in Hemingway's fiction. Author and conservation activist Terry Tempest Williams's keynote address, a tribute to Hemingway as a figure who exerted a strong influence on her, set the tone for many of the seventeen essays that explore Hemingway's use of animals, natural settings, and native peoples. Outliers in the volume—Robert Stoneback's examination of the importance of "the road" (the peripatetic) in Hemingway, Joseph Flora's analysis of the rather obsessive animosity felt toward Hemingway by Idaho writer Vardis Fisher, and John Bittner's extensive examination of the press coverage given to Hemingway's death—helped flesh out the overarching notion of what the West meant to Hemingway. It is no surprise that, reviewing the volume for the *Hemingway Review*, Larry Grimes (2000) called it "a must-read collection of essays" (104) that issues "a call to work" (108) for Hemingway scholars to continue exploring the importance of nature and place in the Hemingway canon. The importance of place was once again a topic at the 1998 conference, where distinguished geographer Ann Buttimer (2000) delivered a paper on the sense of place in Hemingway's fiction that would be published in *Cultural Encounters with the Environment*, a collection of essays on cultural geography.

By the end of the century, even novels that were routinely judged Hemingway's weakest were receiving renewed attention from scholars. Witness, for example, Toni Knott's (1999) collection of essays, *One Man Alone: Hemingway and "To Have and Have Not"*. Although half the book consists of essays by Knott, other contributors confirmed her judgment that the novel has merits often overlooked by those too easily willing to dismiss it either for its overly macho protagonist or its ham-handed approach to socialist themes.

Hemingway and Modernism

In a sophisticated analysis of American writers who "acted on the deep conviction that the principal obstacles to real understanding of experiential reality were the culture's certified knowledge and the habits and techniques by which that knowledge was produced" (xi), Ronald Martin (1991) singled out Hemingway as "the most serious knowledge destroyer" of all the moderns (216). Martin said Hemingway was convinced that "civilization's judgments and principles are bankrupt" (219). Knowledge and wisdom could only be acquired through disciplined behavior—hence, the importance of the code in Hemingway's writings. In Martin's assessment, Hemingway is less the "dumb ox" described by

Wyndham Lewis than a thoughtful analyst of human behavior who consciously rejects mainstream ideology and epistemology.

In his study of the importance of the past to the modernists, Herbert Schneidau (1991) went out of his way to show how much Hemingway depended on his mentors, especially Sherwood Anderson, for the development of his unique style. Schneidau gave him considerable credit, however, for changing the course of American literature. Whether there was an autobiographical element to Hemingway's fictional characters was ultimately not relevant, Schneidau said; whatever the cause, Hemingway made Freudian "repetition-compulsion a standard part of twentieth-century psychic imagery as well as of its stylistic armory" (185). Schneidau insisted, however, that Hemingway's fascination with the past was something he learned from Anderson; but unlike Anderson, who seemed to want to recapture the past, Hemingway was intent on exorcising it.

In *Authority and Speech*, a study of the way speech functions in American fiction, Louise Barnett (1993) described Hemingway as the quintessential example of the modernist writer. Unlike his modernist predecessors or his contemporaries, Hemingway rejected the notion that one can achieve self-actualization through immersion in society. His characters—especially in the early fiction—all come to some sense of an integrated self only by becoming alienated. As a result, Barnett argued, in a novel like *The Sun Also Rises*, "both responsibilities of ordinary speech—that language mean something and that this meaning be communicated—are atrophied" (150). The novel exhibits a "dialectic of discourse" in which "the felt necessity of imposing discipline on speech wars with the desire to express and communicate" (150–51).

J. Gerald Kennedy's (1993) long chapter on Hemingway in *Imagining Paris* traced the impact that the city and its writing community had on the young Hemingway. Kennedy also traced vestiges of Hemingway's Paris memories in the later fiction (including *The Garden of Eden*) and critiques the vision of Paris—and Hemingway—presented in *A Moveable Feast*. In his discussion, Kennedy makes an important observation about technique that helps explain how his work should be read: "His omission of exposition—the so-called 'iceberg' theory by which he submerged meaningful information—produced an almost systematic displacement of emotional content onto the terrain of fictive experience" (111).

In Malcolm Bradbury's (1995) *Dangerous Pilgrimages*, a book that examines the cross-pollination of imagination and myth between Europe and America, Hemingway's years in Europe between 1921 and 1926 become the touchstone for examining the way American expatriates were influenced by life in Paris. Hemingway was also a major subject of Donald Pizer's (1996) *American Expatriate Writing and the Paris Movement*, in which Pizer argued that the theme of *A Moveable Feast* is a "variation on the myth of the fortunate fall" (27). In Paris Hemingway gained his potency as a writer but at the expense of personal happiness, such that in his view Paris is the lost Eden. In *The Sun Also Rises*, the "mythic Paris" (75) serves as creative inspiration for the novel, even though many scenes take place elsewhere.

Marc Dolan (1996) admitted that *A Moveable Feast* is a highly reconstructed account of Hemingway's early years in Paris, a "mythic account of his literary apprenticeship" (80) that shares affinities with much of his fiction, particularly *In Our Time*. These Paris sketches developed two important themes: "the steady growth of an artist's talents" and the simultaneous "slow death of an artist's marriage" (81). Dolan's sympathetic reading even offered an explanation for one of the most distasteful scenes, Hemingway's "cheap shot at Fitzgerald's feelings of genital inadequacy." Dolan read this incident metaphorically, suggesting that Hemingway's "main concern is with the labor of art and the need for discipline," a subtler comment on Fitzgerald's "feelings of *aesthetic* inadequacy" (76).

In Christopher Knight's (1995) *The Patient Particulars*, a study reliant on the theoretical work of Paul de Man, Hemingway's *In Our Time* is used as a representative text of modernist literature. Knight suggested this new form of writing differed from earlier forms, collectively standing as an "end of a way of seeing, of thinking about the world as something out there, waiting to be discovered and redeemed," filled with "interpretative frustrations" that "signal the beginning of a way of being in the world in which the relation between mind and object is construed as less oppositional than as interlaced" (13).

Hemingway's debt to other writers is the subject of Jonathan Quick's (1999) chapter on him in *Modern Fiction and the Art of Subversion*. Calling Hemingway "one of the most literary writers of the modern period" (129), Quick traced his use of models in a number of important works: the *Aeneid* as a model for *A Farewell to Arms*, the *Inferno* as inspiration for *Across the River and Into the Trees*, and the New Testament as the source for *The Old Man and the Sea*. "At its strongest," he said, "Hemingway's fiction displays a radical reworking of received narrative patterns; in decline, it is absorbed by them" (129). Where Quick crosses swords with other critics is in his unwillingness to accept Kenneth's Lynn's claim that Hemingway's insistence on treating writing as a contest revealed "some deep emotional disorder." He argued that doing so tends to "oversimplify the complex, ambiguous motives of a man" set on "making his way—sometimes using elbows and fists—in the society of writers of his day" (131).

Studies of Gender and Race

Although some softening seemed to be occurring in feminists' views of Hemingway by the beginning of the 1990s, Nina Baym's (1992) provocative critique of "The Short Happy Life of Francis Macomber," first published in Jackson Benson's 1990 essay collection but revised for Baym's own volume *Feminism and American Literary History*, continued the feminist assault launched in the 1970s. Baym pointed out that, as early as the 1920s, critics had commented on Hemingway's dismissive treatment of women; what feminists had done, she says, is expose Hemingway's values "as defective rather than admirable" (71). Recognizing that "the technique of scanning men's writings for evidence of male chauvinism has largely vanished from feminist criticism" in the 1990s, Baym insisted that the diminishment of this approach to reading literature by men did not obligate feminists "to read Hemingway sympathetically merely to make him acceptable to an audience that is aware of the policing functions of hostile feminist portraiture" (72). Baym offered a reading of Hemingway's story that emphasizes the play of different voices. Paying close attention to details of the text, Baym entered the argument as to Margot Macomber's actions and motives. Nevertheless, Margot ends up accepting her role as a submissive wife, a condition that remains irritating and unacceptable. The story provides "an indoctrination" into a "self-styled male ethos"—as Baym showed by citing an example from a classroom discussion in which a young female student who offers a nonstandard interpretation of the story is immediately silenced by a male teacher (80).

Until recently one could find relatively few commentaries on Hemingway by critics interested in questions of race; however, Toni Morrison's (1992) assessment in *Playing in the Dark* provides a striking example of how his work was often dismissed as insensitive to African Americans. Focusing on *To Have and Have Not* and *The Garden of Eden*, Morrison exposed Hemingway's unconscious use of stereotypes that ignore the humanity of his African American figures (and his African ones, as Morrison notes in passing). Instead, African Americans are portrayed as servants, helpers, or, most appropriately in the context of Hemingway's fiction, as nurses—those who aid wounded heroes without calling attention to themselves. In a brilliant analogy certain to have resonated with her contemporaries, Morrison described Hemingway's African Americans as "Tontos" whose roles are "to do everything possible to serve the Lone Ranger without disturbing his indulgent delusion that he is indeed alone" (82).

By far the topic dominating critical commentary during the 1990s was Hemingway's fascination with androgyny. In a somewhat less ambitious fashion than Spilka, J. Gerald Kennedy (1991) explored the issue in "Hemingway's Gender Trouble." Looking for imaginative links between *A Moveable Feast* and *The Garden of Eden*, Kennedy called the treatment of androgyny in these texts "contradictory" (193). While generic differences offered a possible explanation, Kennedy believed that both works "display an interesting tension between revelation and concealment, between self-recrimination and self-exculpation" (194). Quoting at length from an unpublished manuscript fragment, Kennedy argued that the memoir contains "traces of gender ambivalence" (201). Consequently, when taken together, the unpublished fragment, memoir, and novel "disclose the intensity of Hemingway's preoccupation with androgyny and the persistence of his fantasies about crossing the gender line" (207).

Shorter than Spilka's *Hemingway's Quarrel with Androgyny* but no less revolutionary in its critique of Hemingway's fiction, Nancy Comley and Robert Scholes' (1994) *Hemingway's Genders: Rereading the Hemingway Text* created a postmodernist reading of what the authors called "the Hemingway Text," by which they mean "a cultural matrix that we share with Hemingway" (x). Concerned principally with "the representation of human character in Hemingway's writing" (11), Scholes and Comley demonstrated that beneath the macho image Hemingway projected lay a sensitive artist whose attitudes were decidedly more complex than previously acknowledged. Hemingway worked with relatively few types of male and female figures, they argued, modifying them constantly to try to capture the essence of "human sexuality." For Hemingway, who always touted his desire to write truthfully, "the bond between sexuality and truth" was "a matter of the primitive or primal" (77). Understandably, his most powerful fiction emerged from his struggles to represent sexuality truthfully. Comley and Scholes placed great emphasis on *The Garden of Eden*, but they discovered Hemingway's vacillating attitudes in many other works as well, hints that reveal psychological distress that is not simply a manifestation of an oedipal complex. In exploring Hemingway's interest in homoeroticism, Comley and Scholes showed that Hemingway was "much more interested" in matters of sexuality (and bisexuality) "than has usually been supposed," and "much more sensitive and complex in his consideration of them" (144). However, while the authors' concluding claim that "the Hemingway you were taught about in high school is dead" (146) may be an accurate assessment for the critical community, much written during the next twenty years would make one wonder if the death of the macho Hemingway was, as Mark Twain announced after learning about his own supposed demise, a bit premature.

In fact, not everyone in the scholarly community found *Hemingway's Genders* as revolutionary as its authors argued. While Quentin Miller (1996) considered the book "a valuable introduction" to the topic of Hemingway's attitudes toward gender (260), Jamie Barlowe (1994), writing in the *Hemingway Review*, suggested that Comley and Scholes overstated their case and ignored much recent scholarship that accounts for some, if not all, of the discoveries in their study. Stephen Clifford (1997) said the Hemingway they sought to bury has been dead for thirty-five years, and the "nuevo Hemingway" they celebrated was often obscured "behind their own codification of the biographical authority and its influence over the fiction" (173). The divergence of opinion was explained rather sardonically by Rose Marie Burwell (1996b), who called *Hemingway's Genders* "a little jewel of a book" (259) that opens up new ways of looking at Hemingway and provides a new methodology for examining his writings. Of course, she observed, it was likely to upset those trained in old-school critical methods who simply cannot accept new ways of looking at canonical authors and texts. Her prediction was borne out by the reaction of many Hemingway fans to the appearance of Christopher Lehmann-Haupt's (1994) review. He actually had much good to say about *Hemingway's Genders*, calling Comley and Scholes's study "richly rewarding" (C21). But many traditionalists may not have gotten past the headline, no doubt written (as most newspaper headlines are) by an editor wishing to generate readership by creating controversy: "Was Hemingway Gay?"

One can see how far Hemingway's reputation had shifted from the "man's man" image predominant from the 1920s through the 1960s in Nancy McCampbell Grace's (1995) *The Feminist Male Character in Twentieth-Century Literature*. Grace wrote extensively about the protagonists of *The Sun Also Rises* and *The Garden of Eden* as examples of feminized males—characters whose sex, a biological fact, may be defined but whose gender, a cultural construct, is amorphous and never clearly fixed. More remarkable, perhaps, is Grace's claim that of the four authors whose works she discusses—Hemingway, James Joyce, Saul Bellow, and Jack Kerouac—Hemingway "took the greatest risks when he dared to explore the psychic and social dimensions of gender reformation in *The Garden of Eden*," a novel that illustrates his "complex and conflict-ridden resolutions of the complexities created by the feminized male" (37).

In another essay using a blend of gender and ecological criticism, Louise Westling (1996) saw Hemingway fighting against gender inclusiveness in favor of an American male myth that promotes individualism and confrontation. Westling looked to biography and psychology to explain why Hemingway may have felt as he did about women's role in society and the importance of the natural world as a place where men tested their mettle. Concentrating on stories set in Upper Michigan, she explored "the question of their power and the values they encode" (89). She described Nick Adams as "a battered American Adam" who "needs to be restored by the wholesome American landscape in a series of carefully controlled rituals that stop his mind from working on the past" (92). Hemingway's male-centered texts and his refusal to acknowledge the feminine qualities of the landscapes in which his protagonists are placed make it probable that "most women" will not "see ourselves in Hemingway's encoding of subjectivity" (100).

In her sociological investigation of the woman hunter, Mary Zeiss Stange (1997) used several of Hemingway's African stories to illustrate her point that, traditionally, women had been excluded from hunting as "a necessary counterpart to their social and psychological subordination to men" (57). Hemingway was never able to reconcile the notion that a woman could be a good hunter (not even with his fourth wife, who seemed fairly adept at the sport), because psychologically "the mere notion that a woman could handle a gun" was "just too unsettling to patriarchally constructed masculinity" (60).

Stephen Clifford's (1998) reading of Hemingway's early fiction in *Beyond the Heroic "I": Reading Lawrence, Hemingway, and Masculinity* relied on narrative theories of Teresa de Lauretis that focus attention on ways readers engender texts. Clifford wished to get beyond biographical readings, which he said continue to plague Hemingway criticism and get in the way of understanding Hemingway's texts *as* texts independent of their author. Though he claimed to be revising a wide range of readings, Clifford's repeated target was the interpretation of Hemingway advanced by Comley and Scholes in *Hemingway's Genders*, which Clifford believed misreads the Hemingway canon by focusing on traditional understandings of gender.

Other Critical Approaches

A survey of some of the other critical articles and chapters on Hemingway's writing published during the 1990s reveals how he was being appropriated to illustrate a wide variety of critical—and political—positions. For example, Harley Oberhelman (1994) traced Hemingway's influence on the Colombian writer Gabriel García Márquez, whose acknowledged interest in Hemingway was evident in a series of articles Márquez wrote over four decades. In "Bulls, Balls, and Booze," John Crowley (1994) examined the role drinking plays in defining characters in *The Sun Also Rises*—and in shaping Hemingway's life, which Crowley described as the downward spiral of an alcoholic. Warner Berthoff (1994) provided a brief, positive assessment of Hemingway's place in American literary history, offering historical as well as technical reasons for his early success and his inability to sustain the level of his early achievements in later work. Scott Donaldson's (1995) essay in J. Gerald Kennedy's *Modern American Short Story Sequences* outlined the publication history of *In Our Time* and offered cogent suggestions for reading the loosely connected sequence of Nick Adams stories. Jopi Nyman (1997, 1998) demonstrated how Hemingway made use of the hard-boiled tradition of American fiction in *To Have and Have Not* to explore themes of tragedy and change.

One of the more intriguing readings of the Hemingway canon is Kim Moreland's (1996) in *The Medievalist Impulse in American Literature*.

Moreland claimed Hemingway's "hard-boiled approach disguises his desperate affection for medieval traditions, traditions that no longer work" in his era (162). Though Moreland found the most striking parallels (and contrasts) between Nick Adams and the medieval knight, she also highlighted veiled allusions to medievalism in almost every major work by Hemingway—including "titles that resonate with chivalric suggestiveness" (175)—revealing how Hemingway used medieval chivalry and medieval warfare as an idealistic contrast to the horrors of modern conflict. She argued, too, that much of what critics had dismissed as hopelessly idealistic love in Hemingway's works was actually based on ideals of courtly love.

In an article published in *Literature and Psychology*, Pamela Boker (1995) argued for a reappraisal of *For Whom the Bell Tolls*, which she said had fallen in critics' estimation. Boker claimed that most of Hemingway's fiction focuses on a male protagonist "who strives toward masculine individuation" by associating with higher ideals or engaging in traditional male activities. In *For Whom the Bell Tolls* Hemingway succeeds in "work[ing] through his hero's separation-individual process," making the novel "psychologically, if not artistically, integrated, and by the strength of the coherent psychological narrative, we are given new reason to judge the novel as a serious fictional enterprise" (85). A year later Boker (1996) made Hemingway a principal focus of *The Grief Taboo in American Literature*, a book in NYU Press's newly inaugurated Literature and Psychoanalysis series. Boker's thesis is that American male writers often work under a taboo that prevents them from expressing genuine grief in their work, especially grief over the loss of parents. Among the best American writers, Hemingway's "commitment to the taboo against grief was perhaps the most dedicated, artistically refined, and ultimately self-devastating of any figure in American literature" (166). Employing techniques of neo-Freudian critical analysis, Boker explained how his constant refusal to come to grips with grief over the loss of his parents—and with the internal turmoil caused by his relationship with his domineering mother and inadequate father—led him into a state of retarded adolescence that also drew him to create his famous style that features the "art of repression" (249).

Michael Kowaleski (1993) titled his chapter on Hemingway in *Deadly Musings: Violence and Verbal Form in American Fiction* "The Purity of Execution in Hemingway's Fiction"—perhaps to signal his disdain for those who question either Hemingway's talent or his motives. One by one, he picked off those who form the "long tradition of disliking Hemingway's work" (131). He asserted that "conceptions of Hemingway's 'masculine' style often have more to do with his biographical posturings than with his prose" (133). Kowaleski provided a bevy of examples to show that Hemingway was a gifted stylist, verbally adept and capable of constructing prose appropriate for any situation. Unfortunately, he said, too many critics come to Hemingway with predetermined attitudes; unless those are dealt with, it may not be possible to "describe the full range of his fictional abilities" (161).

Perhaps no one has been a stronger defender of Hemingway's aesthetic (or his character and moral outlook) in the past twenty years than Albert Murray, the African American novelist and critic of jazz and American culture. In *The Blue Devils of Nada* Murray (1996) offered a sweeping panegyric to Hemingway's artistry, carefully outlining the components of an aesthetic built on the principles of knowing a subject well, writing carefully so as to express one's true feelings about it, and investing personal experience with the attention that makes it representative of the human condition at large. What set Murray's celebration apart from others—besides his ability to find in Hemingway's nonfiction statements that corroborate judgments gleaned from reading the fiction—was his castigation of intellectuals who in his view simply misunderstand what Hemingway was about. Murray insisted that "facts just simply do not support those intellectuals who charge Hemingway with being preoccupied with the hard-boiled nonreflective hero" (188). Most intellectuals, "more interested in substantiating their own theories than in coming to terms with actuality" (191), perpetuated wrongheaded stereotypes, having convinced themselves that the Hemingway hero lives by an outmoded and stultifying code that "represents a fundamental evasion of intellectual responsibility" (200–201). The facts as Murray saw them are simple: "The sentiments of a typical Hemingway hero, like those of Hemingway himself, are almost always those of a man involved with the *refinement* of experience" (200).

Murray believed Hemingway's fiction "always expresses essentially the same fundamental sense of life as that which underlies the spirit of the blues" (179–80). While not overstating his case, Murray bestowed on Hemingway "honorary Negrohood" (180), pointing out how close his attitude toward life was mirrored in African American music (before the age of rap, apparently). In Murray's judgment, "nobody was ever more firmly dedicated to the accurate definition of the eternal condition of man" than Hemingway, and "certainly no twentieth-century U.S. writer ever stated the fundamental issues of human existence more comprehensively" (219).

A provocative chapter on Hemingway closes Michael Boardman's (1992) *Narrative Innovation and Incoherence*, a study of narrative innovation as a reflection of "changes in an author's worldview over the course of a career" (ix). Boardman's examination of Hemingway's career during the 1930s provided an explanation of what happened to the highly successful author of *The Sun Also Rises* and *A Farewell to Arms* that prompted him to produce nonfiction works that cost him a good part of his readership and led critics to question if he had spent his creative powers. During this decade, Hemingway attempted to answer critics' (and friends') charges that his work was not socially relevant. Boardman identified the power of Hemingway's early work in his ability to appeal to readers' shared assumptions about "the omnipresence of suffering" (159). When Hemingway tried to deal with specific social issues directly, his style changed and his appeal seemed diminished. In another study of narrative, *Narrative as Rhetoric,* James Phelan (1996a, 1996b) explored the rhetorical qualities of narrative in Hemingway's fiction. In a chapter reprinted from Scott Donaldson's (1990) collection on the novel, Phelan looked at Hemingway's handling of voice in *A Farewell to Arms* to explain "how voice contributes to the novel's progression" (59). He demonstrated that the novel "traces a coherent process of growth and change in Frederic Henry that culminates, tragically and ironically, in the moment of his greatest loss" (60). In a second chapter originally published in the *Hemingway Review,* he asked how a study of rhetorical theory may help illuminate Hemingway's methods and confirm his artistry—and how Hemingway's works could be used as examples to explain the way a theory of narrative functions.

In her study of the ideological underpinnings of omniscient narration, *Authorial Divinity in the Twentieth Century,* Barbara Olson (1997) examined Hemingway's work to see how he handled the task of what he himself called "writing like God" (quoted in Olson, 37). Olson's careful readings of several stories explained how Hemingway developed confidence in using third-person narration. She was not hesitant to challenge earlier critiques (like Susan Lanser's interpretation of narration in "The Killers") when she felt Hemingway had been misjudged. The most daring assertion Olson makes, however, is that Hemingway's "nagging faith in God" (48) eventually convinced him that he needed the "stability of a knowing divine presence" in his world (51). Though he never fully reconciled himself to writing from an omniscient point of view, both *For Whom the Bell Tolls* and *The Old Man and the Sea* reflected a new attitude toward suffering and belief not present in his earlier work. Especially in this latter work Olson detected "the consolation of a divine power's immanent presence, however vaguely defined" (63).

It is no surprise that Hemingway would figure somewhat prominently in cultural studies of the twentieth century. David Minter (1994) offered a tribute to him in *A Cultural History of the American Novel,* a sweeping analysis of "the structures and procedures of society as well as the structures and procedures of imagining" between the 1880s and 1940 (xiii). Minter found Hemingway the best example of the postwar generation that discovered loss and alienation were their principal inheritance from the conflict. Consequently, he focused "his life and his art" on "grappling with the task" of being a distinguished writer and a "citizen of society," knowing all the while that "a not ignoble failure" was the best he could hope for (137). Convinced that the public persona was crucial to Hemingway's attempt to make his art meaningful, Minter explained how he "mov[ed] in harm's way" (138) all his life to mirror what he was producing in his art: a chronicle of death that inevitably wins in the end. "Nothing Hemingway ever wrote"—not even works that display a certain "wit and nostalgia," like *A Moveable Feast*—"wholly escapes" the sense of "darknesses born of fear" (140). Minter believed Hemingway's originality lay in "forging relations, between writer and work and between reader and writer, in which care and restraint become necessary for the preservation of our shared humanity." Hence, his distinctive style was "a stronghold against formidable forces that threatened to inculcate a sense of disillusionment and cynicism and obliterate a sense of hope and purpose" (141–42).

Hemingway and his work also figured prominently in Paul Civello's (1994) *American Literary Naturalism and Its Twentieth-Century Transformations*. Civello argued that naturalism, a literary movement often identified as historically bound to the late nineteenth century, was actually carried into the next century by a number of authors, including Hemingway. Civello identified elements of *A Farewell to Arms* and *The Sun Also Rises* that reveal Hemingway's appropriation of the ideology and techniques of literary forebears who saw the world as governed by impersonal forces. In a complementary study, Stanley Corkin (1996) placed Hemingway in the realist tradition by showing his ties not only to literary figures such as Sherwood Anderson and Gertrude Stein, but also to realist movements in other art forms, notably the cinema. Corkin argued that Hemingway's *In Our Time* could be linked with D. W. Griffith's *The Birth of a Nation* as works of art that attempt to objectify experience and eliminate extraneous emotions from the presentation of factual detail.

New studies of the impact of the First World War on Hemingway's writing achieved prominence during the decade. In her deconstructive critique of *A Farewell to Arms* in *Representing War: Form and Ideology in First World War Narratives*, Evelyn Cobley (1993) relied heavily on the spadework of Michael Reynolds to point out how Hemingway's imaginative re-creation of historical events served as a literary device rather than a realistic portrait of warfare. The clever use of realist details obscured the ideological framework of a novel where realism and romanticism collide. The novel illustrated better than almost any other that "descriptive detail assists less in the reproduction of the spontaneously given than in the production of ideologically conflicting attitudes" (61). More conventional in approach than Cobley, in *Writing after War*, a study of the elements of war literature that turn an ugly reality into beautiful art, John Limon (1994) explored Hemingway's love-hate relationship with combat, demonstrating how the three novels that reflect his feelings about warfare—*The Sun Also Rises, A Farewell to Arms,* and *For Whom the Bell Tolls*—reflected Hemingway's modernist approach, using the perfection of style as a means of rejecting the chaos of the battlefield.

Marxist critics remained interested in Hemingway's fiction as well. In *The Politics and Poetics of Journalistic Narrative,* Phyllis Frus (1994) offered an unconventional examination of Hemingway's career as a journalist, arguing that neither he nor others who began their careers as journalists should be viewed as creating two separate and hierarchically different forms of literature. Frus's Marxist reading of Hemingway and other writers suggested that their journalism should be evaluated in its own right as a legitimate form of social discourse and not judged inferior to literature simply because it may be time-bound in its recording of contemporary information. Epifanio San Juan's (1995) "Ideological Form, Symbolic Exchange, Textual Production: A Reading of Hemingway's *For Whom the Bell Tolls*" reinterprets the novel that, in San Juan's estimation, transcends both historicist and hermeneutic criticism by viewing "the production of ideology" as "the project of the text" (91). The result is a politicized—heavily Marxist—reading exposing the weaknesses of Hemingway's political consciousness.

Hemingway's suicide was not the only subject of interest to medical professionals. In 1999 Alex Vardamis and Justine Owens coauthored an article in the *Journal of Medical Humanities* on Hemingway's near-death experience, which they believed occurred when he was wounded in the First World War. Carefully examining available evidence and concentrating on *A Farewell to Arms* and "The Snows of Kilimanjaro," the authors explained how Hemingway's experiences shaped the creation of the protagonists of these stories and lent further insight into this medical phenomenon that began to receive serious attention from the medical community decades after Hemingway wrote about it.

Frequently one sees critics using Hemingway's fiction (and on occasion his biography) to illustrate a theoretical principle. But critics have not been the only ones to appropriate Hemingway, as Peter Hays (1999) pointed out in his critique of Tennessee Williams's last Broadway drama, *Clothes for a Summer Hotel.* In this 1980 play about Scott and Zelda Fitzgerald, Williams makes Hemingway and Fitzgerald homosexuals. As such, they could be (as Williams saw himself) "more sensitive, especially to women" (253). In Hays's estimation, Hemingway, a minor character, is not treated well, and comes off poorly as a foil for Fitzgerald.

Another examination of Hemingway's *A Moveable Feast* appeared in Susanna Egan's (1999) *Mirror Talk: Genres of Crisis in Contemporary Autobiography.* Egan explored Hemingway's re-creation of his relationship with Fitzgerald, demonstrating (not to Hemingway's advantage) the many ways Hemingway manipulated the past as he moved from "crude early scribblings" through various revisions to "the tightly controlled writing of the final text in print" (47). The lesson to be taken from such a study, Egan said, is that Hemingway's autobiography, like all others, is really an "explanatory myth" rather than a factual account (47).

True at First Light

While academic critics were scrambling to find new angles from which to revise older versions of Hemingway and refine newer ones, Hemingway's heirs and Scribner continued to work diligently at publishing the remaining unpublished work. The last major manuscript, written during the 1950s after Hemingway returned from his ill-fated 1953 safari, became the basis for *True at First Light*, a heavily redacted version edited by Hemingway's son Patrick. The book was hyped in the *New York Times* months before it appeared (Blumenthal 1998) and was released in the centennial year of Hemingway's birth.

The immediate response was far from positive. In what must have been an embarrassment for those at the paper who chose to promote the book before its appearance, Joan Didion (1998) called Scribner's actions a betrayal; the published text, significantly reduced from its original length by editor Patrick Hemingway, "does not provide the reader with the essence of what the author intended, but instead provides publishers with a great deal of publicity" (74). *New York Times* reviewer Michiko Kakutani (1999) resorted to a bit of wordplay (clever or hackneyed, depending on one's perspective) in claiming that *True at First Light* shows Hemingway "in the worst of all possible lights"; she believed it "never should have seen the light of day." James Wood (1999) thought the book was closer to parody than to the best of Hemingway's writing. Still, he admitted, *True at First Light* possesses "a kind of mottled glamour, made up of bullying integrity and nonsense, of truth and falsity, which always makes the least of Hemingway's books compelling." Describing all of the posthumous publications as Hemingway's "in a loose sense" only, William Cain (1999) believed the book "says nothing fresh or noteworthy" about the Africa Hemingway loved, and the few good passages in it "cannot redeem the clunky dialogue and cartoonish sketches of whites and Africans alike" (C1). Robert Murray Davis (2000) was even more negative, complaining about virtually every aspect of the book but singling out for special condemnation the dialogue between Hemingway and his wife: "Anyone who speaks to a loved one in this kind of revolting babytalk deserves to be beaten with a large stick" (365). Morris Friedman (2000) suggested that "Hemingway deserves no less homage than leaving the man, his life, his work less pawed over" (82).

Two of Hemingway's biographers wrote long reviews of the book, and while neither had much good to say about it, their responses differed in several respects. Kenneth Lynn (1999) aimed his criticism at

Hemingway's sons, arguing that Patrick Hemingway's misguided effort to create a novel from the unfinished manuscript that his father abandoned showed disrespect for an artist who understood this material was not worthy of publication. Jeffrey Meyers (1999) was less harsh on Patrick Hemingway but found even this condensed version "too long and repetitive"; the fault lay with Hemingway, however, who "didn't seem to know where the book was going or how to finish it" (68). Meyers found the new African story had the same faults as the earlier one—Hemingway's egoism got in the way of what might have been a good story—but believed there were passages that redeemed *True at First Light* from being unadulterated dreck: "The best passages are tempered by [Hemingway's] classic virtues: intense curiosity, passion for learning and for mastery, testing of himself and others" (71). Viewed in tandem with *Green Hills of Africa*, Meyers said the new book "inevitably wakens a sense of loss" (72).

The publication of *True at First Light* sparked a lively debate among Hemingway scholars, and in less than a year after the work appeared the *Hemingway Review* ran a special issue compiling responses to what would almost certainly be the last word from Hemingway. The issue began with the record of a conversation at the centennial conference of the Hemingway Society held in Oak Park, Illinois, between conference director Michael Seefeldt and editor Patrick Hemingway. In expansive remarks Hemingway's son explained the many difficulties he had in reducing the mass of manuscript material to a book "that the publisher wished" would be "between two and three hundred pages"; that meant "cutting the manuscript by at least one quarter." Patrick Hemingway ("An Evening" 1999) argued that his editing was done "essentially" to "strengthen the story line because in a commercial cut, people want a story." He believed "the essential quality" of the book he produced "is an action story with a love interest" (10).

Essays by nearly a dozen established and emerging Hemingway scholars give some idea of how troubled some in the academic community were by the publication of this posthumous book and how excited others were at the prospect of having another Hemingway work to pore over. Some commented on the publication (and critiqued Patrick Hemingway's editing). Others, like Robert Gajdusek's (1999) "One Blind Man Exploring a Pretty Big Elephant" and Hilary Justice's (1999) "The Lion, the Leopard, and the Bear" offered literary interpretations. Still others, notably Carl Eby's (1999b) "Hemingway's Truths and Tribal Politics" dealt with the vexing problem of genre: Is this a journal, as the title of the excerpts printed sometime earlier called the book? Is it a memoir? Is it fiction? Patrick Hemingway's subtitle "A Fictional Memoir"—not one Hemingway himself selected—is one likely to drive literary purists to distraction. Linda Miller (1999) suggested in her contribution, "What's Funny about

True at First Light" that, in their zeal to discover "a lyrical tragedy" in every Hemingway work, critics and readers at large "have overlooked the sophisticated interplay of humor and mythology in this one." The truth is, she said emphatically, "*True at First Light* is a rollicking good read" (48). To complete this first scholarly book—for that is what this special issue really is—Stephen Plotkin (1999), an archivist at the John F. Kennedy Library, provided a summary of the manuscripts extant at the time of Hemingway's death.

The value of this special issue goes beyond the sophisticated and enlightened commentaries on *True at First Light*. The list of contributors—Rose Marie Burwell, Eby, Robert Fleming, Gajdusek, del Gizzo, Justice, Robert W. Lewis, Miller, Debra Moddelmog, and Michael Reynolds—is a representative sampling of Who's Who in Hemingway scholarship past, present, and future. The confluence of work by these scholars offers a snapshot into the academic community's interest in Hemingway—the writer and the man—at century's end.

Centenary Publications

Perhaps because there had been a spate of new biographies published in the 1980s and early 1990s, relatively little new biographical work was published in 1999, the centenary of Hemingway's birth. The major exception, of course, was the final volume of Michael Reynolds's biography, discussed earlier in this study. One is tempted to say that Reynolds's work is the last word on Hemingway biographical studies. Yet in the same year it appeared, James Plath and Frank Simons (1999) brought out a collection of reminiscences by people who knew Hemingway at various stages of his life. Almost to a person, family and friends interviewed for *Remembering Ernest Hemingway* were adamant that, despite the myriad of biographies available, the essence of this complex man and gifted writer had not yet been fully captured and explained. Perhaps, as Scott Donaldson (1991) suggested nearly a decade earlier, while Hemingway remained "an irresistible subject" for scholars, "there isn't going to be a definitive biography of Hemingway" (95, 93), partly because no one can guarantee accuracy of any life story but more especially because Hemingway is simply too elusive a subject. Even Michael Reynolds (1991b) admitted as much before he published the last three volumes of his biography. He said a very good biographer reaches a point where he realizes "the limits of his genre and the fictive nature of his trade" (170).

One writer who did take advantage of the centenary was British writer Aubrey Dillon-Malone (1999). Intended primarily for a British audience, Malone's *Hemingway: The Grace and the Pressure* stressed Hemingway's Americanness and zeroed in on his celebrity status. Unfortunately for Dillon-Malone, few reviewers found anything new in his book or had much good to say about its author. Mark Ott (2002) called it a "vulture biography" because it "feeds without attribution" on more serious biographical studies (138). Its only saving grace was that it demonstrated once again how much Hemingway's life and his fiction are intertwined in the public consciousness.

If Dillon-Malone's book was cobbled together from previously published sources and designed to glorify the traditional image of Hemingway as a celebrity, the opposite—or at least an opposing—view was laid out with exceptional insight and considerable scholarly acumen by Debra Moddelmog (1999) in *Reading Desire: In Pursuit of Ernest Hemingway*. Anyone wishing to see how critical theory can inform discussion of Hemingway's work will find Moddelmog's study a model of new critical practice. The work of European theorists and American feminists, as well as that of Hemingway scholars who have revised earlier conclusions about Hemingway's macho image, underlie Moddelmog's investigation—or as she calls it, pursuit—of "Hemingway," at once a real historical person who wrote novels and stories and a construct of critics and readers who created an image of him to fulfill their own desires. Hemingway is a particularly good case study, she said, for examining the entire process by which readers understand and interpret texts, especially ones by authors whose biographies have become part of the national consciousness. The conflict between Hemingway's traditional image as a model of masculinity and the more recent revisionist approaches that have stressed his interest in (and perhaps affinity for) themes of homosexuality make it practically impossible to read him without at least subconsciously being influenced by these preconceived notions about his motivations for writing.

In the course of her study, Moddelmog challenged what she called the "conservative lot" of Hemingway scholars, most of whom rejected poststructuralist readings of his work (14). Her interpretations of texts like *The Garden of Eden*, *The Sun Also Rises*, and "The Snows of Kilimanjaro" demonstrated how reading Hemingway through the lenses of various critical methodologies (deconstruction, feminism, postcolonialism) could provide a new understanding of him—and, more importantly, a better understanding of the critical process itself. The aim of such reading, she argued, was not to arrive at a totalizing interpretation of Hemingway's oeuvre or to force readers (particularly students) "to choose between a homosexual and a heterosexual Hemingway." Instead, one should aim at getting students (and readers in general, by inference) to become "more aware of the presumptions of our sexual system," to "think about how identities are constructed," and to "consider the cultural, pedagogical, and personal uses to which such constructions are put" (143).

One might have thought that by the end of the twentieth century, studies of Hemingway employing techniques of psychoanalysis to explore issues of gender would have raised no more controversy among

Hemingway scholars than studies of symbolism and structure would have in the 1960s. However, Carl Eby's (1999a) *Hemingway's Fetishism* proved that one can always jolt the usually comfortable academic world. In a psychoanalytic analysis of Hemingway's life and fiction, Eby explained how certain recurrent images—the fetishes of his title—help identify Hemingway's lifelong anxiety about issues of gender. He wanted to demythologize Hemingway without "trashing" him (4); he was even apologetic for putting Hemingway on the psychoanalyst's couch. "It is not as fashionable as it once was to psychoanalyze artists while analyzing their art," he admitted, "but this is simply unavoidable in any thorough consideration of fetishism" (7). Eby's close readings and his reexamination of the details of Hemingway's life explain how Hemingway's fetishes (hair, bisexuality, homosexuality, androgyny, castration) reveal not only his characters' motivation but his own, and explain why he chose his subjects. Eby also suggested that the psychological traumas underlying these fetishes help explain the development of the famous Hemingway style.

It is possible to see Eby's work as just another study among the growing number employing theories of psychology and psychoanalysis as tools for unraveling the mysteries of Hemingway's life and fiction. Eby made reference to (and occasional use of) work by Spilka, Lynn, and Comley and Scholes—although he shied away from any reliance on Philip Young, perhaps because Young's focus on the importance of the wounded hero is an example of the kind of totalizing reading he wished to avoid. The reaction of scholars to Eby's work suggested it was more than "more of the same," however. Three reviews illustrate this point. Writing in the *Hemingway Review*, Greg Forter (1999) called *Hemingway's Fetishism* "a persuasive and even a moving book" that "attempts nothing less than a complete reinterpretation of Hemingway's life and work in the context of his basic hypothesis" (133). Joseph Fruscione (1999) said Eby's study "will be a valuable one for Hemingway scholars in the coming years" (124). Furthermore, Fruscione argued, Eby had begun "the process that can potentially turn Hemingway studies in a new direction," issuing "a call for a new type of scholarship that is much more immersed in Hemingway's fiction and which is cognizant of the thematic 'secrets' contained therein" (125). On the other hand, Matthew Stewart (2001a) complained that the "psychoanalytic paradigms on which [Eby] relies are themselves groundless and have been thoroughly disproved" (191). Eby is guilty of a fault shared by many psychoanalytic critics: "things said, done, and felt by fictional characters are attributed to their author, sometimes with justification, sometimes unconvincingly, but always without hesitation" (191). Even if one were to excuse this overzealous attempt to find clues to Hemingway's psychological states in the action and thoughts of his characters, the "insurmountable problem" with Eby's study "stems from its adherence to the psychoanalytic model as pioneered by Freud and developed by the subsequent analysts upon whose backs Eby builds his case" (191). Stewart said, "Flatly put, the psychoanalytical model pioneered by Freud has no validity" (191–92). Just as Eby apologized—probably without really meaning it—for putting Hemingway on the couch for Freudian analysis, Stewart apologized—again without meaning it—for harping on the many faults of Freudian theory. But he must, he said, since the validity of Eby's study "depends on the validity of psychoanalytical methodology." Hence, "to point out the fallacies of psychoanalysis is to point out the fatal flaw in [Eby's] critical practice" (193). Looking back after more than a decade, it appears that the story of *Hemingway's Fetishism* and its reviewers is a case study in critical overkill on both sides.

Finally, in 1999 Scott Donaldson revisited the Hemingway-Fitzgerald friendship in *Hemingway vs. Fitzgerald*, examining many of the materials Matthew Bruccoli collected to try to understand the nature of the complex relationship between two writers now considered among the best of their generation. Donaldson was interested in ferreting out the reasons—psychological as well as social and professional—that a seemingly close friendship deteriorated over the years. The resulting portrait of two writers and their times intertwined cultural criticism with psychological analysis that offers deep understanding of what it was like to be Hemingway or Fitzgerald, and to be an aspiring writer in the first half of the twentieth century.

Notes

[1] Not one to let anything he wrote go to waste, in 2002 Bruccoli published *Classes on Ernest Hemingway*, the edited transcription of a seminar he taught in 1982. Despite the seemingly self-serving nature of this volume, the book is actually a creditable critique of Hemingway's career.

[2] Reynolds may have also been envisioning his own *Hemingway: An Annotated Chronology* (Reynolds 1991a). In fewer than 150 pages—remarkably short when one considers Reynolds's five-volume biography—he provides a useful checklist of the major (and some minor) events in Hemingway's life.

[3] Spilka's essay was originally delivered as a paper at the conference, which accounts for its inclusion in this volume. However, the essay appeared a year earlier in Kenneth Rosen's (1994) *Hemingway Repossessed*.

9: Old Themes, New Discoveries (2000–2010)

IN HER INTRODUCTION TO *Hemingway: Eight Decades of Criticism* Linda Wagner-Martin (2009) calls the twenty-first century "the century of the blend," with "many strands of theoretical readings coalesc[ing] to provide an enriched view of the way critique can enhance both reading and textual work" (xv). Wagner-Martin is right in more ways than one about the blending that took place during this decade. While interrogations of Hemingway texts using new critical methodologies and exploring issues of contemporary interest dominated scholars' attention, more traditional assessments of topics such as the Hemingway code and the Hemingway style continued to appear. The breadth of interest in Hemingway's work can best be illustrated by examining criticism published during the decade by genre or topic rather than strictly chronologically.

Handbooks and Essay Collections

A sure sign of the strength of Hemingway studies is the ongoing initiative by both academic and popular publishers to bring out handbooks and essay collections, the latter frequently filled with previously published materials. In Wagner-Martin's (2000) *Historical Guide to Ernest Hemingway* a brief biographical essay by Michael Reynolds headed a list of contributions that examine themes from a historical perspective. Wagner-Martin's note on influence suggested how literature as well as life provided inspiration for Hemingway. By contrast, the handbook produced by Reynolds (2000), *Ernest Hemingway*, in Gale's Literary Masters series, has a wider focus; it was intended to introduce Hemingway to a new generation of readers. Reynolds brought together comments from a number of critics whose work influenced Hemingway studies during the twentieth century. Published at the end of the decade, classic and contemporary essays in Eugene Goodheart's (2010) *Critical Insights: Ernest Hemingway* provided a sense of how criticism has shaped views about Hemingway and his work. One comes away from reading the book cover to cover with the sense that it is impossible to separate the writer from his fiction, and the man of action from the writer.

A number of new handbooks were devoted to analyzing a single book. Certainly the most ambitious was the two-volume *Comprehensive*

Companion to Hemingway's "A Moveable Feast": Annotation to Interpretation. With painstaking attention to detail, Gerry Brenner (2000) annotated every word or passage that might be puzzling to readers unfamiliar with Hemingway's Paris, identified every person or publication (real or fictional) to which Hemingway alludes, and provided brief interpretations to suggest how one might understand this highly personal memoir. Matthew Stewart's (2001b) *Modernism and Tradition in Hemingway's "In Our Time": A Guide for Students and Readers* was another book designed to help those less familiar with Hemingway's work make sense out of a volume that is markedly experimental and shows early evidence of Hemingway's distinct style and iconic stance against the tragic dimensions of life. Linda Wagner-Martin's (2002) *Ernest Hemingway's "The Sun Also Rises": A Casebook* collected ten essays on the novel, more than half from the preceding two decades. The book's value for scholars and students lies in the diversity of critical perspectives represented in the essays: formalist analysis; psychological investigation; feminist critique; as well as gender, race, and cultural studies demonstrate the multiplicity of viewpoints from which this novel can be examined. More broadly focused, Keith Newlin's (2011) *Critical Insights: "The Sun Also Rises"* in the brief-lived Salem Press Critical Insights series is best considered a student handbook rather than a new contribution to Hemingway studies. Several of the essays commissioned for this volume, however, offer insight into the social milieu and the current 'hot' issue, gender relationships.

Two guides on *A Farewell to Arms* are also noteworthy. Linda Wagner-Martin's (2003) *Ernest Hemingway's "A Farewell to Arms": A Reference Guide* displayed its author's considerable knowledge of the critical tradition and exceptional insight into Hemingway's work. Wagner-Martin offered an intriguing new analysis and took advantage of her colleagues' recent work to explain how the novel transforms not only Hemingway's experiences but the general experience of the First World War into compelling, complex fiction. In 2005 Charles Oliver assembled another collection on *A Farewell to Arms* for the *Dictionary of Literary Biography* series. *Ernest Hemingway's "A Farewell to Arms": A Documentary Volume* (Oliver 2005) provided technical analysis of the novel and a healthy selection of critical commentary organized to illustrate the critical reception of the novel and changing attitudes toward its merits.

Miriam Mandel (2004) described her *A Companion to Hemingway's "Death in the Afternoon"* as "a groundbreaking publication," the "first book to focus on a volume of Hemingway's nonfiction" (1). One might immediately wonder if she was intentionally ignoring earlier studies of the nonfiction, but her point is that hers is the first critical collection focused exclusively on a single nonfiction book by Hemingway. Essays in the volume range from the traditional (on composition, sources, and background) to ones employing new theoretical approaches. For example,

Hilary Justice's "'Prejudiced through Experience': *Death in the Afternoon* and the Problem of Authorship" addressed the complex issue of authority and voice in the complex narrative, while Amy Vondrak's "'The Sequence of Motion and Fact': Cubist Collage and Filmic Montage in *Death in the Afternoon*" suggested a new way of understanding the workings of the narrative by comparing it to film techniques.

Complementing collections centered on single works were ones focused on thematic issues. For example, the nineteen essays and long introduction in Rena Sanderson's (2006) *Hemingway's Italy: New Perspectives*, compiled from papers presented at the 2002 International Hemingway Conference held in Stresa, Italy, examined the way Hemingway's experience in Italy shaped his art. As one might expect, many contributors focused on *A Farewell to Arms*, but other works received attention as well, including the Nick Adams stories and *Across the River and Into the Trees*. Some of the essays place his work in a wider cultural context; others concentrated on technical issues that illuminate Hemingway's craftsmanship. For the present study, notable among the essays is Italian Professor Vito Fortunati's, in which he investigated "what Hemingway meant for intellectuals and writers working in Italy after World War I and through the 1980s" (225). Fortunati concluded that, while Hemingway's reputation in America may have suffered during the last half of the century, "many Italian writers continue to find in his style an inspirational model for their own work" (231).

Kirk Curnutt and Gail Sinclair's (2009) *Key West Hemingway* brought together essays first presented at the 2004 Hemingway Society Conference held in Key West. The editors provided a useful chronology of Hemingway's years there and an introduction outlining the influence of the Keys on his writing. The seventeen essays are a mix of traditional literary criticism and scholarship, postmodern analysis, and biographical studies that flesh out suggestions made in the introduction about the influence of Key West on Hemingway's work. Perhaps the most valuable section is the one in which five contributors revisited *To Have and Have Not*, a novel often disparaged as ham-handed socialism. These essayists argued that the novel is more complex than it appeared to earlier critics but still not among Hemingway's finest. Such candor among devotees of Hemingway is refreshing.

Another collection, which grew out of a 2005 seminar at the American Literature Association meeting, was Mark Cirino and Mark Ott's (2010) *Ernest Hemingway and the Geography of Memory*. Arguing that memory is a "pervasive feature" in all of Hemingway's work, the editors suggested that he used it as "an element of a broader authorial strategy that allows him to separate himself from his narrative alter egos" (xi). Fourteen contributors examined how Hemingway's various uses of memory allow him to get at the larger truths that he claimed great writing can produce. Of special interest, perhaps, is the range of works examined by these essayists and the relative emphasis placed on them. The early novels and stories are explored in some detail, as are *Death in the Afternoon* and *Green Hills of Africa*. What is more noteworthy, however, is the significant attention paid to the posthumous publications, a trend that continued to grow as critics discovered these works to be of greater interest to those pursuing current ideological interests.

Perhaps because she was aware that so many other collections were available (and new ones seem to appear nearly every month or so), Linda Wagner-Martin (2009) organized *Hemingway: Eight Decades of Criticism* topically in sections with titles like "New Critical Approaches to the Wound" and "Places for Continuing Reassessment." Essays and chapters reprinted in the volume—fourteen of the twenty-six were from the *Hemingway Review*, and all but one were published within the past decade—reexamined Hemingway's works from new perspectives, often blending new critical approaches to offer fresh readings and place the fiction and nonfiction in wider cultural contexts. Recognized Hemingway scholars—Paul Smith, J. Gerald Kennedy, Joseph Flora, H. R. Stoneback, Wagner-Martin herself—are represented, but many essays are by the newest generation of critics whose familiarity and comfort with new critical theories make their essays both insightful and readable. The special attention paid by critics to *A Farewell to Arms* in the new century is reflected in her choice of five essays that show not only how critics have reacted to that novel but also to each other. It is worth noting, too, that the twenty-six essays selected for *Eight Decades* take up nearly 600 pages, demonstrating there is still great interest in Hemingway, his work, and his times.

Whereas most collections contain essays by different hands, three published in the first decade of the century are the life's work of individuals whose names have loomed large in the community of Hemingway scholars. The first appeared in 2000, when Jeffrey Meyers assembled essays he had published over two decades in a single volume, *Hemingway: Life into Art*. The fourteen pieces complement Meyers's biography by expanding information on a number of topics only briefly covered in that book (Meyers 1985). The essays stressed once again Meyers's belief that to understand Hemingway's fiction one must first learn all one can about his life.

In 2002 Robert Gajdusek finally collected the essays he had published over two decades into a single volume, *Hemingway in His Own Country*. The "country" to which Gajdusek refers is the imagination, which he said Hemingway inhabited regardless of where he lived. Gajdusek's book is about Hemingway's works, not the man, though inevitably details of Hemingway's life emerge on the periphery (and sometimes close to the center) of some essays. In the introduction, Robert W. Lewis, Gajdusek's contemporary, asserted that his essays provide "a postgraduate course for even the seasoned Hemingway devotees" (xii). Gajdusek's coverage is wide and his readings close. Furthermore, though he seldom has use or high regard for new theoretical approaches, he is aware of the revolution in critical studies and often writes as if he is defending Hemingway from a new pack of hyenas determined to devour his work and neuter the author in the process.

No doubt critics prone to dismiss what they might call the fatally flawed belief in bias-free aesthetics would find *Hemingway in His Own Country* problematic. Furthermore, Gajdusek made no significant efforts to link these disparate essays into an overarching portrait of Hemingway's art, relying on readers to form their own opinions based on the detailed information he provides about individual works. What does come through quite clearly is his admiration for Hemingway, a feeling so strong that it prompted him to chide his mentor Carlos Baker for writing a biography that failed to reveal more about Hemingway as an artist. In a sense, *Hemingway in His Own Country* is Gajdusek's effort to perform that task. He may well have known it would also be a summing-up of his life's work as a critic; he died the year after it was published.

For Hemingway scholars active since the 1970s, Scott Donaldson's (2009) *Fitzgerald & Hemingway: Works and Days* might evoke a sense of déjà vu, but for those starting out in the profession the volume is a godsend. In it Donaldson collected some of his more important fugitive pieces. Unlike his biographical study *Hemingway vs. Fitzgerald* (Donaldson 1999), the new volume focused principally on works by both authors, and as a consequence, young scholars have access to Donaldson's considerable insights gleaned over forty years of study. Donaldson admitted that he revised many of the essays, not simply to create a consistent style but also to make the volume a more coherent assessment based on two principles that characterize his methodology and belief. First, as one might expect from a scholar who invested much of his career in writing biography, "the essays are unified" by "an awareness of the interconnectedness between biography and criticism" (6). Second, Donaldson highlights the fact that Hemingway and Fitzgerald were "compulsive revisers" (7), so that the craftsmanship for which each is famous is shown to be the result of arduous labor over early drafts. In the section on Hemingway, Donaldson concentrated on the early fiction, though the one essay appearing first in this volume explored Hemingway's fascination with the Spanish Civil War. To close the volume, Donaldson reprints the introduction to his 1996 collection of essays, revising "Hemingway and Fame" to highlight the continuing interest scholars have in reconciling Hemingway's quest for fame with his pursuit of literary excellence.

New Editions of Hemingway's Work

In 2005 Robert W. Lewis and Robert Fleming brought out a new edition of Hemingway's fictionalized account of his 1953–54 safari. Titled

Under Kilimanjaro (Hemingway 2005), the Lewis-Fleming collaboration restored many of the cuts made by Patrick Hemingway in his 1999 edition of the tale, *True at First Light*. The magnitude of the changes can be seen simply by picking up both volumes simultaneously. *True at First Light* is just over 300 pages; *Under Kilimanjaro* is nearly 500. The scholar's penchant for preservation is evident in the editors' inclusion of material that Hemingway may have cut out or revised, but Lewis and Fleming argued that they were providing a record of a work in progress that has unity of sorts but is in no way finished.

Unlike *True at First Light*, *Under Kilimanjaro* received notably good reviews, especially from those who understood the editors' intent. The *New York Times* printed only a brief notice (Wyatt 2005)—perhaps because the book was published by a university press rather than a commercial publisher, but more likely because the paper had celebrated the publication of *True at First Light*, which did not receive many favorable reviews. While one can find an occasional review in the popular press that considered Patrick Hemingway's version better than Lewis and Fleming's (e.g., Wakefield 2005), the scholarly community—especially the Hemingway community—was ecstatic about the new version. Within months of publication, the *Hemingway Review* (2005) brought out a special issue devoted to a study of *Under Kilimanjaro*. Included are articles by both editors and ones on masculinity, whiteness, the environment, multiculturalism, and celebrity. Apparently *Under Kilimanjaro* gave the community of Hemingway scholars another chance to locate evidence that Hemingway was sensitive (perhaps even prescient) regarding issues that concern twenty-first-century readers (or critics, at least).

The publication of *Under Kilimanjaro* prompted G. T. Dempsey (2007) to write a lengthy defense of Hemingway and a stern critique of his heirs and publishers. Dempsey believed *Under Kilimanjaro* was the first posthumous publication actually to do justice to Hemingway, who he believed "has been badly served by the commercial publication of a mass of manuscripts" that Hemingway obviously had no intention of publishing (239). Dempsey believed Hemingway went into a steep decline after publishing *For Whom the Bell Tolls*. *Across the River and Into the Trees* was execrable; *The Old Man and the Sea* "a masterpiece despite its awfulness," albeit marred throughout by "sentimentalizing excesses" (244). *Islands in the Stream* was simply "a bad book" (249). Dempsey believed only two posthumous works were truly worth reading. One was *The Garden of Eden*, a "remarkably well written" and "complex book" that distills "the essence of life itself from the simplest everyday experiences" (251). The other was *A Moveable Feast*—and that too, he said, should be reedited by academics who would do a greater service to Hemingway than his widow did.

In fact, a reedited version of *A Moveable Feast* appeared two years later, but few members of the academic community were fully satisfied with the revision. Hemingway's grandson Seán, who served as editor, admits in his commentary on the book that his emendations restore some dignity to his grandmother, Hemingway's second wife, Pauline Pfeiffer, who is vilified in the final chapter of the 1964 version. The *New York Times* notice of the publication was considerably longer than the one about *Under Kilimanjaro*; its author, Motoko Rich (2009), quoted scholars Sandra Spanier, Ann Douglas, and Jacqueline Tavernier-Courbin about the relative merits of the new edition. The *Times* also gave space to Hemingway's longtime friend A. E. Hotchner (2009), who claimed in his diatribe against the new edition that the manuscript was "ready for publication" when Hemingway died and that Mary Welsh Hemingway produced a version faithful to her husband's intentions. Of course, Hotchner also claimed to have suggested the title to Mary.[1]

Reviewers with no particular ax to grind offered a mixed assessment. The *Spectator*'s Allan Massie (2009) believed the additions weakened the original text; Seán Hemingway "may have done his grandma justice" but it comes "at his grandfather's expense." Brenda Wineapple (2009) wrote in the *Wall Street Journal* that the new version may or may not be closer to what Hemingway would have produced; unfortunately, it is nearly impossible to reconstruct an author's intention. What is more certain, she said, is that Scribner "invented an anniversary—the fiftieth year since Hemingway completed a draft of the Paris sketches—to burnish Hemingway's image and, of course, sell books." Christopher Hitchens (2009) believed the restored edition of *A Moveable Feast* was an improvement in some ways over the 1964 edition, which, in his view, revealed Mary Hemingway's heavy hand in downplaying the importance of Hemingway's previous wives. Ultimately Hitchens found the book best read as a piece of nostalgia, not a major literary performance. Leo Robson (2010) was not so convinced, however, that the new version was substantially better than the first. Furthermore, he was annoyed with Seán Hemingway's penchant for footnoting and his insistence on blaming Mary Hemingway for altering the manuscript to suit her own needs—a claim Robson found unsubstantiated.

Scholars would not have to wait long to learn the extent of the changes. In the Fall 2009 issue of the *Hemingway Review*, Robert Trogdon (2009) published a long article cataloging the many alterations that he said made the new version substantially different from the 1964 book. Like Dempsey, Trogdon lamented the absence of "a true scholarly edition of all of Hemingway's works." Yet he claimed this restored edition of *A Moveable Feast* may be seen as "a first tentative step toward a true critical edition" (28).

Kent State's Publishing Initiative

Lewis and Fleming's 2005 edition of *Under Kilimanjaro* was the first book on Hemingway issued by Kent State University Press as part of its initiative to create a niche for Hemingway studies.[2] Encouraged by Kent State professor Robert Trogdon, KSU Press director Will Underwood agreed to continue the two series that had initially been planned at the University of Idaho Press before that press closed in 2004: "Teaching Hemingway" and "Reading Hemingway." At the time only one title had been commissioned. Being selected as the publisher for *Under Kilimanjaro* was something of a coup for KSU Press, as commercial houses were also interested in bringing out the work.

Apparently Hemingway scholars took note as well, as KSU Press became the publisher for more than a dozen important new titles over the next decade. In 2007 the press initiated its Reading Hemingway series with the publication of H. R. Stoneback's (2007) *Reading Hemingway's "The Sun Also Rises": Glossary and Commentary*. The new series was intended, as the first series editor Robert W. Lewis explained in his foreword, "to gloss or annotate, page by page, word by word, if necessary" the primary text, not "tell Hemingway readers what to think and feel about an action, a character or a place" (Stoneback 2007, vii). Stoneback's exegesis—which runs longer than Hemingway's novel—carefully explicates passages to provide important background and offer information designed to help readers "avoid *mis*understanding" it (169). Like Stoneback's book, Joseph Flora's (2008) *Reading Hemingway's "Men without Women"* is not primarily analytical; rather, as Flora noted, borrowing editor Lewis's metaphor, the study is "intended as a tourist guide" (xi). The Reading Hemingway books feature a single scholar's perspective. By contrast, the Teaching Hemingway series involves the collective efforts of a number of college teachers, many of whom are also outstanding Hemingway scholars. The essays in Lisa Tyler's (2008) *Teaching Hemingway's "A Farewell to Arms"* and Peter Hays's (2008) *Teaching Hemingway's "The Sun Also Rises"* are aimed at helping classroom teachers use Hemingway's novels as icons of cultural history and existential investigations of timeless human issues.

Perhaps even more significant than these series is a third one initiated by KSU Press: Hemingway Studies. Planned as a showcase for some of the best contemporary criticism and scholarship on Hemingway, the series got off to an auspicious start with the publication of the initial title, Hilary Justice's (2006) *The Bones of the Others*, a groundbreaking study in which Justice argued for a new reading of Hemingway's corpus. Rather than privilege individual works, she suggested that each story or novel be read in relation to other published and unpublished work. Relying on, but not foregrounding, contemporary theories of authorship and writing, Justice called for treating all of Hemingway's writing as "the Hemingway Text" (6), his "lifelong exploration of the public and the private" (4). Justice's metatextual approach provided some intriguing, nuanced readings of works that simply do not emerge when read independently. Justice repeatedly stressed that Hemingway doubled back frequently, reflecting on his early work in later texts as he tried to reconcile his desire to write truly and authentically with his reading public's demand for fiction that reflected his public image. Her challenge to fellow scholars was to unravel these relationships in order to better understand Hemingway's lifelong project to explore his world (inner and outer) through his writing. The importance of Justice's volume was immediately recognized by fellow Hemingway scholars. In her review, Linda Patterson Miller (2007) called *The Bones of the Others* "a model of its kind," one that "every serious Hemingway scholar will want to read" (144). Linda Wagner-Martin was equally high on Justice's study, which she described as "a strikingly contemporary way to approach this never-dated modernist"; Wagner-Martin believed "there is no work that competes with this" (quoted in Miller, 145).

KSU Press followed up this truly first-rate work with another one, Robert Trogdon's (2007) *The Lousy Racket: Hemingway, Scribner's, and the Business of Literature*, one of the finest contextual studies of Hemingway (or any writer, for that matter). Building on a suggestion by Michael Reynolds (with whom he studied while pursuing a master's), Trogdon addressed the economics of Hemingway's relationship with his publisher (a topic that no doubt satisfied his dissertation director, Matthew Bruccoli). Hemingway is a fruitful subject for Trogdon's approach, because he wanted to be both a highly regarded literary artist and a popular writer. Complementing the work of Hemingway biographers and Maxwell Perkins's biographer Scott Berg, Trogdon demonstrated how research into archives at Princeton and the Kennedy Library can still yield fresh insights. *The Lousy Racket* teems with new information about Hemingway's relationship with people at Scribner's, particularly Perkins. Trogdon included statistics that put to rest much earlier speculation about the monetary value of Hemingway's work during his lifetime. *The Lousy Racket* demonstrates that the creation of the "Hemingway" brand (to use a marketing term sometimes offensive to literary purists) was the result of a conscious collaboration between the artist (and Hemingway was an artist), the professional writer (Hemingway always intended to make his living by writing), the editor (Perkins knew great talent when he saw it, and knew how to nurture it), and the Scribner's team of production specialists, marketers, and publishing executives that made many of Hemingway's works best sellers in his lifetime and staples of the literary world in the decades that followed.

Over the next decade the press continued to issue studies that enriched the scholarly community's understanding of Hemingway. The following titles, several of which are discussed later in this narrative, make clear the contributions of KSU Press in keeping alive scholarship on Hemingway and his work: Mark Ott's (2008) *Sea of Change*; David Earle's (2009) *All Man! Hemingway, 1950s Men's Magazines, and the Masculine Persona*; René Villareal's (2009) *Hemingway's Cuban Son*; Mark Cirino and Mark Ott's (2010) *Ernest Hemingway and the Geography of Memory*; Mark Dudley's (2012) *Hemingway, Race, and Art*; Suzanne del Gizzo and Frederick Svoboda's (2012) *Hemingway's "The Garden of Eden": Twenty-five Years of Criticism*; Steven Florczyk's (2013) *Hemingway, the Red Cross, and the Great War*; Larry Grimes and Bickford Sylvester's (2014) *Hemingway, Cuba, and the Cuban Works*; and Steve Paul, Gail Sinclair, and Steven Trout's (2014) *War & Ink*.

Biographical Studies

With the exception of Michael Reynolds's concluding volume and Aubrey Dillon-Malone's derivative tribute, no major biography appeared in the centenary year of Hemingway's birth (most unusual for a literary figure of his stature) or during the first decade of the new century. Two interesting studies of Hemingway's wartime experiences in China, Peter Moreia's (2006) *Hemingway on the China Front*, and in Cuba, Terry Mort's (2009) *The Hemingway Patrols*, provided extensive detail about brief periods in his adventurous life. Kirk Curnutt's (2007) clever creation of an imagined conversation with Hemingway made *Coffee with Hemingway* a pleasant diversion; Curnutt's introductory essay offered a sound review of the major events of Hemingway's life, while John Updike's foreword provided an assessment of Hemingway by another giant of twentieth-century American fiction.

Chief among the critical biographies produced during the decade is Linda Wagner-Martin's (2007) *Ernest Hemingway: A Literary Life*. Despite the constraints normally placed on authors of volumes in Palgrave Macmillan's Literary Lives series, Wagner-Martin managed to provide a perspective on Hemingway's career that makes her study more than a recapitulation of biographical material. While she borrows heavily from previous biographers for details of Hemingway's life, the insights she developed from years of study allowed her to offer an intriguing perspective on his career. Claiming Hemingway was particularly capable of adapting to the wide range of personal and professional situations in which he found himself, Wagner-Martin stressed the importance of his conscious effort to create his own persona through his life and art: "Perhaps," she speculated, one of his "most successful creations was himself, as both living person and fictional character" (ix). Given that perspective, it is not surprising that Wagner-Martin reads much of the fiction autobiographically, painting Hemingway's father rather than his mother as the authority figure against whom the youthful Ernest rebelled. Wagner-Martin judged the early fiction considerably more meritorious than the later work, and has little good to say about the nonfiction, which she suggests Hemingway wrote strictly for commercial purposes (an opinion some not shared by all Hemingway scholars). Nevertheless, her final assessment revealed her deep-seated admiration for Hemingway's work: "There is little question," she asserted unequivocally, "that Hemingway will be read and loved even into the twenty-second century" (xi).

Less ambitious and more narrowly focused than Wagner-Martin's assessment was Loren Glass's (*Authors, Inc.* 2004) "Being Ernest," a brief but particularly thought-provoking analysis of Hemingway's career as serious writer and public celebrity. Observing that "the principal challenge to Hemingway critics has always been located in the vexed relation between literary biography and literary criticism" (139), Glass claimed that for many literary critics Hemingway's "public personality" became "an embarrassment" (140). In an extended and insightful reading of *Death in the Afternoon*, Glass traced ways Hemingway created that personality through an "exaggerated feminization of his audience" (144); he also explained how and why Hemingway expresses extreme homophobia, especially in his later work. Glass's most intriguing discussion, however, revolves around Hemingway's obsession with death.

Glass claimed that biographies begun during Hemingway's lifetime "exposed the degree to which textual and human identities become conflated in the phenomena of celebrity" (159). He analyzed the relationship between Hemingway and Philip Young, whose early psychoanalytical work bothered Hemingway immensely. What Glass posits, however, is that Hemingway was not averse to psychoanalytic criticism—only its application to living authors, especially ones trying to create works that would outlive them. In essence, Hemingway was afraid that if everything he wrote were read merely as an extension of himself, his work would not be of lasting value. With this idea in mind, Glass offered a reading of *The Garden of Eden* focused on the conflict between the personal (sexual) lives of the protagonists and the growing public life of David Bourne as an author. This is the conflict that Hemingway struggled with as he aged, and while the critics did not literally kill him, he became paralyzed by the thought that his work might not live on after his death.

Hemingway's continuing obsession with death also figured largely in Christopher Martin's (2006) essay "Ernest Hemingway: A Psychological Autopsy of a Suicide." Psychiatrist Martin reviewed much of the same evidence available to biographers, but by applying tools of clinical psychiatry documented the pathologies that eventually drove Hemingway to commit suicide: bipolar disorder, alcohol dependence, traumatic brain injury, and "probably borderline and narcissistic personality traits" (351).

Hemingway's relationships with others—both direct and indirect—were explored in two studies that also shed light on his personality. Stephen

Koch's (2005) *The Breaking Point*, an investigation of the links connecting Hemingway, John Dos Passos, and Spanish activist José Robles, painted an unflattering portrait. Koch argued that Hemingway was duped into believing Robles was a fascist, further demonstrating his superficial understanding of the civil war that gave him material for one of his most popular novels. Although Debra Moddelmog's (2008) examination of Hemingway's relationship with FBI director J. Edgar Hoover covered a topic previously discussed by other critics (e.g., Robins 1992), she made some intriguing observations about this issue. Hoover initially distrusted Hemingway because of his loose association with leftist publications in the 1930s and his overt anti-FBI remarks during the 1940s. Eventually Hoover dismissed the idea that Hemingway had Communist sympathies. Yet, Moddelmog argues, had he known what Hemingway was writing in the postwar years he might have not been so kind toward him. After the Second World War Hemingway was writing the kind of subversive literature that would have caused Hoover to become apoplectic, and had he known the contents of such manuscripts as *The Garden of Eden*, he might have attempted to suppress Hemingway's work. In Moddelmog's view, Hemingway's willingness to explore antimasculine themes showed his true courage.

Searching for Sources of Genius

Critical works that might be described by the old-fashioned term "influence studies" appeared with regularity during the decade. Among these was Robert Crunden's (2000) commentary in *Body & Soul: The Making of American Modernism*. Crunden examined once more the influence of Stein and Anderson on Hemingway, creating a none-too-favorable portrait of Hemingway as a young sycophant ready to stab his mentors in the back once he no longer needed them. In a much more nuanced assessment of influence, Eric Haralson (2003) explored Henry James's "monumental presence" (175) in Hemingway's early fiction, particularly *The Torrents of Spring* and *The Sun Also Rises*. Predictably, perhaps, the club that Hemingway used to bludgeon his literary forebear is homosexuality. For Hemingway, James's "queer nature" and "early unmanning" (a wound James suffered that was generally thought to have been some form of castration) made him "almost predestined to write an overrefined prose" and "offer a fictional universe populated by femmy 'fairies'" (195). Yet, as Haralson demonstrated, underneath the criticism there was deep ambivalence about James as a writer and about sexual identity. Hence, the Hemingway-James relationship provides literary scholars "an exemplary instance of modern straight masculinity (as it seems) reading Victorian gay masculinity" (175).

As one might expect, many influence studies reviewed old ground looking for new clues to explain the sources of Hemingway's genius. For example, in another assessment of Hemingway's debt to Cézanne, Lawrence Standley (2004) explained how Hemingway "had to learn the tricks of traditional fiction writing and then had to break those tricks before the present tense sense could be constructed within the text and consequently be experienced by the reader" (211). Maria DeGuzmán (2005) examined anew the influence of Spain on Hemingway's work as representative—her word is "symptomatic"—of the "larger cultural agonism with Spain as totemic ground" (194). DeGuzmán believed the intense popular interest in Hemingway's benign portrayal had often blinded scholars to the mythmaking that is going on in Hemingway's prose. The contrast implied between the sophisticated and corrupt Anglo-European society outside the country and the primitivism that Hemingway celebrates in the portrait of Spain he creates in his work is simply another example of postcolonial appropriation. Covering ground less well tread, Kim Fortuny (2009) in *American Writers in Istanbul* examined Hemingway's adventures during the Greco-Turkish War and explained how his experience as a journalist aided in his development as a writer of fiction.

In a reinvention of Charles Fenton's 1954 study, David Humphries's (2006) chapter on *The Sun Also Rises* and *In Our Time* in *Different Dispatches: Journalism in American Modernist Prose* also examined the influence of Hemingway's career as a journalist on his early fiction. Although he draws on journalism to explore this relationship in both works, his treatment is decidedly different. He theorizes that the short story collection "reflects the newsreel form and illustrates the changes in perception brought about by new forms of mass media, new scientific conceptions of perception, and the cultural shocks of the Great War." In writing these stories, however, Hemingway eventually came to "challenge the shortcomings of the new journalistic form." Hence, his novel "represents the growing acceptance that it was better to acknowledge the inevitability of subjectivity than uphold an idea of objectivity which was increasingly seen as a disabling illusion" (123).

Mark Ott's (2008) brief but exceptionally well written and well argued *A Sea of Change: Ernest Hemingway and the Gulf Stream: A Contextual Biography* demonstrated what careful manuscript study can do to illuminate the creative process. In Ott's case the manuscript materials, hitherto scarcely mentioned by scholars, are Hemingway's fishing logs from the 1930s. Working from the hypothesis that "the exact observations in the logs explain the stylistic transformation—the shift in his writing method" that occurred between the publication of *A Farewell to Arms* and *The Old Man and the Sea*, Ott produced meaningful comparisons that demonstrate how observations made in the heat of activity on the water became sources for some of Hemingway's creative work.

Continuing interest in Hemingway's relationship to the expatriate community in Paris during the 1920s was the justification for Kirk

Curnutt's (2000) *Ernest Hemingway and the Expatriate Modernist Movement* (2000) in the Gale Study Guides Literary Topics series. While acknowledging the problematic nature of historically grounded literary studies, Curnutt provides extensive background on this important period when literary modernism replaced realism and naturalism as the dominant ideology in Western literary circles. Curnutt explains how Hemingway was influenced by the expatriate community—and how he, in turn, influenced others—and offers readings of stories and novels Hemingway published during the 1920s and beyond. Similarly, Michael Soto's (2004) discussion of *The Sun Also Rises* in *The Modernist Nation* examined the novel as an example of work produced by a writer committed to creating fiction out of experience. In his brief analysis, Soto relies on the work of several earlier Hemingway scholars to explain how Hemingway transformed his experiences in Paris and Spain into a larger exposé of differences between pre- and postwar generations.

As Ben Stoltzfus (2010) astutely argued in *Hemingway and French Writers*, it was not simply the City of Light that influenced Hemingway during his formative years as a writer. Before looking at what Stoltzfus discovers, it is worth pointing out at this point that anyone wishing to understand how new critical theories can lead to a deeper appreciation of Hemingway's achievement need look no farther than this book. The community of Hemingway scholars got a sense of Stoltzfus's deep understanding of the reciprocal relationship between Hemingway and French writers from his earlier *Hemingway and Gide* (Stoltzfus 1978) and from "Sartre, *Nada*, and Hemingway's African Stories" (Stoltzfus 2005). Steeped in the work of French theorists, Stoltzfus assembled a number of previously published essays and ones written specifically for this volume to reveal how Hemingway's apprenticeship in Paris shaped his career in multiple ways. Stoltzfus argued that the Paris years not only provided Hemingway a chance to hone his craft; they also provided him the legitimacy he needed to rise above the provincialism that so often limits artists to temporary popularity. Individual essays traced Hemingway's affinity with important French writers and reveal his relationship with modernist and postmodern movements as his career progressed. Among Stoltzfus's more stimulating essays is his analysis of *The Sun Also Rises*. Heavily influenced by the work of Jacques Lacan, this critique (originally published in *Lacan and Literature* [Stoltzfus 1996]) made a compelling case for Hemingway's first major work of fiction as a postmodern novel.

Although not intended as a direct challenge to the many works that look externally for influences that shaped Hemingway's career, in *The Other Hemingway: Master Inventor*, veteran Hemingway scholar James Brasch (2009), cocompiler of *Hemingway's Library: A Composite Record* (1981), extended the kind of scholarship practiced most notably by Michael Reynolds. Claiming Hemingway was not confined to writing disguised autobiography, Brasch made a strong case for Hemingway's intellectual acumen and his penchant for seeking out individuals whose expertise could enrich his writing. Most notable is Brasch's commentary on Hemingway's use of the library he accumulated while at Finca Vigia, a source not available to most contemporary scholars.

Hemingway and Other Writers

A second form of influence study is one that highlight's Hemingway's relationships with other writers and his influence on them. At times, of course, the relationship is reciprocal, as Ronald Berman observed in three books examining Hemingway and Fitzgerald as products of the 1920s. *Fitzgerald, Hemingway, and the Twenties* (Berman 2001), a collection of Berman's previously published essays supplemented by new work, argued persuasively that to understand Hemingway's and Fitzgerald's works one must appreciate the intellectual climate in which they wrote. Berman wrote about Hemingway's first novels and some of the short stories as treatises exploring some of the more important topics of the time, such as "the loss of certainty" in the postwar decade. Displaying his own familiarity with the work of the intellectual giants of the period, Berman was able to explain why *A Farewell to Arms* was "a central intellectual document of the decade" (9), and why Hemingway's fiction of the 1920s reflected the ideas of writers such as William James, John Dewey, Josiah Royce, Walter Lippmann, Bertrand Russell, George Santayana, and even Ludwig Wittgenstein.

Although Hemingway figured less prominently in Berman's (2003) *Fitzgerald-Wilson-Hemingway: Language and Experience*, he was once again accorded the status of intellectual novelist. In a work that examines the influence of revolutionary ideas about the nature of language and its ability to replicate experience, Berman described how the two most prominent American novelists of the 1920s and the decade's rising star among critics reflected ideas of contemporary philosophers. In a compelling chapter on Hemingway, Berman explained how his plain style was not a means of escaping intellectual and emotional difficulties, but instead revealed "the author's sense of the difficulty of turning perception and experience into language" (79). Furthermore, Berman's interpretations show how the central issue for many of Hemingway's characters is the problem of language itself as a reliable form of representing the reality it purports to describe.

In his third study linking Hemingway and Fitzgerald, *Modernity and Progress*, Berman (2005) reprinted a previously published essay on Hemingway and Cézanne along with two original contributions to examine Hemingway's stance on one of the most important topics in American thought: the idea of progress. Hemingway is presented once more as a writer well versed in contemporary ideas and a keen observer of the modern condition. Again Berman defended him from charges of being anti-intellectual, claiming that, while he "rejects thinking, he does not reject thought" (66). Berman was intent on showing the complexity of Hemingway's mind and his deep understanding of the problems of modern life, which in his work frequently interfere with simplistic notions of progress. In his fourth book pairing Hemingway and Fitzgerald, *Translating Modernism*, Berman (2009) discussed Hemingway's techniques for creating landscape and the uses he made of landscape descriptions.

Hemingway's caustic and demeaning treatment of Fitzgerald in *A Moveable Feast* was defended by Sarah Churchwell (2005), who argued that the significance of the famous and somewhat vulgar incident in which Hemingway challenged Fitzgerald to measure their sex organs could be understood fully only by recognizing the real nature of the longstanding rivalry between the two. Hemingway was constantly measuring himself against Fitzgerald as a writer in a highly sexualized environment that recognized commercial success as masculine, purity of art as feminine.

Second only to commentary on the Hemingway-Fitzgerald relationship is criticism on the connections between Hemingway and Faulkner. Although the two were not close in the way Hemingway and Fitzgerald were, several critics have pointed out the ongoing rivalry (especially from Hemingway's point of view) as both strove for acclaim during their lifetimes. Nearly fifty years after both had died, the linkage remained strong enough for Earl Rovit and Arthur Waldhorn (2005) to issue *Hemingway and Faulkner: In Their Time*, a compilation of observations by contemporaries on their achievements and talents. In their introductory remarks, the editors acknowledged that they have "come to believe that the work of Hemingway and Faulkner rises like an arch above the work of their gifted contemporaries, in part, because of the judgments of those very writers themselves" (13). A more extensive critical analysis was provided in Joseph Urgo and Ann Abadie's (2004) *Faulkner and His Contemporaries*, a collection of essays from a 2002 conference on Faulkner that includes two on the Faulkner-Hemingway relationship. In the first, Donald Kartiganer (2004) explored the similarities between the two men who, though notably dissimilar in so many other ways, were alike in using gesture as a signifier of failure, often the failure to accomplish anything valuable. In the second, George Monteiro (2004) analyzed the rivalry between these two literary giants, one that both acknowledged tacitly while praising each other's work.

During the decade several essays on Hemingway's relationship with other important figures also appeared. For example, Hemingway is the subject of four essays in editors Stephen George and Barbara Heavilin's (2007) collection *John Steinbeck and His Contemporaries*, where the two writers' careers are examined for parallels, correspondences, and contradictions. An attempt to expand the context in which Hemingway may be situated was launched in 2007 at a discussion cosponsored by the Hemingway Society and the Robert Frost Society held at the Modern Language Association annual meeting. Four distinguished scholars—two Hemingway specialists and two in Frost studies—offered observations on useful connections that can be made between the two writers and offered suggestions for further study (del Gizzo 2011).

One of the more curious incidences of Hemingway's influence on younger writers was explored by Brian Hochman (2008) in "Ellison's Hemingways." Hochman traced Ralph Ellison's initial appreciation of Hemingway's prose style, his disavowal of that same style as a contributor to racism in America, and his eventual defense of Hemingway as a moralist. John Bak's (2010) study of Hemingway and Tennessee Williams, *Homo Americanus*, highlighted Hemingway's influence (much of it indirect) on Williams's conception of masculinity. Bak's comparative analysis of the concept of manhood in *The Sun Also Rises* and *Cat on a Hot Tin Roof*, however, further exposed some of the androgynous (and at times homoerotic) qualities of Hemingway's fiction that seem to have escaped earlier generations of critics intent on strengthening the image of Hemingway as "a man's man" and author of the code by which real men should live.

Interest also grew in the role Hemingway played in the development of hard-boiled fiction, a term applied to Hemingway's work as early as 1926 by Allen Tate (1926b), as scholars expanded literary study beyond the established canon and focused on cultural production. Among studies published during the decade, Christopher Breu's (2005) chapter on Hemingway in *Hard-Boiled Masculinities* is of interest because he explored affinities between *The Sun Also Rises*—which he says most critics consider "literary"—and a certain strand of pulp fiction. Breu argued that Hemingway's characters help define the kind of hard-boiled masculinity made popular by writers such as Raymond Chandler and Dashiell Hammett.

Catherine Turner (2003) argued that Hemingway was also responsible for a revolution of sorts in book advertising, at least at Scribner's, where the marketing department and editorial staff were forced to come up with a clever campaign to promote his work without damaging the reputation of a publisher long known for moral probity. David Earle's (2009) *All Man! Hemingway, 1950s Men's Magazines, and the Masculine Persona* is another fine study of Hemingway's influence. By his own admission, however, Earle's study was "not about Hemingway's fiction," as he made clear at the outset, "but about Hemingway himself as a fiction"—and about the role Hemingway played either actively or passively in the postwar "construction" of his image as the "new role model of the masculine persona" (4–5). Earle examined Hemingway's relationship with popular magazines, noting how it often seemed at odds with the "canonizing dynamics of academia that perpetuate the elitist idea" of him as a "high-brow modernist" (19), and explained why Hemingway came to represent the he-man persona. Curiously, Earle said, Hemingway became the model for both "the prototypical soldier" (with whom veterans could empathize) and the "savvy connoisseur, privy to the life of leisure" (20). Earle also explained how the creation of this popular image was the result of a symbiotic process between Hemingway's active solicitation of the kind of attention and adulation that men's magazines provided him and our society's need for such a role model in the postwar years.

Gender, Race, and Ethnic Studies

Feminist readings of Hemingway showed a marked decline in hostility during the decade—although there were still occasional instances of unadulterated hostility. The new, more measured approaches can be found in feminist Suzanne Clark's (2000) *Cold Warriors*. Clark posited that the rise of the Cold War with its attendant ideological conflicts was the most effective reason for Hemingway's being dismissed by intellectuals on both the Right and Left. Much of her essay was devoted to tracing Hemingway's debt to Theodore Roosevelt, who provided the model for the kind of heroism (and celebrity) Hemingway found attractive. At the same time, Clark cautioned, Hemingway frequently critiqued the kind of rugged individualism Roosevelt promoted; eventually his critique put him at odds with those in America who wished to use literature as a political tool. Clark pointed out that Hemingway's complex critique of hypermasculinity was recognized first by conservatives. In keeping with ideals of the Cold War that celebrated American values as interpreted by Theodore Roosevelt, they backed away from Hemingway's seeming embrace of values more akin to communism. Clark believed Hemingway "writes from a position that complicates the willful simplicity of Cold War critical judgments" (66). Hemingway became "unreadable" because "a legendary manliness" that leaves no room for questioning its dominant ideology "limited interpretations and occluded the contested history of culture, identity, and gender" that he "so extensively brought into question" (91–92). Unfortunately, over time all interpretation of his work was reduced to issues of male bonding, masculine superiority, and rugged individualism; small wonder that feminists, and intellectuals in general, rejected him. To properly read Hemingway "from a feminist point of view, as an avant-garde writer whose style unsettles identity and sexual relationships," Clark said "one must first address the reduction of his text to a singular and exaggerated masculine coding" (92). Once one discovers the causes for that monolithic interpretation—causes that lie outside the academy and in the larger world of politics, a subject that is interwoven in Hemingway's texts as much as that of gender identity—one can reclaim Hemingway as a writer meriting continued critical attention.

In *Impossible Women: Lesbian Figures and American Literature*, Valerie Rohy (2000) used *The Sun Also Rises* as a jumping-off point to discuss Hemingway's complex attitude toward lesbianism. Rohy's sensitive and historically grounded reading not only revealed much about cultural attitudes toward the New Woman, as she was described by the postwar press and many postwar scholars, but also defended the study of Hemingway by those interested in queer theory: "Hemingway is most useful to lesbian reading," she argued, "not as an instance of individual obsession with neurosis, but as an astute recorder of the compulsions and anxieties of masculine literary modernism and modernist culture" (67).

Blythe Tellefsen (2000) interpreted *The Garden of Eden* as Hemingway's attempt to "reimagin[e] the categories of race and gender, the structure of the family, and the meaning of artistry" (61) in American society. Tellefsen said this novel, like other major Hemingway works, does not valorize the code hero—and by extension, the American hero as he has been thought of traditionally—but instead "evince[s] a profound sense of the instability of the category of white, male American and a deep ambivalence about that identity" (59). Tellefsen refused to speculate about why Hemingway chose to withhold publication of what would have certainly been a controversial work, but she believed that, in the end, it "reconfigures the same old relationships" that reveal "the strength and power of American mythology over its citizens" (91). She insisted that the sensitivity Hemingway displayed in this novel should not be used as an excuse for his boorish behavior, racism, sexism, and anti-Semitism.

Hemingway's treatment of and attitude toward women—fictional and real—received updated treatment in Lawrence Broer and Gloria Holland's (2002) excellent collection *Hemingway and Women: Female Critics and the Female Voice*. Seventeen original essays provide a revaluation of critical responses to Hemingway and commentary on his work and life. Wishing to acknowledge "the salubrious impact" of women scholars on Hemingway's reputation, the editors invited only women to contribute to the volume (though they acknowledged in a footnote the contributions of some male critics to our understanding of Hemingway's interest in women and gender). The contributors were diverse in their opinions about Hemingway's personal relationships and his recreation of the female figure and voice in his fiction. Some appreciated his artistry despite his behavior toward real women, while others remain skeptical that judging the artistry apart from the behavior is possible. Collectively, however, the essays in *Hemingway and Women* provided a short survey of almost the entire Hemingway canon, viewed from a perspective that serves as an important and necessary counterweight to the preponderance of scholarship written between 1935 and 1970 that focuses almost exclusively on Hemingway's understanding about what it meant to be a man.

Betsy Nies (2002) wrote of Hemingway's fascination with the male body in his early work in *Eugenic Fantasies: Racial Ideology in the Literature and Popular Culture of the 1920s*. She claimed *The Torrents of Spring* and *The Sun Also Rises* offer a damning critique of "eugenic mores" while at the same time celebrating the "reassurance" offered by the "male body, pure and clean," as an "assuring response" to the devastating effects of the world war and to the New Woman, whose behavior threatened traditional sexual roles (64). Deirdre Pettipiece (2002) used her brief monograph, *Sex Theories and the Shaping of Two Moderns*, to rescue Hemingway from "myths" that accuse him of "misogyny and morbid preoccupation with masculinity." She believes that if read with "the influence of contemporary sexual and evolutionary theories in mind"—by which she means Havelok Ellis and Charles Darwin—it is possible to see how "Hemingway's texts illustrate an acute awareness of the struggle for meaning, for purpose, for identity, a struggle shared equally by both sexes" (xxi). Pettipiece found in the stories and novels, particularly *The Garden of Eden*, ample evidence that Hemingway was concerned about ways both men and women rise above their animal instincts to establish identity and meaning in their lives.

Relying on theories developed by Berthold Brecht and heavily influenced by a number of modern theorists, in *Hemingway's Theaters of Masculinity* Thomas Strychacz (2003) examined Hemingway's idea of masculinity by looking at ways male protagonists depend on the perception of others to define themselves as masculine.[3] Five years later, in *Dangerous Masculinities: Conrad, Hemingway, and Lawrence*, Strychacz (2008) used Hemingway's work to explain how modernist writers construct theories of masculinity through their writings. However, in this case Hemingway is employed in a larger debate between various groups of feminists and gender-studies critics analyzing the construct of gender.

The effort to revisit virtually all of Hemingway's fiction to discover evidence of what many posited (or hoped) was his lifelong fascination with the complexity of gender identification—often as a means of thoroughly dispelling or moderating his macho public image—was the impetus for yet another revaluation of *For Whom the Bell Tolls*, this one by Marc Hewson (2004). Challenging recent efforts (particularly those by Comley and Scholes and by Pamela Boker) for falling short of providing a true understanding of the novel's importance as a signpost of Hemingway's changing attitudes toward love and gender, Hewson explained how the novel may profitably be read as "the result of Hemingway's growing need to reassess, through writing, his interaction with stereotypical conceptions of masculinity and femininity—his own and others." The novel served as "a rehearsal ground for the more conscious experiments he would undertake in later manuscripts which are now considered to be primary evidence of his conflicted feelings about gender and sexuality" (172). Hewson relied heavily on the theoretical work of French feminist critic Hélène Cixous, specifically her "concepts of *écriture féminine* and gender bisexuality" (172). Disputing Boker's claim that no Hemingway hero truly knows the true nature of love between men and women, Hewson compiled examples from the novel of Jordan's genuine feelings for Maria. For Hewson, *For Whom the Bell Tolls* was "a watershed" in the Hemingway canon, displaying his movement "toward a more confessional, more honest, approach to his art and his questions about gender, sexuality, and identity" (183).

In another extended study combining psychological criticism and gender studies, *Ernest Hemingway: Masochism and Machismo*, Richard Fantina (2005) argued that beneath the rugged, he-man persona Hemingway created in his life and glorified in many of his characters lay another personality trait that, through careful reading, one can discern from his texts and perhaps from some actions in his life as well: masochism. Straining to differentiate his definition of masochism from classical psychological portraits that consider such behavior deviant, Fantina argued that the "heterosexual male masochism" one finds in Hemingway's work "seeks to submit the male body to the female body in an often ritualized exchange of sexual power" (6). Evidence is often latent because, given the social conditions when Hemingway lived and wrote, neither in life nor in fiction would a writer like Hemingway be willing to reveal that aspect of character. Fantina believes Hemingway should be commended for his masochism, which he calls not a "perversion" but "a distinctly nonaggressive and relatively selfless expression of male sexuality" (7). Fantina builds his case carefully, tracing evidence of this side of many of Hemingway's male characters and explaining how females become willing partners in allowing men to experience the pleasures this form of masochism can provide.

Predictably, Fantina found the climax of Hemingway's exploration of masochism in *The Garden of Eden*, where Catherine Bourne emerges as "an accumulation of traits inherited from many of her predecessors [in Hemingway's fiction] and amounts to a quantitative and qualitative synthesis" (117). As Fantina demonstrates, evidence of masochistic traits in Hemingway's men often vitiates the famous Hemingway code, but he takes pains to explain that Hemingway was not consciously subversive; he believed in many of the qualities he assigned to his male protagonists and was happy to celebrate them. However, the presence of masochism in his work reveals that he was more complex in his understanding of human sexuality and human relationships than one might derive from a monolithic reading of his fiction as simple celebration of the (patriarchal) code. "In the last resort," Fantina concludes, "we can be grateful to Hemingway for his radical subversion of some twentieth-century manifestations of patriarchy, even if we can hardly pretend that this was his project" (163).

A year later Fantina (2006) followed up his book with another report on Hemingway's tendency to foreground masochism in his work, citing the importance of dominant women in early and late works.

Amid the many attempts to address Hemingway and gender, Todd Onderdonk's (2006) article on *The Sun Also Rises* is noteworthy as a counter to the many attempts to make Hemingway appear conflicted about matters of gender early in his professional life. Onderdonk argued that Hemingway made it clear that "to be feminized" was "a bad thing" (61), and that "the issue of feminization" is central to understanding Hemingway's first novel. The text "reveals a proliferation of male humiliations and tender masculine intimacies," which Onderdonk called "repeated transgressions" of Hemingway's commitment—real, not feigned—to a macho code of conduct (62). The real problem, as Hemingway recognized, was that in the modern world traditional forms of masculinity were no longer acceptable, and he was forced to construct a new image of the masculine that accounted for elements (particularly feminized elements) of personality and behavior. The image Hemingway constructed of himself "in and beyond his fiction" was based on a notion of "exclusivity" (81)—only a few can claim the distinction of being real men, and of course, Hemingway is one of those elite. Onderdonk believed Hemingway used this novel "to define masculinity in a way that would exalt himself and exclude most of those peers who were, in 1925, regarded as his professional betters" (81).

In her assessment of *The Garden of Eden* in *Anachronism and Its Other*, Valerie Rohy (2009) addressed what she sees as the novel's "concern [with] the way in which white masculinity becomes visible to itself through projections onto a space of 'darkness'" (100). Relying heavily on the theoretical work of Freud, Lacan, and their disciples, Rohy explored "the relation of queer sexuality and gender identity to race, racism, and temporality" (101). Rohy (2011) continued her study of Hemingway's value for transgender studies in "Hemingway, Literalism, and Transgender Reading," tracing ways the "critical conversation" surrounding *The Garden of Eden* "raise[s] questions relevant to transgender studies now" (151).

Focusing more closely on the issue of race than Rohy does, in *Race and Identity in Hemingway's Fiction* Amy Strong (2008) offered strong readings of novels and stories that contain nonwhite figures, suggesting that a better understanding of these characters can sharpen our assessment of Hemingway, whose lifelong interest in matters of race seemed to parallel and at times equal his interest in issues involving gender. Strong was hard on earlier generations of critics (Philip Young comes in for special opprobrium) who either ignored or minimized the importance of these characters in favor of more traditional, patriarchal themes and white male characters. As so many critics had done before her, Strong found the posthumously published *The Garden of Eden* a seminal text for exploring all of the issues repressed or ignored by her predecessors. In writing about the posthumously published *Under Kilimanjaro*, she noted a decided change in Hemingway's vision of race. Where his early works reveal "that American concepts of freedom, power, and identity were constructed in opposition to the lives and experiences of native American and African American characters," in his final book on Africa Hemingway "shows the evils of white imperialism" and respect for African customs. Strong argued that Hemingway withheld publication of this book during his lifetime because it may have damaged "his reputation and public persona." Nevertheless, she said, seeing "his interest in race as a continuum" makes it possible to "revise the way we read some of Hemingway's fiction and challenge his oversimplified status as the quintessential white American male—an assumption that has too long held sway in critical discussions of his life and works" (138).

Two works on Hemingway and race deserve mention because they encourage a more balanced look at the Hemingway canon. In an analysis cleverly titled "The Short Happy Life of Black Feminist Theory," Ann Ducille (2010) revisited Hemingway's story of the Macombers to see how its African setting influences the extraordinary behavior of its characters. She also suggested (rather forcefully) that Hemingway and other writers whose works have been considered canonical—and sometimes dismissed because of that designation—deserve continuing attention. David Wyatt's (2010) brief but sensitive reading of Hemingway's work, "Performing Maleness: Hemingway," began with a cautionary note: "we misrepresent Hemingway when we reduce him to the champion of a 'code' or the rhetoric of 'not talking.'" Hemingway does not *"recommend* the behavior of his central characters"; instead, he uses them to illustrate "the cost of the performance of being male" (54).

The third leg of the triangle of chauvinisms of which Hemingway is often accused—racist attitudes toward ethnic "others," especially Jews—was also revisited by critics during the early 2000s. Gary Martin Levine's (2003) critique of *The Sun Also Rises* in *The Merchants of Modernism* explained how the treatment of Robert Cohn links the novel to a tradition of protest against the growing hegemony of consumerism as a dominant ideology in America. In *Jewishness and Masculinity from the Modern to the Postmodern*, Neil Davison (2010) examined Hemingway's attitude toward Jews and the use he made of them in his writing, particularly *The Sun Also Rises*. Linking his study with ones that focus on Hemingway's obsession with issues of gender, Davison argued that it is "an oversight to undervalue the role of racialized Jewishness in *The Sun Also Rises* as incidental to Hemingway's idiosyncratic gender struggles" (96). The portrayal of the male Jew as other, particularly as feminized other, allows Hemingway to define masculinity in a way that foregrounds his own claims to that characteristic.

Hemingway on War: New Perspectives

By the beginning of the new century, the influence of new interpretations of Hemingway's character, personality, and psychological makeup had taken firm hold on American readers inside and outside the academy. Concerned about this trend, Matthew Stewart (2000) observed in "Ernest Hemingway and World War I: Combatting Recent Psychobiographical Reassessments, Restoring the War," that "invariably, if the graduate students I have taught have read any secondary literature on Hemingway, it has been [Kenneth] Lynn, and just as invariably they are much taken with his conclusions." Lynn's conclusions are "arrived at through a tendentious methodology" (199), Stewart said, and he felt compelled to defend earlier critical commentary about the significant influence the First World War had on Hemingway over Lynn's conclusions that combat was only incidental in shaping Hemingway's fiction. Stewart compiles a thoughtful, well-documented case that Hemingway's experiences in the war were paramount in determining not only his subject matter but also his style. Agreeing with Stewart is Margot Norris (2000), who reprinted her 1988 article about the centrality of the First World War in Hemingway's artistic consciousness in a wider study of the influence of the war on literature, *Writing War in the Twentieth Century*. Norris argued that *A Farewell to Arms* is an early example of how the horrors of modern warfare could paradoxically give rise to great art. Norris's highly self-reflexive, postmodernist critique of war's influence on literature pays special attention to Hemingway's attempts to write truly about its "unknowabilities" (60).

The ways war can shape the literary imagination is also the subject of Alex Vernon's (2004) *Soldiers Once and Still: Ernest Hemingway, James Salter, and Tim O'Brien*, a study of literary responses to three twentieth-century wars by veterans. War had such a defining influence on Hemingway's fiction, Vernon argued, that his novels and stories reflect his combat experiences even when they are ostensibly about other subjects. Nowhere is this more true than in Hemingway's understanding of the concepts of manhood and gender relationships. Vernon believed anyone wishing to understand the literature of war (and veterans' literature) of the twentieth century must come to grips with Hemingway's treatment of war and its impact, because "every post-Hemingway American war veteran who has attempted to write serious fiction about war and the military has had to contend with Hemingway's looming shadow" (23).

The publication of Seán Hemingway's (2003) anthology of his grandfather's writings on war prompted a lengthy tribute from Thomas Putnam (2006), who praised Hemingway's ability to report accurately on battlefield events and describe the impact of war on populations affected by it. However, James Meredith (2004) argued that Hemingway's attitude toward armed conflict "was profoundly conflicted throughout his life"

(197). Meredith's analysis of the multiple voices Hemingway employs to render conflict realistically points out the ambivalence present in both his early fiction and later publications.

Those attributing Hemingway's creative imagination to his "war wound," already a dwindling number by the twenty-first century, were delivered a body blow by Keith Gandal (2008) in *The Gun and the Pen: Hemingway, Fitzgerald, Faulkner and the Fiction of Mobilization*. Gandal argued for a major reinterpretation of these novelists' work based on a careful understanding of the historical record and their personal experiences during the First World War. Such study reveals that the real motivation for novels like *The Sun Also Rises* and *A Farewell to Arms* was not Hemingway's "experiences of the horrors of World War I," but rather his "inability to have such experiences." The "famous sense of woundedness, diminishment, and loss" stemmed not from "the disillusionment or the alienation from traditional values" brought about by the war, but "instead from personal rejection by the U.S. Army." All three writers were "deemed unsuitable for full military service," and as a result felt "emasculated" (5). Gandal's reading of *The Sun Also Rises* and *A Farewell to Arms* placed great stress on Hemingway's feelings of inadequacy and his prejudices against minorities.

Hemingway's view of war again came in for scrutiny in Karsten Heige Piep's (2009) *Embattled Home Fronts: Domestic Politics and the American Novel of World War I*. Piep argued that Hemingway was not so much disillusioned by the war as he was by the postwar political situation that turned him against politics, leftist movements, and the women's movement emerging at the time. The bitter, fatalistic *A Farewell to Arms* could only have been written, she argued, after Hemingway experienced the disappointments of postwar society, which he witnessed firsthand through his assignments as a journalist.

Readings Applying New Critical Theories

Susanna Pavloska's (2000) *Modern Primitives: Race and Language in Gertrude Stein, Ernest Hemingway, and Zora Neale Hurston* is a good example of how cultural criticism had affected readers' understanding and appreciation of Hemingway's work. Defining primitivism as "the viewing of one culture through the eyes of another" (vii), Pavloska showed how Hemingway "embraced traditional primitivism" (59), using it to highlight the "insubstantial values of modern consumer society" (61) in *The Sun Also Rises*. The bulk of Pavloska's critique, however, focused on the stories in which Native Americans play a role. In these, Hemingway's view of the "primitive" is "drenched in nostalgia" (71), leaving him open to charges of naïveté or outright blindness to the true plight of native peoples. In *Border Modernism: Intercultural Readings in American Literary*

Modernism, Christopher Schedler (2002) combined psychoanalytic and cultural approaches in his discussion of the Nick Adams stories. Arguing that these tales reflect not only an "attempt to recapture the father of his boyhood years" but also a series of "attempts to 'select his own ancestors,'" Hemingway "employs the figure of the Indian as an imagined ancestor" to establish a "paternal legacy" that places Nick within a tribal culture. Schedler argued that Hemingway's "identification with Indians" not only allows him to "choose his own personal ancestors," but at the same time gives him a vehicle to "critique and renew" his own "culture" (57). This early effort becomes "the paradigmatic model" for Hemingway's "lifelong quest for 'tribal fathers'" (58), and helps explain his later interest in Africans.

Hemingway's political texts and subtexts sparked several commentaries during the decade. Michael Szalay's (2000) *New Deal Modernism: American Literature and the Invention of the Welfare State*, a Marxist reading that searches for the political subtext in postwar art, painted Hemingway as a conservative interested primarily in the textual integrity of his novels and stories. Relying heavily on the theoretical work of Theodor Adorno and Fredric Jameson (who advanced a similar theory about Hemingway in 1971), Szalay presented a strong case for Hemingway's rejection of leftist ideology in favor of creating texts that value aesthetic unity over social commentary. In explaining how Hemingway worked almost savagely to create this kind of fiction, Szalay provided interesting insights into how the image of the wound actually functions—as "a threat that writing is meant to alleviate" by showing its superiority to the human body (95). He also made a strong case for Hemingway's rejection of New Deal politics in favor of more Republican (the capitalization is intentional) ideals. Another political study, Lauretta Frederking's (2010) *Hemingway on Politics and Rebellion*, revealed that Hemingway's work appeals to scholars outside the realm of literary and cultural studies. The nine essays in Frederking's volume were all written by professors of politics, economics, or business, who use Hemingway's fiction as a means of expanding the boundaries of their disciplines, examining ways political struggle becomes a way for "an individual to discover his or her natural or authentic self" (4).

In an intriguing blend of psychoanalytic, gender, and environmentalist criticism, Cary Wolfe (2002) explored Hemingway's work from the viewpoint of "the discourse of species" (226), the way humans interact with animals. Wolfe argued that, where Hemingway criticism had highlighted the complexities of his understanding of issues relating to gender and identity, little had been done to examine his treatment of other species. Analyzing *The Garden of Eden*, Wolfe exposed Hemingway's transgression of norms, including norms in dealing with species, and exposed not only the highly charged quality of Hemingway's writing about identity and sexual relationships (and "cross-species identification" [243]) but also the antiromantic ideology that informs his fiction.

The most detailed assessment of Hemingway from an ecocritical perspective, however, may be Glen Love's (2003) chapter on him in *Practical Ecocriticism*. Love argued that, despite Hemingway's claims to be a champion of nature, the "two essential elements" of his "unique" consciousness—"a primitivistic conception of the natural world and one's proper behavior in it" and "a theory of literary tragedy"—are fundamentally "warring" principles (119). Love believed the tension between these two ideas was best expressed in *The Old Man and the Sea*, a novel he explicated in detail, explaining how Hemingway's primitivism paradoxically "arises from its countertendency to war against the earth, to exploit the natural world for self-aggrandizement" (122). Love did not fault Hemingway too harshly for adopting a view of the natural world that contemporary environmentalists would find objectionable. Instead, he concluded that "the great power of much of [Hemingway's] work arises from the tensions between the competing pulls of defiant individualism and the abiding earth" (133). Yet, he cautioned, "part of the cost of that greatness is a diminished earth" and a "version of primitivism" that even Hemingway began to question in his later years. An ecocritical reading of Hemingway's fiction is valuable, Love suggested, because in addition to making us "see and feel" and teaching us "how it was," it is now possible to see how Hemingway also "dramatize[d] for us how we have reached our precarious present" (132).

Contributing significantly to Hemingway scholarship during this decade were new assessments of Hemingway's short stories and short story collections. James Phelan's (2005) reading of "Now I Lay Me" in *Living to Tell about It: A Rhetoric and Ethics of Character Narration* explained how the components of lyric narratives, in which readers are invited to engage in the emotional experiences of narrators who are also characters in the story, work to give the story its exceptional power and immediacy. Among the more persuasive postmodern reinterpretations of Hemingway as a writer of short stories is Peter Donahue's (2003) "The Genre Which Is Not One: Hemingway's *In Our Time*, Difference, and the Short Story Cycle." Donahue argued that Hemingway's collection cannot be considered a conventional cycle, largely because Hemingway violated the modernist (and formalist) code of seeking to control within the cycle what T. S. Eliot called "the anarchy which is the contemporary world" (quoted in Donahue, 162). Instead, Donahue said, *In Our Time* served "the postmodernist purpose of upending control, order, shape, and significance to achieve its meaning" (162).

Milton Cohen's (2006) *Hemingway's Laboratory: The Paris "in our time"* demonstrates how new appreciation of early works can be achieved when these are read in the context of later achievements. Analyzing the sketches in Hemingway's slim volume *in our time*, Cohen explained how these "experiments" made possible the "consolidation of his mature style" (xiv). Kerry McSweeney's (2007) chapter on Hemingway in *The Realist Short Story of the Powerful Glimpse* focused on his development of the short story sequence featuring Nick Adams. McSweeney argued that the chronology established in Young's 1972 edition was open to question. McSweeney looked instead for unity and coherence based on *affect*, the creation of emotional intensity that works within a story and across story lines to bind individual tales into a sequence that exposes something larger than any individual unit is able to convey.

The thesis of Donald Bouchard's (2010) *Hemingway: So Far from Simple* is not startling, but his methodology for proving it marked another turn in the continual process of revaluating Hemingway's fiction by new critical standards. Bouchard's objective was "to show that Hemingway was a serious writer and that his simplicity—if in fact that adequately describes his life's work, his style, and his experiments with narrative form—was the conscious product of a complex and evolving practice" (18). Concentrating on the first two decades of Hemingway's career and the two works published after the Second World War, Bouchard gave Hemingway the kind of "attention" he said is promoted by theorists Michel Foucault, Gilles Deleuze, and Edward Said. Bouchard examined Hemingway's life and writing in a broad cultural context to explain how individual works emerged from the intersection of Hemingway's imagination and the events and ideas that influenced his writing life. The result is a book that gives prominence to Hemingway the writer and craftsman over Hemingway the classic writer institutionalized by academics.

Traditional Approaches

Although among the first approaches to be employed by Hemingway critics as early as the 1920s and 1930s, traditional studies of characterization, theme, style, and technique remained of interest nearly a hundred years later. Few twenty-first-century studies are as traditional, however, as William Ferrell's (2000) assessment of the Hemingway hero in *Literature and Film in Modern Mythology*. Revisiting this oft-discussed topic, Ferrell found that Hemingway's hero is modeled on Odysseus, a figure forced to expose himself to great dangers and repeatedly prove himself a man. John Vickery (2009) discussed Hemingway's two early novels in *The Prose Elegy*, a traditional study of genre and "the modern elegiac temper" (1). Elegiac elements abound in *The Sun Also Rises*, he noted, but these are "played out against a view of romantic love that deflates the conventional view of pre-war times by elevating the physical over the emotional and consummation over commitment" (65). In *A Farewell to*

Arms, Hemingway "locates the elegiac in the physical loss of a sexual and emotional partner amid a civilization scarcely worthy of the name" (93).

More often, new approaches added nuance to critics' understanding of older concepts. For example, in a study influenced equally by theories of history such as Frederick Jackson Turner's on the significance of the American frontier and by Roland Barthes's theory of mythic speech, Patricia Ross (2006) examined Hemingway's concept and use of "wilderness" as an ideological principle underlying his fiction. Ross said that Hemingway is "chief among the American Modernists to focus on wilderness as a literal signification"; his code hero is "nothing more than a rendition of the frontier/wilderness man" who "symbolizes wilderness without any ambiguity" (17). Ross argued that Hemingway's development of the code hero relied on accepting the myth of wilderness; unfortunately, that ideology cannot withstand too much scrutiny. Hemingway willfully ignored the complexity of the myth, always looking nostalgically at its importance as a counterweight to the messiness and ambiguities of modern life.

Two studies illuminate the way critics in the twenty-first century approached larger thematic issues. William Cain's (2006) "Death Sentences: Rereading *The Old Man and the Sea*" challenged those who dismiss the novella as slight and sentimental and suggested that this "most misunderstood" (112) work represented a new departure in Hemingway's career, an attempt "to make the tragic and the comic coincide" (114). In his own close reading of the work, Cain argued that "Hemingway's ideal audience consists of readers who pause over sentences and savor the spaces in between" (114)—presumably, one senses, not ones who attack the novels looking for evidence to support theoretical principles they espouse. Cain saw links between Santiago and his creator; like Santiago going out every day to fish even though he has caught nothing for months, at this point in his career Hemingway was "rising with the sun to write and count that day's allotment of prose" (116) even though he seemed unable to create fiction that met his own high standards. Far from being sentimental, the book's harsh language and powerful scenes "expose dimensions of experience that are almost impossible to face and that bring home with intensity the feelings that Hemingway explored" (118). Cain was even bold enough to reinterpret the obvious Christ-imagery of the novel, suggesting that "for Hemingway, Jesus was not the Redeemer but the peerless embodiment of a life of pain" who "accepted a mission" although "he knew he was dead the moment he was born" (123). Cain argued that for Hemingway the act of writing was a death-defying experience: "Inside the world of the book while it was being written, it was possible for Hemingway to feel nothing else mattered, including the reality of death" (125). Cain's Hemingway is a truly tragic figure working to produce great art in the face of inevitable defeat.

Notes

[1] An account of the publication, including commentary on Seán Hemingway's motivations for creating the new edition, Scribner's role in the publication, and scholars' observations on the project was written by journalist Steve Paul (2009) and published in the *Hemingway Review* under the clever title "'New Coke vs. Old Coke': The Debate over *A Moveable Feast: The Restored Edition*." Those enamored with the uniqueness of *A Moveable Feast* might do well to consult Craig Monk's (2008) *Writing the Lost Generation: Expatriate Autobiography and American Modernism*, in which Hemingway's memoir is treated as one of many attempts to capture the experiences and attitudes of the postwar generation.

[2] Information about Kent State University Press becoming a major publisher of Hemingway studies is based on a personal interview conducted on April 12, 2013, with Will Underwood, KSU Press director, and acquisitions editor Joyce Harrison.

[3] Some in the community of Hemingway scholars, weary of having to plod through so many studies of "Hemingway and gender," applauded Strychacz for his insight. That weariness was front and center in Kirk Curnutt's (2004) review of *Hemingway's Theaters of Masculinity*: "The heart frankly wearies," he began, "at the prospect of yet another full-length volume on Hemingway and gender" (103). Robert Trogdon (2005) asked that, after two decades of touting the new, sexually confused Hemingway, "What more, one is tempted to ask, need be said about Hemingway and masculinity?" (367). Both gave Strychacz high marks, however, for adding to an understanding of Hemingway's methodology in dealing with gender issues.

10: The Undisputed Champ Once More (2011–2014)

The status of Hemingway's reputation in the broad academic community fifty years after his death was succinctly described by Robert Lamb (2010) in the introduction to *Art Matters: Hemingway, Craft, and the Creation of the Modern Short Story*. Despite the proliferation of scholarship on Hemingway, "there remains a strong antipathy among academic critics toward him and his work, sometimes resulting in downright dismissal, especially among generalists and non-twentieth-century scholars" (1–2). Lamb countered Hemingway's detractors with a litany of praise he assembled from twentieth-century authors worldwide who openly acknowledged their admiration of Hemingway's work and their debt to him as an influence on their own fiction and nonfiction. These tributes, Lamb said, are convincing proof that Hemingway is "a towering figure whose art matters enormously" (6).

Anniversary Tributes

The fiftieth anniversary of Hemingway's death served as the occasion for the publication of several retrospectives—some in what might be considered unusual places. *USA Today* ran an article enumerating reasons Hemingway had "turned into a cottage industry since his death" (Wilson 2011). Jeffrey Meyers (2011) wrote a brief tribute for the online edition of the *Wall Street Journal*, noting the highlights of Hemingway's life in the spotlight and offering the opinion that his best works stand with those of Fitzgerald and Faulkner as "the literary gold standard for the 20th century." *Los Angeles Times* culture critic Reed Johnson's (2011) assessment of Hemingway's legacy stressed his larger-than-life presence fifty years after his death and his continuing influence on popular culture and literature. Johnson ended his article with a comment by Junot Diaz, author of the 2007 Pulitzer Prize–winning novel *The Brief Wondrous Life of Oscar Wao*: "[Hemingway] had an enormous influence on male writing in America, and his echoes, I suspect, are to be found almost everywhere." On the other side of the Atlantic, in a long piece for Britain's *Independent*, John Walsh (2011) explored the reasons for Hemingway's suicide, finding them in Hemingway's inability to "sustain[] the myth of Hemingway the Man's Man." Also interested in the cause for

Hemingway's decision to take his own life, the *Observer*'s Peter Beaumont (2011) suggested that constant hounding by FBI Director J. Edgar Hoover played a more significant role than previously acknowledged.

One of the more intriguing retrospectives is David Walsh's (2011) Marxist critique, posted on the World Socialist Web Site. Known for bashing many contemporary American authors for their capitulation to Western capitalist ideas, Walsh was surprisingly gentle on Hemingway. Noting that Hemingway "has largely dropped out of favor" in recent decades after being branded "homophobic and misogynistic, if not racist and anti-Semitic," Walsh insisted that "his sensibility at its best is compassionate and his view of the world one to be reckoned with." Some of his works are "staggeringly beautiful"; he was a writer who worked "powerfully and elegantly to represent life as it is." Of course, Walsh was quick to note that Hemingway was popular in the Soviet Union—suggesting that his work has left-leaning tendencies compatible with Marxist thinking. He was "a product of America in its transition to being an imperial power," and his early work reacted against much of the rhetoric that surrounded that movement. Given Walsh's own ideological bent, it is hardly surprising that he attributed Hemingway's decline to his unwillingness to confront the consequences of America's rise to world dominance. Still, Walsh argued, "he deserves to be read widely."

The Hemingway Letters

In 2011 the first volume of a comprehensive edition of Hemingway's letters appeared. Volume 2, covering the years 1923 to 1925, was published two years later. In the introduction to the first volume, General Editor Sandra Spanier (2011) called the 6,000-plus letters "the last great unexplored frontier of Hemingway studies" (xii). As she acknowledged, many important letters had been destroyed, most notably ones to Agnes von Kurowsky, Hadley Richardson, and Pauline Pfeiffer. What survived, however, sketched out a portrait of Hemingway not always captured in the many published biographies. Readers would be surprised at "the extent to which the letters contradict the common image of Hemingway the solitary artist, adventurer, and tough guy, unencumbered by if not estranged from his family." The correspondence reveals a "loving husband," a "proud father," a "playful and devoted brother," and (perhaps most remarkably, though Spanier does not emphasize the point) an "affectionate and ever-dutiful son." They also present Hemingway as a "political observer," "natural historian," "astute businessman," "infatuated lover," an "instigator and organizer of festivities"—in sum, the "everyday Hemingway" (xxix).

Predictably, the publication of Hemingway's letters—something he had expressly forbidden before he died—met with mixed reactions. *New*

York Times reviewer Arthur Phillips (2011) called the *Letters* "a spectacular scholarly achievement" (BR8). Hemingway biography Jeffrey Meyers (2012) was less enthusiastic, grousing that the first volume "has its faults" and "does not cast important new light on Hemingway's life," though it "confirms in great detail what is already known" (174–75). Reviewing the second volume for the British magazine the *Spectator*, Alexander Fiske-Harrison (2013) admitted that many people would take an interest in the correspondence, but speculated that this massive edition might be "too much of a good thing." Although he was fascinated with the letters, Edward Mendelson (2014) complained that these volumes "seem[ ] to have been edited for readers who do not exist," as they contain many unnecessary notes (some of which he says misrepresent Hemingway).

Studies of Life and Relationships

The book that caught the attention of contemporary reviewers and the reading public in 2011 was Paul Hendrickson's *Hemingway's Boat: Everything He Loved in Life and Lost, 1934–1961*. A former journalist, Hendrickson used a clever angle to approach his subject: through Hemingway's relationship with his boat, the *Pilar*, which he bought in 1934. With the attention of a scholar, Hendrickson explored the most troublesome decades of Hemingway's life, tracing Hemingway's erratic behavior with family, friends, and associates as he spiraled deeper into the depression that finally drove him to take his life. Light on literary criticism (except for an extended justification for Hendrickson's claim that *Across the River and Into the Trees* is Hemingway's "most autobiographical" novel [316]), the biography is expansive in examining a number of side issues that touched Hemingway's life, such as the history of the boatyard that built *Pilar* and Hemingway's relationships with Arnold Samuelson and Walter Houk. Despite his disclaimers, Hendrickson tried to get inside Hemingway's mind to understand what motivated him during the decades when only the publication of *For Whom the Bell Tolls* and *The Old Man and the Sea* temporarily staved off the constant drumbeat of negative criticism that he was finished as a writer. In a claim that will amaze (and possibly infuriate) readers familiar with Hemingway's life from other sources, Hendrickson admitted that he had "come to believe deeply that Ernest Hemingway, however unpostmodern it may sound, was on a lifelong quest for sainthood"—yet, "at nearly every turn, he defeated himself" (16).

In a sense, Hendrickson's book is an example of resistant reading—resistant to the trend in Hemingway criticism since the advent of the feminist movement and the posthumous publication of works that led academics to focus on a more complex, sexually conflicted Hemingway than the image he projected while he was alive. Hendrickson's Hemingway is once again the macho, chest-beating, hard-drinking adventure-seeker who realized that to write truly and well, he had to cloister himself away from the world so the words would come to him. In Hemingway, Hendrickson explained, it is possible to see "the irresolvable contradictions of the life and the glories of the work—some of it." Yet, he continued, "the Hemingway myth, however much oversold and devalued, can still powerfully stand in a new century for a great many tensions unresolved in American males"—at least, he qualified, "so I believe" (17–18).

One might expect a biography crafted to support that premise would generate considerable controversy. Maureen Dowd (2011), certainly no supporter of the traditional macho Hemingway, called Hendrickson's book "captivating" (SR 11). *Washington Post* reviewer Howell Raines (2011) said it was "a large-minded, rigorously fair summation of the best thought on Hemingway's writing, his life, traumas, pathologies, his family and friends, his even more abundant cast of personal, literary and cultural enemies." Raines thought Hendrickson had succeeded, where many "very able scholars" had failed, in demonstrating that "a writer's life can contain two conflicting existences, one purely original genius and one of irreversible destructiveness." *New York Times* reviewer Arthur Phillips (2011) believed the book "includes some of the most moving, beautiful pieces of biography I have ever read"—but immediately qualified his praise by adding "except when the book is discussing Ernest Hemingway and his boat" (BR8). Instead, Phillips suggested, the portraits of minor figures are the strong points of Hendrickson's study. Jeffrey Meyers (2012) seemed genuinely put out by this book. The descriptions of "the endless fishing expeditions become extremely boring" (176); the supposed compassionate portrait of Hemingway is as "vulturine" (177) as many of the works Hendrickson criticized; the study is "heavily dependent on previous critics" and "has nothing new to say about Hemingway's work" (178). A hint about the real sources of Meyers's prejudice against *Hemingway's Boat* may be found in his observation that "the best part of the book, on Gregory," is a synthesis of works by Gregory Hemingway's third wife and his children—and "my own essay" (178). Possibly, however, Hendrickson's book is further proof that veteran Hemingway scholar Robert Gajdusek (2002) was right on the mark ten years earlier in observing that "despite a continuing series of biographies, the mystery of Hemingway the man seems radically unexplored" (1).

Less noticed outside academe, Lyle Larsen's (2011) *Stein and Hemingway: The Story of a Turbulent Friendship* focused on a relationship that helped shape Hemingway's career. Although virtually every biographer of Hemingway had commented on this important connection, Larsen's incorporation of materials from a wide array of published and unpublished materials in the Hemingway collection demonstrated just how important Stein was in getting Hemingway to focus on his career and develop the style for which he became famous. Larsen also pointed the finger of blame directly at Stein's companion Alice B. Toklas as the cause of deteriorating relations between the two writers. In a similar study, John Cohassey (2014) explained in *Hemingway and Pound: A Most Unlikely Friendship*, how what started out as a mentor-pupil relationship grew into a real friendship between the avant-garde poet and the revolutionary young novelist.

Joseph Fruscione's (2012) *Faulkner and Hemingway: Biography of a Literary Rivalry* made use of sophisticated critical tools developed in the later decades of the twentieth century to explore ways the two writers consciously—and more often unconsciously—competed to be viewed as the premier writer of their generation. Working within the critical framework constructed by Dennis Brown (1990) in *Intertextual Dynamics within the Literary Group*, Fruscione examined "the tense, shared, and psychological influence between Faulkner and Hemingway in an intragenerational context, coupled with notions of rivalry and masculine performativity" (7). Following their careers through the 1920s into the years following the Second World War, Fruscione demonstrated that each read the other's' work and commented on it privately and publicly. Hence, many of their most important novels and stories can be read as responses to previously published works, a kind of textual sparring that led to two competing versions of modernism. By the end of the 1940s, both had "created their respective artistic worlds, imaginative realms in which they had established patterns of style, theme, characterization, subject, and place," all the while drawing "sharp contrasts with one another, with each implying the primacy of his own aesthetic vision" (151). While they may have felt "the desire to outperform each other," Fruscione concluded, the rivalry had decidedly beneficial effects for American literature: "In their own ways, Faulkner and Hemingway sought after—and frequently achieved—the perfection of craft for which all artists strive in one another's shadow" (244).

Hemingway's work inspired by Africa was the topic of a collection ably assembled by Miriam Mandel (2011). The ten contributors to *Hemingway and Africa* surveyed Hemingway's knowledge of the customs and natural terrain, revisited his exploits on safari, and assessed his sometimes unrealistic views of the continent. Essays on individual works concentrated on posthumously published work with African settings. It should be pointed out, however, that James Plath's "Barking at Death: Hemingway, Africa, and the Stages of Dying" provided a nuanced reading of the oft-anthologized and oft-critiqued "Snows of Kilimanjaro." Another very useful essay is the final one from Kelli Larson: an annotated bibliography of scholarship on Hemingway's African writings published between 1989 and 2010. The collection made it possible to get a sense of both the best and the worst of Hemingway's encounter with the Dark Continent.

Interest in other people, places, events, and ideas that shaped Hemingway's fiction continued to motivate scholars. In *The Last Good Land*, a study in which Hemingway's works are used to examine the importance of Spain in the American literary imagination, Eugenio Suárez-Galbán (2011) mounted a spirited, if somewhat tendentious, defense of Hemingway's unshakable belief in Spain as "the last good land" (223). In *Paris and American Literatures*, Jonathan Austad (2013) explored connections and parallels between Hemingway's early work and the Dadaist movement, which he said "played a key role in the Parisian mind-set" after the First World War (54). Austad believed Hemingway "appropriates the movement's nihilist sentiments" (54) and employs some of their techniques, such as the juxtaposition of contradictory imagery, to argue that "ideals are meaningless and irrelevant" (64). Nancy Sindelar's *Influencing Hemingway* (2014) documented the many people and places that shaped his work; her commentary also explained how Hemingway transposed his real-life experiences into fiction.

The forty-plus essays in Debra Moddelmog and Suzanne del Gizzo's (2013) *Ernest Hemingway in Context* explored "influence" in a broader context: biography, initial reception of Hemingway's work, adaptations, intellectual movements, ailments and accidents, the environment, politics, race (to which several chapters are devoted), religion, sexuality and marriage, war, women—and more. While the roster of contributors reads like a Who's Who in Hemingway studies, as Michael DuBose pointed out in his review of the volume for the *Hemingway Review*, "there is only so much that can be said in ten pages" (110), the uniform length of each entry. Nevertheless, *Ernest Hemingway in Context* offered an accurate and reasonably comprehensive snapshot of the best that was being thought and said about Hemingway as the century moved into its second decade.

On War (Once More)

Seven years after publishing a sensitive study of Hemingway's use of his war experiences to fashion early works like *A Farewell to Arms*, Alex Vernon (2011) wrote in *Hemingway's Second War: Bearing Witness to the Spanish Civil War* a similar assessment of the way firsthand experiences shaped his second great war novel, *For Whom the Bell Tolls*. Vernon's literary biography examined the dispatches Hemingway wrote from the battlefield, critiques the 1937 film *The Spanish Earth*, to which Hemingway contributed significantly, and described how the facts Hemingway amassed in these roles served to spark his imagination in creating his novel. Vernon also made some cogent observations about the status of this novel in the Hemingway canon, hinting that his admiration for *For Whom the Bell Tolls* may place him at odds with the current community of Hemingway scholars who have elevated *The Garden of Eden* to a place beside *The Sun Also Rises* as Hemingway's most important works. Although *For Whom the Bell Tolls* was an "instant critical and commercial success," Vernon said, it has "since garnered far less attention by scholars, perhaps because of its apparently traditional attitude of soldierly martyrdom" (199), or simply because it deals with "a war increasingly fading from American memory" (200). Certainly Vernon's study, particularly in his careful comparison of the novel with *A Farewell to Arms*, went far in restoring the book to a place of prominence among Hemingway's novels.

Viewed in light of the history of Hemingway criticism, Vernon's book is an example of what a scholar committed to careful, exhaustive research—and blessed with what reviewer Earl Rovit (2011) called "quicksilver creative agility" (lxxiii)—can produce. Like Michael Reynolds's 1976 groundbreaking study *Hemingway's First War: The Making of "A Farewell to Arms,"* from which Vernon derived his title, *Hemingway's Second War* is likely to have notable influence on future generations of scholars. Rovit called it simply "hands-down the definitive study of this aspect of Hemingway's career" (lxxi).

Interested in the impact of war on Hemingway, first as a participant and then as a journalist, Doug Underwood (2011) focused on Hemingway's career as a journalist in *Chronicling Trauma*. Underwood explained how Hemingway was able to turn traumatic experience to his advantage as a writer. In *Authoring War: The Literary Representation of War from the Iliad to Iraq*, Kate McLoughlin (2011) constructed a postmodernist reading of Hemingway's story "On the Quai at Smyrna," focusing on the importance of lacunae, silences, and other "avoidance tropes" (151) that convey the story's principal theme: the atrocity and senselessness of war.

In a revisionist assessment of Hemingway and war, Steven Florczyk (2013) made personal papers of Hemingway's commanding officer, Captain Robert W. Bates, the centerpiece of *Hemingway, the Red Cross, and the Great War*, re-creating an almost day-by-day account of Hemingway's time in Italy. Although Florczyk seemed to delight in pointing out the minor errors of other scholars, his principal aim was to restore the notion, once commonplace but discredited after Michael Reynolds published *Hemingway's First War* in 1978, that Hemingway relied heavily on personal experience to write stories and novels about the war. Florczyk makes a compelling case that Hemingway's war literature "is significantly informed by personal experience and historical research, both of which he transformed into fiction according to a highly crafted literary technique" (142).

The eighteen essays in *War & Ink*, edited by Steve Paul, Gail Sinclair, and Steve Trout (2014), revisited the early years of Hemingway's career, during which he developed his keen eye for observation, pithy style, and obsession with questions of mortality and violence. At the center of these essays is the question of the role Hemingway's time as a reporter for the

Kansas City Star played in his early emergence as a writer whose powers of observation, combined with a journalistic style that strips away ornamentation to record core issues involving human emotions, set him apart from others in his generation. Rather than repeat scholarship that explains and interprets Hemingway's personal experiences, contributors examined the context in which Hemingway served during the First World War and described the confluence of style and experience as it was expressed in some of the early stories. In *Understanding War*, Doug Underwood (2013) expanded observations about Hemingway made in his earlier *Journalism and the Novel* (Underwood 2010), exposing the epistemological basis for Hemingway's rejection of journalism in favor of fiction as the best way to represent truth. Because his goal was "to identify and convey felt emotions in the way they truly are," Underwood said, Hemingway found journalism inadequate; journalists are "restrained from telling the truth about life in its entirety" (126). Underwood linked Hemingway to the philosophical tradition of David Hume and Walter Lippmann, who argued that custom and habit keep people from perceiving life as it actually is. These books suggest that the work of scholars interested in Hemingway's journalism may not yet be at an end.

New Views on Race and Gender

The growing interest in Hemingway's attitudes toward race and the importance of race in his understanding of gender is evident in another fine scholarly study from Kent State University Press, Marc Dudley's (2011) *Hemingway, Race, and Art: Bloodlines and the Color Line*. Dudley adopted as his starting point for his interrogation of the Hemingway canon observations made by Toni Morrison in her influential 1992 study of American literature, *Playing in the Dark*, and by inference if not direct quotation, Edward Said's studies on the notion of the outsider in European fiction. Although the presence of minorities sometimes "is seemingly nonexistent" (6) in much of his fiction, Hemingway's attempts to construct male identity—which, Dudley said, means white male identity—are inexorably bound up in his understanding of other races. Dudley analyzed several short stories and the African writings, citing examples of Hemingway's depiction of Native Americans, African Americans, and Africans in works that deal with issues of race and the construction of identity. Dudley's book exposed Hemingway's lifelong interest in one of the three subjects that were "on his mind for much of his literary career: masculinity, nationality, and race" (159).

Gary Holcomb and Charles Scruggs's (2012) *Hemingway and the Black Renaissance*, a collection of nine essays, traced Hemingway's influence on several notable African American writers of the early twentieth century. One might have expected African Americans to distance themselves from Hemingway; yet, as the contributors demonstrate, he had demonstrable influence on James Baldwin, Richard Wright, and Ralph Ellison. The volume also contains an intriguing essay arguing for Jean Toomer's *Cane* as inspiration for the structure of Hemingway's first major collection of stories. Holcomb's essay on Hemingway and Claude McKay, a reprint of an article originally published in the *Journal of Modern Literature* (Holcomb 2007), placed both authors in a transnational and transatlantic context. Also of note is an essay suggesting that Hemingway influenced Toni Morrison (a fact she might find hard to acknowledge).

In a provocative chapter on *The Sun Also Rises* in his *Gender, Race, and Mourning in American Modernism*, Greg Forter (2011) argued that Hemingway fetishizes the ideal of manhood, idealizing it at the same time as he recognizes the impossibility of attaining it in the modern world. For Hemingway, "the modern world is defined by the unmournable loss of the manhood the bullfighter represents." Forter claimed the novel "develops a set of techniques for memorializing without mourning" this ideal man; these techniques "bespeak" what he called "a *fetishistic* melancholia: they turn upon a disavowed knowledge of modern manhood's double 'castration,' insisting that men are cut off from both (racialized) primality and expressive 'femininity' while preserving these in rigidified, affectively deadened, unenlivening forms" (57).

Benjamin West (2013) offered a different perspective on this subject in *Crowd Violence in American Modernist Fiction*. Examining the three novels in which war and its aftermath are central to the plot, West concluded that Hemingway does not endorse "a particular version of idealized masculinity," but instead points out "various failures of traditional masculine identity" (127). This more nuanced understanding, based on careful analysis of Hemingway's most iconic protagonists—Jake Barnes, Frederic Henry, and Robert Jordan—reveals how far critics have come in appreciating the subtleties of Hemingway's artistry.

Hemingway's fiction provides Sarah Anderson (2012) several useful examples for her study of depictions of trauma in modernist fiction. Reading "his trauma narratives as sites of resistance" (15), Anderson built on the long-established tradition of seeing the wounded hero as suffering from trauma but focused on Hemingway's female characters to see if his portrayal of trauma might be gender based—and gender biased.

Exploring Old and New Territory

Veteran Hemingway scholar Lawrence Broer (2011) offered a psychological critique of Hemingway's fiction in his comparative study *Vonnegut and Hemingway: Writers at War*. Broer explored the intriguing question of why Vonnegut, considered by many the writer of his generation most closely allied with Hemingway, was adamant in distancing himself from

Hemingway and finding fault with his work. Carefully pairing novels by each author, Broer provided a reading of the Hemingway canon that explains how deep-seated, repressed feelings drive Hemingway to write about a meaningless universe. Broer also argued for the importance of the publication of *Under Kilimanjaro* for Hemingway critics, because the frank self-portrait in this book allows for a more complete view of Hemingway as a writer and a man.

In a challenge to environmentalist readings that celebrate Hemingway's view of the natural world, Lloyd Willis (2011) argued that in his fiction Hemingway "practiced a politics of environmental evasion," opting for a simplistic belief that the unspoiled, virgin land "will always be available in the world for those who are willing to pursue a Thoreauvian plan of environmental imperialism" (126–27). To illustrate his point, Willis offered close readings of *In Our Time* and *Green Hills of Africa*. The former, he said, "betrays an awareness of environmental destruction, looks away from it, and creates an image of perpetually available and pristine space that it encloses within its generic structure" (130). What seemed even worse in Willis's view is Hemingway's view of the environment in *Green Hills of Africa*, in which, he says, Hemingway "recommends an environmental imperialism that fulfills, in the worst possible ways, Thoreau's command to encounter wilderness at any cost" (130).

Hemingway's works continue to prove useful subjects of study by scholars interested in narratology. In "Recalcitrant Simplicity: Thin Characters and Thick Narration in *A Farewell to Arms*," Alexander Hollenberg (2012) used the novel to explain "how a simply drawn character can suggest the terms of our rhetorical relation to the larger text while also causing us to think self-consciously about the relative importance we assign to mimetic, thematic, and synthetic character dimensions" (301). Building on—and in some ways expanding and correcting—the analysis of the novel offered by James Phelan, Hollenberg argued that "Hemingway's simple style serves as a way to disimagine Frederic" while at the same time producing what Hollenberg calls "*thick narration*: a mode of narrative communication that is characterized by a complex, oscillating relationship between the implied author and narrator," thereby making it hard to distinguish between them and forcing readers to "consider the role of interpretation as a central concern of the text" (307).

In another attempt to explain the rhetorical qualities of Hemingway's fiction, James Phelan (2013) examined his use of voice and characterization in *A Farewell to Arms*, a novel in which Hemingway transforms personal experience into a narrative dealing with wider issues. Phelan argued that it is possible to have a more optimistic worldview than Hemingway's and still be moved deeply by this novel, largely because, by manipulating voice, Hemingway is able to generate exceptional empathy and sympathy for his main characters. Phelan also claimed that Catherine "provides a model" for Frederic to show him "how to live with the knowledge of the world's destructiveness" (86). Not content to simply assert what could be construed as a chauvinist position, Phelan addressed some of the more strident attacks launched by feminists against the novel, answering critics like Judith Fetterley by acknowledging the truth of many of her observations. Catherine does seem to be a male fantasy, subservient to Frederic; in this, Phelan said, "Hemingway's representation of Catherine is ethically flawed." And yet, "to focus only on that flaw is to miss some of the genuine power of Hemingway's handling of Catherine's character" (100). Phelan believed the tension created by Catherine's dual role—as servant and guide—is what allows the novel to appeal to modern readers: "The combination of intellectual resistance and emotional suasion has the potential of making one rethink—and rejustify or revise—one's own world view" (102).

Editors Suzanne del Gizzo and Frederic Svoboda's (2012) collection *Hemingway's "The Garden of Eden": Twenty-Five Years of Criticism* contains a generous selection of important critical commentary on what is perhaps the most controversial publication to bear Hemingway's name. The editors claimed their collection "capture[s] the dynamic of the critical conversations as they unfolded" (x) and shows how critical commentary is built on previous scholarship. The volume includes an essay by Tom Jenks, who assembled the published 70,000-word version from Hemingway's manuscripts (which ran more than 200,000 words), in which he explains the methodology he used to create this "new" Hemingway work. Noteworthy in this collection is an observation by the editors: *The Garden of Eden* is "quickly becoming one of Hemingway's most frequently taught works." Though they qualified this by saying the novel is helping readers develop new understandings of Hemingway's other works, the fact remains: If future generations get their idea of Hemingway from a manuscript he chose not to publish, in a version he did not authorize, what impact will that have on his reputation?

In his multidisciplinary study of Hemingway's fiction, *In Paris or Paname*, Jeffrey Herlihy (2011) employed recent theoretical work in psychology, anthropology, and literary studies to examine what he calls an "overdetermined characteristic" of Hemingway's fiction: the "foreignness" of his main characters (1). As place was so important to Hemingway, Herlihy's study of displacement as a plot device offered yet another way to discover patterns and themes that complement the more traditional interpretations that focus on psychological wholeness and social conflict. His work suggests that, as the scope of literary critics expands to make use of disciplines outside literature, it may be possible to find additional ways to make Hemingway's fiction accessible to new readers.

Finally, in *Hemingway, Cuba, and the Cuban Works* editors Larry Grimes and Bickford Sylvester (2014) collected twenty-one essays by

American and Cuban scholars that explore Hemingway's time in Cuba, examine the influence the island and its people had on him, and analyze his fiction based in or around Cuba. Like Miriam Mandel's *Hemingway and Africa*, this volume offered nuanced readings of Hemingway's work, particularly *The Old Man and the Sea*, and corrected some misconceptions about his activities in Cuba (especially during the 1930s). Kelli Larson's extensive annotated bibliography made clear the continuing interest in Hemingway's association with Cuba and its influence on his fiction. In a companion piece annotating criticism published in Cuba, Ned Quevedo Arnaiz provided similar documentation for Cubans' fascination with Hemingway, a man who, Arnaiz said, has become part of that island's mythology.

Challengers to Mainstream Twenty-First-Century Approaches

Amid the torrent of critical commentary inspired by new forms of critical theory, Harold Kaplan's (2011) chapter in *The Solipsism of Modern Fiction: Comedy, Tragedy, and Heroism* seems like a throwback to a simpler age in Hemingway criticism—or a reversion to critical premises that appear inadequate, if one believes advances in theory make earlier forms of critical inquiry incomplete, suspect, or wrongheaded. Kaplan's brief review of Hemingway's fiction, focused principally on early works, showed how the body of Hemingway's oeuvre is designed to record "a favorite myth of our time," the "story of the wounded hero, by turns a man of sensibility and man of action, helpless and strenuously active" (94). Kaplan demonstrated how "natural experience is the object of both attraction and revulsion for Hemingway's characters" (96). In this highly metaphysical reading, Kaplan found that sport—especially bullfighting—becomes "a religious service" that gives "resolution to conflict." If one reads Hemingway in this way, one can see him "as a symbolist writer transcribing a metaphysical search"; this characteristic, Kaplan said, is what makes his work lasting (105).

In a critique of both Hemingway and his critics, Thomas Gordon Perrin (2012) explained why, in his later career, Hemingway may have been ahead of his time in addressing "the increasingly visible incoherences of modernist aesthetics" (152). Using *The Old Man and the Sea* as his principal example, Perrin offered reasons for Hemingway's increasing distaste for symbolic readings of his texts—while at the same time he was creating works that cry out for symbolic readings, ones whose failure to be sufficiently grounded in the real world make more literal readings difficult. Like T. S. Eliot's *The Cocktail Party*, another work Perrin investigated in his essay, *The Old Man and the Sea* seems to exude indeterminacy and demand multiple readings—a characteristic, Perrin argued, that is "the open secret of mainstream 1950s modernism" (168).

Certainly Matthew Nickel's (2013) *Hemingway's Dark Night* must have seemed like a hostile missile launched into the midst of a love feast. Taking on a fairly large segment of the community of Hemingway scholars, Nickel argued forcefully (perhaps at times tendentiously) that Hemingway had an interest in Catholicism that predates his wounding, that his conversion to Catholicism was real, and that his fiction—including the later works—reveals "patterns of sin and redemption, the dark night, and the possibility of love and salvation attained through the medium of art" (212). All of Hemingway's completed novels "portray characters deep in the dark night seeking reconciliation," who in their moments of suffering are offered "an image beyond the darkness, the possibility that through love (*eros* and *agape*), there may be a light in the dark night" (245). At the center of Nickel's argument is his interpretation of *The Old Man and the Sea*, where "a closer look at how Catholicism informs the deep structure and iceberg of the text reveals a clearly Christian story" (217). More surprising, perhaps, is his claim that *The Garden of Eden* reveals the same "Christian pattern" in its focus on "betrayal, darkness, and the quest to strike light in darkness, to create out of the past a form of atonement" (234).

While in some scholarly circles Nickel's approach may have seemed dated—even outmoded—the continuing fascination with "all things Hemingway" garnered for him a number of favorable reviews. As one might expect, Nicholas Ripatrazone's (2014) assessment for *CatholicFiction.net* was highly supportive; he was especially thankful that Nickel has "help[ed] recover Hemingway from being relegated to a nondescript Protestant individualist ethos" that Hemingway had "personally rejected before 1918," but which has "remained in criticism of his work." More noteworthy, perhaps, was Mark Von Cannon's (2014) judgment in the *Hemingway Review* that, despite some omissions and sketchy analysis caused in part by Nickel's effort to be inclusive, the book will be "an immense aid" (154) to general readers and scholars interested in Hemingway's attitudes toward religion.

A strong advocate for Hemingway's preeminence among American writers, Robert Lamb spent years examining Hemingway's fiction and publishing his findings in a number of scholarly journals (see, for example, his lengthy article "Hemingway and the Creation of Twentieth-Century Dialogue" [Lamb 1996]). Beginning in 2010, he restructured his work in two studies that challenge assumptions not only about Hemingway but also about the practice of criticism by Lamb's contemporaries. Lamb's (2010) *Art Matters* provided a new critical vocabulary to explain how Hemingway's short stories achieve the impact they have had for nearly a century. The second part of Lamb's extended study of the short stories,

The Hemingway Short Story: A Study in Craft for Writers and Readers (Lamb 2013), called for a "new" kind of scholarship that returns to practices that characterized earlier study while making use of insights derived from recent literary theorists. Lamb's close readings of individual stories are based on premises to which he alludes in *Art Matters* and articulated forcefully in the preface to *The Hemingway Short Story*: that "a writer is not merely a social construction, a site upon which cultural forces contend, but a complex human being, a professional in his or her craft" (xiii); that the "bifurcation" of the study of a writer between examination of craft and "cultural critique" is "spurious" (xiv); and that the short study is "a distinct literary genre, complete with its own conventions" and not simply a shorter version of a novel. With these in mind, Lamb undertook his analysis of "the aesthetic principles and techniques of the most influential fiction writer of the past hundred years" (xii).

Conclusion: The Enduring Master

IN CONCLUDING THIS STUDY, I wish to pose and answer briefly two questions important for the future of Hemingway studies. First, can more be said about Hemingway and his fiction? Second, has nearly a century of critical commentary justified the exalted place claimed for him by his devoted admirers? While there is no way to be definitive in responding to either of these queries, recent scholarship and commentary suggest that, at this time at least, the answer to both questions is "yes."

Given the exhaustive exploration of Hemingway's work over nearly a century, it may be hard to imagine entirely new readings or avenues of inquiry into his fiction opening up. Nevertheless, the possibility exists that more sophisticated examination of well-worn stereotypes may yield surprising results. Certainly such is the case with Mark Cirino's (2012) *Ernest Hemingway: Thought in Action*, a slim but provocative examination of Hemingway's fiction written from the premise that "Hemingway's work constitutes a revolution in the fictional investigation of modern consciousness, not an avoidance of it" (80). Hemingway's characters often find themselves in situations where action is called for and time to think a luxury. Instead, "this apparent conflict—between the man of action and the man of thought—not only defines Hemingway's public persona but also represents the essential tension in his work" (79). His "focus on action incorporates consciousness into an urgent external situation and does not ignore it or fail to understand the functioning of the mind" (80).

Perhaps the most daring claim Cirino makes in his book is that Hemingway has a right to be considered a psychological novelist, interested in exploring the life of the mind as much as his more celebrated contemporary psychological novelists Marcel Proust, James Joyce, and William Faulkner. Using Michael Reynolds's *Hemingway's Reading* (1981) as his guide, Cirino scrutinizes the catalog of books Hemingway owned or borrowed over three decades to demonstrate that he had a continuing interest in the topic. Coupling this information with comments Hemingway made in letters to family and friends about the aims of his fiction, Cirino lays out a powerful case for readings that offer new ways of understanding some of Hemingway's most celebrated works and appreciating some that have not fared so well with critics. For example, he describes "Big Two-Hearted River" as "a silent drama of metacognition" in which the "condition of Nick's consciousness becomes the narrator's primary concern" (21). He asserts that Santiago's real quest in *The Old Man and the Sea* "is related not to the physical act of fishing but rather to the internal sustenance of mental solvency, mental control, sanity, the mastery of consciousness" (39–40). *A Farewell to Arms* should be seen as comparable to Faulkner's *The Sound and the Fury*, "an incisive investigation into the psychological or philosophical implications of time" (57). In *The Sun Also Rises*, "Hemingway's subtle evocation of Jake Barnes's interiority" signals "profound character development" (132). A wide array of sources—philosophers Henri Bergson, Georges Poulet, and Emile Boutroux; psychologists Sigmund Freud and William James—buttress Cirino's argument that critics who dismissed Hemingway as lightweight and consecrated Joyce, Proust, and Faulkner as leading lights of the modern psychological novel did not look deeply enough at the strong current of interest in the mind flowing through all his novels where surface action captures readers' immediate attention. If one agrees with Cirino's arguments, there is still much about Hemingway to be discovered, and much in his work to merit continued study.

Turning to my second question: Is Hemingway worth the effort, and will he last? Again, there is no way to predict what literary critics will do in a hundred years (or even a decade, for that matter). However, one prediction can be made with some certitude: Hemingway will remain a staple in college classrooms, either for his own value as an artist or as a "cultural text" to assist students in understanding the past, appreciating the present, and shaping the future. Thanks to the continuing efforts of Kent State University Press, new titles published in 2015—Alex Vernon's (2015) *Teaching Hemingway on War* and Joseph Fruscione's (2015) *Teaching Hemingway and Modernism* in the "Teaching Hemingway" series—will offer useful assistance to teachers of Hemingway's work.

It would be hard to find a better endorsement of Hemingway's value to twenty-first-century readers than that offered by the writer Andre Dubus in his 2012 PEN Hemingway keynote address. "In this digital present where so many human faces are lit with the glow of one screen after another," Dubus told the audience assembled at the Kennedy Library in Boston, at "a time when the notion of individuality and the truly real is beginning to blur, more than ever before we need the life's work of Ernest Hemingway, a writer whose daily surrendering of himself to his novels and stories and the lives being lived inside them achieves precisely what he hoped it would, to 'make it alive,' which miraculously, still has the enduring power to make *us* more alive in that precious allotment of time we are all given on this earth" (15).

Major Works by Ernest Hemingway

Three Stories and Ten Poems, 1923.
in our time, 1924.
In Our Time, 1925.
The Torrents of Spring, 1926.
The Sun Also Rises, 1926.
Men without Women, 1927.
A Farewell to Arms, 1929.
Death in the Afternoon, 1932.
Winner Take Nothing, 1933.
Green Hills of Africa, 1935.
To Have and Have Not, 1937.
The Fifth Column and the First Forty-nine Stories, 1938.
For Whom the Bell Tolls, 1940.
Across the River and Into the Trees, 1950.
The Old Man and the Sea, 1952.
A Moveable Feast, 1964.
Islands in the Stream, 1970.
The Dangerous Summer, 1985.
The Garden of Eden, 1986.
True at First Light, 1999.
Under Kilimanjaro, 2005.
A Moveable Feast: The Restored Edition, 2009.

Works Cited

Abrahams, William. 1972. "Hemingway: The Posthumous Achievement." *Atlantic Monthly*, June, 98, 100–101.
Adams, J. Donald. 1937. "Ernest Hemingway's First Novel in Eight Years." *New York Times Book Review*, October 17, 2.
———. 1939. "Ernest Hemingway." *English Journal* 28, no. 2 (February): 87–94.
———. 1940. "The New Novel by Hemingway." *New York Times*, October 20, 1.
Adams, John R. 1932. "New Hemingway Story Increases Writer's Prestige." *San Diego Union*, October 2, 6.
———. 1933. "Literary Guidepost." *San Diego Union*, November 19, 9.
Aiken, Conrad. 1926. "Expatriates." *New York Herald Tribune Books*, October 31, Section 7, 4.
Aldridge, John. 1951. "Hemingway: Nightmare and the Correlative of Loss." In *After the Lost Generation: A Critical Study of the Writers of Two Wars*, 23–43. New York: McGraw-Hill.
———. 1954a. "Before the Sun Began to Rise." *New York Times Book Review*, July 11, 4.
———. 1954b. "Hemingway: The Etiquette of the Berserk." *Mandrake* 2 (Autumn–Winter): 331–41. Reprinted in *In Search of Heresy: American Literature in an Age of Conformity*, 149–65. New York: McGraw-Hill, 1956.
———. 1970. "Hemingway between Triumph and Disaster." *Saturday Review*, October 10, 23–26, 39.
Algren, Nelson. 1964. "Who's Who at the Lost and Found." *Nation*, June 1, 560–61.
———. 1965. *Notes from a Sea Diary: Hemingway All the Way*. New York: Putnam.
"All Stones End . . ." 1937. *Time*, October 18, 79–85.
Allen, Hugh. 1940. "The Dark Night of Ernest Hemingway." *Catholic World* 151 (February): 522–29.
Allen, Mary. 1983. "The Integrity of Animals: Ernest Hemingway." In *Animals in American Literature*, 177–96. Urbana: University of Illinois Press.
"An Anderson Parody." 1926. *Springfield Sunday Union & Republican*, August 29, 7F.
Anastas, Benjamin. 1993. "Three Ways of Being Modern: The Lost Generation Trilogy by James Mellow." *Iowa Review* 23, no. 1 (Winter): 161–74.

Anders, Smiley. 1970. "Three Good Stories Will Not Harm Writer's Standing." *Baton Rouge Advocate*, November 8, 2F.
Anderson, Quentin. 1972. "Devouring the Hemingway Corpus." *New Leader*, May 15, 13–15.
Anderson, Sarah. 2012. "Readings of Gender and Madness in Hemingway's *Across the River and Into the Trees* and *The Garden of Eden*." In *Readings of Trauma, Madness, and the Body*, 69–83. New York: Palgrave Macmillan.
Angoff, Charles. 1950. "The Library: Ernest Hemingway." *American Mercury*, November, 619–25.
Anibal, C. E. 1933. Review of *Death in the Afternoon*. *Hispania* 16, no. 1 (February–March): 112–13.
Arnold, Lloyd. 1968. *High on the Wild with Hemingway*. Caldwell, ID: Caxton.
Astro, Richard, and Jackson Benson, eds. 1974. *Hemingway in Our Time*. Corvallis: Oregon State University Press.
Aswell, James. 1929. "Critic Lavishes Praise on New Hemingway Novel." *Richmond Times-Dispatch*, October 6, 25.
Atkins, John A. 1952. *The Art of Ernest Hemingway: His Work and Personality*. London: Nevill.
Atkinson, Brooks. 1964. "Gertrude Stein and Scott Fitzgerald Are Defended against Hemingway's Attack." *New York Times*, July 7, 32.
Austad, Jonathan A. 2013. "From Dada to Nada: The Dadaist Influence on Hemingway's Works between 1922 and 1926." In *Paris in American Literatures: On Distance as a Literary Resource*, edited by Jeffrey Herlihy-Mera and Vamsi K. Koneru, 53–68. Lanham, MD: Fairleigh Dickinson University Press.
"Authors and Critics Appraise Works." 1961. *New York Times*, July 3, 6.
Bak, John. 2010. *Homo Americanus: Ernest Hemingway, Tennessee Williams, and Queer Masculinities*. Madison, NJ: Farleigh Dickinson University Press.
Baker, Carlos. 1940. "The Hard Trade of Mr. Hemingway." *Delphian Quarterly* 23, no. 3 (July): 12–16, 45.
———. 1942. "Anthologies of Mars and Midas." *Sewanee Review* 51, no. 1 (January–March): 160–63.
———. 1952a. *Hemingway: The Writer as Artist*. Princeton, NJ: Princeton University Press.
———. 1952b. "The Marvel Who Must Die." *Saturday Review*, September 6, 10–11.
———. 1954. "The Palmy Days of Papa." *Saturday Review*, May 29, 14–15.
———, ed. 1961. *Hemingway and His Critics: An International Anthology*. New York: Hill and Wang.
———, ed. 1962. *Ernest Hemingway: Critiques of Four Major Novels*. New York: Scribner.
———. 1964. "A Search for the Man as He Really Was." *New York Times Book Review*, July 26, 4.

———. 1967. "His Beat Was the World." *New York Times Book Review*, May 28, 1, 16.

———. 1969a. Review of *Ernest Hemingway and the Little Magazines. American Literature* 40, no. 4 (January): 572–74.

———. 1969b. Review of *Ernest Hemingway and the Pursuit of Heroism. American Literature* 41, no. 1 (March): 129–30.

———. 1969c. *Ernest Hemingway: A Life Story*. New York: Scribner.

———, ed. 1981. *Ernest Hemingway: Selected Letters, 1917–1961*. New York: Scribner.

Baker, Sheridan. 1967. *Ernest Hemingway: An Introduction and Interpretation*. New York: Holt, Rinehart and Winston.

Bakker, Jan. 1972. *Ernest Hemingway: The Artist as a Man of Action*. Assen, Neth.: Van Gorcum.

———. 1983. *Fiction as Survival Strategy: A Comparative Study of the Major Works of Ernest Hemingway and Saul Bellow*. Amsterdam: Rodopi.

Balassi, William. 1990. "Hemingway's Greatest Iceberg: The Composition of *The Sun Also Rises*." In *Writing the American Classics*, edited by James Barbour and Tom Quirk, 125–55. Chapel Hill: University of North Carolina Press.

Baldwin, Marc. 1997. *Reading "The Sun Also Rises": Hemingway's Political Unconscious*. New York: Lang.

Barlowe, Jamie. 1994. Review of *Hemingway's Genders. Hemingway Review* 14, no. 1 (Fall): 84–87.

———. 1996. Review of *Hemingway: The Postwar Years and the Posthumous Novels. Novel* 30, no. 1 (Fall): 138–40.

Barnes, Lois. 1953. "The Helpless Hero of Ernest Hemingway." *Science and Society* 17, no. 1 (Winter): 1–25.

Barnett, Louise. 1993. "The Dialectic of Discourse in *The Sun Also Rises*." In *Authority and Speech: Language, Society, and Self in the American Novel*, 149–64. Athens: University of Georgia Press.

Barton, Bruce. 1927. Review of *The Sun Also Rises. Atlantic Monthly*, April, 12, 14.

Batliner, Doris. 1993. "Author Explores Hemingway's Life." *Rockford Register*, February 7, 4F.

Baym, Nina. 1992. "'Actually, I Felt Sorry for the Lion': Reading Hemingway's 'The Short Happy Life of Francis Macomber.'" In *Feminism and American Literary History: Essays*, 71–80. New Brunswick, NJ: Rutgers University Press.

Beach, Joseph Warren. 1932. "The Cult of the Simple." In *The Twentieth-Century Novel: Studies in Technique*, 530–43. New York: Century.

———. 1951. "How Do You Like It Now, Gentlemen?" *Sewanee Review* 59, no. 2 (Spring): 311–28.

Beaumont, Peter. 2011. "Fresh Claim over Role the FBI Played in Suicide of Ernest Hemingway." *Observer*, July 2.

Beckerman, Marty. 2011. *The Heming Way: How to Unleash the Booze-Inhaling, Animal-Slaughtering, War-Glorifying, Hairy-Chested, Retro-Sexual Legend Within*. New York: St. Martin's Press.

Beebe, Maurice, and John Feaster. 1968. "Criticism of Ernest Hemingway: A Selected Checklist." *Modern Fiction Studies* 14, no. 3 (Autumn): 337–69.

Beegel, Susan F. 1988. *Hemingway's Craft of Omission: Four Manuscript Examples.* Ann Arbor, MI: UMI Research Press.

———, ed. 1989. *Hemingway's Neglected Short Fiction: New Perspectives.* Tuscaloosa: University of Alabama Press.

———. 1990. "Hemingway and Hemochromatosis." In Wagner-Martin 1998, 375–88.

———. 1996. "Conclusion: The Critical Reputation of Ernest Hemingway." In Donaldson 1996, 269–99.

Bellow, Saul. 1953. "Hemingway and the Image of Man." *Partisan Review*, May–June, 338–42.

Bennett, Arnold. 1929. Review of *A Farewell to Arms. Evening Standard*, November 14, 5.

Bennett, Warren. 1970. "Character, Irony, and Resolution in 'A Clean, Well-Lighted Place.'" *American Literature* 72, no. 1 (March): 70–79.

Benson, Frederick. 1967. *Writers in Arms: The Literary Impact of the Spanish Civil War.* New York: New York University Press.

Benson, Jackson. 1969. *Hemingway: The Writer's Art of Self-Defense.* Minneapolis: University of Minnesota Press.

———, ed. 1975. *The Short Stories of Ernest Hemingway: Critical Essays.* Durham, NC: Duke University Press.

———. 1989. "Ernest Hemingway: The Life as Fiction and the Fiction as Life." *American Literature* 61, no. 3 (October): 345–58.

———, ed. 1990. *New Critical Approaches to the Short Stories of Ernest Hemingway.* Durham, NC: Duke University Press.

Berg, A. Scott. 1978. *Max Perkins: Editor of Genius.* New York: Dutton.

Berman, Ronald. 2001. *Fitzgerald, Hemingway, and the Twenties.* Tuscaloosa: University of Alabama Press.

———. 2003. *Fitzgerald-Wilson-Hemingway: Language and Experience.* Tuscaloosa: University of Alabama Press.

———. 2005. *Modernity and Progress: Fitzgerald, Hemingway, Orwell.* Tuscaloosa: University of Alabama Press.

———. 2009. *Translating Modernism: Fitzgerald and Hemingway.* Tuscaloosa: University of Alabama Press.

Berthoff, Warner. 1994. "'The Flight of the Rocket' and 'The Last Good Country': Fitzgerald and Hemingway in the 1920s, and After." In *American Trajectories: Authors and Readings 1790–1970*, 101–16. University Park: Penn State University Press.

Bessie, Alvah. 1940. "Hemingway's *For Whom the Bell Tolls.*" *New Masses*, November 5, 25–29.

Bilyeu, Jack. 1950. "Hemingway's Latest Work Is Called Disappointment." *Richmond Times-Dispatch*, October 15, 11A.

Bloom, Harold, ed. 1985. *Ernest Hemingway.* New York: Chelsea House.

———, ed. 1987a. *Ernest Hemingway's "A Farewell to Arms."* New York: Chelsea House.

———, ed. 1987b. *Ernest Hemingway's "The Sun Also Rises."* New York: Chelsea House.

———, ed. 1991. *Brett Ashley.* New York: Chelsea House.

———, ed. 1996a. *Ernest Hemingway's "A Farewell to Arms."* Broomall, PA: Chelsea House.

———, ed. 1996b. *Ernest Hemingway's "The Old Man and the Sea."* Broomall, PA: Chelsea House.

———, ed. 1996c. *Ernest Hemingway's "The Sun Also Rises."* Broomall, PA: Chelsea House.

———, ed. 1999a. *Ernest Hemingway.* Broomall, PA: Chelsea House.

———, ed. 1999b. *Ernest Hemingway's "The Old Man and the Sea."* Broomall, PA: Chelsea House.

———, ed. 2003a. *Ernest Hemingway.* Philadelphia: Chelsea House.

———. 2003b. "Ernest Hemingway." In *Genius: A Mosaic of One Hundred Exemplary Creative Minds,* 569–74. New York: Warner.

———, ed. 2004. *Nick Adams.* Philadelphia: Chelsea House.

———, ed. 2005. *Ernest Hemingway.* Philadelphia: Chelsea House.

———, ed. 2007. *Ernest Hemingway's "The Sun Also Rises."* Philadelphia: Chelsea House.

———, ed. 2008. *Ernest Hemingway's "The Old Man and the Sea."* New York: Bloom's Literary Criticism.

———, ed. 2009. *Ernest Hemingway's "A Farewell to Arms."* New York: Bloom's Literary Criticism.

———, ed. 2010. *Ernest Hemingway's "A Farewell to Arms."* New York: Bloom's Literary Criticism.

———, ed. 2011a. *Ernest Hemingway.* New York: Bloom's Literary Criticism.

———, ed. 2011b. *Ernest Hemingway's "The Sun Also Rises."* New York: Bloom's Literary Criticism.

Blumenthal, Ralph. 1998. "A New Book by Hemingway: Blend of Life and Fiction Tells of African Bride." *New York Times,* August 24.

Boardman, Michael. 1992. "Innovation as Pugilism: Hemingway and the Reader after *A Farewell to Arms.*" In *Narrative Innovation and Incoherence: Ideology in Defoe, Goldsmith, Austen, Eliot, and Hemingway,* 146–88. Durham, NC: Duke University Press.

Boker, Pamela A. 1995. "Negotiating the Heroic Paternal Ideal: Historical Fiction as Transference in Hemingway's *For Whom the Bell Tolls.*" *Literature and Psychology* 41, nos.1–2 (Spring–Summer): 85–112.

———. 1996. *The Grief Taboo in American Literature: Loss and Prolonged Adolescence in Twain, Melville, and Hemingway.* New York: New York University Press.

Booth, Bradford. 1953. Review of *Hemingway: The Writer as Artist. American Literature* 25, no. 1 (March): 95–96.

Boreth, Craig. 2012. *The Hemingway Cookbook.* Chicago: Chicago Review Press.

Bouchard, Donald F. 2010. *Hemingway: So Far from Simple.* Amherst, NY: Prometheus Books.

Boyd, Ernest. 1926. Review of *The Torrents of Spring*. *Independent*, June 12, 694.
Bradbury, Malcolm. 1968. "Sad Voyage." *New Statesman*, March 22, 386.
———. 1970. "Broken Stoic." *Manchester Guardian*, October 24, 18.
———. 1983. *The Modern American Novel*. Oxford: Oxford University Press.
———. 1995. "A Generation Lost and Found: Hemingway, Fitzgerald, and the Paris of the Twenties." In *Dangerous Pilgrimages: Trans-Atlantic Mythologies and the Novel*, 295–358. London: Secker & Warburg.
Bradbury, Malcolm, and David Palmer, eds. 1971. *The American Novel and the Nineteen Twenties*. London: Edward Arnold.
Brasch, James D. 2009. *That Other Hemingway: The Master Inventor*. Victoria, BC: Trafford.
Brasch, James D., and Joseph Sigman. 1981. *Hemingway's Library: A Composite Record*. New York: Garland.
Bredahl, A. Carl, and Susan Drake. 1990. *Hemingway's "Green Hills of Africa" as Evolutionary Narrative: Helix and Scimitar*. Lewiston, NY: Mellen.
Breit, Harvey. 1952. "*The Old Man and the Sea.*" *Nation*, September 6, 194.
Brenner, Gerry. 1982. "Are We Going to Hemingway's Feast?" *American Literature* 54, no. 4 (December): 528–44.
———. 1983. *Concealments in Hemingway's Works*. Columbus: Ohio State University Press.
———. 1991. *"The Old Man and the Sea": Story of a Common Man*. New York: Twayne.
———. 2000. *A Comprehensive Companion to Hemingway's "A Moveable Feast"*. Lewiston, NY: Mellen.
Breu, Christopher. 2005. "The Hard-Boiled Male Travels Abroad." In *Hard-Boiled Masculinities*, 83–114. Minneapolis: University of Minnesota Press.
Brian, Denis. 1988. *The True Gen: Intimate Portraits of Ernest Hemingway by Those Who Knew Him*. New York: Grove.
Brickell, Herschel. 1925. "Tales Galore by Writers from Lands Near and Far." *New York Evening Post Literary Review*, October 16, 3.
———. 1932. "What Bullfighting Means to the Spaniard." *New York Herald Tribune*, September 25, 3, 12.
Bridgman, Richard. 1966. "Ernest Hemingway." In *The Colloquial Style in America*, 195–230. New York: Oxford University Press.
"Brief Mention." 1964. *American Literature* 36, no. 1 (November): 401.
"Briefer Mention." 1927. *Dial*, January, 73.
Britton, Beverly. 1941. "Balancing the Books." *Richmond Times-Dispatch*, November 27, 4.
Broer, Lawrence R. 1973. *Hemingway's Spanish Tragedy*. Tuscaloosa: University of Alabama Press.
———. 1989. "'On Writing': A Portrait of the Artist as Nick Adams." In *Hemingway's Neglected Short Fiction: New Perspectives*, edited by Susan Beegel, 107–22. Tuscaloosa: University of Alabama Press.

———. 2011. *Vonnegut and Hemingway: Writers at War.* Columbia: University of South Carolina Press.
Broer, Lawrence R., and Gloria Holland, eds. 2002. *Hemingway and Women: Female Critics and the Female Voice.* Tuscaloosa: University of Alabama Press.
Brooks, Cleanth. 1943. "Mr. Kazin's America." *Sewanee Review* 51, no. 2 (January–March): 52–61.
———. 1963. "Ernest Hemingway: Man on His Moral Uppers." In *The Hidden God: Studies in Hemingway, Faulkner, Yeats, Eliot and Warren,* 6–21. New Haven, CT: Yale University Press.
Brooks, Cleanth, and Robert Penn Warren. 1943. *Understanding Fiction.* New York: Crofts.
Brooks, Van Wyck. 1953. *The Writer in America.* New York: Dutton.
Brooks, Walter R. 1929. "Behind the Blurbs." *Outlook and Independent,* October 16, 270.
Brown, Dennis. 1990. *Intertextual Dynamics within the Literary Group— Joyce, Lewis, Pound and Eliot: The Men of 1914.* New York: St. Martin's Press.
Broyard, Anatole. 1970. "Papa's Disappointing 'Big One.'" *Life,* October 9, 10.
Bruccoli, Matthew J., ed. 1970. *Ernest Hemingway, Cub Reporter: Kansas City Star Stories.* Pittsburgh: University of Pittsburgh Press.
———, ed. 1971. *Ernest Hemingway's Apprenticeship: Oak Park, 1916–1917.* Washington, DC: Microcard Editions.
———, ed. 1973. *Hemingway at Auction, 1930–1973.* Detroit: Gale.
———. 1978. *Scott and Ernest: The Authority of Failure and the Authority of Success.* Carbondale: Southern Illinois University Press.
———, ed. 1986a. *Conversations with Ernest Hemingway.* Jackson: University Press of Mississippi.
———. 1986b. "Portrait of the Writer as a Liar." *National Review,* January 31, 58–60.
———. 1994. *Fitzgerald and Hemingway: A Dangerous Friendship.* New York: Carroll & Graf.
———, ed. 1996. *The Only Thing That Counts: The Ernest Hemingway/Maxwell Perkins Correspondence, 1925–1947.* New York: Scribner, 1996.
———. 2002. *Classes on Ernest Hemingway.* Columbia: Thomas Cooper Library, University of South Carolina.
———, ed. 2004. *The Sons of Maxwell Perkins: Letters of F. Scott Fitzgerald, Ernest Hemingway, Thomas Wolfe, and Their Editor.* Columbia: University of South Carolina Press.
Bruccoli, Matthew J., and Judith Baughman, eds. 2006. *Hemingway and the Mechanism of Fame.* Columbia: University of South Carolina Press.
Bryer, Jackson. 1967. *The Critical Reputation of F. Scott Fitzgerald: A Bibliographical Study.* Hamden, CT: Archon Books.
———, ed. 1969. *Fifteen Modern American Authors: A Survey of Research and Criticism.* Durham, NC: Duke University Press.

———, ed. 1989. *Sixteen Modern American Authors, Volume 2: A Survey of Research and Criticism since 1972.* Durham, NC: Duke University Press.

Budick, Emily Miller. 1989. "*The Sun Also Rises*: Hemingway's New Covenant of History." In *Fiction and Historical Consciousness: The American Romance Tradition,* 164–84. New Haven, CT: Yale University Press.

Burgum, Edwin Berry. 1938. "Hemingway's Development." *New Masses,* November 22, 21–24.

Burhans, Clinton. 1968. "The Complex Unity of *In Our Time.*" *Modern Fiction Studies* 14, no. 3 (Autumn): 313–28.

Burwell, Rose Marie. 1992. Review of *Hemingway's Quarrel with Androgyny. Style* 26, no. 2 (Summer): 351–55.

———. 1996a. *Hemingway: The Postwar Years and the Posthumous Novels.* New York: Cambridge University Press.

———. 1996b. Review of *Hemingway's Genders. Novel* 29, no. 2 (Winter): 259–61.

Busch, Frederick. 1992. "Reading Hemingway without Guilt." *New York Times,* January 12.

Butcher, Fanny. 1950. "That Old Black Magic That Is Hemingway's." *Chicago Sunday Tribune,* September 17, Magazine of Books, 3, 14.

———. 1952. "Hemingway at His Incomparable Best." *Chicago Sunday Tribune,* September 7, Magazine of Books, 1.

Butcher, Maryvonne. 1968. "Occasional Pieces." *Tablet,* March 23, 285.

Buttimer, Ann. 2000. "Place Metaphor and Milieu in Hemingway's Fiction." In *Cultural Encounters with the Environment,* ed. Alexander Murphy and Douglas Johnson, 203–19. Lanham, MD: Rowman & Littlefield.

Butts, Leonard. 1986. Review of *Along with Youth* and *Hemingway: A Biography. Studies in the Novel* 18, no. 3 (Fall): 333–38.

———. 1991. Review of *Hemingway's Quarrel with Androgyny. Studies in the Novel* 23, no. 4 (Winter): 509–12.

Cain, William E. 1999. "Hemingway in Decline." *Boston Globe,* July 11, C1.

———. 2006. "Death Sentences: Rereading *The Old Man and the Sea.*" *Sewanee Review* 114, no. 1 (Winter): 112–25.

Calder-Marshall, Arthur. 1952. Review of *The Old Man and the Sea. Listener,* September 18, 477.

Callaghan, Morley. 1964. Review of *A Moveable Feast. Spectator,* May 22, 696.

Calverton, V. F. 1939. "Steinbeck, Hemingway, and Faulkner." *Modern Quarterly* 11, no. 4 (Fall): 36–44.

Capers, Julian. 1929. "Love and War Are Basic Elements of New Hemingway Novel." *Dallas Morning News,* October 13, Books, 3.

Carpenter, Frederick. 1954. "Hemingway Achieves the Fifth Dimension." *PMLA* 69, no. 4 (September): 711–18.

Carver, Raymond. 1985. "Coming of Age, Going to Pieces." *New York Times,* November 17. Reprinted in *Call If You Need Me: The Uncollected Fiction and Other Prose,* 276–85. New York: Vintage, 2001.

Catton, Bruce. 1937. "A Book a Day." *Greensboro Record,* October 16, 4.

Chamberlain, John. 1933. "Books of the Times." *New York Times*, October 27, Art Books, 17.
———.1935. "Books of the Times." *New York Times*, October 25, 19.
Chase, Cleveland. 1926. "Out of Little, Much." *Saturday Review of Literature*, December 11, 420–21.
Chase, Richard. 1957. *The American Novel and Its Tradition*. Garden City, NY: Doubleday.
"Cheapening Boston." 1929. *Boston Herald*, July 24, 14.
Churchwell, Sarah. 2005. "'4000 a Screw': The Prostituted Art of F. Scott Fitzgerald and Ernest Hemingway." *European Journal of American Culture* 24, no. 2 (August): 105–29.
Cirino, Mark. 2012. *Ernest Hemingway: Thought in Action*. Madison: University of Wisconsin Press.
Cirino, Mark, and Mark P. Ott, eds. 2010. *Ernest Hemingway and the Geography of Memory*. Kent, OH: Kent State University Press.
Civello, Paul. 1994. *American Literary Naturalism and Its Twentieth-Century Transformations: Frank Norris, Ernest Hemingway, Don DeLillo*. Athens: University of Georgia Press.
Claridge, Henry, ed. 2012. *Ernest Hemingway*. 4 vols. New York: Routledge.
Clark, Suzanne. 2000. "Theodore Roosevelt and the Postheroic Era: Reading Hemingway Again." In *Cold Warriors: Manliness on Trial in the Rhetoric of the West*, 59–96. Edwardsville: Southern Illinois University Press.
Clarke, Phil. 1953. "Maugham Issues a Frank Warning." *Richmond Times-Dispatch*, January 25, 4A.
Cleaton, Allen. 1932. "Mr. Hemingway's New Book: Introduction to Bullfighting." *Richmond Times-Dispatch*, October 2, 5.
Clifford, Stephen. 1997. "The Tyranny of Biography: Hemingway's Readers and the Fascination for Papa." *College Literature* 24, no. 2 (June): 172–82.
———. 1998. *Beyond the Heroic "I": Reading Lawrence, Hemingway, and "Masculinity."* Cranbury, NJ: Associated University Press.
Cobley, Evelyn. 1993. *Representing War*. Toronto: University of Toronto Press.
Cochran, Robert. 1968. "Circularity in *The Sun Also Rises*." *Modern Fiction Studies* 14, no. 3 (Autumn): 297–305.
Cohassey, John. 2014. *Hemingway and Pound: A Most Unlikely Friendship*. Jefferson, NC: McFarland.
Cohen, Milton. 2006. *Hemingway's Laboratory: The Paris "in our time"*. Tuscaloosa: University of Alabama Press.
Colvert, James B. 1955. "Ernest Hemingway's Morality in Action." *American Literature* 27, no. 3 (November): 372–85.
Comley, Nancy. 1979. "The Economics of Survival." *Novel* 12, no. 3 (Spring): 244–53.
———. 1998. Review of *Hemingway: The Postwar Years and the Posthumous Novels*. *Studies in the Novel* 30, no. 3 (Fall): 454–56.
Comley, Nancy, and Robert Scholes. 1994. *Hemingway's Genders: Rereading the Hemingway Text*. New Haven, CT: Yale University Press.

Connolly, Cyril. 1937. Review of *To Have and Have Not*. *New Statesman & Nation*, October 16, 606.
———. 1950. Review of *Across the River and Into the Trees*. *Times* (London), September 3, 3.
———. 1952. Review of *The Old Man and the Sea*. *Sunday Times* (London), September 7, 5.
———. 1953. "Earnest Work." *Times Literary Supplement*, February 8, 5.
———. 1964. "Bull on the Left Bank." *Sunday Times* (London), May 24, 36.
Cooper, Stephen. 1987. *The Politics of Ernest Hemingway*. Ann Arbor, MI: UMI Research Press.
Cooperman, Stanley. 1967. "Death and *Cojones*: Frederic Henry (Ernest Hemingway)." In *World War I and the American Novel*, 181–90. Baltimore: Johns Hopkins University Press.
Corbett, Edward. 1970. Review of *Islands in the Stream*. *America*, November 7, 382–84.
Corkin, Stanley. 1996. "Ernest Hemingway's *In Our Time* and the Objectification of the Modern." In *Realism and the Birth of the Modern United States: Cinema, Literature, and Culture*, 160–220. Athens: University of Georgia Press.
Cottrell, Robert C. 2010. "The Cinematic Artist and the Literary Lion." In *Icons of American Popular Culture*, 64–85. New York: Sharpe.
Cowley, Malcolm. 1932. "A Farewell to Spain." *New Republic*, November 30, 76–77.
———. 1937. "Hemingway: Work in Progress." *New Republic*, October 20, 305–6.
———. 1938. "Hemingway in Madrid." *New Republic*, November 2, 367–68.
———. 1941. "Death of a Hero." *New Republic*, January 20, 89–90.
———. 1944a. "Hemingway and His Hero." *New Republic*, December 4, 754–58.
———. 1944b. "Introduction." *The Viking Portable Hemingway*. New York: Viking. Reprinted in Weeks 1962, 40–51.
———. 1949. "A Portrait of Mr. Papa." *Life*, January 10. Reprinted in McCaffery 1950, 31–56.
———. 1950. Review of *Across the River and Into the Trees*. *New York Herald Tribune Book Review*, September 10, 1, 16.
———. 1952. "Hemingway's Novel Has Rich Simplicity of a Classic." *New York Herald Tribune Book Review*, September 7, 1, 17.
———. 1967. "Papa and the Parricides." *Esquire*, June, 101–3, 160–62.
———. 1970. "A Double Life, Half Told." *Atlantic Monthly*, December, 105–8.
———. 1973. "Hemingway: The Old Lion." In *A Second Flowering: Works and Days of the Lost Generation*, 216–32. New York: Viking.
———. 1984. "Hemingway's Wound—and Its Consequences for American Literature." *Georgia Review* 38, no. 2 (Summer): 223–39.

Cox, James. 1984. "Of Books on Hemingway." *Sewanee Review* 92, no. 3 (Summer): 484–92.
Crews, Frederick C. 1987. "Pressure under Grace." *New York Review of Books*, August 13, 30–37.
Crowley, John W. 1994. "Bulls, Balls, and Booze: *The Sun Also Rises*." In *The White Logic: Alcoholism and Gender in American Modernist Fiction*, 43–64. Amherst: University of Massachusetts Press.
Crozier, Robert. 1984. "The Mask of Death, the Face of Life: Hemingway's Feminique." *Hemingway Review* 4, no. 1 (Spring): 2–13.
Crunden, Robert M. 2000. *Body & Soul: The Making of American Modernism*. New York: Basic Books.
Curnutt, Kirk. 2000. *Ernest Hemingway and the Expatriate Modernist Movement*. Detroit: Gale.
———. 2004. Review of *Hemingway's Theaters of Masculinity*. *Hemingway Review* 23, no. 2 (Spring): 103–7.
———. 2007. *Coffee with Hemingway*. London: Duncan Baird.
Curnutt, Kirk, and Gail D. Sinclair, eds. 2009. *Key West Hemingway: A Reassessment*. Gainesville: University Press of Florida.
Curran, Ronald. 1986. Review of *The Dangerous Summer*. *World Literature Today* 60, no. 1 (Winter): 115.
Dabney, Crystal. 1927. "Ernest Hemingway's Short Stories Are Patterns of Stark Simplicity." *Dallas Morning News*, November 6, 3.
Daiches, David. 1941. "Ernest Hemingway." *English Journal* 30, no. 3 (March): 175–86.
Daniel, Robert. 1947. "Hemingway and His Heroes." *Queen's Quarterly* 5, no. 4 (Winter): 471–85.
Davenport, Guy. 1970. "Hemingway as Walter Pater." *National Review*, November 17, 1214–15.
Davis, Elmer. 1938. "He Has Ground a New Edge." *Saturday Review of Literature*, October 15, 6.
Davis, Robert Gorham. 1952. "Hemingway's Tragic Fisherman." *New York Times Book Review*, September 7, 1, 20.
Davis, Robert Murray. 1969. "Entering Literary History: Hemingway." *Southern Humanities Review* 3, no. 4 (Fall): 382–95.
———. 1993. Review of *Hemingway: A Life without Consequences*. *World Literature Today* 67, no. 3 (Summer): 615.
———. 2000. Review of *True at First Light: A Fictional Memoir*. *World Literature Today* 74, no. 2 (Spring): 364–65.
Davison, Neil. 2010. "The Feminized Jewish Pugilist: Racial Ambivalence and Weak Muscle-Jews." In *Jewishness and Masculinity from the Modern to the Postmodern*, 92–120. London: Routledge.
DeFalco, Joseph. 1963. *The Hero in Hemingway's Short Stories*. Pittsburgh: University of Pittsburgh Press.
DeFazio, Albert J. 1991. Review of *Hemingway's Quarrel with Androgyny*. *Hemingway Review* 10, no. 2 (Spring): 78.

DeGuzmán, Maria. 2005. "Hemingway in the Dirt: Spanish Earth and the Ingestion of Authenticity." In *Spain's Long Shadow: The Black Legend, Off-Whiteness, and Anglo-American Empire*, 209–24. Minneapolis: University of Minnesota Press.

Del Gizzo, Suzanne. 1999. "A Lie by Noon?" *Hemingway Review* 19, no. 1 (Fall): 35–38.

Del Gizzo, Suzanne, and Camille Roman. 2011. "A Frost/Hemingway Roundtable Co-Sponsored by the Robert Frost Society and the Hemingway Society." *Hemingway Review* 30, no. 2 (Spring): 99–117.

Del Gizzo, Suzanne, and Frederic J. Svoboda, eds. 2012. *Hemingway's "The Garden of Eden": Twenty-Five Years of Criticism*. Kent, OH: Kent State University Press.

Dempsey, G. T. 2007. "Justice for Ernest Hemingway." *Antioch Review* 65, no. 2 (Spring): 239–55.

DeVoto, Bernard. 1929. "*A Farewell to Arms*." *Bookwise* 1 (November): 5–9.

———. 1935. "Hemingway in the Valley." *Saturday Review of Literature*, October 26, 5.

Dewing, Arthur. 1931. "The Mistake about Hemingway." *North American Review* 232, no. 4 (October): 364–71.

Didion, Joan. 1998. "Last Words." *New Yorker*, November 9, 74–80.

Diehl, Digby. 1972. "New Helping of Unissued Hemingway." *Los Angeles Times Calendar*, April 16, 45.

Diliberto, Gioia. 1992. *Hadley*. New York: Ticknor & Fields.

Dillon-Malone, Aubrey. 1999. *Hemingway: The Grace and the Pressure*. New York: Robson.

Doctorow, E. L. 1986. "Braver Than We Thought." *New York Times Book Review*, May 18, 1, 44–45.

Dolan, Marc. 1996. "Becoming an Artist: Modern(ist) Life and *A Moveable Feast*." In *Modern Lives: A Cultural Re-reading of "The Lost Generation,"* 49–86. West Lafayette, IN: Purdue University Press.

Donahue, Peter. 2003. "The Genre Which Is Not One: Hemingway's *In Our Time*, Difference, and the Short Story Cycle." In *The Postmodern Short Story: Forms and Issues*, edited by Farhat Iftekharrudin, Joseph Boyden, Mary Rohrberger, and Jale Claudet, 161–72. Westport, CT: Greenwood.

Donaldson, Scott. 1971. "Hemingway's Morality of Compensation." *American Literature* 43, no. 3 (November): 399–420.

———. 1977. *By Force of Will: The Life and Art of Ernest Hemingway*. New York: Viking.

———, ed. 1990. *New Essays on "A Farewell to Arms"*. New York: Cambridge University Press.

———. 1991. "Toward a Definitive Biography." In Scafella 1991, 93–104.

———. 1995. "Hemingway's *In Our Time*: The Biography of a Book." In *Modern American Short Story Sequences*, edited by J. Gerald Kennedy, 35–51. Cambridge: Cambridge University Press.

———, ed. 1996. *The Cambridge Companion to Hemingway*. New York: Cambridge University Press.

———. 1999. *Hemingway vs. Fitzgerald: The Rise and Fall of a Literary Friendship*. Woodstock, NY: Overlook.

———. 2009. *Fitzgerald & Hemingway: Works and Days*. New York: Columbia University Press.

Doorly, Margaret. 1926. "Among the New Books." *Omaha World Herald*, January 10, 6.

Dos Passos, John. 1929. Review of *A Farewell to Arms*. *New Masses*, December 1, 16.

Dowd, Maureen. 2011. "A Farewell to Macho." *New York Times*, October 16, SR 11.

DuBose, Michael. 2013. Review of *Ernest Hemingway in Context*, edited by Debra Moddelmog and Suzanne del Gizzo. *Hemingway Review* 33, no.1 (Fall): 110–13.

Dubus, Andre. 2012. "Ernest Hemingway: Why His Work Matters Now More than Ever, a Love Letter from the Digital World." *Hemingway Review* 32, no. 1 (Fall): 7–16.

Ducille, Ann. 2010. "The Short Happy Life of Black Feminist Theory." *Differences: A Journal of Feminist Cultural Studies* 21, no. 1 (Spring): 32–47.

Dudley, Marc K. 2011. *Hemingway, Race, and Art: Bloodlines and the Color Line*. Kent, OH: Kent State University Press.

Duffus. R. L. 1932. "Hemingway Now Writes of Bull-Fighting as an Art." *New York Times Book Review*, September 25, 5, 17.

Duggan, Francis X. 1953. "The Obsession of Violence." *Commonweal*, March 13, 583–84.

Duke, Maurice. 1970. "Papa's Last Novel Will Sell Well, But It Is Not Good Hemingway." *Richmond Times-Dispatch*, October 11, F5.

Dupee, F. W. 1953. "Hemingway Revealed." *Kenyon Review* 15, no. 1 (Winter): 150–55.

Earle, David. 2009. *All Man! Hemingway, 1950s Men's Magazines, and the Masculine Persona*. Kent, OH: Kent State University Press.

Eastman, Max. 1933. "Bull in the Afternoon." *New Republic*, June 7, 94–97.

Eby, Carl. 1995. "'Come Back to the Beach Ag'in, David Honey!': Hemingway's Fetishization of Race in *The Garden of Eden*." In Wagner-Martin 1998, 329–48.

———. 1996. Review of *Hemingway: The Postwar Years and the Posthumous Novels*. *Hemingway Review* 15, no. 2 (Spring): 108–11.

———. 1999a. *Hemingway's Fetishism: Psychoanalysis and the Mirror of Manhood*. New York: SUNY Press.

———. 1999b. "Hemingway's Truth and Tribal Politics." *Hemingway Review* 19, no. 1 (Fall): 24–27.

Egan, Susanna. 1999. "Lies, Damned Lies and Autobiography: Hemingway's Treatment of Fitzgerald in *A Moveable Feast*." In *Mirror Talk: Genres in Crisis in Contemporary Autobiography*, 31–47. Chapel Hill: University of North Carolina Press.

Emmett, Elizabeth. 1927. "A Reader in Revolt." *McNaught's Monthly* 7 (April): 114–15.

Epstein, Joseph. 1970. "The Importance of Being Young—and Ernest." *Washington Post Book World*, October 11, 1, 3.
"Ernest, Good and Bad." 1969. *Time*, April 18, 104–6.
"*Ernest Hemingway and the Pursuit of Heroism*, by Leo Gurko." 1968. *Kirkus*, August 16.
"Ernest Hemingway Displays New Technique of the Short Story." 1927. *Seattle Daily Times*, December 25, F5.
"Ernest Hemingway Hurt in Motor Crash." 1930. *Boston Herald*, November 3, 5.
"Ernest Hemingway's Stories Protest the Cruelties of the Universe." 1933. *Dallas Morning News*, November 5, Features, 4.
Erskine, John. 1933. "The Hollow Life." *Brooklyn Daily Eagle*, November 5, Sunday Review, 17.
Evans, Robert. 1966. "Hemingway and the Pale Cast of Thought." *American Literature* 38, no. 2 (May): 161–75.
Evans, Robert C. 2010. "In His Time (and Later): Ernest Hemingway's Critical Reputation." In Goodheart 2010, 34–48.
"An Evening with Patrick Hemingway." 1999. *Hemingway Review* 19, no. 1 (Fall): 8–16.
Fadiman, Clifton. 1928. "The Whole Duty of the Young Novelist." *Nation*, April 18, 445–47.
———. 1929. "A Fine American Novel." *Nation*, October 30, 497–98.
———. 1933a. "Ernest Hemingway: An American Byron." *Nation*, January 18, 63–64.
———. 1933b. "A Letter to Mr. Hemingway." *New Yorker*, October 28, 74–75.
———. 1937. Review of *To Have and Have Not*. *New Yorker*, October 16, 100–101.
———. 1938. Review of *The Fifth Column and the First Forty-Nine*. *New Yorker*, October 22, 94–95.
———. 1964. Report on *A Moveable Feast*. *Book-of-the-Month Club News*, May, 1–2, 4–5.
———. 1970. Report on *Islands in the Stream*. *Book-of-the-Month Club News*, Fall, 2–4.
Fantina, Richard. 2005. *Ernest Hemingway: Machismo and Masochism*. New York: Palgrave.
———. 2006. "Pegging Ernest Hemingway: Masochism, Sodomy, and the Dominant Woman." In *Straight Writ Queer: Non-Normative Expressions of Heterosexuality in Literature*, 46–67. Jefferson, NC: McFarland, 2006.
Farquhar, Robin. 1968. "Dramatic Structure in the Novels of Ernest Hemingway." *Modern Fiction Studies* 14, no. 3 (Autumn): 271–82.
Faulkner, William. 1952. Review of *The Old Man and the Sea*. *Shenandoah* 3, no. 1 (Autumn): 55.
Fellner, Harriet. 1986. *Hemingway as Playwright: The Fifth Column*. Ann Arbor, MI: UMI Research Press.
Fenstermaker, John. 2013. "Ernest Hemingway in *Esquire*." In *Literature and Journalism: Inspiration, Intersections and Inventions from Ben

Franklin to Stephen Colbert, edited by Mark Canada, 187–208. New York: Palgrave Macmillan.

Fenton, Charles A. 1954. *The Apprenticeship of Ernest Hemingway: The Early Years*. New York: Farrar, Straus & Young.

Ferguson, Charles. 1927. "Five Rising Stars in American Fiction." *Bookman*, May, 251–57.

Ferguson, Mary Anne, ed. 1973. *Images of Women in Literature*. Boston: Houghton Mifflin.

Ferrell, William K. 2000. "Finding Morality in a Bullring: *The Sun Also Rises* by Ernest Hemingway." In *Literature and Film as Modern Mythology*, 167–80. Westport, CT: Praeger.

Fetterley, Judith. 1977. "*A Farewell to Arms*: Ernest Hemingway's 'Resentful Cryptogram.'" In *The Authority of Experience: Essays in Feminist Criticism*, edited by Arlyn Diamond and Lee R. Edwards, 257–73. Amherst: University of Massachusetts Press.

Fiedler, Leslie. 1960. *Love and Death in the American Novel*. New York: Criterion.

———. 1964. *Waiting for the End*. New York: Stein and Day.

"Fiesta." 1927. *Times Literary Supplement*, June 30, 454.

Finch, John. 1952. "Full Scale Study of Hemingway." *Boston Herald*, November 30, Christmas Book Section, 18.

Firestone, Shulamith. 1970. *The Dialectic of Sex*. New York: William Morrow.

Fischer, Heinz, ed. 2007. The Pulitzer Prize Archive, Part G, Supplement. Volume 21, *Chronicle of the Pulitzer Prize for Fiction*. Munich: Saur Verlag.

Fishkin, Shelley Fisher. 1985. "Ernest Hemingway." In *From Fact to Fiction: Journalism and Imaginative Writing in America*, 135–64. Baltimore: Johns Hopkins University Press.

Fiske-Harrison, Alexander. 2013. "Does the World Need 17 Volumes of Hemingway's Letters?" *Spectator*, October 26.

Fitzgerald, F. Scott. 1926. "How to Waste Material: A Note to My Generation." *Bookman*, May, 262–65.

Fleming, Robert E. 1978. Review of *By Force of Will*. *Journal of English and Germanic Philology* 77, no. 4 (October): 603–5.

———. 1994. *The Face in the Mirror: Hemingway's Writers*. Tuscaloosa: University of Alabama Press.

———, ed. 1999. *Hemingway and the Natural World*. Moscow: University of Idaho Press.

Flora, Joseph. 1982. *Hemingway's Nick Adams*. Baton Rouge: Louisiana State University Press.

———. 1989. *Ernest Hemingway: A Study of the Short Fiction*. Boston: Twayne.

———. 2008. *Reading Hemingway's "Men Without Women."* Kent, OH: Kent State University Press.

Florczyk, Steven. 2013. *Hemingway, the Red Cross, and the Great War*. Kent, OH: Kent State University Press.

Flower, Desmond. 1941. Review of *For Whom the Bell Tolls*. *Observer*, March 9, 4.
"Foolish Fuel." 1933. *August Chronicle*, May 22, 4.
"Forceful as a Pile Driver." 1925. *Trenton Sunday Times*, October 18, 5.
Forter, Greg. 1999. Review of *Hemingway's Fetishism*. *Hemingway Review* 18, no. 2 (Spring): 133–36.
———. 2011. "Redeeming Violence in *The Sun Also Rises*: Phallic Embodiment, Primitive Ritual, Fetishistic Melancholia." In *Gender, Race, and Mourning in American Modernism*, 54–95. New York: Cambridge University Press.
Fortunati, Vito. 2004. "Hemingway, the Embodiment of the American Myth, and Italian Leftist Writers." In Sanderson 2006, 225–32.
Fortuny, Kim. 2009. *American Writers in Istanbul*. Syracuse, NY: Syracuse University Press.
Frakes, James R. 1983. "Hemingway's Mama Rescued." *Cleveland Plain Dealer*, August 14, B17.
Frederking, Lauretta, ed. 2010. *Hemingway on Politics and Rebellion*. New York: Routledge.
Freedman, Morris. 2001. "Disparaging Hemingway." *Virginia Quarterly Review* 77, no. 1 (Winter): 78–84.
Friedrich, Otto. 1957. "Ernest Hemingway: Joy through Strength." *American Scholar* 26, no. 4 (Autumn): 470, 518–30.
Frohock, W. M. 1947a. "Ernest Hemingway: Violence and Discipline: I." *Southwest Review* 32, no. 2 (Winter): 89–97.
———. 1947b. "Ernest Hemingway: Violence and Discipline: II." *Southwest Review* 32, no. 3 (Spring): 184–93.
Frus, Phyllis. 1994. "'News That Stays': Hemingway, Journalism, and Objectivity in Fiction." In *The Politics and Poetics of Journalistic Narrative: The Timely and the Timeless*, 53–89. Cambridge: Cambridge University Press.
Fruscione, Joseph. 1999. Review of *Hemingway's Fetishism*. *American Studies International* 37, no. 3 (October): 124–25.
———. 2012. *Faulkner and Hemingway: Biography of a Literary Rivalry*. Columbus: Ohio State University Press.
———. 2015. *Teaching Hemingway and Modernism*. Kent, OH: Kent State University Press.
Frye, Northrop. 1951. "Novels on Several Occasions." *Hudson Review* 3, no. 4 (Winter): 611–19.
Fulford, Robert. 1964. "On Hemingway: His Last Sad Book Gives Him Back His Early Stature." *Macleans*, June 6, 47–48.
Fuller, Edmund. 1970. "Hemingway: The Good and the Bad." *Wall Street Journal*, November 3, 10.
———. 1972. "Hemingway's Nick Adams Tales." *Wall Street Journal*, June 8, 10.
Gaggin, John. 1988. *Hemingway and Nineteenth-Century Aestheticism*. Ann Arbor, MI: UMI Research Press.
Gajdusek, Robert. 1978. *Hemingway's Paris*. New York: Scribner.

———. 1984. *Hemingway and Joyce: A Study in Debt and Payment.* Corte Madera, CA: Square Circle.

———. 1987. "Elephant Hunt in Eden: A Study in New and Old Myths and Other Strange Beasts in Hemingway's Garden." *Hemingway Review* 7, no. 1 (Fall): 14–19.

———. 1994. Review of *The Face in the Mirror: Hemingway's Writers* by Robert Fleming. *Hemingway Review* 13, no. 2 (Spring): 101–6.

———.1999. "One Blind Man Exploring a Pretty Big Elephant." *Hemingway Review* 19, no. 1 (Fall): 31–34.

———. 2002. *Hemingway in His Own Country.* Notre Dame, IN: University of Notre Dame Press.

Galantière, Lewis. 1930. "The Brushwood Boy at the Front." *Hound & Horn* 3 (January–March): 259–62.

———. 1964. "'There Is Never Any End to Paris.'" *New York Times Book Review*, May 10, 1, 26.

Galligan, Edward. 1993. "Biographies and Biographers." *Sewanee Review* 101, no. 2 (Spring): 282–89.

Gandal, Keith. 2008. *The Gun and the Pen: Hemingway, Fitzgerald, Faulkner, and the Fiction of Mobilization.* New York: Oxford University Press.

Gannett, Lewis. 1950. Review of *Across the River and Into the Trees.* *New York Herald Tribune*, September 7, 23.

Garcia, Wilma. 1984. *Mothers and Others: Myths of the Female in the Works of Melville, Twain, and Hemingway.* New York: Lang.

Gardiner, Harold. 1952. "Pathetic Fallacy." *America*, September 13, 569.

Garlington, Jack. 1959. "The Intelligence Quotient of Lady Brett Ashley." *San Francisco Review* 1 (September): 23–28.

Garnett, David. 1934. Review of *Winner Take Nothing.* *New Statesman & Nation*, February 10, 192.

———. 1935. Review of *Green Hills of Africa.* *New Statesman & Nation*, April 4, 529.

Geismar, Maxwell. 1941. "No Man Alone Now." *Virginia Quarterly Review* 17, no. 4 (Fall): 517–34.

———. 1942. "Ernest Hemingway: You Could Always Come Back." In *Writers in Crisis: The American Novel 1925–1940*, 37–86. Boston: Houghton Mifflin.

———. 1949. "The Position of Ernest Hemingway." *New York Times Book Review*, July 31, 1.

———. 1950. "To Have and to Have and to Have." *Saturday Review*, September 9, 18–19.

———. 1962. "Was 'Papa' a Truly Great Writer?" *New York Times Book Review*, July 1, 1, 16.

———. 1964. "When He Was Good." *Cosmopolitan*, May, 8–9.

———. 1970. "Hemingway's 'Lost' Novel: Illuminating Self-Portrait." *Chicago Sun-Times Showcase*, October 4, 1, 19.

Gellens, Jay, ed. 1970. *Twentieth Century Interpretations of "A Farewell to Arms."* Englewood Cliffs, NJ: Prentice-Hall.

Gellhorn, Martha. 1978. *Travels with Myself and Another.* New York: Dodd, Mead.
George, Stephen, and Barbara Heavilin, eds. 2007. *John Steinbeck and His Contemporaries.* Lanham, MD: Scarecrow Press.
Gifford, William. "Ernest Hemingway: The Monsters and the Critics." *Modern Fiction Studies* 14, no. 3 (Autumn): 255–70.
Gill, Brendan. 1952. Review of *The Old Man and the Sea. New Yorker*, September 6, 115.
Gladstein, Mimi. 1986. *The Indestructible Woman in Faulkner, Hemingway, and Steinbeck.* Ann Arbor, MI: UMI Research Press.
Glass, Loren. 2004. "Being Ernest." In *Authors, Inc.: Literary Celebrity in the United States, 1880–1980*, 139–74. New York: New York University Press.
Glasser, William. 1966. "*A Farewell to Arms.*" *Sewanee Review* 74, no. 2 (Spring): 453–69.
Godden, Richard. 1990. "'You've Got to See It, Feel It, Smell It, Hear It,' Buy It: Hemingway's Commercial Forms." In *Fictions of Capital: The American Novel from James to Mailer*, 39–77. New York: Cambridge University Press.
Goldstein, Albert. 1940. "Literature and Less." *New Orleans Times-Picayune*, November 3, Section 2, 11.
Goodheart, Eugene. 1956. "The Legacy of Ernest Hemingway." *Prairie Schooner* 30, no. 3 (Fall): 212–18.
———, ed. 2010. *Critical Insights: Ernest Hemingway.* Englewood Cliffs, NJ: Salem Press.
Gordon, Caroline. 1949. "Notes on Hemingway and Kafka." *Sewanee Review* 57, no. 2 (Spring): 215–26.
Gordon, David. 1966. "The Son and the Father: Patterns of Response to Conflict in Hemingway's Fiction." *Literature and Psychology* 16, nos. 3–4 (Fall–Winter): 122–38.
Gorman, Herbert. 1926. "Hemingway Keeps His Promise." *New York World*, November 14, 10M.
———. 1942. "How Men Have Fought and Died." *New York Times Book Review*, November 8, 1, 37.
Gould, Gerald. 1926. Review of *In Our Time. Observer*, November 7, 8.
———. 1927. "New Novels." *Observer*, June 12, 8.
Grace, Nancy McCampbell. 1995. *The Feminized Male Character in Twentieth-Century Literature.* Lewiston, NY: Mellen.
Gratton, C. Harley. 1932. "The Slump in Letters." *North American Review* 234, no. 1 (July): 49–57.
"A Great New Hemingway." 1952. *Trenton Evening Times*, August 31, pt. 4, 10.
Grebstein, Sheldon. 1973. *Hemingway's Craft.* Carbondale: Southern Illinois University Press.
Green, James. 1968. "Symbolic Sentences in 'Big Two-Hearted River.'" *Modern Fiction Studies* 14, no. 3 (Autumn): 307–12.

Greene, Graham. 1941. Review of *For Whom the Bell Tolls*. *Spectator*, March 7, 258.
Greene, Philip. 2012. *To Have and Have Another: A Hemingway Cocktail Companion*. New York: Perigee.
Greer, Germaine. 1970. *The Female Eunuch*. New York: McGraw-Hill.
Griffin, Peter. 1985. *Along with Youth: Hemingway, the Early Years*. Oxford: Oxford University Press.
———. 1987. "Pressure under Grace." *New York Review of Books*, August 13, 30–37.
———. 1990. *Less than Treason: Hemingway in Paris*. Oxford: Oxford University Press.
Grimes, George. 1927. "Hemingway's Short Stories." *Omaha World Herald*, November 13, Sunday Magazine, 6.
———. 1932. "The Art of Fighting the Bull, Explained by Ernest Hemingway." *Omaha World Herald*, September 4, Sunday Magazine, 6.
———. 1935. "With Hemingway in Africa, Thinking as He Goes Hunting." *Omaha World Herald*, November 10, 7E.
Grimes, Larry. 1985. *The Religious Design of Hemingway's Early Fiction*. Ann Arbor, MI: UMI Research Press.
———. 2000. Review of *Hemingway and the Natural World*. *Hemingway Review* 20, no. 1 (Fall): 104–8.
Grimes, Larry, and Bickford Sylvester, eds. 2014. *Hemingway, Cuba, and the Cuban Works*. Kent, OH: Kent State University Press.
Grissom, Candace. 2014. *Fitzgerald and Hemingway on Film: A Critical Study of the Adaptations, 1924–2013*. Jefferson, NC: McFarland.
Gullason, Thomas A. 1984. "The 'Lesser' Renaissance: The American Short Story in the 1920s." In *The American Short Story 1900–1945: A Critical History*, edited by Philip Stevick, 71–102. Boston: Twayne.
Gurko, Leo. 1968. *Ernest Hemingway and the Pursuit of Heroism*. New York: Crowell.
Gurko, Leo, and Miriam Gurko. 1944. "The Essence of F. Scott Fitzgerald." *College English* 5, no. 7 (April): 372–76.
Haas, Victor P. 1950a. "Hemingway's New Novel." *Omaha World Herald*, September 10, 28C.
———. 1950b. "American Tragedy." *Omaha World Herald*, September 24, 29C.
Hackett, Alice Payne. 1967. *Seventy Years of Best Sellers, 1895–1965*. New York: Bowker.
Haight, Anne Lyon. 1954. *Banned Books*. 2nd ed. New York: Bowker.
Halliday, E. M. 1952. "Hemingway's Narrative Perspective." *Sewanee Review* 60, no. 2 (April–June): 202–18.
———. 1964. Review of *Ernest Hemingway*. *American Literature* 36, no. 3 (November): 388–89.
———. 1966. Review of *Hemingway on Love*. *American Literature* 38, no. 2 (May): 259–61.
Hand, Harry. 1966. "Transducers and Hemingway's Heroes." *English Journal* 55, no. 7 (October): 870–71.

Hanneman, Audre, comp. 1967. *Ernest Hemingway: A Comprehensive Bibliography*. Princeton, NJ: Princeton University Press.
———, comp. 1975. *Supplement to Ernest Hemingway: A Comprehensive Bibliography*. Princeton, NJ: Princeton University Press.
Hansen, Harry. 1926. "An American Parody." *New York World*, May 30, 4M.
———. 1940. "First Reader." *Greensboro Daily News*, October 24, 6.
Haralson, Eric L. 2003. "'The Other Half Is the Man': The Modern Triangle of Gertrude Stein, Ernest Hemingway, and Henry James." In *Henry James and Queer Modernity*, 173–204. New York: Cambridge University Press.
Hardy, Richard, and John Cull. 1977. *Hemingway, A Psychological Study*. New York: Irvington.
Harlow, Benjamin. 1966. "Some Archetypal Motifs in *The Old Man and the Sea*." *McNeese Review* 17: 74–79.
Harold, Brent. 1980. "The Marxist Survey of American Fiction." *Radical Teacher* 15 (March): 43–51.
Hart, Jeffrey. 1964. "Hemingway's Code." *National Review*, June 2, 450–52.
———. 1972. "Vintage Hemingway." *National Review*, July 21, 801–2.
Hartwick, Harry. 1934. "Grace under Pressure." In *The Foreground of American Fiction*, 151–59. New York: American Book.
Hawkins, Ruth A. 2012. *Unbelievable Happiness and Final Sorrow*. Fayetteville: University of Arkansas Press.
Hays, Peter L. 1966. "Hemingway and the Fisher King." *University Review* (Kansas City) 32, no. 3 (Spring): 225–28.
———. 1990. *Ernest Hemingway*. New York: Continuum.
———. 1999. "Tennessee Williams 'Outs' Scott and Ernest." In *The Author as Character: Representing Historical Writers in Western Literature*, edited by Paul Franssen and A. J. Hoenselaars, 253–63. Cranbury, NJ: Associated University Press.
———. 2008. *Teaching Hemingway's "The Sun Also Rises."* Kent, OH: Kent State University Press.
———. 2011. *The Critical Reception of Hemingway's "The Sun Also Rises."* Rochester, NY: Camden House.
Hemingway, Ernest. 1990. "Lack of Passion," edited by Susan Beegel. *Hemingway Review* 9, no. 2 (Spring): 57–68.
———. 1990. "Philip Haines Was a Writer," edited by Donald Junkins. *Hemingway Review* 9, no. 2 (Spring): 2–9.
———. 1999. *True at First Light*, edited by Patrick Hemingway. New York: Scribner.
———. 2000. *Hemingway on Fishing*, edited by Nick Lyons. New York: Lyons Press.
———. 2003a. *Hemingway on Hunting*, edited by Seán Hemingway. New York: Scribner.
———. 2003b. *Hemingway on War*, edited by Seán Hemingway. New York: Scribner.

———. 2005. *Under Kilimanjaro*, edited by Robert W. Lewis and Robert Fleming. Kent, OH: Kent State University Press.
Hemingway, Gregory. 1976. *Papa: A Personal Memoir*. Boston: Houghton Mifflin.
Hemingway, John Patrick. 2007. *Strange Tribe: A Family Memoir*. Guilford, CT: Lyons.
Hemingway, Leicester. 1962. *My Brother, Ernest Hemingway*. Cleveland: World Publishing.
Hemingway, Mary Welsh. 1976. *How It Was*. New York: Knopf.
Hemingway, Valerie. 2004. *Running with the Bulls: My Years with the Hemingways*. New York: Ballantine.
"Hemingway: Making of a Master." 1954. *Newsweek*, May 17, 104, 106.
"Hemingway Dead of Shotgun Wound." 1961. *New York Times*, July 3, 1.
"Hemingway Novel Brings Suit." 1941. *San Francisco Chronicle*, June 3, 13.
Hemingway Review. 2006. Special issue on *Under Kilimanjaro*. Vol. 25, no. 2 (Spring).
"Hemingway's Biographer." 1961. *New York Times*, November 4, 16.
"Hemingway Seems Out of Focus in *The Sun Also Rises*." 1926. *Chicago Daily Tribune*, November 27, 13.
"Hemingway's Fine Book on Africa." 1935. *Richmond Times-Dispatch*, November 17, Sunday Magazine, 10.
"Hemingway Slaps Eastman." 1937. *New York Times*, August 14, 15.
"Hemingway's Power in Finer Revelation." 1940. *Springfield Union*, October 31, 8.
"Hemingway's Tale." 1937. *Springfield Republican*, October 21, 8.
"Hemingway's Unstill Waters." 1970. *Times Literary Supplement*, October 16, 1193–94.
Hendrickson, Paul. 2011. *Hemingway's Boat: Everything He Loved in Life, and Lost, 1934–1961*. New York: Knopf.
Henricksen, Bruce. 1989. "The Bullfight Story and Critical Theory." In *Hemingway's Neglected Short Fiction: New Perspectives*, edited by Susan Beegel, 131–40. Tuscaloosa: University of Alabama Press.
Herlihy, Jeffrey. 2011. *In Paris or Paname: Hemingway's Expatriate Nationalism*. New York: Rodopi.
"Hero as Celebrity." 1967. *Time*, May 19, 133–34, 136.
Herrick, Robert. 1929. "What Is Dirt?" *Bookman*, November 29, 258–62.
Hewson, Marc. 2004. "A Matter of Love or Death: Hemingway's Developing Psychosexuality in *For Whom the Bell Tolls*." *Studies in the Novel* 26, no. 2 (Summer): 170–84.
Hicks, Granville. 1930. "The World of Hemingway." *New Freeman*, March, 40–42.
———. 1932. "Bulls and Bottles." *Nation*, November 9, 461.
———. 1935a. *The Great Tradition: An Interpretation of American Literature since the Civil War*. New York: Macmillan.
———. 1935b. "Small Game Hunting." *New Masses*, November 19, 23.

———. 1944. "Twenty Years of Hemingway." *New Republic*, October 23, 524–25.

———. 1951. "Our Novelists' Shifting Reputations." *English Journal* 40, no. 1 (January): 1–7.

———. 1952. "Hemingway's 'Happy Conspiracy with Permanence.'" *New York Times Book Review*, October 12, 4.

———. 1958. "The Shape of a Career." *Saturday Review*, December 13, 16, 38.

———. 1967. "The Novelist as Newspaperman." *Saturday Review*, May 27, 23–24.

Higgins, George V. 1972. "Rooting in Papa's Closet to Discover . . . 14 Pages?!" *National Observer*, April 19, 21.

Highet, Gilbert. 1952. "New Books." *Harper's*, October, 102, 104.

Hitchens, Christopher. 2009. "The Man in Full." *Atlantic*, June, 83–87.

Hochman, Brian. 2008. "Ellison's Hemingways." *African American Review* 42, nos. 3–4 (Fall–Winter): 513–32.

Hoffer, Bates L., ed. 1976. *Hemingway's Experiments in Structure and Style*. San Antonio: Trinity University Press.

Hoffman, Frederick. 1951. *The Modern Novel in America 1900–1950*. Chicago: Regnery.

———. 1954. Review of *Ernest Hemingway*. *American Literature* 25, no. 4 (January): 514–15.

———. 1969. "Ernest Hemingway." In Bryer 1969, 275–300.

Holcomb, Gary Edward. 2007. "The Sun Also Rises in Queer Black Harlem: Hemingway and McKay's Modernist Intertext." *Journal of Modern Literature* 30, no. 4 (Summer): 61–81.

Holcomb, Gary Edward, and Charles Scruggs, eds. 2012. *Hemingway and the Black Renaissance*. Columbus: Ohio State University Press.

Holcombe, Wayne. 1986. "Philip Young or Youngerdunger?" *Hemingway Review* 5, no. 2 (Spring): 24–33.

Holder, Alan. 1963. "The Other Hemingway." *Twentieth-Century Fiction* 9 (October): 153–57.

Holland, Laurence. 1955. Review of *The Apprenticeship of Ernest Hemingway*. *American Literature* 26, no. 4 (January): 590–92.

Holland, Robert. 1968. "Macomber and the Critics." *Studies in Short Fiction* 5, no. 1 (Winter): 171–78.

Hollenberg, Alexander. 2012. "Recalcitrant Simplicity: Thin Characters and Thick Narration in *A Farewell to Arms*." *Narrative* 20, no. 3 (October): 302–21.

Hotchner, A. E. 1966. *Papa Hemingway: A Personal Memoir*. New York: Random House.

———. 2009. "Don't Touch 'A Moveable Feast.'" *New York Times*, July 19.

Hovey, Richard B. 1966. "*The Old Man and the Sea*: A New Hemingway Hero." *Discourse* 9, no. 3 (Summer): 283–94.

———. 1968. *Hemingway: The Inward Terrain*. Seattle: University of Washington Press.

———. 1978. Review of *By Force of Will: The Life and Art of Ernest Hemingway*. *American Literature* 49, no. 4 (January): 667–68.

Howe, Irving. 1961. "In Search of a Moral Style." *New Republic*, September 25, 21–23, 26–27.

———. 1969. "The Wounds of All Generations." *Harper's*, May, 96–102. Reprinted in *Celebrations and Attacks: Thirty Years of Literary and Cultural Commentary*, 155–60. New York: Horizon, 1979.

———. 1970. "Great Man Going Down." *Harper's*, October, 120–25.

Howell, John M. 1969. *Hemingway's African Stories: The Stories, Their Sources, Their Critics*. New York: Scribner.

Hubbell, Jay B. 1972. *Who Are the Major American Writers?* Durham, NC: Duke University Press.

Humphries, David. 2006. "The Camera Eye and Reporter's Conscience in Ernest Hemingway's *In Our Time* and *The Sun Also Rises*." In *Different Dispatches: Journalism in American Modernist Prose*, 83–124. New York: Routledge.

Hutchinson, Percy. 1927. "Mr. Hemingway Shows Himself a Master Craftsman in the Short Story." *New York Herald Tribune Books*, October 16, 9, 27.

———. 1929. "Love and War in the Pages of Mr. Hemingway." *New York Times Book Review*, September 29, 5.

Hyman, Stanley Edgar. 1947. "The Marxist Criticism of Literature." *Antioch Review* 7, no. 4 (Winter): 541–68. Reprinted in *Karl Marx's Social and Political Thought*, vol. 8, edited by Bob Jessop and Russell Wheatley, 263–86. New York: Routledge, 1989.

———. 1964. "Ernest Hemingway with a Knife." *New Leader*, May 11, 8–9.

Idema, Henry. 1990. "Ernest Hemingway: From Religious Communities to the Privatization of Religion." In *Freud, Religion, and the Roaring Twenties: A Psychoanalytic Theory of Secularization in Three Novelists: Anderson, Hemingway, and Fitzgerald*, 135–78. Savage, MD: Rowman & Littlefield.

"In the Wind." 1940. *Nation*, December 21, 634.

Jack, Peter Monro. 1938. "Hemingway's Play and Stories." *New York Times Book Review*, October 23, 4.

Jackson, Joseph Henry. 1937. "A Bookman's Notebook." *San Francisco Chronicle*, October 19, 8.

———. 1950. Review of *Across the River and Into the Trees*. *San Francisco Chronicle*, September 7, 18.

Jameson, Fredric. 1971. *Marxism and Form: Twentieth-Century Dialectical Theories of Literature*. Princeton, NJ: Princeton University Press.

Jameson, Storm. 1934. "The Craft of the Novelist." *English Review*, January, 28–43.

Janeway, Elizabeth. 1971. *Man's World, Woman's Place: A Study in Social Mythology*. New York: William Morrow.

Jenks, Tom. 1987. "Editing Hemingway: *The Garden of Eden*." *Hemingway Review* 7, no. 1 (Fall): 30–33.

Jensen, Arthur. 1950. "Critical Essays on Hemingway." *Boston Herald*, December 3, Book Section, 27.
Jobes, Katharine T., ed. 1968. *Twentieth Century Interpretations of "The Old Man and the Sea."* Englewood Cliffs, NJ: Prentice-Hall.
Johnson, Edgar. 1940. "Farewell the Separate Peace: The Rejections of Ernest Hemingway." *Sewanee Review* 48, no. 3 (July–September): 289–300.
Johnson, Paul. 1988. "The Deep Waters of Ernest Hemingway." In *Intellectuals*, 143–72. New York: Harper Collins.
Johnson, Reed. 2011. "Rethinking Hemingway 50 Years after His Death." *Los Angeles Times*, July 2.
Johnston, Kenneth. 1987. *The Tip of the Iceberg: Hemingway and the Short Story*. Gainesville, FL: Penkeville.
Jones, Howard Mumford. 1940. "The Soul of Spain." *Saturday Review of Literature*, October 26, 5, 19.
———. 1942. "Minority Report on Hemingway." *Saturday Review of Literature*, December 12, 11.
Jones, John A. 1959. "Hemingway: The Critics and the Public Legend." *Western Humanities Review* 13, no. 1 (January): 387–400.
Jones, Robert. 1987. "Mimesis and Metafiction in Hemingway's *The Garden of Eden*." *Hemingway Review* 7, no. 1 (Fall): 2–13.
Joost, Nicholas. 1968. *Ernest Hemingway and the Little Magazines: The Paris Years*. Barre, MA: Barre Publishers.
———. 1970. "Ernest Hemingway." *Contemporary Literature* 11, no. 2 (Spring): 293–302.
Josephs, Allen. 1986. Review of *The Garden of Eden*. *Hemingway Review* 6, no. 1 (Fall): 112–14.
———. 1994. *"For Whom the Bell Tolls": Ernest Hemingway's Undiscovered Country*. New York: Twayne.
———. 1995. Review of *The Face in the Mirror: Hemingway's Writers*. *American Literature* 67, no. 1 (March): 60–61.
Justice, Hilary K. 1999. "The Lion, the Leopard, and the Bear." *Hemingway Review* 19, no. 1 (Fall): 39–42.
———. 2004. "'Prejudiced through Experience': *Death in the Afternoon* and the Problem of Authorship." In Mandel 2004, 237–56.
———. 2006. *The Bones of the Others: The Hemingway Text from the Lost Manuscripts to the Posthumous Novels*. Kent, OH: Kent State University Press.
Kakutani, Michiko. 1986. "'*Garden of Eden*.'" *New York Times*, June 15, E8.
———. 1999. "The Hunter Returns, Weary but Still Macho." *New York Times*, June 22, E6.
Kaplan, Harold. 2011. "Hemingway and the Passive Hero." In *The Solipsism of Modern Fiction: Comedy, Tragedy, and Heroism*, 93–110. New Brunswick, NJ: Transaction.
Kartiganer, Donald. 2004. "'Getting Good at Doing Nothing': Faulkner, Hemingway, and the Fiction of Gesture." In Urgo and Abadie 2004, 54–73.

Kashkeen, Ivan. 1935. "Ernest Hemingway: A Tragedy of Craftsmanship." *International Literature* 5 (May): 72–90. Reprinted in McCaffery 1950, 76–108.
Kauffmann, Stanley. 1964. "Paris and Hemingway in the Spring." *New Republic*, May 9, 17–18, 20–21, 23–24.
Kaupke, Ellen. 1952. "'Old Man' and 'Papa' Come Back." *Daily Northwestern*, September 25, 6.
Kazin, Alfred. 1937. "Hemingway's First Book on His Own People." *New York Herald Tribune Books*, October 17, 3.
———. 1938. "What Spain Has Made of Ernest Hemingway." *New York Herald Tribune Books*, October 16, 5.
———. 1942. *On Native Grounds: An Interpretation of Modern American Prose Literature*. New York: Reynal & Hitchcock.
———. 1950. "The Indignant Flesh." *New Yorker*, September 9, 101–3.
———. 1964. "Hemingway as His Own Fable." *Atlantic Monthly*, June, 54–57.
———. 1984. "Hemingway the Painter." In *An American Procession*, 357–73. New York: Knopf.
Kennedy, J. Gerald. 1991. "Hemingway's Gender Trouble." *American Literature* 63, no. 2 (June): 187–206.
———. 1993. "City of Danger: Hemingway's Paris." In *Imagining Paris: Exile, Writing, and American Identity*, 79–141. New Haven, CT: Yale University Press.
Kennedy, J. Gerald, and Jackson Bryer, eds. 1998. *French Connections: Hemingway and Fitzgerald Abroad*. New York: St. Martin's Press.
Kennedy, William. 1967. "The 'Clear Heart' of Reporter Hemingway." *National Observer*, May 29, 19.
———. 1985. "The Last Ole." *New York Times Book Review*, June 9, 1, 32–33, 35.
Kenner, Hugh. 1975. *A Homemade World: The American Modernist Writers*. New York: Knopf.
Kermode, Frank. 1964. "Hemingway's Last Novel." *New York Review of Books*, June 11, 4–6.
Kert, Bernice. 1983. *The Hemingway Women*. New York: Norton.
Kiley, Jed. 1965. *Hemingway: An Old Friend Remembers*. New York: Hawthorn Books.
Killinger, John. 1960. *Hemingway and the Dead Gods: A Study in Existentialism*. Lexington: University Press of Kentucky.
Knight, Christopher J. 1995. "Ernest Hemingway and *In Our Time*." In *The Patient Particulars: American Modernism and the Technique of Originality*, 117–51. Cranbury, NJ: Associated University Press.
Knott, Toni D. 1999. *One Man Alone: Hemingway and "To Have and Have Not."* Lanham, MD: University Press of America.
Kobler, J. F. 1970. "Hemingway's 'The Sea Change': A Sympathetic View of Homosexuality." *Arizona Quarterly* 26, no. 4 (Winter): 318–24.
———. 1985. *Ernest Hemingway: Journalist and Artist*. Ann Arbor, MI: UMI Research Press.

Koch, Stephen. 2005. *The Breaking Point: Hemingway, Dos Passos, and the Murder of José Robles*. New York: Counterpoint.
Kowaleski, Michael. 1993. "The Purity of Execution in Hemingway's Fiction." In *Deadly Musings: Violence and Verbal Form in American Fiction*, 131–61. Princeton, NJ: Princeton University Press.
Krim, Seymour. 1952. "Ernest Hemingway: Valor and Defeat." *Commonweal*, September 19, 584–86.
Kronenberger, Louis. 1926. "A New Novelist." *Saturday Review of Literature*, February 13, 555.
———. 1933. "Hemingway's New Stories and Other Recent Works of Fiction." *New York Times Book Review*, November 5, 6.
———. 1937. "When He Thinks—." *Nation*, October 23, 439–40.
Krutch, Joseph Wood. 1927. "The End of Art." *Nation*, November 16, 548.
———. 1940. Review of *The Fifth Column*. *Nation*, March 16, 371–72.
Kupferberg, Herbert. 1986. "Books." *Parade*, June 15, 17.
Kyle, Frank. 1995. *Hemingway and the Post-Narrative Condition: An Unauthorized Commentary on "The Sun Also Rises and Other Essays."* Huntington, WV: University Editions.
Lamb, Robert Paul. 1996. "Hemingway and the Creation of Twentieth-Century Dialogue." *Twentieth Century Literature* 42, no. 4 (Winter): 453–90.
———. 2010. *Art Matters: Hemingway, Craft, and the Creation of the Modern Short Story*. Baton Rouge: Louisiana State University Press.
———. 2013. *The Hemingway Short Story: A Study in Craft for Writers and Readers*. Baton Rouge: Louisiana State University Press.
Lanser, Susan Sniader. 1981. *The Narrative Act: Point of View in Prose Fiction*. Princeton, NJ: Princeton University Press.
Larsen, Lyle. 2011. *Stein and Hemingway: The Story of a Turbulent Friendship*. Jefferson, NC: McFarland.
Larson, Kelli A. 1990. *Ernest Hemingway: A Reference Guide 1974–1989*. Boston: G. K. Hall.
———. 1992. "Stepping into the Labyrinth: Fifteen Years of Hemingway Scholarship." *Hemingway Review* 11, no. 2 (Spring): 19–24.
"The Last by Hemingway: Very Good and All His." 1970. *San Diego Union*, October 4, E8.
Latham, Aaron. 1977. "A Farewell to Machismo." *New York Times Magazine*, October 16, 54–55, 80, 82, 90–99.
Latimer, Margery. 1926. "A Burlesque of Sherwood Anderson." *New York Herald Tribune Books*, July 18, 16.
Laurence, Frank M. 1981. *Hemingway and the Movies*. Jackson: University Press of Mississippi.
Lawrence, D. H. 1927. Review of *In Our Time*. *Calendar of Modern Letters* 4 (April): 72–73.
LeBost, Barbara. 1965. "'The Way It Is': Something Else on Hemingway." *Journal of Existentialism* 6 (Winter): 175–80.

Lee, A. Robert, 1971. Review of *Ernest Hemingway: A Life Story* and *Islands in the Stream*. *Studies: An Irish Quarterly Review* 60, no. 238 (Summer): 220–23.

———, ed. 1983. *Ernest Hemingway: New Critical Essays*. Totowa, NJ: Barnes and Noble.

Lee, Charles. 1940. "Hemingway's Finest Novel—'For Whom the Bell Tolls.'" *Boston Herald*, October 26, 13.

Leff, Leonard J. 1997. *Hemingway and His Conspirators: Hollywood, Scribner's, and the Making of American Celebrity Culture*. Lanham, MD: Rowman & Littlefield.

Lehan, Richard. 1977. Review of *Hemingway's First War: The Making of A Farewell to Arms*. *American Literature* 49, no. 3 (November): 471–73.

Lehmann-Haupt, Christopher. 1969. "A Replica of Hemingway So Real It Moves." *New York Times*, April 21, 45.

———. 1970. "The Case of the Missing Annotations." *New York Times*, September 30, 41.

———. 1983. "Books of the Times." *New York Times*, June 23.

———. 1985. "Books of the Times." *New York Times*, October 21.

———. 1992. "A Life of Hemingway, the Esthete and Loner." *New York Times Book Review*, November 2.

———. 1994. "Was Hemingway Gay? There's More to the Story." *New York Times*, November 10, C21.

Levin, Harry. 1951. "Observations on the Style of Ernest Hemingway." *Kenyon Review* 13, no. 4 (Autumn): 581–609.

Levine, Gary Martin. 2003. "'A Single Window': First-Person Narrators and Consuming Jews in F. Scott Fitzgerald's *The Great Gatsby*, Ernest Hemingway's *The Sun Also Rises*, and Willa Cather's *The Professor*." In *The Merchant of Modernism: The Economic Jew in Anglo-American Literature, 1864–1939*, 109–30. New York: Routledge.

Lewis, R. W. B. 1953. Review of *The Old Man and the Sea*. *Hudson Review* 6, no. 1 (Spring): 146–48.

———. 1985. "Who's Papa?" *New Republic*, December 2, 31–34.

Lewis, Robert W. 1965. *Hemingway on Love*. Austin: University of Texas Press.

———. 1987. "Hemingway's Lives: A Review." *Hemingway Review* 7, no. 1 (Fall): 45–62.

———, ed. 1990. *Hemingway in Italy and Other Essays*. New York: Praeger.

———. 1992. *"A Farewell to Arms": The War of the Words*. New York: Twayne.

Lewis, Sinclair. 1937. Review of *To Have and Have Not*. *Newsweek*, October 18, 34.

Lewis, Wyndham. 1934. "The Dumb Ox: A Study of Ernest Hemingway." *Life and Letters* 10 (April): 33–45. Reprinted in Meyers 1982, 186–207.

"Library Expert Finds Public Taste Turning from Realism to Romance." 1936. *Boston Herald*, December 28, 2.

Limon, John. 1994. "Temporal Form and Wartime: Modernism after World War I." In *Writing after War: American War Fiction from Realism to Postmodernism*, 84–127. New York: Oxford University Press.

Lippmann, Walter. 1929. *A Preface to Morals*. New York: Macmillan.

Lisca, Peter. 1966. "The Structure of Hemingway's *Across the River and Into the Trees*." *Modern Fiction Studies* 12, no. 2 (Summer), 232–50.

Littell, Robert. 1927. "Notes on Hemingway." *New Republic*, August 10, 303–6.

———. 1941. Review of *For Whom the Bell Tolls*. *Yale Review* 30, no. 2 (Winter): vi, viii.

Locklin, Gerald, and Charles Stetler. 1992. Review of *Hemingway's Quarrel with Androgyny*. *Studies in Short Fiction* 29, no. 1 (Winter): 138.

Lodge, David. 1980. "Analysis and Interpretation of the Realist Text: A Pluralist Approach to Ernest Hemingway's 'Cat in the Rain.'" *Poetics Today* 1, no. 4 (Summer): 5–22.

Loesberg, Jonathan. 1972. "Nick Adams as a Consistent Hero." *Providence Sunday Journal*, June 11, H21.

Long, Robert Emmet. 1964. "Hemingway and His Contemporaries in Paris." *North American Review* 249, no. 3 (Autumn): 69–72.

———. 1970. Review of *Islands in the Stream*. *Commonweal*, October 23, 99–100.

Love, Glen A. 1987. "Hemingway's Indian Virtues: An Ecological Reconsideration." *Western American Literature* 22, no. 3 (November): 201–13.

———. 1990. "*The Professor's House*: Cather, Hemingway, and the Chastening of American Prose Style." *Western American Literature* 24: 295–311.

———. 2003. "Hemingway among the Animals." In *Practical Ecocriticism: Literature, Biology, and the Environment*, 117–34. Charlottesville: University of Virginia Press.

Lovett, Robert Morss. 1932. "Ernest Hemingway." *English Journal* 21, no. 8 (October): 609–17.

Lowe, John Livingston. 1927. *The Road to Xanadu: A Study in the Ways of the Imagination*. Boston: Houghton Mifflin.

Ludington, Townsend. 1977. Review of *By Force of Will*. *New Republic*, June 4, 35–36.

Lutz, Mark. 1926. "Clever Story Is Well Done." *Richmond Times-Dispatch*, November 7, 9.

Lynn, David H. 1989. *The Hero's Tale: Narrators in the Early Modern Novel*. New York: St. Martin's Press.

Lynn, Kenneth S. 1981. "Hemingway's Private War." *Commentary* 72, no. 1 (July): 24–33.

———. 1987. *Hemingway*. New York: Simon & Schuster.

———. 1999. "Hemingway, Ltd." *National Review*, June 28, 50–52.

Lyons, Donald. 1994. Review of *Ernest Hemingway: A Life without Consequences*. *American Spectator* 27, no. 10 (October): 72–73.

Lyons, Leonard. 1950. "Broadway Gazette: The Editor Had a Footnote." *Repository*, September 29, 28.

Macaulay, Alistair. 2013. "It's Ballet, with Booze and Bulls." *New York Times,* May 13, C2.
Macauley, Robie. 1970. "100-Proof Old Ernest, Most of It, Anyway." *New York Times Book Review*, October 4, 50–51.
Macdonald, Dwight. 1941. "Reading from Left to Right." *Partisan Review*, January–February, 24–28.
———. 1962. "Ernest Hemingway." *Against the American Grain*, 167–84. New York: Random House.
Mailer, Norman. 2003. "Oddments on Hemingway." In *The Spooky Art: Essays on Writing*, 260–62. New York: Random House.
Maloff, Saul. 1969. "The Impotence of Being Ernest." *Commonweal*, May 9, 235–36.
Mandel, Miriam B. 1995. *Reading Hemingway: The Facts in the Fictions.* Metuchen, NJ, Scarecrow Press.
———. 2004. *A Companion to Hemingway's "Death in the Afternoon."* Rochester, NY: Camden House.
———, ed. 2011. *Hemingway and Africa.* Rochester, NY: Camden House.
Maner, William. 1950. "Shakespeare's Runner-Up Is Topic of Brisk Brawl." *Richmond Times-Dispatch*, November 19, A9.
———. 1952. "Hemingway Wins Praise on 'Old Man'." *Richmond Times-Dispatch*, September 7, 8A.
Mann, Thomas. 1932. Dust jacket remarks on *A Farewell to Arms*. Quoted in *Richmond Times-Dispatch*, February 14.
Manning, Margaret. 1972. "Nick Adams—a Reminder." *Boston Globe*, April 24, 23.
Mansfield, Harvey. 2006. *Manliness.* New Haven, CT: Yale University Press.
Maris, Ronald W., and Bernard Lazerwitz. 1981. *Pathways to Suicide: A Survey of Self-Destructive Behaviors.* Baltimore: Johns Hopkins University Press.
"Marital Tragedy." 1926. *New York Times,* October 31, 7.
Mark Twain Journal. 1962. Vol. 9 (Summer). Special Hemingway tribute issue.
Marsden, Malcolm. 1969. "Hemingway's Symbolic Pattern: The Basis of Tone." *Discourse* 12, no. 1 (Winter): 16–28.
Marshall, Margaret. 1940. "Notes by the Way." *Nation*, October 26, 395–96.
Martin, Christopher D. 2006. "Ernest Hemingway: A Psychological Autopsy of a Suicide." *Psychiatry: Interpersonal & Biological Processes* 69, no. 4 (Winter): 351–61.
Martin, Ronald. 1991. "Ezra Pound and Ernest Hemingway: The Discipline of Destruction." In *American Literature and the Destruction of Knowledge: Innovative Writing in the Age of Epistemology*, 208–30. Durham, NC: Duke University Press.
Martin, Wendy. 1972. "Seduced and Abandoned in the New World: The Fallen Woman in American Fiction." In *The American Sisterhood: Writings of the Feminist Movement from Colonial Times to the Present*, 257–72. New York: Harper & Row.

Marx, Paul. 1980. "Hemingway and Ethnics." In *Seasoned Authors for a New Season: The Search for Standards in Popular Writing*, edited by Louis Filler, 43–50. Bowling Green, OH: Bowling Green University Popular Press.

Massie, Allan. 2009. "Rewrites and Wrongs." *Spectator*, August 8.

Matthews, T. S. 1929. "Nothing Ever Happens to the Brave." *New Republic*, October 9, 208–10.

———. 1935. "A Hemingway You'll Never Be." *New Republic*, November 27, 79–80.

Maurois, André. 1929. "Ernest Hemingway." *This Quarter* 2, no. 2 (October–December): 212–15. Reprinted in Meyers 1982, 48–49.

Maxwell, D. E. S. 1963. *American Literature: The Intellectual Background*. New York: Columbia University Press.

Mayberry, George. 1952. "Truth and Poetry." *New Republic*, October 13, 21–22.

McCaffery, John K. M., ed. 1950. *Ernest Hemingway: The Man and His Work*. Cleveland, OH: World.

McCarthy, Harold. 1974. "Hemingway and Life as Play." In *The Expatriate Perspective: American Novelists and the Idea of America*, 136–55. Rutherford, NJ: Fairleigh Dickinson University Press.

McClure, John. 1926. "Literature and Less." *New Orleans Times-Picayune*, December 5, 4.

McClurg, Jocelyn. 1992. "Not Just Another Hemingway Bio." *Mobile Register*, December 20, 10G.

McConnell, Frank. 1986. "Hemingway: Stalking Papa's Ghost." *Wilson Quarterly* 10, no. 1 (January): 160–72.

McCormick, John. 1957. *Catastrophe and Imagination: English and American Writing 1870 to 1930*. London: Longmans, Green.

———. 1971. *The Middle Distance: A Comparative History of American Imaginative Literature 1919–1932*. New York: Free Press.

———. 1975. "The Anachronous Hero: Hemingway and Montherlant." In *Fiction as Knowledge: The Modern Post-Romantic Novel*, 109–31. New Brunswick, NJ: Rutgers University Press.

McDermott, William. 1929. "On Hemingway's Best Seller." *Cleveland Plain Dealer*, October 19, 19.

———. 1950. "McDermott on Hemingway." *Cleveland Plain Dealer*, September 15, 13.

———. 1952. "McDermott on Hemingway." *Cleveland Plain Dealer*, September 11, 17.

McDowell, Edwin. 1985. "New Hemingway Novel to Be Published in May." *New York Times*, December 17.

McFarland, Ron. 2012. "The World's Most Interesting Man." *Midwest Quarterly* 54, no. 4 (Summer): 414–30.

———. 2014. *Appropriating Hemingway: Using Him as a Fictional Character*. Jefferson, NC: McFarland.

McIntyre, O. O. 1929. "New York by Day." *Tampa Morning Tribune*, March 9, 8.

McKelly, James C. 1992. Review of *Hemingway's Quarrel with Androgyny*. *American Literature* 64, no. 1 (March): 177–78.
McLaughlin, Richard. 1954. "Years When Famous Novelist Was Learning How to Write." *Springfield Republican*, June 6, 7C.
McLemore, Henry. 1952. "The Great Gift of Narrative." *Rockford Morning Star*, October 24, 6A.
McLendon, James.1972. *Papa: Hemingway in Key West*. Miami: Seeman.
McSweeney, Kerry. 2007. "Affects in Hemingway's Nick Adams Sequence." In *The Realist Short Story of the Powerful Glimpse*, 56–73. Columbia: University of South Carolina Press.
Meier, Thomas. 1997. Review of *Hemingway; The Postwar Years and the Posthumous Novels*. *American Literature* 69, no. 1 (March): 234–35.
Mellow, James R. 1992. *Hemingway: A Life without Consequences*. Boston: Houghton Mifflin.
Mencken, H. L. 1928. "Fiction." *American Mercury*, May, 127.
———. 1930. "Fiction by Adept Hands." *American Mercury*, January 19, 127.
———. 1932. "The Spanish Idea of a Good Time." *American Mercury*, December, 507–8.
Mendelson, Edward. 2014. "Who Was Ernest Hemingway?" *New York Review of Books*, August 14.
"Men without Women." 1927. *Time*, October 24, 38.
Meredith, James H. 2004. "Understanding Hemingway's Multiple Voices of War: A Rhetorical Study." In *War and Words: Horror and Heroism in the Literature of Warfare*, edited by Sara Munson Deats, Lagretta Tallent Lenker, and Merry G. Perry, 197–214. Lanham, MD: Lexington Books.
Merrill, Robert. 1988. "Demoting Hemingway: Feminist Criticism and the Canon." *American Literature* 60, no. 2 (May): 255–68.
Merritt, Robert. 1986. "Projects Should Have Been Untouched." *Richmond Times-Dispatch*, June 1, F5.
Messenger, Christian. 1981. *Sport and the Spirit of Play in American Fiction: Hawthorne to Faulkner*. New York: Columbia University Press.
Messent, Peter B. 1990. "Slippery Stuff: The Construction of Character in *The Sun Also Rises*." In *New Readings of the American Novel: Narrative Theory and Its Application*, 86–129. New York: Macmillan.
———. 1992a. *Ernest Hemingway*. New York: St. Martin's Press.
———. 1992b. "Reconstructing Papa: New Directions in Hemingway Criticism." *Journal of American Studies* 26, no. 2 (August): 269–75.
Meyers, Jeffrey. 1977. Review of *Hemingway's First War: The Making of "A Farewell to Arms."* *Criticism* 19, no. 3 (Summer): 269–73.
———, ed. 1982. *Hemingway: The Critical Heritage*. Boston: Routledge & Kegan Paul.
———. 1983. "A Trail of Destruction." *National Review*, August 19, 1027–28.
———. 1985. *Hemingway: A Biography*. New York: Harper & Row.
———. 1986a. "A Conventional Chap." *National Review*, January 31, 60–61.

———. 1986b. "Tonsorial." *National Review*, May 23, 44–46.
———. 1999. "Nubile Savage." *New Criterion* 18, no. 1 (September): 68–72.
———. 2000. *Hemingway: Life into Art*. New York: Cooper Square.
———. 2011. "Hemingway's Achievement." *Wall Street Journal Online*, June 30. http://online.wsj.com/news/articles.
———. 2012. "Ernest Becoming Hemingway." *Yale Review* 100, no. 3 (July): 167–80.
Miller, D. Quentin. 1996. Review of *Hemingway's Genders*. *Studies in the Novel* 28, no. 2 (Summer): 258–60.
Miller, Linda Patterson. 1999. "What's Funny about *True at First Light*?" *Hemingway Review* 19, no. 1 (Fall): 48–52.
———. 2007. Review of *The Bones of the Others*. *Hemingway Review* 27, no. 1 (Fall): 140–45.
Miller, Madelaine Hemingway. 1975. *Ernie: Hemingway's Sister "Sunny" Remembers*. New York: Crown.
Miller, Max. 1940. "Hemingway Regains Mastery as Novelist." *San Diego Union*, October 27, 7C.
Miller, Neil. 2010. *Banned in Boston: The Watch and Ward Society's Crusade against Books, Burlesque, and the Social Evil*. Boston: Beacon Press.
Millett, Kate. 1970. *Sexual Politics*. Garden City, NY: Doubleday.
Millis, Walter. 1942. "The Red Face of War: From Goliath to Hitler." *New York Herald Tribune Books*, October 25, 3.
Minot, John Clair. 1932. "A Novelist Becomes an Expert on the 'Sport' of Bullfighting." *Boston Herald*, September 26, 10.
———. 1935. "Hemingway's African Safari." *Boston Herald*, November 2, 9.
Minter, David. 1994. "War as Metaphor: The Example of Ernest Hemingway." In *A Cultural History of the American Novel*, 133–45. Cambridge: Cambridge University Press.
Mizener, Arthur. 1952. "Prodigy into Peer." *Saturday Review*, October 18, 25.
Moddelmog, Debra. 1993. "Reconstructing Hemingway's Identity: Sexual Politics, the Author, and the Multicultural Classroom." In Wagner-Martin 1998, 239–63.
———. 1999. *Reading Desire: In Pursuit of Ernest Hemingway*. Ithaca, NY: Cornell University Press.
———. 2008. "Telling Stories from Hemingway's FBI File: Conspiracy, Paranoia, and Masculinity." In *Modernism on File: Writers, Artists, and the FBI, 1920–1950*, edited by C. A. Culleton and K. Leick, 53–72. New York: Palgrave Macmillan.
Moddelmog, Debra, and Suzanne del Gizzo, eds. 2013. *Ernest Hemingway in Context*. New York: Cambridge University Press.
Modern Fiction Studies. 1955. Vol. 1, no. 3 (Winter). Special issue on Hemingway.
———. 1968. Vol. 14, no. 3 (Autumn). Special issue on Hemingway.
Monk, Craig. 2008. *Writing the Lost Generation: Expatriate Autobiography and American Modernism*. Iowa City: University of Iowa Press.

Monteiro, George. 1978. "Hemingway's Hemingway." *Novel* 11, no. 3 (Spring): 286–88.
———, ed. 1994. *Critical Essays on Ernest Hemingway's "A Farewell to Arms."* New York: G. K. Hall.
———. 2004. "The Faulkner-Hemingway Rivalry." In Urgo and Abadie 2004, 74–92.
Montgomery, Constance Cappel. 1966. *Hemingway in Michigan*. New York: Fleet.
Moore, Harry T. 1971. "Hemingway and a Chronology without Characterization." In *Age of the Modern and Other Literary Essays*, 89–91. Edwardsville: Southern Illinois University Press.
———. 1972. "Hemingway Trove, Nick Adams Back." *St. Louis Globe-Democrat*, April 15, 4D.
Moran, Joe. 2000. *Star Authors: Literary Celebrity in America*. Sterling, VA: Pluto.
Moreira, Peter. 2006. *Hemingway on the China Front*. Washington, DC: Potomac Books.
Moreland, Kim I. 1996. "Ernest Hemingway: Knighthood in Our Time." In *The Medievalist Impulse in American Literature: Twain, Adams, Fitzgerald, and Hemingway*, 161–202. Charlottesville: University of Virginia Press.
Morgan, Kathleen. 1990. *Tales Plainly Told: The Eyewitness Narratives of Hemingway and Homer*. Columbia, SC: Camden House.
Morris, Lawrence. 1926a. "Frolicking on Olympus." *New Republic*, September 15, 101.
———. 1926b. "Warfare in Man and among Men." *New Republic*, December 22, 142–43.
Morris, Wright. 1963. "Hemingway: The Function of Style." In *The Territory Ahead*, 133–46. New York: Athenaeum.
Morrison, Toni. 1992. "Disturbing Nurses and the Kindness of Sharks." In *Playing in the Dark: Whiteness and the Literary Imagination*, 61–91. Cambridge, MA: Harvard University Press.
Morrow, Lance.1986. "A Quarter Century Later, the Myth Endures." *Time*, August 25, 70.
Mort, Terry. 2009. *The Hemingway Patrols*. New York: Scribner.
Morton, Brian. 1992. Review of *Hemingway: A Life without Consequences*. *New Leader*, December 14, 22–23.
Moseley, Edwin. 1962. "Christ as the Old Champion: Hemingway's *The Old Man and the Sea*." *Pseudonyms of Christ in the Modern Novel*, 205–14. Pittsburgh: University of Pittsburgh Press.
Moylan, Thomas. 1955. "Violence in Hemingway." *Catholic World* 181 (July): 287–93.
"Mr. Hemingway Writes Some High-Spirited Nonsense." 1926. *New York Times Book Review*, June 13, 8.
Mudrick, Marvin. 1964. "A Farewell to Spring and Paris." *Hudson Review* 17, no. 4 (Winter): 572–79.

Muir, Edwin. 1927. "Fiction." *Nation & Athenaeum*, July 2, 450, 452.
———. 1952. "Two Novelists." *Observer*, September 7, 7.
Murray, Albert. 1996. "The Storyteller as Blues Singer: Ernest Hemingway Swinging the Blues and Taking Nothing." In *The Blue Devils of Nada: A Contemporary American Approach to Aesthetics*, 141–221. New York: Pantheon.
Murray, G. E. 1972. "New Discoveries: Papa's Tales of Nick Adams, His Heroic Alter Ego." *Chicago Sun-Times Book Week*, April 16, 18.
Muste, John. 1966. *Say That We Saw Spain Die: Literary Consequences of the Spanish Civil War*. Seattle: University of Washington Press.
Nagel, James, ed. 1984. *Ernest Hemingway: The Writer in Context*. Madison: University of Wisconsin Press.
———, ed. 1995. *Critical Essays on Ernest Hemingway's "The Sun Also Rises."* New York: G. K. Hall.
———, ed. 1996. *Ernest Hemingway: The Oak Park Legacy*. Tuscaloosa: University of Alabama Press.
Nagel, James, and Henry S. Villard, eds. 1989. *Hemingway in Love and War: The Lost Diary of Agnes von Kurowsky*. Boston: Northeastern University Press.
Nelson, Raymond. 1979. *Hemingway, Expressionist Artist*. Ames: Iowa State University Press.
Nelson, Valerie J. 2005. "Bernice Kert, 81." *Los Angeles Times*, July 26.
"The New Books: Fiction." 1926. *Saturday Review of Literature*, July 31, 12.
Newlin, Keith, ed. 2011. *Critical Insights: "The Sun Also Rises."* Pasadena, CA: Salem Press.
"New Novels: The War and After." 1929. *Times* (London), November 15, 20.
Nickel, Matthew. 2013. *Hemingway's Dark Night: Catholic Influences and Intertextualities in the Work of Ernest Hemingway*. Wickford, RI: New Street Communications.
Nies, Betsy L. 2002. "Hemingway, Eugenic Terror, and the 'Newest New Woman.'" In *Eugenic Fantasies: Racial Ideology in the Literature and Popular Culture of the 1920s*, 45–66. New York: Routledge.
Noble, David. 1968. *The Eternal Adam and the New World Garden: The Central Myth of the American Novel since 1830*. New York: Braziller.
Noble, Donald R., ed. 1983. *Hemingway: A Revaluation*. Troy, NY: Whitson.
Nolan, Charles J., Jr. 1984. "Hemingway's Women's Movement." *Hemingway Review* 3, no. 2 (Spring): 14–22.
Nolan, William F. 1972. "Papa as Nick." *WGA [Writers Guild of America/West Newsletter]*, June, 21–22.
Nordell, Roderick. 1970. "The Sea as a Mirror: Hemingway's View of Himself." *Christian Science Monitor*, October 8, 13.
Norris, Margot. 2000. "Lies and Truth in Hemingway's *A Farewell to Arms*." In *Writing War in the Twentieth Century*, 58–77. Charlottesville: University of Virginia Press.
Notice. 1932. *Boston Herald*, May 21, 13.

Nuffer, David. 2008. *The Best Friend I Ever Had: Revelations about Ernest Hemingway from Those Who Knew Him*. Bloomington, IN: Xlibris.
Nyman, Jopi. 1997. *Men Alone: Masculinity, Individualism, and Hard-Boiled Fiction*. Costerus New Series, 3. Atlanta: Rodopi.
———. 1998. *Hard-Boiled Fiction and Dark Romanticism*. New York: Lang.
Oberhelman, Harley D. 1994. *The Presence of Hemingway in the Short Fiction of Gabriel García Márquez*. Fredericton, NB: York Press.
O'Connor, William Van. 1964. "Hemingway's Sad Memoir." *Massachusetts Review* 5, no. 4 (Summer): 789–91.
O'Faolin, Sean. 1956. "Ernest Hemingway." In *The Vanishing Hero: Studies of Novelists of the Twenties*, 121–45. Boston: Little, Brown.
O'Hara, John. 1950. "The Author's Name Is Hemingway." *New York Times Book Review*, September 10, 1, 30.
Oldsey, Bernard. 1970. "The Novel in the Drawer." *Nation*, October 19, 376, 378.
———. 1974. Review of *Ernest Hemingway: Five Decades of Criticism*. *College Literature* 1, no. 2 (Spring): 146–48.
———. 1979. *Hemingway's Hidden Craft: The Writing of "A Farewell to Arms."* University Park: Penn State University Press.
———, ed. 1981. *Ernest Hemingway: The Papers of a Writer*. New York: Garland.
"The Old Values and the New Story." 1952. *Baton Rouge Advocate*, September 5, 4A.
Oliver, Charles M., ed. 1989. *A Moving Picture Feast: The Filmgoer's Hemingway*. New York: Praeger.
———. 1990. Review of *Hemingway's "Green Hills of Africa" as Evolutionary Narrative: Helix and Scimitar*. *Hemingway Review* 10, no.1 (Fall): 73.
———, ed. 2005. *Ernest Hemingway's "A Farewell to Arms": A Documentary Volume*. Detroit: Thomson Gale.
———.2007. *Critical Companion to Ernest Hemingway: A Literary Reference Guide to His Life and Work*. New York: Facts on File.
———. 2013. "*The Hemingway Review* and the Ernest Hemingway Foundation and Society." In Moddelmog and del Gizzo 2013, 429–34.
Olson, Barbara K. 1997. "'I Don't Like to Write like God': Hemingway's Omniscient Narration." In *Authorial Divinity in the Twentieth Century: Omniscient Narration in Woolf, Hemingway, and Others*, 37–63. Cranbury, NJ: Associated University Press.
Onderdonk, Todd. 2006. "'Bitched': Feminization, Identity, and the Hemingwayesque in *The Sun Also Rises*." *Twentieth Century Literature* 52, no. 1 (Spring): 61–91.
Ott, Mark. 2002. Review of *Hemingway: The Grace and the Pressure*. *Hemingway Review* 22, no. 1 (Fall): 138–39.
———. 2008. *A Sea of Change: Ernest Hemingway and the Gulf Stream: A Contextual Biography*. Kent, OH: Kent State University Press.
Ozick, Cynthia. 1969. "Women and Creativity: The Demise of the Dancing Dog." *Motive* 29 (March–April): 7–16. Reprinted in *Woman in Sexist*

Society: Studies in Power and Powerlessness, edited by Vivian Gornick and Barbara K. Moran, 307–22. New York: Basic Books, 1970.

Parker, Dorothy. 1927. "A Great Book of Short Stories." *New Yorker*, October 29, 92–94.

———. 1940. Review of *For Whom the Bell Tolls*. *PM*, October 20, 42.

Pattee, Fred Lewis. 1930. *The New American Literature, 1890–1930: A Survey*. New York: Century.

Paul, Elliott. 1937. "Hemingway and the Critics." *Saturday Review of Literature*, November 6, 3–4.

———. 1950. Review of *Across the River and Into the Trees*. *Providence Sunday Journal*, September 10, IV: 8.

Paul, Steve. 2009. "'New Coke vs. Old Coke': The Debate over *A Moveable Feast: The Restored Edition*." *Hemingway Review* 29, no. 1 (Fall): 16–23.

Paul, Steve, Gail Sinclair, and Steven Trout, eds. 2014. *War & Ink: New Perspectives on Ernest Hemingway's Life and Writings*. Kent, OH: Kent State University Press.

Pavloska, Susanna. 2000. *Modern Primitives: Race and Language in Gertrude Stein, Ernest Hemingway, and Zora Neale Hurston*. New York: Garland.

Peckham, Morse. 1971. "Ernest Hemingway: Sexual Themes in His Writing." *Sexual Behavior* 1, no. 4 (July): 62–70.

Perrin, Thomas Gordon. 2012. "The Old Men and the 'Sea of Masscult.'" *American Literature* 84, no. 1 (March): 151–74.

Petersen, Clarence. 1986. "Surely You're Joking, Mr. Feynman." *Chicago Tribune*, February 2.

Peterson, Richard K. 1969. *Hemingway, Direct and Oblique*. The Hague: Mouton.

Pettipiece, Deirdre Anne. 2002. *Sex Theories and the Shaping of Two Moderns: Hemingway and H. D.* New York: Routledge.

Pettit, Robert. 1986. "A New Hemingway Now Emerges." *Greensboro News & Record*, May 25, E5.

Phelan, James. 1996a. "Voice, Distance, Temporal Perspective, and the Dynamics of *A Farewell to Arms*." In *Narrative as Rhetoric: Technique, Audiences, Ethics, Ideology*, 59–84. Columbus: Ohio State University Press.

———. 1996b. "What Hemingway and a Rhetorical Theory of Narrative Can Do for Each Other: The Example of 'My Old Man.'" In *Narrative as Rhetoric: Technique, Audiences, Ethics, Ideology*, 87–104. Columbus: Ohio State University Press.

———. 2005. "Progression and Audience Engagement in Lyric Narratives." In *Living to Tell about It: A Rhetoric and Ethics of Character Narration*, 158–82. Ithaca, NY: Cornell University Press.

———. 2013. "*A Farewell to Arms* (1929): *Bildung*, Tragedy, and the Rhetoric of Voice." In *Reading the American Novel 1920–2010*, 61–84. Malden, MA: Wiley-Blackwell.

Phelps, William Lyon. 1941. "*Esquire*'s Five-Minute Shelf." *Esquire*, February, 76, 135–38.

Phillips, Arthur. 2011. "A Swell Life." *New York Times*, November 13, BR8.
Phillips, H. L. 1927. "A Happy New Year: 'In the Ernest Hemingway Manner.'" *Richmond Times-Dispatch*, December 31, 6.
Phillips, K. J. 1990. "Ernest Hemingway, *The Sun Also Rises*." In *Dying Gods in Twentieth-Century Fiction*, 65–75. Lewisburg, PA: Bucknell University Press.
Piep, Karsten Helge. 2009. "Ernest Hemingway, *A Farewell to Arms*, and Personal War." In *Embattled Home Fronts: Domestic Politics and the American Novel of World War I*, 83–105. New York: Rodopi.
Pintarich, Paul. 1983. "One at a Time: Hemingway's Women." *Northwest Magazine*, July 26, 16, 23.
Pizer, Donald. 1996. *American Expatriate Writing and the Paris Movement*. Baton Rouge: Louisiana State University Press.
Plath, James, and Frank Simons. 1999. *Remembering Ernest Hemingway*. Key West, FL: Ketch & Yawl Press.
Plimpton, George. 1958. "Ernest Hemingway: The Art of Fiction No. 21." *Paris Review* 18 (Spring): 60–89.
———. 1964. Review of *A Moveable Feast*. *New York Herald Tribune Book Week*, May 3, 1, 12–13.
Plotkin, Stephen. 1999. "The *True at First Light* Manuscripts." *Hemingway Review* 19, no. 1 (Fall): 61–63.
"Poignant Love Story Told by Ernest Hemingway." 1929. *Springfield Sunday Union & Republican*, November 10, 7E.
Poore, Charles. 1935. "Ernest Hemingway's Story of His African Safari." *New York Times Book Review*, October 27, 3, 27.
———. 1937. "Books of the Times." *New York Times*, October 15, 21.
———. 1952. "Books of the Times." *New York Times*, October 9, 29.
———. 1953. Books of the Times." *New York Times*, February 26.
———. 1961. "Hemingway." *New York Times*, July 3, 6.
———. 1964. "Ernest Hemingway's Memoir of Paris in the Twenties." *New York Times*, May 5, 41.
"Pressure under Grace: An Exchange." 1987. *New York Review of Books*, October 22.
Price, Reynolds. 1972. "For Ernest Hemingway." *New American Review* 14: 38–66.
"Princeton Names Dr. Baker Leader of English Group." 1952. *Trenton Evening Times*, September 28, pt. 2, 4.
Pritchard, William. 1988. "The Trouble with Ernest." *Hudson Review* 41, no. 1 (Spring): 218–24.
Pritchett, V. S. 1941. Review of *For Whom the Bell Tolls*. *New Statesman & Nation*, March 15, 275–76.
Pryce-Jones, Alan. 1964. "Poor and Very Happy Hemingway." *New York Herald Tribune*, May 5, 23.
"Punk and Incense." 1950. *Trenton Sunday Times*, October 15, Section 4, 10.
Putnam, Thomas. 2006. "Hemingway on War and Its Aftermath." *Prologue* 38, no. 1 (Spring): 22–29.

Quick, Jonathan. 1999. "Literary Hemingway." In *Modern Fiction and the Art of Subversion*, 129–65. New York: Lang.
Quinn, Patrick. 1952. "Measure of Hemingway." *Commonweal*, October 24, 73–75.
Rabkin, Eric. 1977. "Spatial Form and Plot." *Critical Inquiry* 4 (1977): 253–70.
Raeburn, John. 1974. "Ernest Hemingway: The Public Writer as Popular Culture." *Journal of Popular Culture* 3, no. 1 (Summer): 91–98.
———. 1984. *Fame Became Him: Hemingway as Public Writer*. Bloomington: Indiana University Press.
Rahv, Philip. 1937. "The Social Muse and the Great Kudu." *Partisan Review*, December, 62–64.
———. 1950. "*Across the River and Into the Trees*, by Ernest Hemingway." *Commentary*, October, 400–402.
Raines, Howell. 2011. Review of *Hemingway's Boat*. *Washington Post*, September 22.
Rascoe, Burton. 1926. "The Wylies, Bromfields, and Hemingways." *New York Sun*, November 7, 10.
———. 1927. "Daybook of a New Yorker." *Evansville Courier*, January 22.
———. 1929. "The Fall Books—Read and Talked About." *Art & Decoration*, November, 124.
———. 1934. Review of *Winner Take Nothing*. *Esquire*, January, 86.
———. 1940. "Wolfe, Farrell, and Hemingway." *American Mercury*, December, 493–98.
Register, Cheri. 1975. "American Feminist Literary Criticism: A Bibliographical Introduction." In *Feminist Literary Criticism: Explorations in Theory*, edited by Josephine Donovan, 1–28. Lexington: University Press of Kentucky.
Rendezvous. 1970. Special issue on Hemingway.
Renza, Louis. 1988. "The Importance of Being Ernest." *South Atlantic Quarterly* 88, no. 3 (Summer): 661–85.
Reynolds, Michael. 1976. *Hemingway's First War: The Making of "A Farewell to Arms."* Princeton, NJ: Princeton University Press.
———. 1980. "Unexplored Territory: The Next Ten Years of Hemingway Studies." *College Literature* 7, no. 3 (Fall): 189–201.
———. 1981. *Hemingway's Reading 1910–1940: An Inventory*. Princeton, NJ: Princeton University Press.
———, ed. 1983. *Critical Essays on Ernest Hemingway's "In Our Time."* Boston: G. K. Hall.
———. 1986. *The Young Hemingway*. Oxford: Basil Blackwell.
———. 1988. *"The Sun Also Rises": A Novel of the Twenties*. Boston: Twayne.
———. 1989. *Hemingway: The Paris Years*. Oxford: Basil Blackwell.
———. 1991a. *Hemingway: An Annotated Chronology*. Detroit, MI: Omnigraphics.
———. 1991b. "Up Against the Crannied Wall: The Limits of Biography." In Scafella 1991, 170–78.

———. 1992. *Hemingway: The American Homecoming*. Cambridge, MA: Blackwell.

———. 1997. *Hemingway: The 1930s*. New York: Norton.

———. 1999. *Hemingway: The Final Years*. New York: Norton.

———. 2000. *Ernest Hemingway*. Detroit: Gale.

Rich, Motoko. 2009. "'Moveable Feast' Is Recast by Hemingway Grandson." *New York Times Book Review*, June 28, A1.

Riemer, James D. 1987. "Rereading American Literature from a Men's Studies Perspective: Some Implications." In *The Making of Masculinities: The New Men's Studies*, ed. Harry Brod, 289–300. Boston: Allen & Unwin.

Ripatrazone, Nicholas. 2014. Review of *Hemingway's Dark Night*. CatholicFiction.net, March 23. http://catholicfiction.net/book-review/hemingway-s-dark-night-catholic-influences-and-intertextualities-in-the-work-of-ernest-hemingway.php.

Robins, Natalie. 1992. *Alien Ink: The FBI's War on Freedom of Expression*. New York: Morrow.

Robinson, Ted. 1926a. "Hemingway Book Is Masterpiece." *Cleveland Plain Dealer*, November 14, Features, 7.

———. 1926b. Review of *The Torrents of Spring*. *Cleveland Plain Dealer*, June 20, Features, 3.

———. 1929. "Living Figures Writhe on Hemingway's Pages as His Stark Art Tears at You." *Cleveland Plain Dealer*, October 6, Amusement & Art, 6.

———. 1932. "Bully Book by Hemingway Gores All Notions That Bullfighting Is Brutal." *Cleveland Plain Dealer*, September 25, 11.

Robson, Leo. 2010. "*A Moveable Feast: The Restored Edition*." *New Statesman*, July 12, 48.

Rohy, Valerie. 2000. "Modernist Perversity: The Repetition of Desire in *The Sun Also Rises*." In *Impossible Women: Lesbian Figures and American Literature*, 65–90. Ithaca, NY: Cornell University Press.

———. 2009. "A Darker Past in *The Garden of Eden*." In *Anachronism and Its Other*, 99–120. Albany: SUNY Press.

———. 2011. "Hemingway, Liberalism, and Transgender Reading." *Twentieth Century Literature* 57, no. 2 (Summer): 148–79.

Romer, Sam. 1940. "Hemingway—a Political Review." *Socialist Call*, November 30, 8.

Rosen, Kenneth, ed. 1994. *Hemingway Repossessed*. Westport, CT: Praeger.

Rosenfield, Isaac. 1951. "A Farewell to Hemingway." *Kenyon Review* 13, no. 1 (Winter): 147–53.

Ross, Lillian. 1950. "How Do You Like It Now, Gentlemen?" *New Yorker*, May 13, 36–62.

———. 1961. *Portrait of Hemingway*. New York: Simon & Schuster.

Ross, Patricia Ann. 2006. "Lamenting the Last Good Country: The Hemingway Script of the American Wilderness." In *The Spell Cast by Remains: The Myth of Wilderness in American Literature*, 23–46. New York: Taylor & Francis.

Rothman, N. L. 1928. "Hemingway Whistles in the Dark." *Dial*, April 1, 336–38.
Rovere, Richard. 1950. Review of *Across the River and Into the Trees*. *Harper's*, September, 104–6.
Rovit, Earl. 1963. *Ernest Hemingway*. New York: Twayne.
———. 1965. Review of *A Moveable Feast*. *Books Abroad* 39, no. 1 (Winter): 91–92.
———. 1997. "Hemingway in Our Time." *Sewanee Review* 105, no. 3 (Summer): 431–35.
———. 2011. "The Tip of the Iceberg." *Sewanee Review* 119, no. 4 (Fall): lxxii–lxxiii.
Rovit, Earl, and Gerry Brenner. 1986. *Ernest Hemingway*. Boston: Twayne.
Rovit, Earl, and Arthur Waldhorn, eds. 2005. *Hemingway and Faulkner: In Their Time*. New York: Continuum.
Ruark, Robert. 1950. "Hemingway's Latest like Boyish Stuff Where Talent Stumbles over Clumsy Feet." *Boston Traveler*, September 19, 71.
———. 1952. "Ruark Says." *Baton Rouge Times Advocate*, August 28, 4A.
Rubin, Louis. 1970. "New Hemingway Novel Poses Questions." *Washington Sunday Star*, October 4, E1.
———. 1972. "A Portrait of Nick Adams and How He Happened." *Washington Sunday Star*, April 23, C6.
Rudat, Wolfgang. 1990. *A Rotten Way to Be Wounded: The Tragicomedy of "The Sun Also Rises."* New York: Lang.
———. 1992. *Alchemy in "The Sun Also Rises": Hidden Gold in Hemingway's Narrative*. Lewiston, NY: Mellen.
Russ, Joanna. 1972. "What Can a Heroine Do? Or, Why Women Can't Write." In *Images of Women in Fiction: Feminist Perspectives*, ed. Susan Koppelman Cornillon, 3–20. Bowling Green, OH: Bowling Green State University Popular Press.
Russell, H. K. 1955. "The Catharsis in *A Farewell to Arms*." *Modern Fiction Studies* 1, no. 3 (Winter): 25–30.
Russell, Phillips. 1935. "The Literary Lantern." *Greensboro Daily News*, November 17, B5.
Ryan, Alan. 1986. "Hemingway's Fine Novel of Early Sorrow." *Cleveland Plain Dealer*, May 25, 12P.
Ryan, Frank L. 1980. *The Immediate Critical Reception of Ernest Hemingway*. Washington, DC: University Press of America.
Ryan, William J. "Uses of Irony in *To Have and Have Not*." *Modern Fiction Studies* 14, no. 3 (Autumn): 329–36.
"Sad Young Man." 1926. *Time*, November 1, 48.
Said, Edward. 1978. *Orientalism*. New York: Pantheon.
———. 1985. Review of *The Dangerous Summer*. *London Review of Books*, November 21, 19–20. Reprinted as "How Not to Get Gored" in *Reflections on Exile and Other Essays*, 231–38. Cambridge, MA: Harvard University Press.

Samuels, Charles Thomas. 1970. "The Heresy of Self-Love." *New Republic*, April 26, 28–32.
Samuelson, Arnold. 1984. *With Hemingway: A Year in Key West and Cuba*. New York: Random House.
Sanderson, Rena, ed. 1992. *Blowing the Bridge: Essays on Hemingway and "For Whom the Bell Tolls."* New York: Greenwood.
———, ed. 2006. *Hemingway's Italy: New Perspectives*. Baton Rouge: Louisiana State University Press.
Sanderson, Stewart. 1961. *Ernest Hemingway*. New York: Grove.
Sanford, Marcelline Hemingway. 1962. *At the Hemingways: A Family Portrait*. Boston: Little, Brown.
San Juan, Epifanio. 1995. "Ideological Form, Symbolic Exchange, Textual Production: A Reading of Hemingway's *For Whom the Bell Tolls*." In *Hegemonies and Strategies of Transgression*, 91–119. Albany: SUNY Press.
Satterfield, Archie. 1970. "Hemingway Legend Lives in New Book." *Seattle Times*, October 18, H4.
Savage, D. S. 1948. "Ernest Hemingway." *Hudson Review* 1, no. 3 (Autumn): 380–401. Reprinted in *The Withered Branch: Six Studies in the Modern Novel*. New York: Pellegrini & Cudahy, 1952.
Scafella, Frank. 1987. "Clippings from *The Garden of Eden*." *Hemingway Review* 7, no. 1 (Fall): 20–29.
———, ed. 1991. *Hemingway: Essays of Reassessment*. New York: Oxford University Press.
Schedler, Christopher. 2002. "Ernest Hemingway: Modernist 'Tribalism.'" In *Border Modernism: Intercultural Readings in American Literary Modernism*, 54–72. New York: Routledge.
Schmidt, Dolores Barracano. 1971. "The Great American Bitch." *College English* 32, no. 8 (May): 900–905.
Schneidau, Herbert N. 1991. *Waking Giants: The Presence of the Past in Modernism*, 184–201. New York: Oxford University Press.
Schneider, Daniel. 1967. "The Symbolism of *The Sun Also Rises*." *Discourse* 10, no. 1 (Summer): 334–42.
———. 1968. "Hemingway's *A Farewell to Arms*: The Novel as Pure Poetry." *Modern Fiction Studies* 14, no. 3 (Autumn): 283–96.
Schneider, Isidor. 1931. "The Fetish of Simplicity." *Nation*, February 18, 184–86.
Scholes, Robert. 1982. "Decoding Papa: 'A Very Short Story' as Work and Text." In *Semiotics and Interpretation*, 110–26. New Haven, CT: Yale University Press.
Schorer, Mark. 1941. "The Background of a Style." *Kenyon Review* 3, no. 1 (Winter): 101–5.
———. 1952. "With Grace under Pressure." *New Republic*, October 6, 19–20.
———. 1953. "Criticism of Hemingway." *Sewanee Review* 61, no. 3 (Summer): 514–18.

———. 1954. "Mr. Hemingway & His Critics." *New Republic*, November 15, 18–20.
———. 1970. Review of *Ernest Hemingway: A Life Story*. *American Literature* 41, no. 4 (January): 592–94.
Schwartz, Delmore. 1938. "Ernest Hemingway's Literary Situation." *Southern Review* 3, no. 4 (Autumn): 769–82. Reprinted in McCaffery 1950, 114–29.
———. 1952. "Long after Eden." *Partisan Review*, November–December, 702–3.
———. 1953. "One for the Author." *New York Times Book Review*, March 8, 6.
Schwenger, Peter. 1979. "The Masculine Mode." *Critical Inquiry* 5, no. 4 (Summer): 621–33.
Scott, Nathan A. 1966. *Ernest Hemingway: A Critical Essay*. Grand Rapids, MI: Eerdmans.
Selby, John. 1933. "Book a Day." *Rockford Morning Star*, October 29, 6.
———. 1937. "Book a Day." *Rockford Morning Star*, October 15, 10.
"Several Hundred Hear Lyle Saxon's Discussion of Books and Writers." 1933. *Baton Rouge State-Times*, January 30, 12.
Seward, William. 1969. *My Friend, Ernest Hemingway: An Affectionate Reminiscence*. South Brunswick, NJ: Barnes.
Shaw, Samuel. 1972. *Ernest Hemingway*. New York: Ungar.
Sherwood, Robert E. 1940. Review of *For Whom the Bell Tolls*. *Atlantic Monthly*, November, front section, n.p.
Simon, Kate. 1950. "Old Age of a Hero." *New Republic*, September 18, 20–21.
"Sinclair Lewis Says Hemingway Will Win Future Nobel Prize." 1930. *Cleveland Plain Dealer*, December 1, 14.
Slabey, Robert. 1965. "The Structure of *In Our Time*." *South Dakota Review* 3, no. 1 (Autumn): 38–52.
Smith, Agnes W. 1929. "Mr. Hemingway Does It Again." *New Yorker*, October 12, 120.
Smith, Harrison. 1950. "Pattern Is Familiar, but Hemingway Is Different." *New Orleans Times-Picayune*, September 10, Section 2, 7.
Smith, Julian. 1969. "Christ Times Four: Hemingway's Unknown Spanish Civil War Stories." *Arizona Quarterly* 25, no. 1 (Spring): 5–17.
———. 1970. "More Products of the Hemingway Industry." *Studies in Short Fiction* 7, no. 4 (Fall): 638–46.
Smith, Paul. 1989. *A Reader's Guide to the Short Stories of Ernest Hemingway*. Boston: G. K. Hall.
———. 1993. Review of *Hemingway: A Life without Consequences*. *Hemingway Review* 12, no. 2 (Spring): 83–87.
———, ed. 1998. *New Essays on Hemingway's Short Fiction*. New York: Cambridge University Press.
Snell, George. 1947. *Shapers of American Fiction 1798–1947*. New York: Dutton.

Solomon, Barbara. 1986. "Where's Papa?" *New Republic*, March 9, 30–34.
"Some Italian Novels." 1929. *Times Literary Supplement*, November 28, 998.
Soto, Michael. 2004. *The Modernist Nation: Generation, Renaissance, and Twentieth-Century American Literature*, 142–51. Tuscaloosa: University of Alabama Press.
Spanier, Sandra, and Robert W. Trogdon, eds. 2011–. *The Letters of Ernest Hemingway*. Cambridge: Cambridge University Press.
Spilka, Mark. 1958. "The Death of Love in *The Sun Also Rises*." In *Twelve Original Essays on Great American Novels*, edited by Charles Shapiro, 238–56. Detroit: Wayne State University Press.
———. 1982. "Hemingway and Fauntleroy: An Androgynous Pursuit." In *American Novelists Revisited: Essays in Feminist Criticism*, edited by Fritz Fleischman, 339–70. Boston: G. K. Hall.
———. 1987. "Hemingway's Barbershop Quintet: *The Garden of Eden* Manuscripts." In Wagner-Martin 1998, 349–72.
———. 1990. *Hemingway's Quarrel with Androgyny*. Lincoln: University of Nebraska Press.
Spolsky, Ellen. 1993. *Gaps in Nature: Literary Interpretation and the Modular Mind*. Albany: SUNY Press.
Sprague, Claire. 1969. "*The Sun Also Rises*: Its 'Clear Financial Basis.'" *American Quarterly* 21, no. 2, pt. 1 (Summer): 259–66.
Squire, John. 1941. "A Full Length Novel on the Spanish War." *Illustrated London News*, March 29, 420.
Stafford, William. 1981. "Benjy Compson, Jake Barnes, and Nick Carraway: Replication in Three 'Innocent' American Narrators of the 1920s." In *Books Speaking to Books: A Contextual Approach to American Fiction*, 27–50. Chapel Hill: University of North Carolina Press.
Stallings, Laurence. 1932. "Dissertation on Pride." *New York Sun*, September 23, 34.
Stanley, Lawrence. 2004. "Hemingway, Cézanne and Writing." In *Literature and the Writer*, edited by Michael J. Meyer, 204–26. New York: Rodopi.
Stange, Mary Zeiss. 1997. *Woman the Hunter*. Boston: Beacon Press.
Stanton, Edward. 1989. *Hemingway and Spain: A Pursuit*. Seattle: University of Washington Press.
Stanzel, F. K. 1984. *A Theory of Narrative*. Cambridge: Cambridge University Press.
Stark, Bruce. 1989. "Ernest Hemingway." In Bryer 1989, 404–79.
Stein, Gertrude. 1923. Review of *In Our Time*. In Wagner-Martin 1998, 17.
———. 1933. "Ernest Hemingway and the Post-War Decade." *Atlantic Monthly*, August, 197–208.
Steiner, George. 1969. "*Across the River and Into the Trees*." *New Yorker*, September 13, 147–50.
Stephens, Robert O. 1958. "Hemingway's 'Across the River and Into the Trees': A Reprise." *Texas Studies in English* 37: 92–101.
———. 1968. *Hemingway's Nonfiction: The Public Voice*. Chapel Hill: University of North Carolina Press.

———. 1977a. Review of *Hemingway's First War: The Making of "A Farewell to Arms."* *Journal of English and Germanic Philology* 76, no. 2 (April): 280–82.

———, ed. 1977b. *Ernest Hemingway: The Critical Reception.* New York: Burt Franklin.

Stephens, Rosemary. 1966. "'In Another Country': *Three* as Symbol." *University of Mississippi Studies in English* 7: 40–47.

Stewart, Matthew C. 2000. "Ernest Hemingway and World War I: Combatting Recent Psychobiographical Reassessments, Restoring the War." *Papers on Language & Literature* 36, no. 2 (Spring): 198–217.

———. 2001a. "The Measure of What You Bring: Three Recent Books on Hemingway." *College Literature* 28, no. 1 (Winter): 190–201.

———. 2001b. *Modernism and Tradition in Ernest Hemingway's "In Our Time": A Guide for Students and Readers.* Rochester, NY: Camden House.

"Stirs Paris." 1927. *San Diego Evening Tribune*, February 17, 9.

Stoltzfus, Ben. 1978. *Gide and Hemingway: Rebels against God.* Port Washington, NY: Kennikat.

———. 1996. *Lacan and Literature: Purloined Texts.* Albany: SUNY Press.

———. 2005. "Sartre, *Nada*, and Hemingway's African Stories." *Comparative Literature Studies* 42, no. 3: 205–28.

———. 2010. *Hemingway and French Writers.* Kent, OH: Kent State University Press.

Stoneback, H. R. 2007. *Reading Hemingway's "The Sun Also Rises": Glossary and Commentary.* Kent, OH: Kent State University Press.

Strong, Amy. 1996. "Screaming through Silence: The Violence of Race in 'Indian Camp' and 'The Doctor and the Doctor's Wife." In Wagner-Martin 1998, 29–44.

———. 2008. *Race and Identity in Hemingway's Fiction.* New York: Palgrave Macmillan.

Strychacz, Thomas. 1989. "Dramatizations of Manhood in Hemingway's *In Our Time*." In Wagner-Martin 1998, 45–60.

———. 2003. *Hemingway's Theaters of Masculinity.* Baton Rouge: Louisiana State University Press.

———. 2008. *Dangerous Masculinities: Conrad, Hemingway, and Lawrence.* Gainesville: University Press of Florida.

Suárez-Galbán, Eugenio. 2011. "Hemingway: Stories of the Last Good Land." In *The Last Good Land: Spain in American Literature*, 199–223. Amsterdam: Rodopi.

Sugg, Richard. 1972. "Hemingway, Money, and *The Sun Also Rises*." *Fitzgerald/Hemingway Annual*, 257–67.

Sullivan, Walter. 1977. "The Rose in the Fist: Hemingway Once Again." *Sewanee Review* 83, no. 4 (Fall): 675–81.

Sutherland, Fraser. 1972. *The Style of Innocence: A Study of Hemingway and Callaghan.* Toronto: Clarke, Irwin.

Svoboda, Frederic J. 1983. *Hemingway and "The Sun Also Rises": The Crafting of a Style*. Lawrence: University Press of Kansas.

Svoboda, Frederic J., and Joseph Waldmeir, eds. 1995. *Hemingway: Up in Michigan Perspectives*. East Lansing: Michigan State University Press.

Sylvester, Bickford. 1966. "Hemingway's Extended Vision: *The Old Man and the Sea*." *PMLA* 81 (March): 130–38.

Szalay, Michael. 2000. "The Politics of Textual Integrity: Ayn Rand, Gertrude Stein, and Ernest Hemingway." In *New Deal Modernism: American Literature and the Invention of the Welfare State*, 75–119. Durham, NC: Duke University Press.

Tanner, Tony. 1964. "Tough and Tender." *Encounter* 23 (June): 71–75.

———. 1965. *The Reign of Wonder: Naivety and Reality in American Literature*. Cambridge: Cambridge University Press.

Tate, Allen. 1926a. "Good Prose." *Nation*, February 10, 160–62.

———. 1926b. "Hard-Boiled." *Nation*, December 15, 642, 644.

Tavernier-Courbin, Jacqueline. 1991. *Ernest Hemingway's "A Moveable Feast": The Making of a Myth*. Boston: Northeastern University Press.

Tellefsen, Blythe. 2000. "Rewriting the Self against the National Text: Ernest Hemingway's *The Garden of Eden*." *Papers on Language & Literature* 36, no. 1 (Winter): 58–92.

Tetlow, Wendolyn. 1992. *Hemingway's "In Our Time": Lyrical Dimensions*. Cranbury, NJ: Associated University Press.

"This Novelist Is a Bull Fighter." 1927. *Dallas Morning News*, February 27, Section 3, 3.

Thompson, Ralph. 1940. "Books of the Times." *New York Times*, October 21, 15.

Thorp, Willard. 1960. *American Writing in the Twentieth Century*. Cambridge, MA: Harvard University Press.

Tinkle, Lon. 1950. "Latest Testament of Hemingway Hero Yet Another Portion of Primitivism." *Dallas Morning News*, September 10, Section 5, 3.

Tinsley, James. 1975. Review of *Ernest Hemingway: Five Decades of Criticism*. *Great Lakes Review* 2, no. 1 (Summer): 117–18.

Todd, B. E. 1929. "Farewell and Return." *Spectator*, November 16, 727.

"To Discuss Hemingway." 1939. *Omaha World Herald*, June 23, 17.

Toole, William. 1967. "Religion, Love and Nature in *A Farewell to Arms*: The Dark Shape of Irony." *CEA Critic* 29 (May): 10–11.

"Toughness Is All." 1937. *Times Literary Supplement*, October 9, 733.

Trilling, Lionel. 1939. "Hemingway and His Critics." *Partisan Review* (Winter): 52–60. Reprinted in Baker 1961, 61–70.

———. 1941. "An American in Spain." *Partisan Review*, January–February, 63–67.

Trogdon, Robert W. 1999. *Ernest Hemingway: A Documentary Volume*. Detroit: Gale.

———. 2005. Review of *Hemingway's Theaters of Masculinity*. *Studies in the Novel* 37, no. 3 (Fall): 367–69.

———. 2007. *The Lousy Racket: Hemingway, Scribner's, and the Business of Literature*. Kent, OH: Kent State University Press.

———. 2009. "*A Moveable Feast: The Restored Edition*: A Review and a Collation of Differences." *Hemingway Review* 29, no. 1 (Fall): 24–45.

Troy, William. 1933. "Mr. Hemingway's Opium." *Nation*, November 15, 570.

Turner, Catherine. 2003. "Changing America's Literary Taste: Scribner's and Ernest Hemingway." In *Marketing Modernism between the Two World Wars*, 145–72. Amherst: University of Massachusetts Press.

Tuttleton, James. 1977. "'Combat in the Erogenous Zone': Women in the American Novel between the Two World Wars." In *What Manner of Woman: Essays on English and American Life and Literature*, edited by Marlene Springer, 271–97. New York: New York University Press.

———. 1988. "Emasculating Papa: Hemingway at Bay." In *Vital Signs: Essays on American Literature and Criticism*, 240–61. New York: Dee.

———. 1992. "Hemingway Unbound." *New Criterion* 11, no. 4 (December): 23–30.

Tyler, Lisa, ed. 2008. *Teaching Hemingway's "A Farewell to Arms."* Kent, OH: Kent State University Press.

Underwood, Doug. 2010. *Journalism and the Novel: Truth and Fiction, 1700–2000*. New York: Cambridge University Press.

———. 2011. *Chronicling Trauma: Journalists and Writers on Violence and Loss*. Urbana: University of Illinois Press.

———. 2013. "Hemingway as Seeker of 'The Real Thing' and the Epistemology of Art." In *The Undeclared War between Journalism and Fiction*, 123–52. New York: Palgrave Macmillan.

Unfried, Sarah P. 1976. *Man's Place in the Natural Order: A Study of Hemingway's Major Works*. New York: Gordon.

Updike, John. 1970. "Papa's Sad Testament." *New Statesman*, October 16, 489.

Urgo, Joseph, and Ann Abadie. 2004. *Faulkner and His Contemporaries*. Jackson: University Press of Mississippi.

Valentine, Ross. 1952. "Over the Sea and into Our Hearts." *Richmond Times-Dispatch*, September 1, 6.

Van Doren, Carl. 1935. "Ernest Hemingway, Singing in Africa." *New York Herald Tribune Books*, October 27, 3.

Vardamis, Alex A., and Justine E. Owens. 1999. "Ernest Hemingway and the Near-Death Experience." *Journal of Medical Humanities* 20, no. 3 (Fall): 203–17.

Vaughan, J. N. 1940. "Two Tales." *Commonweal*, December 13, 20.

Vernon, Alex. 2004. *Soldiers Once and Still: Ernest Hemingway, James Salter & Tim O'Brien*. Iowa City: University of Iowa Press.

———. 2011. *Hemingway's Second War: Bearing Witness to the Spanish Civil War*. Iowa City: University of Iowa Press.

———. 2015. *Teaching Hemingway on War*. Kent, OH: Kent State University Press.

"Versatile Hemingway." 1929. *Daily Northwestern*, October 1, 2.

Vickery, John B. 2009. *The Prose Elegy: An Exploration of Modern American and British Fiction*. Baton Rouge: Louisiana State University Press.

Villarreal, René. 2009. *Hemingway's Cuban Son: Reflections on the Writer by His Longtime Majordomo*. Kent, OH: Kent State University Press.

Von Cannon, Michael. 2014. Review of *Hemingway's Dark Night*. *Hemingway Review* 33, no. 2 (Spring): 151–54.

Vondrak, Amy. 2004. "'The Sequence of Motion and Fact': Cubist Collage and Filmic Montage in *Death in the Afternoon*." In Mandel 2004, 257–79.

Waggoner, Hyatt. 1955. "Ernest Hemingway." *Christian Scholar* 38 (June): 114–20.

Wagner, Linda Welshimer, ed. 1974. *Ernest Hemingway: Five Decades of Criticism*. East Lansing: Michigan State University Press.

———. 1975. *Hemingway and Faulkner: Inventors/Masters*. Metuchen, NJ: Scarecrow Press.

———. 1977. *Ernest Hemingway: A Reference Guide*. Boston: G. K. Hall.

———. 1985. Review of *The Hemingway Women*. *Hemingway Review* 4, no. 2 (Spring): 56–57.

———, ed. 1987. *Ernest Hemingway: Six Decades of Criticism*. East Lansing: Michigan State University Press.

Wagner-Martin, Linda, ed. 1987. *New Essays on "The Sun Also Rises."* New York: Cambridge University Press.

———. 1991. "Hemingway Regendered." *Novel* 24, no. 3 (Spring): 323–24.

———. 1995. "The Hemingway-Stein Story." In Wagner-Martin 1998, 389–402.

———, ed. 1998. *Ernest Hemingway: Seven Decades of Criticism*. East Lansing: Michigan State University Press.

———, ed. 2000. *A Historical Guide to Ernest Hemingway*. New York: Oxford University Press.

———, ed. 2002. *Ernest Hemingway's "The Sun Also Rises": A Casebook*. New York: Oxford University Press.

———. 2003. *Ernest Hemingway's "A Farewell to Arms": A Reference Guide*. Westport, CT: Greenwood.

———. 2007. *Ernest Hemingway: A Literary Life*. New York: Palgrave Macmillan.

———, ed. 2009. *Ernest Hemingway: Eight Decades of Criticism*. East Lansing: Michigan State University Press.

Wain, John. 1970. "No Surprises." *London Observer*, October 11, 33.

Wakefield, Richard. 2005. "'*Under Kilimanjaro*: Papa, without Restraint, Is Too Wooly to Decipher." *Seattle Times*, September 9.

Waldhorn, Arthur. 1972. *A Reader's Guide to Ernest Hemingway*. New York: Farrar, Straus & Giroux.

———, ed. 1973. *Ernest Hemingway: A Collection of Criticism*. New York: McGraw-Hill.

Walpole, Hugh. 1927. "Contemporary American Letters." *Nation*, June 4, 302–3.

———. 1929. "The Best Books of 1929." *Saturday Review* (London), December 21, 747–48.
Walsh, David. 2011. "Fifty Years since the Death of Ernest Hemingway." *World Socialist Web Site*, July 6. http://www.wsws.org/en/articles/2011/07/hemi-j06.html.
Walsh, Jeffrey. 1982. *American War Literature: 1914 to Vietnam.* London: Macmillan.
Walsh, John. 2011. "Being Ernest." *Independent*, June 11.
Ward, A. C. 1932. *American Literature 1880–1930.* New York: Dial.
Warren, Robert Penn. 1947. "Ernest Hemingway." *Kenyon Review* 9, no. 1 (Winter): 1–28.
Warshow, Robert. 1950. Review of *Across the River and Into the Trees. Partisan Review*, November–December, 876–84.
"War Story." 1929. *Greensboro Record*, October 26, 8.
Wasserstrom, William. 1969. "The Hemingway Problem." *Virginia Quarterly Review* 45, no. 3 (Summer): 531–37.
Watkins, Floyd C. 1971. *The Flesh and the Word: Eliot, Hemingway, Faulkner.* Nashville, TN: Vanderbilt University Press.
Watts, Emily Stipes. 1971. *Ernest Hemingway and the Arts.* Urbana: University of Illinois Press.
Waugh, Evelyn. 1950a. "*Winner Take Nothing.*" *Tablet*, September 30, 291–92.
———. 1950b. "The Case of Mr. Hemingway." *Commonweal*, November 3, 97–98.
Weber, Brom. 1971. "Ernest Hemingway's Genteel Bullfight." In Bradbury and Palmer 1971, 151–64.
Weber, Ronald. 1990. *Hemingway's Art of Nonfiction.* New York: St. Martin's Press.
Weeks, Edward. 1935. Review of *Green Hills of Africa. Atlantic Monthly*, November, 36.
———. 1952. Review of *The Old Man and the Sea. Atlantic Monthly*, September, 72.
Weeks, Robert, ed. 1962. *Hemingway: A Collection of Critical Essays.* Englewood Cliffs, NJ: Prentice-Hall.
———. 1967. Review of Recent Books on Hemingway. *American Quarterly* 19, no. 2 (Summer): 260–65.
Weiss, Daniel. 1985. "Ernest Hemingway: The Stylist of Stoicism." In *The Critic Agonistes: Psychology, Myth and the Art of Fiction*, 138–60. Seattle: University of Washington Press.
West, Benjamin. 2013. "The Crowd at War and at Home in Hemingway's and Fitzgerald's Fiction." In *Crowd Violence in American Modernist Fiction: Lynchings, Riots and the Individual under Assault*, 103–27. Jefferson, NC: McFarland.
West, Ray B. 1944. "Ernest Hemingway: Death in the Evening." *Antioch Review* 4 (Winter): 569–80.
———. 1952. "Hemingway and Faulkner: Two Masters of the Modern Short Story." In *The Short Story in America*, 85–106. Chicago: Regnery.

———. 1953. "The Sham Battle over Ernest Hemingway." *Western Review* 17 (Spring): 234–40.
Westling, Louise. 1996. "Pastoral Regression in Hemingway and Faulkner." In *The Green Breast of the New World: Landscape, Gender, and American Fiction*, 82–124. Athens: University of Georgia Press.
Wexler, Joyce. 1981. "E.R.A. for Hemingway: A Feminist Defense of *A Farewell to Arms*." *Georgia Review* 35, no. 1 (Spring): 111–23.
Wheelan, Joe. 1986. "Latest Posthumous Hemingway Novel Weak." *Trenton Evening Times*, June 1, DD2.
White, W. M., ed. 1967. *By-Line: Ernest Hemingway: Selected Articles and Dispatches of Four Decades*. New York: Scribner.
———. 1969. "The Crane-Hemingway Code: A Reevaluation." *Ball State University Forum* 10, no. 2 (Spring): 15–20.
Whitlow, Roger. 1984. *Cassandra's Daughters: The Women in Hemingway*. Westport, CT: Greenwood.
"Whole Technic of Bullfighting." 1932. *Springfield Sunday Union & Republican*, October 9, 7E.
Wickes, George. 1969. "Ernest Hemingway in Montparnasse." In *Americans in Paris*, 149–88. Garden City, NY: Doubleday.
Wilkinson, Myler. 1986. *Hemingway and Turgenev: The Nature of Literary Influence*. Ann Arbor, MI: UMI Research Press.
Williams, Wirt. 1981. *The Tragic Art of Ernest Hemingway*. Baton Rouge: Louisiana State University Press.
Willingham, Kathy. 1993. "Hemingway's *The Garden of Eden*: Writing with the Body." In Wagner-Martin 1998, 293–310.
Willis, Lloyd. 2011. "Ernest Hemingway and American Literature's Legacy of Environmental Disengagement." In *Environmental Evasion: The Literary, Critical, and Cultural Politics of "Nature's Nation,"* 125–34. Albany: SUNY Press.
Willson, Norma. 1974. "Majority Report: A Liberated Glossary: Guide to Feminist Writings." *English Journal* 63, no. 6 (September): 14–15.
Wilson, Craig. 2011. "'Papa' Hemingway Still Casts a Long Shadow." *USA Today*, June 29.
Wilson, Edmund. 1924. "Mr. Hemingway's Dry-Points." *Dial* 77 (October): 340–41.
———. 1927. "The Sportsman's Tragedy." *New Republic*, December 14, 102–3.
———. 1935. "Letter to the Russians about Hemingway." *New Republic*, December 11, 135–36.
———. 1938. "Hemingway and the Wars." *Nation*, December 10, 628, 630.
———. 1939. "Hemingway: Gauge of Morale." *Atlantic Monthly*, July, 36–46.
———. 1940. "Return of Ernest Hemingway." *New Republic*, October 28, 591–92.
Wilson, Robert N. 1979. *The Writer as Social Seer*. Chapel Hill: University of North Carolina Press.

Wineapple, Brenda. 2009. "Paris in a New Light." *Wall Street Journal*, July 24.
Wolf, Robert. 1926. "*In Our Time*." *New York Herald Tribune Books*, February 24, 3.
Wolfe, Cary. 2002. "Fathers, Lovers, and Friend Killers: Rearticulating Gender and Race via Species in Hemingway." *Boundary2* 29, no. 1 (Spring): 223–57.
Wood, James. 1999. "The Lion King." *New York Times*, July 11.
Woolf, Virginia. 1927. "An Essay in Criticism." *New York Herald Tribune*, October 9, 1, 8.
Wyatt, David. 2010. "Performing Maleness: Hemingway." In *Secret Histories: Readings in Twentieth-Century American Literature*, 53–67. Baltimore: Johns Hopkins University Press.
Wyatt, Edward. 2005. "Hemingway Recycled." *New York Times*, February 8.
Wycherley, Alan. 1969. Review of *Ernest Hemingway: A Life Story*. *AN&Q* 8 (September): 15–16.
———. 1976. Review of *Ernest Hemingway: Five Decades of Criticism*. *AN&Q* 15 (July): 78–80.
Wylder, Delbert E. 1969. *Hemingway's Heroes*. Albuquerque: University of New Mexico Press.
Yardley, Jonathan. 1970. "How Papa Grew." *New Republic*, October 10, 25–26, 30.
Young, Philip. 1950. Review of *Across the River and Into the Trees*. *Tomorrow*, November, 55–56.
———. 1952. *Ernest Hemingway*. New York: Rinehart.
———. 1959a. "Ernest Hemingway." In *Seven Modern Novelists: An Introduction*, edited by William Van O'Connor, 153–88. Minneapolis: University of Minnesota Press.
———. 1959b. *Ernest Hemingway*. Minneapolis: University of Minnesota Press.
———. 1964. "Our Hemingway Man." *Kenyon Review* 26, no. 1 (Autumn): 676–707.
———. 1966a. *Ernest Hemingway: A Reconsideration*. New York: Harcourt.
———. 1966b. "On Dismembering Hemingway." *Atlantic Monthly*, August, 45–49.
———. 1967. "Hemingway by Moonlight." *Chicago Tribune Book Week*, May 28, 6.
———. 1972. "'Big World Out There': The Nick Adams Stories." *Novel* 6, no. 1 (Autumn): 5–19.
———. 1987. "Pressure under Grace." *New York Review of Books*, August 13, 30–37.
———. 2000. *American Fiction, American Myth: Essays*. University Park: Penn State University Press.
Young, Stark. 1940. "Mr. Tone and Mr. Hemingway." *New Republic*, March 25, 408.

Zabel, Morton Dauwen. 1950. "A Good Day for Mr. Tolstoy." *Nation*, September 9, 230.

Zuckert, Catherine. 1990. "Hemingway on Being in Our Time." In *Natural Right and the American Imagination: Political Philosophy in Novel Form*, 161–95. Savage, MD: Rowman & Littlefield.

Index

Abadie, Ann, 200
Abrahams, William, 101
Adams, J. Donald, 32, 33, 37
Adams, John R., 24, 27
Adams, Nick (Hemingway character), 21, 87, 100, 118, 126, 147, 149, 150, 172, 173, 174, 187, 210, 212
Adorno, Theodor, 210
Aeneid (Virgil), 169
aesthetics (aesthetic qualities), 5, 27, 36, 52, 68, 75–76, 87, 88, 98, 121, 152, 169, 175, 189, 210, 219, 226, 228
Africa, 29–31, 36, 73, 114, 121, 160, 173, 179–80, 198, 207, 219, 222
African Americans, 170, 175, 222–23
Africans, 170, 210, 222
Ahab (literary character), 84
Aiken, Conrad, 13
alcoholism, 173, 195
Alderman, Taylor, 96
Aldridge, John, 50, 60, 62–63, 94, 148
Algren, Nelson, 74, 76–77
Allen, Hugh, 35,
Allen, Mary, 123
The Ambassadors (Henry James), 66
America, 8, 12, 14, 15, 17, 19, 20–21, 26, 30, 32, 34, 37, 38, 39, 49, 52, 54, 57, 59, 62, 63, 65, 66, 71, 75, 76, 78, 87, 89, 103, 105, 113, 118, 119, 121, 122, 131, 137, 139, 140, 142, 146, 157, 158, 168, 172, 181, 182, 187, 199, 201, 202, 203, 207, 208, 209–10, 213, 216, 218, 221
American Dream, 63, 139
American Library Association, 32
Americans. *See* America
Anastas, Benjamin, 159
Anders, Smiley, 95
Anderson, Quentin, 101
Anderson, Sarah, 223
Anderson, Sherwood, 12, 13, 26, 168, 177, 196
androgyny, 67, 115, 126, 136, 153–55, 156, 157, 159, 160, 170–71, 183, 201
Angoff, Charles, 48
Anibal, C. E., 25
animals, 36, 38–39, 98, 123, 131, 167, 201–11
Anthony Adverse (Hervey Allen), 32
anti-Americanism, 62
anti-intellectualism, 36, 61, 72, 83, 87, 200
anti-romanticism, 104
anti-Semitism, 122, 203, 216
Arnaiz, Ned Quevedo, 226
Arnold, Lloyd, 91
Arnold, Matthew (Arnoldian criticism), 5, 34, 35, 67, 102
Ashley, Brett (Hemingway character), 50, 65, 71, 126, 152
Astro, Richard, 105
Aswell, James, 17
Atkins, John A., 59–61
Atkinson, Brooks, 74
Austad, Jonathan A., 220
Austen, Jane, 32
autobiography, 29, 34, 74, 140–41, 178–79, 199

Bacall, Lauren, 2
Bak, John, 201

Baker, Carlos, 3, 35–36, 40, 52, 55, 56–59, 61, 69, 72, 75, 79, 80, 81, 86, 88–92, 99, 102, 109, 111–12, 114, 120, 124, 126–27, 129, 132–33, 137, 138, 140, 146, 153, 156, 189
Baker, Sheridan, 77
Bakhtin, Mikhail, 150
Bakker, Jan, 99, 119
Balassi, William, 147
Baldwin, James, 223
Baldwin, Marc, 163
Barkley, Catherine (Hemingway character), 18, 71, 103–4, 109, 127, 130, 150, 154, 224–25
Barlowe, Jamie, 161, 171
Barnes, Jake (Hemingway character), 71, 81, 85, 146, 223
Barnes, Lois, 61–62, 64
Barnett, Louise, 168
Barthes, Roland, 213
Barton, Bruce, 13, 14
Bates, Robert W., 221
Batliner, Doris, 158
Baughman, Judith, 97
Baym, Nina, 151, 169–70
Beach, Joseph Warren, 4, 22, 49–50, 52
Beach, Sylvia, 50
Beaumont, Peter, 216
Beckerman, Marty, 1
Beegel, Susan F., 7, 144, 150–51, 156, 165, 166
Bell, Millicent, 126
Bellow, Saul, 59, 119, 135, 172
Bennett, Arnold, 18
Bennett, Joan, 2
Bennett, Warren, 83–84, 102
Benson, Frederick, 85
Benson, Jackson, 81–82, 95, 102, 105–6, 125, 143, 150–51, 170
Beowulf, 86
Berg, A. Scott, 111–12, 193
Bergman, Ingrid, 2
Bergson, Henri, 230
Berman, Ronald, 199–200
Berthoff, Warner, 173
Bessie, Alvah, 38

best-seller, 3, 90, 193
Bilyeu, Jack, 47
biography, 3, 60, 69, 72, 88–91, 109, 110, 112, 114, 117, 118, 129, 132, 133–34, 137–42, 143, 155, 158–61, 172, 178–79, 181–82, 184, 188, 189, 194–96, 197, 217–20
Birth of a Nation (film), 177
bisexuality. *See* androgyny
Bittner, John, 167
Bloom, Harold, 121, 126
Blumenthal, Ralph, 179
Boardman, Michael, 175–76
Bogart, Humphrey, 2
Boker, Pamela A., 174, 204–5
Boni & Liveright, 12
Book-of-the-Month Club, 37, 73, 93
Booth, Bradford, 58
Boreth, Craig, 1
Bouchard, Donald F., 212
Bourne, Catherine (Hemingway character), 137, 154, 205
Bourne, David (Hemingway character), 137, 155, 160, 195, 205
Boutroux, Emile, 230
boxing, 19, 105, 141
Boyd, Ernest, 12
Bradbury, Malcolm, 95, 98, 122, 168
Brasch, James D., 117, 198–99
bravery, 36, 63, 64
Brecht, Berthold, 204
Bredahl, A. Carl, 144–45
Breit, Harvey, 55
Brenner, Gerry, 119, 135, 143, 156, 186
Breu, Christopher, 201
Brian, Denis, 141–42
Brickell, Herschel, 12, 24
Bridgman, Richard, 83, 107
The Brief Wondrous Life of Oscar Wao (Junot Diaz), 215
Britton, Beverly, 39
Broch, Hermann, 66
Broer, Lawrence R., 97–98, 150, 203–4, 223–24

Brontë, Emily, 154
Brooks, Cleanth, 41–42, 43, 45, 84, 102
Brooks, Van Wyck, 62, 69
Brooks, Walter R., 17
Brothers, Joyce, 129
Brown, Dennis, 219
Broyard, Anatole, 95
Bruccoli, Matthew J., 96–97, 133, 159, 184, 193
brutality, 25, 27, 57, 63, 65, 123
Bryer, Jackson, 4, 7, 91, 166
Budick, Emily Miller, 146
bullfighting, 19, 24–26, 36, 65, 67, 91, 105, 131, 141, 150, 223, 226
Burgum, Edwin Berry, 33
Burnett, Frances Hodgson, 154
Burwell, Rose Marie, 126, 155, 159–61, 172, 181
Busch, Frederick, 158
Butcher, Fanny, 47, 55
Butcher, Maryvonne, 86
Butler, Nicholas Murray, 39
Buttimer, Ann, 167
Butts, Leonard, 133, 155
Byron, Lord (George Gordon), 26, 30, 32, 146

Cain, William E., 179, 213
Calder-Marshall, Arthur, 55
Callaghan, Morley, 74
Calverton, V. F., 34
Campbell, Joseph, 75
Camus, Albert, 68
Cane (Jean Toomer), 223
canon (literary), 40, 46, 55, 57, 61, 65, 79, 95, 99, 102, 108, 109, 110, 112, 113, 115, 148, 149, 150, 151, 152, 165, 167, 172, 173, 201, 202, 203, 205, 207, 220, 222, 224
Cantwell, Richard (Hemingway character), 49
Capers, Julian, 17
Carpenter, Frederick I., 62
Cartland, Barbara, 103
Carver, Raymond, 133–34
castration, 71, 183, 196, 223

Cat on a Hot Tin Roof (Tennessee Williams), 201
Catholicism, 4, 35, 63, 227
Catton, Bruce, 31
celebrity, 1, 5, 6, 19, 38, 49, 53, 57, 86, 89, 108, 109, 120, 138, 163, 165, 181, 182, 190, 195, 202
censorship, 4, 19
Cézanne, Paul, 112, 197, 199
Chamberlain, John, 27, 29, 30
Chandler, Raymond, 201
characters (characterization), 1, 2, 7, 12, 13, 14, 15–16, 18, 19, 21, 22–23, 27, 28, 29, 30, 31, 32, 34, 35, 37, 38, 39, 43–44, 45, 47, 49, 56, 57, 61, 65, 66, 67, 71, 72, 77, 79, 80, 81, 82–83, 84, 85, 87, 89, 102, 104, 109, 110, 113, 114–15, 118, 125, 127, 129–31, 136–37, 138, 139, 140, 146, 147, 148, 149, 154, 160, 162, 163, 168, 171, 172, 173, 178, 183, 192, 194, 199, 201, 205, 206, 207, 211, 212, 219, 223, 224–25, 226, 227, 229, 230
The Charterhouse of Parma (Stendhal), 108
Chase, Cleveland, 13
Chase, Richard, 64
Christ (Jesus Christ), 84–85, 153, 213
Christianity, 63, 84–85, 98, 118, 130, 154, 155, 227
Churchwell, Sarah, 200
Cirino, Mark, 187–88, 194, 229–30
Civello, Paul, 177
Cixous, Hélène, 205
Claridge, Henry, 7
Clark, C. E. Frazer, Jr., 96
Clark, Suzanne, 202–3
Clark, Walter van Tilburgh, 39
Clarke, Phil, 55
Cleaton, Allen, 24
Clifford, Stephen, 171–72, 173
Clothes for a Summer Hotel (Tennessee Williams), 178
Cobley, Evelyn, 177
The Cocktail Party (T. S. Eliot), 226
code. *See* Hemingway code

code hero (in Hemingway's fiction), 28–29, 56–57, 67, 78, 81, 203
Cohassey, John, 219
Cohen, Milton, 211–12
Cold War, 202
Coleridge, Samuel Taylor, 118
Colvert, James B., 63–64
Comley, Nancy, 156, 161, 171–72, 173, 183, 204
Communism, 38, 196, 202
Connolly, Cyril, 31, 48, 55, 59, 74
Conrad, Joseph, 44, 146
Cooper, Gary, 2, 43
Cooper, James Fenimore, 66
Cooper, Stephen, 121
Cooperman, Stanley, 84
Copperfield, David (literary character), 86
Corbett, Edward, 95
Corkin, Stanley, 177
Cottrell, Robert C., 2
courage, 32, 35, 63, 69, 81, 89, 105, 127, 153, 196
courtly love, 174
Cowley, Malcolm, 4, 25, 29, 31, 33, 37, 42, 47, 52–53, 55, 73, 76, 87, 94, 99, 126, 127, 141
Cox, James, 116
Craik, Dinah Mulock, 154
Crane, Stephen, 85, 108
Crews, Frederick C., 141
Crowley John W., 173
Crozier, Robert, 148
cruelty, 12, 16, 28, 35, 74, 135
Crunden, Robert M., 196
Cuba, 94, 117, 194, 225–26
Cull, John, 111
cultural criticism (cultural studies), 7, 8, 98, 99, 115, 122, 142, 152, 153–54, 165–66, 167, 171, 172, 176, 182, 184, 186, 187, 188, 192, 197, 201, 202, 203, 204, 205–6, 210, 212, 215, 228, 230
Curnutt, Kirk, 187, 194, 198, 214
Curran, Ronald, 131

Dabney, Crystal, 15
Dadaist movement, 220
Daiches, David, 40, 42
Daniel, Robert, 44–45
Darwin, Charles, 204
Davenport, Guy, 94
Davis, Elmer, 33
Davis, Robert Gorham, 55
Davis, Robert Murray, 90–91, 159, 179
Davison, Neil, 207
De Falco, Joseph, 75–76
De Fazio, Albert J., 155
De Gourmont, Remy, 34
de Lauretis, Teresa, 173
de Man, Paul, 169
De Maupassant, Guy, 45
De Voto, Bernard, 18, 30
death (in Hemingway's fiction), 25, 27, 29, 35, 36, 40, 41, 42, 64, 66, 69, 76, 78, 79, 84, 87, 95, 97–98, 99, 103, 104, 105, 123, 131, 154, 158, 177, 178, 195, 213, 219
deconstruction (deconstructionist criticism), 149, 164, 177, 182
The Deerslayer (James Fenimore Cooper), 66
DeGuzmán, Maria, 197
Del Gizzo, Suzanne, 5, 115, 181, 194, 201, 220, 225
Deleuze, Gilles, 212
Dempsey, G. T., 190, 191
Dewey, John, 199
Dewing, Arthur, 22–23
Diamond, Arlyn, 104
Diaz, Junot, 215
Dickens, Charles, 21, 36, 48, 79
Diehl, Digby, 101
dignity, 18, 39, 54, 63, 78, 98
Diliberto, Gioia, 9
Dillon-Malone, Aubrey, 181–82, 194
dissertations (on Hemingway), 34, 56, 60, 75, 76, 121, 130, 132, 144, 193
divorce, 17, 19, 103, 121, 139
Doctorow, E. L., 137
Dolan, Marc, 169
Domingín, Luis Miguel, 131
Donahue, Peter, 211

Donaldson, Scott, 1, 109–10, 137, 148, 156, 157, 165, 173, 176, 184, 189
Donne, John, 76
Doorly, Margaret, 12
Dos Passos, John, 18, 19, 22, 69, 114, 196
Douglas, Ann, 191
Dowd, Maureen, 218
Drake, Susan, 144–45
Dreiser, Theodore, 44, 107
Dubus, Andre, 230
Ducille, Ann, 207
Dudley, Marc K., 194, 222
Duffus. R. L., 24–25
Duggan, Francis X., 59
Duke, Maurice, 94
Dupee, F. W., 55

Earle, David, 201–2
Eastman, Max, 25–26, 33, 46, 52, 60
Eby, Carl, 160–61, 166, 180, 181, 183–84
ecocriticism (environmental criticism), 123, 167, 190, 210–11, 220, 224
economics, 114, 147–48, 156, 193
Edwards, Lee, 104
Egan, Susanna, 178–79
Einstein, Albert, 144
elegy (elegiac works), 25, 212–13
Eliot, George (Marian Evans), 79
Eliot, T. S., 97, 98, 114, 211, 226
Elizabethan writers, 21
Ellis, Havelok, 204
Ellison, Ralph, 201, 223
Emmett, Elizabeth, 14
environmental criticism. *See* ecocriticism
epic, 54, 58, 62, 84
Epstein, Joseph, 95
Erskine, John, 26–27
Esquire (magazine), 27, 38, 52, 67, 120
Evans, Robert, 87–88
Evans, Robert C., 7
existentialism (existentialist criticism), 67, 81, 84, 93, 105, 106, 111, 112, 113, 118, 125, 157, 192
expatriates, 19, 75, 168, 197–98, 214

expressionism (expressionist art), 112, 197

Fadiman, Clifton, 18, 26, 27, 31, 33, 73, 93
Fantina, Richard, 205–6
A Farewell to Arms (film), 2
Faulkner, William, 3, 4, 22, 26, 34, 41, 44, 50, 52, 56, 69, 71, 91, 97, 98, 107, 108, 122, 130, 200, 209, 215, 219, 229, 230
FBI (Federal Bureau of Investigation), 196, 216
Fellner, Harriet, 121
feminism (feminist criticism), 5, 9, 102–4, 105, 112–13, 115, 117, 124, 125, 127–28, 129–30, 135, 137, 148–49, 151, 152–53, 154, 155, 157, 164, 165, 169–70, 172, 182, 186, 202, 204, 205, 207, 217, 225
Fenstermaker, John, 52
Fenton, Charles A., 60–61, 102, 140, 197
Ferguson, Charles, 14–15
Ferguson, Mary Anne, 103
Ferrell, William K., 212
Fetterley, Judith, 104, 115, 127, 148, 225
Fiedler, Leslie, 71, 73, 131
Finca Vigia, 117, 199
Finch, John, 59
Finn, Huckleberry (literary character), 34, 59, 66
The Fire and the Wood (R. C. Hutchinson), 39
Firestone, Shulamith, 103
First World War, 42, 50, 56, 69, 77, 84, 147, 153, 163, 177–78, 186, 187, 204, 208, 209, 220, 222
Fischer, Heinz, 39
Fisher, Vardis, 167
Fishkin, Shelley Fisher, 222
Fiske-Harrison, Alexander, 217
Fitzgerald, F. Scott, 4, 5, 8, 11, 12, 66, 75, 96, 98, 107, 111, 114, 122, 159, 166, 169, 178, 184, 189, 199–200, 209, 215

Fitzgerald, Zelda, 178
Fitzgerald/Hemingway Annual, 96
Fleming, Robert E., 110, 162–63, 167, 191, 189–90, 192
Flora, Joseph, 118, 149, 167, 188, 192
Florczyk, Steven, 194, 221
Flower, Desmond, 37
Flynn, Errol, 2
For Whom the Bell Tolls (film), 2
formalism (formalist criticism), 75, 83, 116, 147, 152, 162, 186, 211
Forter, Greg, 183, 223
Fortunati, Vito, 187
Fortuny, Kim, 197
Foucault, Michel, 212
Frakes, James R., 129
Frank, Waldo, 29
Frederking, Lauretta, 210
Freedman, Morris, 5
Freud, Sigmund, 147, 206, 230
Freudian psychology, 76, 122, 133, 136, 168, 174, 183–84
Friedrich, Otto, 65
Frohock, W. M., 42–43
frontier (in Hemingway). *See* myth of the frontier
Frost, Robert, 69, 201
Frost Society (Robert Frost Society), 201
Frus, Phyllis, 178
Fruscione, Joseph, 183, 219, 230
Frye, Northrop, 47
Fulford, Robert, 74
Fuller, Edmund, 94, 101

Gaggin, John, 121
Gajdusek, Robert, 120, 137, 163, 180, 181, 188–89, 218
Galantière, Lewis, 18, 73–74
Galligan, Edward, 159
Gandal, Keith, 209
Gannett, Lewis, 47, 158
Garcia, Wilma, 130
Gardiner, Harold, 55
Gardner, Ava, 2
Garlington, Jack, 65–66
Garnett, David, 27, 29

Geismar, Maxwell, 40–41, 42, 47, 70, 74, 76, 94
Gellens, Jay, 73
Gellhorn, Martha (Hemingway's third wife), 3, 121, 139
gender (in Hemingway's writings), 17, 67, 102, 104, 115, 126, 130, 140, 152, 157, 162, 183, 208
gender studies, 102, 126, 148, 159, 162, 165, 169–73, 186, 202–6, 210–11, 214, 223
George, Stephen, 200
Gide, Andre, 111, 198
Gill, Brendan, 55
Gilson, Étienne, 97
Gladstein, Mimi, 130–31
Glass, Loren, 195
Glasser, William, 85
God, 63, 67–68, 77, 84, 103, 111, 146, 176
Godden, Richard, 147–48, 156
Gold, Michael, 22
Goldman, Jonathan, 1
Goldstein, Albert, 37
Gone with the Wind (Margaret Mitchell), 32
Goodheart, Eugene, 64–65, 185
Gordon, Caroline, 44
Gordon, David, 84
Gorman, Herbert, 13, 40
Gould, Gerald, 12, 14
Grace, Nancy McCampbell, 172
Gratton, C. Harley, 22
Great Depression, 26, 139
The Great Gatsby (F. Scott Fitzgerald), 66, 146
Great War. *See* First World War
Grebstein, Sheldon, 99–100, 102
Greco-Turkish war, 197
Greene, Graham, 37
Greene, Philip, 1
Greer, Germaine, 103
Griffin, Peter, 90, 132–33, 138, 141, 143, 150, 153
Griffith, D. W., 177
Grimes, George, 15, 21, 24, 29
Grimes, Larry, 121, 167, 194, 225–26
Grissom, Candace, 8

Gullason, Thomas A., 122
Gurko, Leo, 5, 78–79
Gurko, Miriam, 5

Haas, Victor P., 48
Hackett, Alice Payne, 3
Haight, Anne Lyon, 4
Halliday, E. M., 41–42, 72, 76
Hammett, Dashiell, 201
Hand, Harry, 85
Hanneman, Audre, 6, 82–83, 86, 117
Hansen, Harry, 12
Haralson, Eric L., 196
hard-boiled fiction, 20, 22, 33, 173, 174, 175, 201
Hardy, Richard, 111
Hardy, Thomas, 44
Harlow, Benjamin, 84
Harold, Brent, 113
Harrison, Joyce, 214
Hart, Jeffrey, 74, 101
Hartwick, Harry, 28
Hawkins, Ruth A., 10
Hawthorne, Nathaniel, 41, 42, 66, 156
Hayes, Helen, 2
Hays, Peter L., 7, 84, 142–43, 178, 192
Hayward, Susan, 2
Heavilin, Barbara, 200
Heidegger, Martin, 68, 112
Heisenberg, Werner, 144
Heller, Joseph, 103
Hemingway, Clarence (Hemingway's father), 119, 174, 194
Hemingway, Ernest, letters: 7, 38, 88, 89, 97, 114, 126–27, 132, 159, 166, 216–17, 229
Hemingway, Ernest, works by:
 Across the River and Into the Trees, 3, 4, 31, 47–52, 54–55, 57–58, 79, 83, 93, 95, 127, 169, 187, 190, 217
 "After the Storm," 151
 "The Art of the Short Story," 150
 "Big Two-Hearted River," 86, 150, 229–30
 "Cat in the Rain," 116, 151

 "A Clean, Well-Lighted Place," 83, 150
 The Dangerous Summer, 131
 Death in the Afternoon, 23, 24–26, 29, 33, 34, 40, 58, 70, 79, 99, 111–12, 131, 186–87, 188
 "The Doctor and the Doctor's Wife," 165
 A Farewell to Arms, 2, 3, 4, 17–19, 21, 24, 30, 36, 37, 45, 50, 52, 61, 70, 72, 73, 79, 83, 85, 103, 104, 108, 112, 113, 120, 126, 127, 139, 144, 154, 157, 164, 169, 175, 176, 177, 178, 186, 187, 188, 192, 197, 199, 208, 209, 220, 221, 224, 230
 Fiesta, 14
 The Fifth Column and the First Forty-nine Stories, 31–32
 For Whom the Bell Tolls, 2, 3, 37–40, 41, 42–43, 45, 50, 52, 58, 62, 64, 72, 79, 84, 85, 87, 94, 103–4, 105, 107, 112, 113, 127, 139, 144, 164, 174, 176, 178, 190, 204, 205, 217, 220, 221
 The Garden of Eden, 97, 115, 116, 119, 125, 135–37, 140, 153, 154, 155, 156, 157, 160, 166, 168, 170, 171, 172, 182, 190, 194, 195, 196, 203, 204, 205, 206, 210, 220–21, 225, 227
 Green Hills of Africa, 29–30, 34, 58, 79, 120, 143, 144–45, 180, 188, 224
 in our time, 11, 150, 212
 In Our Time, 11–12, 21, 83, 86, 107, 124, 125, 147, 151, 162, 165, 166, 169, 173, 177, 186, 197, 211, 224
 "Indian Camp," 165
 Islands in the Stream, 2, 93–95, 97, 100, 101, 102, 135, 136, 160, 190
 "The Killers," 43, 102, 123, 176
 "The Last Good Country," 101, 154
 Men at War, 40

Hemingway, Ernest, works by—(cont'd)
  Men without Women, 15–16, 141, 192
  A Moveable Feast, 3, 52, 73–75, 76, 77, 79, 87, 91, 93, 106, 147, 156, 159, 160, 161, 162, 163, 168, 169, 170–71, 177, 178–79, 186, 190, 200, 214
  A Moveable Feast: The Restored Edition, 191, 214
  "A Natural History of the Dead," 151
  "Now I Lay Me," 211
  The Old Man and the Sea, 3, 54–56, 58, 63, 68, 72, 73, 79, 84, 85, 88, 95, 97, 111, 118, 120, 126, 143–44, 150, 153, 157, 169, 176, 190, 197, 211, 213, 217, 226, 227, 230
  "Old Man at the Bridge," 151
  "On the Quai at Smyrna," 221
  "Out of Season," 150
  "The Sea Change," 114–15
  "The Short, Happy Life of Francis Macomber," 85, 103, 150, 151, 170, 207
  "The Snows of Kilimanjaro," 150, 162, 178, 182, 219
  The Sun Also Rises, 3, 4, 7, 13–15, 16, 17, 18, 19, 45, 50, 52, 66–67, 70, 71, 72, 79, 84, 86, 119, 122, 126, 139, 143, 145, 146, 147, 148, 149, 153, 154, 162, 163, 164, 168, 169, 172, 173, 175, 177, 178, 182, 186, 192, 196, 197, 198, 201, 203, 204, 206, 207, 209, 212, 223, 230
  Three Stories and Ten Poems, 11, 165
  To Have and Have Not, 4, 31–32, 34–35, 36, 41, 45, 52, 58, 79, 86, 162, 167, 170, 173, 187
  The Torrents of Spring, 12–13, 79, 196, 204
  True at First Light, 179–81, 190
  Under Kilimanjaro, 189–91, 192, 207, 224
  "A Very Short Story," 123, 151
  Winner Take Nothing, 26–28
Hemingway, Grace (mother), 125–26, 138, 174
Hemingway, Gregory (son), 3, 218
Hemingway, Hadley (Hadley Richardson, Hemingway's first wife), 9, 19, 75, 101, 132, 139, 143, 216
Hemingway, John (son), 90, 132
Hemingway, John Patrick (grandson), 3
Hemingway, Leicester (brother), 2
Hemingway, Mary Welsh (Hemingway's fourth wife), 3, 88, 121, 191
Hemingway, Patrick (son), 125, 179, 180, 190
Hemingway, Pauline (Pauline Pfeiffer, Hemingway's second wife), 9–20, 19, 121, 139, 191, 216
Hemingway, Seán (grandson), 191, 208, 214
Hemingway, Valerie, 3
Hemingway code, 32, 35, 43, 45, 50, 56–57, 61, 62, 63, 64, 65, 66, 71, 73, 78, 81, 85, 99, 100, 114, 136, 141, 146, 167, 175, 185, 201, 205, 206, 207
"Hemingway Editor" (web site), 2
Hemingway hero, 2, 21, 28–29, 30, 33, 36, 42, 43, 44–45, 49, 56–57, 58, 59, 61, 63–64, 67–68, 69, 70, 73, 75–76, 77, 79, 81, 84–85, 87–88, 97, 98, 99, 100, 119, 135, 139, 143, 148, 170, 174, 175, 83, 205, 212, 222, 226
Hemingway notes (journal), 96
Hemingway problem, 91–92
Hemingway Review (journal), 5, 9, 96, 115, 120, 129, 137, 155, 159, 160–61, 163, 167, 171, 176, 180, 183, 190, 191, 214, 220
Hemingway Society, 6, 76, 115, 120, 125, 148, 180, 187, 201
Hendrickson, Paul, 217–18
Henry, Frederic (Hemingway character), 18, 28, 73, 85, 104, 127, 223, 224, 225

Herlihy, Jeffrey, 225
hero. *See* code hero; Hemingway hero
The Hero with a Thousand Faces (Joseph Campbell), 75
heroism, 26, 55, 64, 78–79, 81, 86, 123, 130–31, 146, 153–54, 155, 173, 202, 213, 226
Herrick, Robert, 18–19
Hewson, Marc, 204–5
Hicks, Granville, 4, 21, 25, 28–29, 30, 46, 50, 52, 59, 66, 86
Higgins, George V., 101
Highet, Gilbert, 55
Hitchens, Christopher, 191
Hochman, Brian, 201
Hoffer, Bates L., 106
Hoffman, Frederick, 6–7, 50–51, 58, 73
Hohenberg, John, 39
Holcomb, Gary Edward, 222–23
Holcombe, Wayne, 10
Holder, Alan, 71
Holland, Gloria, 203
Holland, Laurence, 60
Holland, Robert, 85
Hollenberg, Alexander, 224
Holmesland, Oddvar, 151
Homer, 144
homophobia, 195, 216
homosexuality, 114–15, 119, 133, 152, 155, 171, 178, 182, 183, 196, 201
honesty, 32, 122, 124, 163, 205
honor, 35, 43, 63, 123
Hoover, J. Edgar, 196, 216
Hotchner, A. E., 3, 10, 137, 191
Houk, Walter, 217
Housman, A. E., 44
Hovey, Richard B., 78, 85, 91, 102, 110, 119
Howe, Irving, 4, 69, 89
Howell, John, M., 73
Hubbell, Jay B., 91
Huckleberry Finn (Mark Twain), 34, 59, 66
Hume, David, 222
Humphries, David, 197
hunting, 2, 29, 55, 89, 91, 102, 173

Hutchinson, Percy, 15. 17
Hutchinson, R. C., 39
Hyman, Stanley Edgar, 4, 52, 74

iceberg theory, 105, 147, 149, 168, 227
Idema, Henry, 147
Inferno (Dante), 169
influence (Hemingway's influence on others), 2, 3, 4, 20, 27, 56, 60, 65, 69, 71, 124, 135, 164, 167, 173, 198, 199, 201, 215, 219, 220, 222–23
influences (on Hemingway), 12, 13, 57, 60, 84, 85, 97, 100, 106–7, 114, 120, 121, 128, 142, 147–48, 149, 153, 154, 166, 168, 169, 185, 187, 196–97, 198, 199, 202, 207, 208, 212, 219, 220, 226
International Brigade, 38
irony (in Hemingway), 43, 62, 63, 67, 77, 81, 83–84, 86, 135, 160
Islands in the Stream (film), 2

Jack, Peter Monro, 33
Jackson, Joseph Henry, 31, 47
James, Henry, 29, 66, 83, 196
James, William, 199, 230
Jameson, Fredric, 105, 210
Jameson, Storm, 28
Janeway, Elizabeth, 103, 131
Jenks, Tom, 135, 136, 137, 155, 160, 225
Jensen, Arthur, 46
Jesus. *See* Christ
Jobes, Katharine T., 73
Johnson, Edgar, 36–37
Johnson, Paul, 145–46
Johnson, Reed, 215
Johnston, Kenneth, 149
Jones, Howard Mumford, 4, 37, 40
Jones, John A., 67
Jones, Robert, 137
Joost, Nicholas, 78, 80, 90, 91, 92
Jordan, Robert (Hemingway character), 42, 58, 85, 87, 205, 223
Josephs, Allen, 137, 144, 162–63

journalism, 60, 79–80, 86–87, 96, 121, 122, 178, 197, 209, 221, 222
Joyce, James, 14, 17, 69, 114, 120, 172, 229, 230
Jung, Carl, 75
Justice, Hilary K., 180, 181, 187, 192–93

Kakutani, Michiko, 137, 179
Kansas City Star, 60, 222
Kaplan, Harold, 226
Kartiganer, Donald, 200
Kashkeen, Ivan, 30–31, 52
Kauffmann, Stanley, 74
Kaupke, Ellen, 54
Kazin, Alfred, 4, 31, 33, 41–42, 48, 67, 69, 74, 123
Kennedy, J. Gerald, 166, 168, 170–71, 173, 188
Kennedy, John Fitzgerald, 69, 70, 116
Kennedy, William, 86
Kennedy Center (Washington, D.C.), 2
Kennedy Library (John F. Kennedy Library, Boston), 6, 96, 115, 116, 119, 125, 128, 136, 149, 156, 157, 166, 181, 193, 230
Kenner, Hugh, 99
Kent State University Press, 192–94, 222, 230
Kermode, Frank, 74
Kerouac, Jack, 172
Kert, Bernice, 128–29
Key West, Florida, 3, 19, 30, 187
Kierkegaard, Søren, 68
Kiley, Jed, 3
The Killers (film), 2
Killinger, John, 67–68, 73
Kipling, Rudyard, 14, 154
Knight, Christopher J., 169
Knott, Toni D., 167
Kobler, J. F., 114–15, 121
Koch, Stephen, 195–96
Kolodny, Annette, 152
Kowaleski, Michael, 174–75
Krim, Seymour, 55
Kronenberger, Louis, 4, 12, 27, 31
Krutch, Joseph Wood, 4, 15–16, 33

Kupferberg, Herbert, 136
Kurowsky, Agnes von, 109, 142, 216
Kyle, Frank, 163

La Farge, Oliver, 18, 69
Lacan, Jacques, 151, 157, 198, 206
Lamb, Robert Paul, 215, 227–28
Lancaster, Burt, 2
Lanser, Susan Sniader, 123, 176
Lardner, Ring, 14
Larsen, Lyle, 218–19
Larson, Kelli A., 6, 219, 226
Latham, Aaron, 115
Latimer, Margery, 12
Laughing Boy (Oliver Lafarge), 18
Laurence, Frank M., 8
Lawrence, D. H., 12, 17, 103, 104, 165, 173, 204
LeBost, Barbara, 84
Lee, A. Robert, 90, 124
Lee, Charles, 37
Leff, Leonard J., 163–64
Lehan, Richard, 106, 109
Lehmann-Haupt, Christopher, 89, 94, 128, 129, 133, 158, 172
Levin, Harry, 46–47, 51
Levine, Gary Martin, 207
Lewis, R. W. B., 53–54
Lewis, Robert W., 76, 95, 102, 132, 133, 143–44, 148, 181, 188, 189–90, 192
Lewis, Sinclair, 4, 14, 20, 31–32
Lewis, Wyndham, 27–28, 29, 33, 45, 46, 52, 62, 73, 168
Life (magazine), 53, 54, 121, 131
Light in August (William Faulkner), 66
Limited Editions Club, 39
Limon, John, 177–78
Lippmann, Walter, 20–21, 199, 222
Lisca, Peter, 83
Littell, Robert, 20, 37
Locklin, Gerald, 155
Lodge, David, 116
Loesberg, Jonathan, 101
Lone Ranger, 170
Long, Robert Emmet, 74–75, 94
Look (magazine), 121

Lost Generation, 12–23, 49, 50, 56, 67, 74, 78, 81, 99, 158, 214
Love, Glen A., 147, 211
love (in Hemingway), 17, 18, 19, 36, 50, 59, 63, 66, 67, 75, 76, 83, 93, 98, 105, 110, 112, 142, 174, 180, 204, 205, 212, 227
Lovett, Robert Morss, 4, 21
Lowe, John Livingston, 118
Ludington, Townsend, 110
Lukács, Georg, 162
Lutz, Mark, 13
Lynn, David H., 146
Lynn, Kenneth S., 126–27, 138, 140–41, 146, 152, 153, 157, 159, 169, 179–80, 183, 208
Lyons, Donald, 158
Lyons, Leonard, 48

MacArthur, Charles G., 19
Macaulay, Alistair, 2
Macauley, Robie, 93
Macdonald, Dwight, 38, 70, 76
MacLeish, Archibald, 114
Macomber, Margot (Hemingway character), 85, 103, 130, 170
The Macomber Affair (film), 2
Mailer, Norman, 3, 102, 103, 126, 135
Maloff, Saul, 89
Malraux, Andre, 66
Mandel, Miriam B., 7, 186, 219, 226
Maner, William, 48, 55
Mann, Thomas, 18
Manning, Margaret, 101
Mansfield, Harvey, 153
manuscripts (Hemingway's), 69, 114, 116, 119, 131, 144, 147, 156, 159–61, 166, 181, 190, 196, 204–5, 225
Maria (Hemingway character), 103–4, 152, 205
Maris, Ronald W., 122
Maritain, Jacques, 97
Mark Twain Journal, 70
Markel, Les, 48
Márquez, Gabriel Garcia, 173

marriage, 17, 19, 50, 75, 121, 129, 139, 143, 169
Marryat, Frederick, 154
Marsden, Malcolm, 84
Marshall, Margaret, 37
Martin, Christopher D., 195
Martin, Ronald, 167–68
Martin, Wendy, 103
Marx, Paul, 122
Marxist criticism, 30–31, 36, 52, 61–62, 67, 103, 104, 105, 113, 147–48, 163, 165, 178, 210, 216
Masefield, John, 154
masculinity, 24, 81, 84, 102, 111, 112, 113, 115, 133, 136, 141, 152, 153, 154, 173, 174, 182, 190, 196, 200, 201, 202, 203, 204, 206, 207, 214, 219, 222, 223
masochism, 205–6
Massie, Allan, 191
Matthews, T. S., 18, 30
Maurois, André, 14, 23
Maxwell, D. E. S., 70
Mayberry, George, 59
Mayo Clinic, 160
McCaffery, John K. M., 46
McCarthy, Harold, 105
McClure, John, 13–14
McClurg, Jocelyn, 158
McConnell, Frank, 124, 135
McCormick, John, 66, 98
McDermott, William, 17, 48–49, 54
McDowell, Edwin, 136
McFarland, Ron, 1, 2
McIntyre, O. O., 19
McKay, Claude, 223
McKelly, James C., 155
McLaughlin, Richard, 60
McLemore, Henry, 55
McLendon, James, 3
McSweeney, Kerry, 212
medievalism, 173–74
Meier, Thomas, 160
Mellow, James R., 154, 158–59
Melville, Herman, 41, 42, 66, 84, 130
Mencken, H. L., 4, 15, 18, 25
Mendelson, Edward, 217
Meredith, James H., 208–9

Mérimée, Prosper, 14
Merrill, Robert, 152
Merritt, Robert, 136
Messenger, Christian, 122
Messent, Peter B., 157, 161–62
Meyers, Jeffrey, 28, 35, 38, 39, 109, 123, 124, 129, 132–34, 137, 140, 146, 152, 153, 180, 188, 215, 217, 218
Michigan (in Hemingway's writings), 77, 118, 164–65, 172
Miller, D. Quentin, 171
Miller, Henry, 103
Miller, Linda Patterson, 180–81, 193
Miller, Madelaine Hemingway (Hemingway's sister), 2
Miller, Max, 37
Miller, Neil, 23
Millett, Kate, 102, 104
Millis, Walter, 40
Minot, John Clair, 25, 30
Minter, David, 176–77
misogyny, 71, 104, 112, 128, 204, 216
Mizener, Arthur, 59
Moby-Dick (Herman Melville), 66
Moddelmog, Debra, 115, 151, 166, 181, 182, 196, 220
Modern Fiction Studies (journal), 61, 85
Modern Language Association, 152, 201
Modernism, 22, 23, 27, 97, 99, 138, 166, 167–69, 178, 186, 193, 196, 197, 198, 200, 202, 203, 204, 207, 209–10, 211, 213, 214, 219, 223, 226–27, 230
Monk, Craig, 214
Monteiro, George, 110, 164, 200
Montgomery, Constance Cappel, 77
Montijo, John Igual, 38
Moore, Harry T., 89–90, 100, 101
moral criticism, 5, 27, 32, 34, 45, 64, 66–67, 69, 72, 75, 78, 146, 152, 163
moralist (Hemingway as), 35, 37, 42, 43, 44, 52, 58, 63, 64, 66–67, 69, 76, 77, 78, 80, 98, 175, 201

Moran, Joe, 1
Moreira, Peter, 194
Moreland, Kim I., 173–74
Morgan, Harry (Hemingway character), 31, 33, 42
Morgan, Kathleen, 144
Morris, Lawrence, 13, 14
Morris, Wright, 83
Morrison, Toni, 170, 222, 223
Morrow, Lance, 136
Mort, Terry, 194
Morton, Brian, 158
Moseley, Edwin, 84–85
Moylan, Thomas, 63
Mudrick, Marvin, 75
Muir, Edwin, 14, 55
multiculturalism (multicultural studies), 166, 190
Murray, Albert, 175
Murray, G. E., 101
Muscular Christianity, 154, 155
Muste, John, 85
myth criticism, 83, 84, 126, 130, 146, 163, 168–69, 212, 213
myth of the American Adam, 57
myth of the American male, 49, 172
myth of the frontier (in Hemingway), 55, 119, 154, 164, 213

nada. *See* nihilism
Nagel, James, 125, 142, 164
narratology (assessments of narrative), 4, 5, 99, 106, 113, 123, 127, 144–45, 147, 148, 151, 157, 163, 169, 173, 174–75, 176, 187, 211, 212, 223, 224–25
Native Americans, 18, 147, 207, 209, 210, 222
naturalism (literary movement), 59, 67, 177, 198
Nelson, Raymond, 112
Nelson, Valerie J., 128
New Criticism, 67, 75, 81, 83, 84, 86, 93
New Deal, 210
New England Society for the Suppression of Vice, 19
new historicist criticism, 5, 9

New Humanism, 67
New Woman (of the 1920s), 112, 123
Newlin, Keith, 186
Nickel, Matthew, 227
Nies, Betsy L., 204
Nietzsche, Friedrich, 66
nihilism, 41, 42, 62, 76, 100, 198, 220
Nobel Prize for Literature, 1, 20, 61, 68, 71, 88, 139
Noble, David, 84
Noble, Donald R., 125
Nolan, Charles J., Jr., 127–28, 148
Nolan, William F., 101
Nordell, Roderick, 94
Norris, Faith, 106
Norris, Frank, 14
Norris, Margot, 208
Nuffer, David, 3
Nyman, Jopi, 173

O. Henry (William Sidney Porter), 15
Oak Park, Illinois, 81, 91, 96, 138, 163, 164, 180
Oberhelman, Harley D., 173
O'Connor, William Van, 68, 74
O'Faolin, Sean, 64
O'Hara, John, 48–49
The Old Man and the Sea (film), 2
Oldsey, Bernard, 94, 101, 107, 112, 116, 125
Oliver, Charles M., 7, 8, 96, 115, 145, 186
Olson, Barbara K., 176
Onderdonk, Todd, 206
O'Neill, Eugene, 41
Ordóñez, Antonio, 131
Ott, Mark, 182, 187, 194, 197
Owens, Justine E., 178
The Ox-Bow Incident (Walter van Tilburgh Clark), 39
Ozick, Cynthia, 102

Paris, France, 11, 14, 15, 19, 30, 73, 75, 91–92, 120, 138–39, 143, 158, 160, 161, 163, 166, 168–69, 186, 191, 197–98, 211–12, 220, 225
Parker, Dorothy, 4, 15, 37

parody, 12, 47, 70, 86, 101, 131, 137, 179
Parsons, Louella, 129
Pattee, Fred Lewis, 22
Paul, Elliott, 32, 47
Paul, Steve, 194, 214, 221
Pavloska, Susanna, 209
Peck, Gregory, 2
Peckham, Morse, 98
PEN Hemingway Awards, 230
Perkins, Max, 97, 111, 193
Perrin, Thomas Gordon, 226–27
Petersen, Clarence, 129
Peterson, Richard K., 80–81
Pettipiece, Deirdre Anne, 204
Pettit, Robert, 136
Pfeiffer, Gus, 139
Pfeiffer, Pauline. *See* Hemingway, Pauline
Phelan, James, 148, 157, 176, 211, 224–25
Phelps, William Lyon, 38–39
Phillips, Arthur, 217, 218
Phillips, H. L., 19
Phillips, K. J., 146
philosophical criticism, 5, 35, 36, 44, 67–68, 82, 84, 97, 106, 112, 163, 222, 230
philosophy (in Hemingway), 25, 35, 36, 40, 42, 81–82, 93, 105, 147, 199
Piep, Karsten Helge, 209
Pietsch, Michael, 131
Pilar (Hemingway's boat), 217
Pintarich, Paul, 129
Pizer, Donald, 168–69
Plath, James, 181, 219
Plimpton, George, 53, 70, 74, 116
Poe, Edgar Allan, 41, 42
politics, 38, 59, 76, 110, 121, 165, 202–3, 209, 210, 220, 224
Poore, Charles, 4, 29, 32, 59, 69, 73
postmodernism, 171, 211, 221
poststructuralist criticism, 5, 182
Poulet, Georges, 230
Pound, Ezra, 11, 106–7, 108, 114, 116, 219
Power, Tyrone, 2

Pratt, Ann, 104
Price, Reynolds, 95
Priestley, J. B., 69
primitivism (in Hemingway's writing), 22, 63, 64–65, 66, 87, 98, 102, 130, 171, 197, 209, 211
Pritchard, William, 141
Pritchett, V. S., 37, 69
Proust, Marcel, 106, 229, 230
Pryce-Jones, Alan, 73
psychological criticism, 56–57, 59, 67, 75–76, 78, 81, 83, 84, 91, 95, 111, 118, 119, 122–23, 125, 133, 157, 160, 165, 171, 172, 173, 174, 183–84, 186, 195, 205, 208, 219, 223–24, 225
psychology (Hemingway's use of), 22, 30, 36, 42, 229, 230
Pulitzer Prize, 18, 39, 56, 215
Pullin, Faith, 124
Putnam, Thomas, 208
Pynchon, Thomas, 135

Quick, Jonathan, 169
Quinn, Patrick, 59

Rabkin, Eric, 113
race (in Hemingway), 122, 165, 170, 186, 201, 203, 206–7, 222–23
Raeburn, John, 1, 120–21
Rahv, Philip, 31, 48
Raines, Howell, 218
Rascoe, Burton, 13, 18, 19, 27, 38
Reader's Digest, 91
realism (literary movement), 13, 14, 18, 22, 27, 32, 33, 48, 65, 67, 103, 112, 116, 177, 198, 212
The Rebel (John Igual Montijo), 38
The Red Badge of Courage (Stephen Crane), 108
Register, Cheri, 104
religion (in Hemingway), 66, 67, 72, 77, 83, 84, 85, 98, 121, 146, 147, 163, 220, 226, 227
Remembrance of Things Past (Proust), 106
Rendezvous (journal), 95
Renza, Louis, 147

Reynolds, Michael, 108–9, 113–14, 117–18, 120, 124, 125, 138–40, 143, 157, 161, 166, 177, 181, 184, 185, 193, 194, 198, 221, 229
Rich, Motoko, 191
Richardson, Hadley. *See* Hemingway, Hadley
Richter, Conrad, 39
Riemer, James D., 153
Ripatrazone, Nicholas, 227
The Road to Xanadu (John Livingston Lowe), 118
Robins, Natalie, 196
Robinson, Lillian, 104
Robinson, Ted, 12–13, 17, 24
Robson, Leo, 191
Rohy, Valerie, 203, 206
Roman Catholicism. *See* Catholicism
Romanticism (Romantic writers), 26, 30, 32, 44, 81, 82, 118, 146
romanticism (sentimental attitude), 32, 33, 50, 61, 65, 70, 76, 100, 103, 104, 154, 177, 211, 212
Romer, Sam, 38
Romero, Pedro (Hemingway character), 67
Roosevelt, Theodore, 202
Rosen, Kenneth, 96, 164, 184
Rosenfield, Isaac, 49
Ross, Lillian, 45–46
Ross, Patricia Ann, 213
Rothman, N. L., 14, 15
Rovere, Richard, 47
Rovit, Earl, 71–72, 73, 75, 99, 102, 135, 161, 200, 221
Royce, Josiah, 199
Ruark, Robert, 47, 54
Rubin, Louis, 94, 101
Rudat, Wolfgang, 145
Russ, Joanna, 103
Russell, Bertrand, 199
Russell, H. K., 61
Russell, Phillips, 29–30
Russian writers, 21
Ryan, Alan, 136
Ryan, Frank L., 7
Ryan, William, 86

Said, Edward, 131
Samuels, Charles Thomas, 90
Samuelson, Arnold, 3, 217
San Juan, Epifanio, 178
Sanderson, Rena, 164, 187
Sanderson, Stewart, 68
Sanford, Marcelline Hemingway (Hemingway's sister), 2
Santayana, George, 199
Santiago (Hemingway character), 55, 84–85, 153, 213, 230
Sartre, Jean Paul, 68, 198
Satterfield, Archie, 93
Savage, D. S., 45, 76
Scafella, Frank, 137, 157
The Scarlet Letter (Nathaniel Hawthorne), 66
Schedler, Christopher, 210
Schmidt, Dolores Barracano, 103, 131
Schneidau, Herbert N., 168
Schneider, Daniel, 84, 85
Schneider, Isidor, 22
Scholes, Robert, 123, 171–72, 173, 183, 204
Schorer, Mark, 4, 39, 45, 54, 55, 61, 90
Schwartz, Delmore, 32, 55, 59, 63, 64
Schwenger, Peter, 113
Scott, George C., 2
Scott, Nathan A., 77
Scott, Walter, 36
Scribner (publisher), 12, 52, 54, 72, 73, 93, 94, 114, 131, 135, 156, 163, 179, 191, 193, 201, 214
Scribner, Charles, 69
Scribner, Charles Jr., 82, 125, 136
Scribner's Magazine, 4, 19
Scruggs, Charles, 222
Second World War, 119, 121, 196, 218, 219
Selby, John, 26, 31
Seward, William, 3
Shakespeare, William, 5, 13, 48, 49
Shaw, Samuel, 100
Shelley, Percy Bysshe, 57
Sherwood, Robert E., 37
short stories, 11–12, 13, 16, 19, 26, 31, 33, 46, 52, 54, 59, 75–76, 99, 106, 107, 122, 123, 140, 141, 144, 149–51, 173, 197, 211, 212, 215, 227–28
Sigman, Joseph, 117
Simon, Kate, 47
Simons, Frank, 181
Sinclair, Gail, 187, 194, 221
Slabey, Robert, 83
Smith, Agnes W., 17–18
Smith, Carol, 126
Smith, Harrison, 47
Smith, Julian, 84, 90
Smith, Paul, 148, 149–50, 151, 159, 166, 188
Snell, George, 43
Snow, C. P., 69
The Snows of Kilimanjaro (film), 2
socialist criticism. *See* Marxist criticism
Solomon, Barbara, 136
Soto, Michael, 198
The Sound and the Fury (Faulkner), 230
Spain, 25, 38, 85, 97, 107, 114 131, 138, 142, 197, 198, 220
Spanier, Sandra, 148, 191, 216
Spanish Civil War, 37, 84, 85, 139, 164, 189, 196, 220
Spilka, Mark, 66–67, 126, 153–55, 156, 157, 159, 165, 166, 170, 171, 183, 184
Spillane, Mickey, 135
sports, 21, 24, 25, 27, 32, 36, 56, 105, 120, 122, 131, 226
Sprague, Claire, 156
Squire, John, 38
Stafford, William, 122
Stallings, Laurence, 24
Standley, Lawrence, 197
Stange, Mary Zeiss, 173
Stanton, Edward, 142
Stanzel, F. K., 123
Stark, Bruce, 7
Stein, Gertrude, 11, 12, 26, 28, 35, 114, 144, 165, 166, 177, 196, 209, 218–19
Steinbeck, John, 34, 200–1
Steiner, George, 90
Stendhal (Marie-Henri Beyle), 45, 108

Stephens, Robert O., 4, 49, 79–80, 91, 109, 145
Stephens, Rosemary, 84
Stetler, Charles, 155
Stevenson, Robert Louis, 43–44
Stewart, Matthew C., 183–84, 186, 208
stoicism, 28, 97, 122, 157
Stoltzfus, Ben, 111, 148, 151, 157, 198
Stoneback, H. R., 167, 188, 192
Stoppard, Tom, 125
Strong, Amy, 165, 206–7
structuralism (structuralist criticism), 83, 116, 147, 151
Strychacz, Thomas, 165–66, 204, 214
style (in Hemingway), 2, 11, 12, 13–14, 16, 18, 19, 21–22, 23, 24–25, 26, 29, 33, 34, 36, 39, 41, 42, 43, 44, 49, 51, 55, 57, 60, 63, 66, 67, 69, 70, 76, 77, 78, 80–81, 83, 86, 93, 94, 97, 99–100, 105, 106, 107, 113, 119, 122, 126, 135, 140, 142, 144, 146, 147, 149, 162, 163, 164, 166, 168, 174, 176, 177, 178, 183, 185, 186, 187, 189, 199, 201, 202, 208, 212, 218–19, 221, 222, 224
Suárez-Galbán, Eugenio, 220
Sugg, Richard, 156
suicide, 68, 69–70, 95, 98, 122, 128, 195, 215
Sullivan, Walter, 109, 110
The Sun Also Rises (ballet), 2
The Sun Also Rises (film), 2
Sutherland, Fraser, 98–99
Svoboda, Frederic J., 119–20, 164–65, 194, 212
Sylvester, Bickford, 84, 194, 225
symbolism, 18, 26, 37, 40, 42, 43, 44, 55, 58, 62, 63, 67, 69, 75, 84, 86, 88, 111, 131, 178, 183, 213, 226
Szalay, Michael, 210

Tanner, Tony, 74, 83
Tate, Allen, 4, 12, 14, 28
Tavernier-Courbin, Jacqueline, 161, 191
Tellefson, Blythe, 203
Tennyson, Alfred, 44
Tetlow, Wendolyn, 162
Thackeray, William Makepeace, 48
theme (thematic studies), 2, 13, 34, 34, 41, 47, 50, 52, 55–56, 58, 61, 66, 67, 71, 75–76, 77, 78, 79, 81, 105, 106, 109, 111, 112, 118, 119, 125, 127, 136, 137, 140, 149, 160, 161–62, 164, 165, 167, 168–69, 173, 182, 183, 185, 187, 196, 206, 212, 213, 219, 221, 224, 225
Thompson, Ralph, 37
Thorp, Willard, 67
Time (magazine), 1, 31, 121
Tinkle, Lon, 48
Tinsley, James, 107
To Have and Have Not (film), 2
Todd, B. E., 18
Toklas, Alice B., 219
Tolkien, J. R. R., 86
Tolstoy, Leo, 9, 17
Tonto, 170
Toole, William, 83
Toomer, Jean, 223
Toronto Star, 116, 138
Tracy, Spencer, 2
tragedy, 17, 58, 66, 71, 97–98, 118, 140, 147, 173, 181, 211, 226
Transcendentalists, 83
trauma, 56–57, 97, 118, 127, 133, 140, 141, 143, 183, 195, 218, 221, 223
The Trees (Conrad Richter), 39
Trilling, Lionel, 4, 34, 38, 67, 69
Trogdon, Robert W., 7, 114, 191, 192, 193, 214
Trout, Steven, 194, 221
Troy, William, 27
Turgenev, Ivan, 45, 121
Turner, Catherine, 201
Turner, Frederick Jackson, 213
Tuttleton, James, 112–13, 152–53, 159
Twain, Mark (Samuel Clemens), 34, 59, 66, 83, 130, 171

Twain Society (Mark Twain Society), 70
Tyler, Lisa, 192

UMI Press, 121, 130, 144
Underwood, Doug, 221, 222
Underwood, William, 192, 214
Unfried, Sarah P., 105
United States of America. *See* America
Updike, John, 95, 194
Urgo, Joseph, 200

Valentine, Ross, 54
Van Doren, Carl, 29
Vardamis, Alex A., 178
Vaughan, J. N., 38
Vernon, Alex, 208, 220–21, 230
Vickery, John B., 212
Victorian values, 13, 63, 81, 154
Villard, Henry Serrano, 142
Villarreal, René, 194
violence, 14, 26, 39, 43, 45, 50, 76, 77, 123, 158, 174, 221, 223. *See also* brutality
Von Cannon, Michael, 227
Vondrak, Amy, 187
Vonnegut, Kurt, 135, 164, 223–24

Waggoner, Hyatt, 63
Wagner, Linda Welshimer (*see also* Wagner-Martin, Linda), 6, 106–7, 108, 117, 129, 148
Wagner-Martin, Linda. (*see also* Wagner, Linda Welshimer), 5, 148, 155, 165–66, 185, 186, 188, 193, 194–95
Wain, John, 95
Wakefield, Richard, 190
Waldhorn, Arthur, 100, 200
Waldmeir, Joseph, 164–65
Walpole, Hugh, 15, 18
Walsh, David, 216
Walsh, Jeffrey, 127
Walsh, John, 215
war, 17, 18–20, 21, 25, 26, 27, 32, 36, 37–39, 40, 41, 42, 45, 46, 50, 56–57, 60, 66, 69, 73, 75–76, 77, 81, 84, 85, 108–9, 110, 118, 119, 121, 127, 133, 138, 139, 142, 147, 153, 163, 164, 174, 177–78, 186, 187, 189, 196, 197, 204, 208–9, 220–22, 223
War and Peace (Leo Tolstoy), 37
Ward, A. C., 21
Warren, Robert Penn, 43–44, 45, 65, 102, 107
Warshow, Robert, 47
Wasserstrom, William, 91
Watch and Ward Society, 19, 23
Watkins, Floyd C., 97
Watson, William Braasch, 151
Watts, Emily Stipes, 97
Waugh, Evelyn, 4, 48
Weber, Brom, 94
Weber, Ronald, 145
Weeks, Edward, 29, 55
Weeks, Robert, 73, 76, 87
Weiss, Daniel, 122
West, Benjamin, 223
West, Ray B., 42, 52, 62, 72, 102
Westbrook, Max, 125–26
Westling, Louise, 172
Wexler, Joyce, 127
Wheelan, Joe, 136–37
White, William M., 6, 85, 86
Whitlow, Roger, 129–30
Wickes, George, 28, 92, 166
Wilder, Thornton, 15
Wilkinson, Myler, 121
Williams, Tennessee, 178, 201
Williams, Terry Tempest, 167
Williams, Wirt, 118
Willis, Lloyd, 224
Willson, Norma, 103–4
Wilson, Craig, 215
Wilson, Edmund, 4, 11, 16, 22, 30, 33, 34–35, 37, 41, 45, 60, 67, 107, 199
Wilson, Robert N., 111
Wineapple, Brenda, 191
Wittgenstein, Ludwig, 199
Wolf, Robert, 12
Wolfe, Cary, 210–11
Wolfe, Thomas, 111

women (in Hemingway's fiction), 16–17, 28, 36, 48, 49, 50, 59, 71, 79, 84, 102–4, 111, 112, 117, 124, 126, 127–31, 141, 148–49, 151–53, 154, 170–73, 203, 204, 205, 206, 220
Wood, James, 179
Woolf, Virginia, 4, 16–17
World War I. *See* First World War
World War II. *See* Second World War
wound (Hemingway's wound), 42, 56–57, 68, 78, 79, 81, 126–27, 139, 140–41, 142, 145, 154, 170, 178, 183, 188, 209, 210, 223, 226, 227
Wright, Richard, 223
Writer's Guild of America, 101
Wyatt, David, 207

Wyatt, Edward, 190
Wycherley, Alan, 90, 107–8
Wylder, Delbert E., 79, 95

Yardley, Jonathan, 94
Yeats, William Butler, 69
Young, Philip, 6, 10, 30, 42, 47, 56–57, 58–59, 60, 61, 62, 68, 73, 75, 77, 78, 81, 85, 86, 92, 95, 96, 97, 99, 100, 101, 102, 117, 118, 124, 125, 126, 132, 133, 138, 140, 141, 143, 150, 154, 155, 183, 195, 206, 212
Young, Stark, 4, 33

Zabel, Morton Dauwen, 47
Zapf, Hubert, 151
Zola, Emile, 44
Zuckert, Catherine, 147

www.ingramcontent.com/pod-product-compliance
Lightning Source LLC
Chambersburg PA
CBHW051602230426
43668CB00013B/1944